W9-ARB-216

BUSINESS STRATEGY & PLANNING

Edited by Bernard Taylor

A handbook of strategic planning

Edited by

Bernard Taylor B.A.

and

Kevin Hawkins M.A., M.Sc.

Longman

LONGMAN GROUP LIMITED
London
Associated companies, branches and representatives throughout the world

First published 1972

ISBN 0 582 44587 6 cased

Set in Monotype Joanna
and printed in Great Britain by
Cox & Wyman Ltd,
London, Fakenham and Reading

Contents

C. *The management of technology*

Contents

Preface

This book was initially based on papers presented to University of Bradford Management Centre Conferences and Seminars over the period 1967–70. In order to achieve a comprehensive coverage of the subject however the material has been supplemented with articles reprinted from various journals, both British and American.

Unlike most of the other published works on corporate planning, this book includes a considerable amount of thought and experience on the subject which has been drawn from *British* companies. Corporate strategy is not a purely American phenomenon: as the articles collected in this book suggest, it can and should be practised by British managers in the same measure as their transatlantic competitors. This is not to imply that American models should be uncritically imitated in British industry – on the contrary it is important that we learn from the mistakes which American companies have made in formulating and applying corporate strategy. The point is that corporate strategic planning should no longer be regarded as an impossibly highbrow exercise which only top-drawer executives in large American corporations can undertake. A strategic approach to the management of a business can be successfully applied in any situation.

Bradford University
Management Centre
March 1971

BERNARD TAYLOR
KEVIN HAWKINS

Acknowledgements

The editors would like to extend their thanks to the following publishers and individual authors for granting permission to reprint articles in this book. We are particularly indebted to Pergamon Press Ltd, and to the Society for Long Range Planning for allowing us to reprint the following articles from their journal *Long Range Planning*:

'The choice of corporate objectives', by M. F. Cantley, Vol. 3 No. 1.

'Setting up corporate planning', by E. von Allmen, Vol. 2 No. 1.

'Does planning pay?' by H. Igor Ansoff *et al.*, Vol. 3 No. 2.

'The role of business in society', by T. Kempner *et al.*, Vol. 2 No. 4.

'People and pollution: the challenge to planning', by Colin Hutchinson, Vol. 3 No. 3.

'Should government and company planners influence each other?' by Sir Fred Catherwood, Vol. 1 No. 4.

'Financial forecasting and strategic planning', by A. L. Kingshott, Vol. 1 No. 2.

'Strategic planning for corporate growth in developing countries', by A. van Dam, Vol. 2 No. 1.

'Management science and strategic planning', by B. Wagle, Vol. 3 No. 3.

'Developing corporate strategy through planning programming and budgeting', by L. A. Dougharty, Vol. 2 No. 3.

We would like to thank the editors of *Harvard Business Review* for allowing us to reprint 'How to evaluate corporate strategy', by Dr S. Tilles, 'Human relations and human resources', by R. E. Miles and 'Patterns of organisation change', by Larry Greiner. We would like to thank the editor of *Business Horizons*, in addition to Stanley S. Thune and Robert J. House, for allowing us to reprint 'Where long range planning pays off'. We are grateful to the Boston Consulting Group Inc. for their kind permission to reprint 'Growth and Financial Strategies' by Dr Alan Zakon.

We are also indebted to Business Publications Ltd, for allowing us to reprint the following articles from *Journal of Business Policy*:

'Setting targets for profit and growth', by Sir Fred Catherwood, Vol. 1 No. 1.

'Meeting social responsibilities: the cost and the implications', by R. A. Long, Vol. 1 No. 1.

'A strategic merger policy', by Dr Gerald Newbould, Vol. 1 No. 2.

'Business and consumerism', by George A. Steiner, Vol. 1 No. 3.

'The multinational enterprise and U.K. economic interests', by John H. Dunning, Vol. 1 No. 4.

We are grateful to Mr A. E. B. Perrigo, Mr David Farmer and Dean H. Igor Ansoff, for allowing us to either publish or reprint articles in this book. The rest of the book is made up of articles reproduced from University of Bradford Management Centre Conference and Seminar Manuals and we are grateful to the university and to the authors concerned for their cooperation in making this publication possible.

Last, but by no means least, we would like to thank Miss Catherine Davies and Mrs Jean Carter for their invaluable help in assembling and typing out the manuscript for this book. For any remaining errors and omissions we alone are responsible.

The remaining contributions were made at conferences organised under the auspices of the Bradford University Management Centre.

BERNARD TAYLOR
KEVIN HAWKINS

Bradford University Management Centre
March 1971

Introduction

Opponents of planning usually tend to argue that no matter how sophisticated and erudite a long-range company (or national) plan may be, the shape of the future is so nebulous and uncertain that any attempt to forecast it and plan for it is likely to be a pretentious and time-wasting exercise. Such objections have never been difficult to refute. Even the most enthusiastic and devoted planner would hardly claim that his function gave him an incontrovertible claim to mastery over the crystal ball. A realistic approach to corporate planning over the long term and to the formulation of business objectives and strategies must be based on the assumption that the combined force of time and circumstance may well cause top management to revise its strategic thinking not only once but perhaps many times during the lifetime of a company plan. As Broom has pointed out:

> The external business environment of any company is subject to frequent changes. Management cannot forecast with certainty a continuation of the cold war; it cannot predetermine the exact course of the business cycle; and it cannot know in advance what new government regulations will be introduced or what new trade union pressures will be brought to bear.*

But all such reservations, while perfectly valid and demonstrably true, imply that a corporate strategic plan – embodying the objectives of a business firm and the methods whereby these are to be achieved – is in itself a guarantee of future growth and prosperity. Only the most naïve theorist of management would argue that any formal system or technique – whether it be strategic planning, management by objectives or job enrichment – can operate independently of the individuals who collectively make up the business organisation. All managers are human and all human beings are fallible, thus management techniques and procedures can never be one iota more effective than the abilities of the people who use them.

* H. N. Broom, *Business Policy and Strategic Action*, Prentice-Hall, 1969, pp. 51–2.

Having said this, it must be clearly established at the outset that there is a growing body of empirical evidence to suggest that a systematic approach to the formulation and achievement of a company's objectives *can* be a positive aid to overall business success. As Broom has said, 'a company must know its goals and the direction and velocity of its movement toward or away from them' (p. 51). Thus corporate objectives may be formulated, written down, communicated to or discussed with all members of the management team and the overall sense of purpose and commitment within the organisation thereby augmented. Obviously this approach will not in itself guarantee the achievement of corporate objectives, but at least the whole management team will be more aware of what they are trying to do and their chances of success should thereby be improved.

Planning, therefore, is no more than the application of common sense to the management of a business firm and thus there is no business operation that cannot be planned. Strategic planning, as the name implies, concerns itself with those managerial decisions which 'affect a firm's chances for growth . . . within the framework of which all minor or daily decisions will rest' (p. 47). In general a company must pay particular attention to the following areas in which strategic decisions can be made:

1 The determination of corporate objectives.
2 The relationship between a company and the economic, social and physical environment in which it operates.
3 The relationship between a company and the various interest groups which form an integral part of its operations.
4 The way in which a company uses its human, financial and technological resources.
5 The problems posed by operating a business on a multinational scale.
6 The shape of the future environment in which companies will have to survive and grow.

This book aims to assist both practising managers and students of management to appreciate how strategic decisions may be made in all these fields within a clear and comprehensive frame of reference. A cross-section of personal opinions and assessments of the strategic planning function is presented, together with case studies of planning in action and an introduction to the use of quantitative techniques as an aid to strategic decision-making. In choosing the material for this book, the editors have been particularly concerned to provide answers for (or at least some food for thought on) the following key issues in corporate decision-making:

1 How can strategic planning reduce, or at least equip managers to face, the uncertainty and insecurity of a business environment subject to an accelerating pace of change?
2 How can strategic planning positively assist companies to grow and prosper

in an age when the formula for business success appears to lie in a mixture of managerial expertise and opportunism?

3 How can strategic planning help companies to discharge their obligations to society as a whole at a time when the social and environmental costs of economic growth are moving up the agenda for government action?

4 How can strategic planning assist top management to accommodate and reconcile the requirements and aspirations of pressure groups such as shareholders, customers and employees?

5 How can strategic planning improve top management's utilisation of a firm's human, financial and technological resources?

6 Is strategic planning as applicable to the small firm as it is to the multi-national corporation and how can it help managers to overcome problems of size and scale?

7 How far can the effectiveness of strategic planning be improved by the application of quantitative, scientific techniques, and how far does it remain a matter of intuitive, subjective judgements and personal 'hunches' on the part of the chief executive?

Finally, and perhaps most important of all, the experience of strategic planning should certainly improve top management's overall knowledge of company activities. As the editors have argued elsewhere,* contemporary management is in danger of becoming excessively oriented towards the various functional specialisms recognised within the firm, such as marketing, finance and personnel. The overall success of the enterprise, however, is dependent upon the coordination of these functional objectives within the framework of a coherent and comprehensive strategy. Consistency of purpose is the key to success. Without a clearly-defined set of guidelines for top management, consistency in the day-to-day conduct of the business can be very difficult to achieve in the absence of a much more centralised control of decision-making. Yet present-day conditions are making such a degree of central control increasingly undesirable and difficult to achieve. The bigger the company and the more sophisticated its specialist functions, the more acute do these problems of overall coordination and control become.

It is as true today as it has ever been that the success of a business depends primarily on the judgement, energy and skill of its top managers. In an age of increasing specialisation there is a growing need for 'broad-ganged' directors and executives who can combine a high degree of competence in one or more functional areas with an ability to recognise the interrelated nature of business problems. There is a clear and present demand for top executives who have not only mastered the growing corpus of management techniques but who also possess a coherent business philosophy and an awareness of all the factors relevant to the success of the company. These top managers should have a broad understanding of the business, a clear idea of where the organisation is or

* In the introduction to *Journal of Business Policy*, 1, no. 1, Autumn 1970.

should be going, and the ability to motivate and control the various depart-ments and divisions of the firm in pursuit of its overall objectives. We submit that the practice of corporate strategic planning will increase the strength of this hitherto rare stream of management thought and the overall performance of British industry should thereby be raised.

Notes on Contributors

ALLMEN, ERWIN VON, Vice President, Precision Products Group, Safeguard Industries Inc.

ANSOFF, H. IGOR, Dean of the Graduate School of Management, Vanderbilt University, Nashville, Tennessee.

CANTLEY, M. F., A lecturer in Operational Research at the University of Lancaster School of Business and Organisational Studies.

CATHERWOOD, SIR H. FREDERICK, Director, Richard Costain Ltd.; formerly Director General of the National Economic Development Council.

COX, JOAN, Head of Scientific and Technological Statistics Branch, Department of Trade and Industry.

DOUGHARTY, L. A., On the staff of the Cost Analysis Department, Rand Corporation, Santa Monica, California.

DUNNING, JOHN H., Professor of International Business, University of Reading.

EZRA, DEREK, Chairman, National Coal Board, and Chairman of the Europe Steering Committee Confederation of British Industry.

FARMER, DAVID, Currently undertaking research at the University of Bath School of Management.

FINNISTON, H. M., Deputy Chairman, British Steel Corporation.

GREINER, L., Associate Professor of Organisational Behaviour, Harvard Business School.

HAWKINS, KEVIN, Lecturer in Industrial Relations, Management Centre, University of Bradford.

HENRY, HARRY, Visiting Professor of Marketing, Management Centre, University of Bradford.

HOUSE, ROBERT J., Associate Professor of Management, the Bernard Baruch College of the City University of New York, and a member of Dunnuck, Folton and Associates, Management Consultants.

HUTCHINSON, COLIN, Chairman, Conservation Society.

KEMPNER, T., Now Principal of The Administrative Staff College, Henley.

KINGSHOTT, A. L., Treasurer of Ford of Europe Inc., Ford Motor Company.

LONG, R. A., Executive Director, British Rail.

MACMILLAN, KEITH, Lecturer in Economics, Trinity and All Saints College, Leeds.

MILES, R. E., Assistant Professor of Business Administration, University of California, Berkeley.

NEAL, L. F., Industrial Relations Director, British Rail, 1967–71. Now Chairman of the Commission on Industrial Relations.

NEWBOULD, GERALD D., Reader, Manchester Business School.

PERRIGO, A. E. B., Head of the Small Business Centre, University of Aston, Birmingham.

PORTMAN, D. R., Managing Director, Serck Radiators.

REDWOOD, H., General Manager, Central Planning Department, Fisons Ltd.

ROBINSON, COLIN, Professor of Economics, University of Surrey.

STEINER, G. A., Professor of Business at the Graduate School of Business Administration, Los Angeles, California.

TAYLOR, BERNARD, Director of Post Experience Programmes, University of Bradford Management Centre.

TILLES, SEYMOUR, Vice President of Boston Consulting Group.

TINDALE, L. V. D., Director and General Manager, Industrial and Commercial Finance Corporation.

THUNE, STANLEY S., Corporate Planning Manager for the Givaudan Corporation.

VAN DAM, ANDRE, Director of Planning, Corn Products, Latin America.

WAGLE, B., Manager, Management Science, IBM Scientific Centre, Peterlee, Co Durham.

WICKENS, J. D., Formerly Personnel Manager, English Electric Ltd., Bradford.

ZAKON, ALAN, On the staff of the Boston Consulting Group Inc.

PART I

Formulating and developing corporate strategy

1

Strategy as a tool for coping with change

H. IGOR ANSOFF

What is the value of a strategic approach to the determination of the future of a business firm, or indeed of any other organisation? Professor Ansoff defines strategy as a set of decision-making rules for the guidance of organisational behaviour, and implies thereby that the latter may be more predictable as a result. This immediately distinguishes strategy from objectives; the latter represents the goals that the organisation is seeking to attain, the former indicates a means by which these may be attained. Although it is common knowledge that many firms in rapidly growing markets fulfil their growth and profit objectives without a clearly defined strategy, Ansoff argues that in a less favourable market environment a strategy may be of particular value for coping with rapid and disruptive change. Though strategy is a complex and costly tool, there is evidence that it more than pays for itself.

This paper is concerned with the role of a quite specific concept of strategy in the management of purposive organisations. But even within this limited area, the subject of strategy as an instrument of change is too broad to be covered in the space available. Thus, I would like to circumscribe even further the area of my analysis.

My first choice is between substance and concept of strategy. It seems to me that today we have much more agreement on substantive answers on major issues than on conceptual and procedural tools by which the issues are to be resolved. Thus we agree that poverty must be eradicated, wars stopped, natural ecological balance restored. We agree that firms should be useful contributors to social welfare, universities peaceful and constructive contributors to social knowledge, and government an effective provider of public service. But we sadly lack the concepts, the social institutions, the processes by which all these desirable ends can be brought about.

At this point in history the 'how' of meeting society's needs is much more difficult than the 'what'. Therefore I chose to limit my remarks to the concept for attacking problems rather than their contents.

Harold Leavitt has suggested that there are three ways in which social problems can be attacked: through designing the process by which society's work is

done, through structuring human relations and behaviour, and through designing the decision-making process. I would like to focus my attention on the
third line of attack and, within it, on a specific decision-making tool called
strategy.

Thirdly, I would like to limit consideration of strategy to what may be called
purposive organisations: the business firm, the university, the hospital, the
executive and service branches of the government. Two features are common to
all of them: each has an identifiable output – a manufactured product, an
educated person, a cured patient; and each has identifiable, although not
always precise, objectives by which the success of the organization is measured.

For all of these purposive organisations, we can usefully employ a decision-
making tool called strategy by some people and policy by others. Basically a
strategy, as I shall define it, is a set of decision-making rules for guidance of
organisational behaviour. There are three distinctive types of rules: (a) rules for
determining the relation between an organisation and its external environment;
in business firms this is frequently called the product-market strategy; (b) rules
for establishing the internal relations and processes *within* the organisation; this
is frequently referred to as the organisational concept; and (c) the rules by which
the organisation conducts its day-to-day business called major operating
policies. A strategy has several distinguishing characteristics:

1 The process of strategy formulation results in no immediate action. Rather
  it sets the general direction in which the organisation will grow and develop.
2 Consequently, strategy is what is commonly called today a *search heuristic*. It
  stimulates members of the organisation to invent and to find certain types of
  opportunities and suppresses invention of others.
3 Because strategy is a heuristic for developing new information for the firm,
  its selection usually occurs under a very special informational environment:
  at best only partial information is available about specific action alternatives.
  Most information available to the decision maker is about groups or classes
  of alternatives. This information is highly aggregated and subject to large
  variance.
4 When search results in discovery of specific alternatives, less aggregated and
  more precise information becomes available. This information may cast
  doubts on the wisdom of the original strategy choice.
5 Thus the process of strategy selection and strategy application is a closely
  coupled two-level decision process which feeds back information and mutual
  adaptation between concrete opportunities and the decision heuristic.
6 There is another and similar set of guidelines found in organisations, called
  objectives. Objectives are yardsticks by which the expected or the past success
  of the organisation is measured. For example, in the business firm these
  commonly include growth, profitability, market share, etc.
7 Strategy and objectives are similar and yet distinct. They are distinct in the
  fact that the objectives represent the *ends* which the firm is seeking to attain,
  while the strategy is the means to these ends. Thus a strategy which is valid

under one set of objectives may lose its validity when the objectives of the organisation change drastically.

8 Finally, strategy and objectives are interchangeable, both at different points in time and at different levels of organisation. Thus some attributes of performance (such as, for example, market share) can be an objective of the firm at one time and its strategy at another. Further, as objectives and strategy are elaborated throughout an organisation, a typical hierarchical relationship results: elements of strategy at a higher managerial level become objectives at a lower one.[1]

In summary, strategy is an elusive and a somewhat abstract concept. Its formulation typically produces no immediate concrete productive action in the firm. Above all, it is an expensive process both in terms of actual dollars and managerial time.

Since management is a pragmatic, result-oriented activity, a question needs to be asked – that of whether an abstract concept, such as strategy, can usefully contribute to the firm's performance.

In the business firm, general recognition of strategy is relatively recent – barely fifteen years old. However, history of business abounds with clear examples of deliberate and successful use of strategy. DuPont's deliberate and successful move from explosives into chemicals in the 1920s is one example. Henry Ford's concentration on the Model T for the emerging mass market was another great success, but his strategy of vertical integration was a failure. As an alternative to Henry Ford's strategy, consider Durant's persistent vision of a firm founded on a full automotive product line and Sloan's subsequent rationalisation of this vision into a clear set of organisational guidelines.[2,3] More recently, Royal Little's clearheaded and deliberate decision guidelines for building a novel type of firm, called a conglomerate, is another instance of success. So is Kircher's strategy for converting a slumbering Singer sewing machine company into a successful growth firm. So is Sears and Roebuck's foresightful move to suburbia.

A skilful business analyst can discern a unique strategy in a majority of successful firms. However, while discernible, in most cases the strategies are not explicit. They are either a private concept shared only by the key management or a diffuse generally understood but seldom verbalised sense of common purposes throughout the firm. It has been argued by some managers, and with good reasons, that strategy, because it represents a unique competitive advantage of the firm, should not be made explicit but kept most private.

Since the middle 1950s American business literature has increasingly reflected an opposing view in favour of carefully and explicitly formulated strategy. Further, this view favours not only making the strategy a matter of concern to many managers throughout the firm but also to many of the workers, particularly sales and R and D personnel since the latter not only have a contribution to make but are also the principal agents of implementation of the strategy.

If the value of a concept is to be measured by its apparent contribution to success, we would have to admit that somehow both views are correct: a great many firms have succeeded and are succeeding without the benefit of an enunciated strategy, while a smaller and growing number appear to have benefited from deliberate strategy formulation.

An explanation can be sought through resolution of another apparent paradox: strategy is a system concept which gives coherence and direction to growth of a complex organisation. How is it possible, then, for a large and complex organisation, such as a business firm, to attain coordination and coherence without making strategy explicit?

One answer is to be found in the nature of the firm's growth. If a firm is operating in products and markets with substantial unfulfilled or growing demand, if the characteristics of demand change slowly, if the technology of products and processes is stable, if all these conditions exist, strategy changes slowly and gradually. Coherence of behaviour and organisational coordination are attained through informal organisational learning and adaptation. New managers and workers are typically given long periods of indoctrination into the nature of the business; their careers are shaped by gradual progression through the firm. In the process they acquire an experiential, almost intuitive, awareness of the firm's strategic guidelines. When environment, technology, or competition changes in an orderly manner, these managers are able to adapt to the change using their accumulated knowledge and experience. A manager in engineering can be expected to adapt in ways similar to a manager in markets or production. A reasonably coherent organisational growth results. It can be questioned whether such loosely coordinated behaviour produces the best possible growth, but it works demonstrably. Thus, given deliberate *extrapolative growth*, an explicit strategy is not essential to coordinated adaptive growth.[4] Given this fact, several questions can be asked concerning the utility of having a strategy.

The first is whether strategy is a viable concept. Some writers, significantly observers not of the firm but of decision processes in the government such as Lindbloom, have argued that organisational complexity, uncertainties of information, and limited human cognition make it impossible to approach strategy formulation in a systematic manner. Their argument is that strategy formulation must of necessity proceed in the adaptive, unsystematic, informal way observed in most organisations. The answer to this contention is that the proof of the pudding is in the eating. The examples cited above, as well as some more recent ones, demonstrate that strategy *can* be formulated systematically.

Given that strategy formulation is feasible, the next question to be asked is whether it produces improvement in organisational performance, if used as an alternative to adaptive growth. Until quite recently we had no satisfactory answer to this question. However, within the last year, two particular conclusive pieces of evidence have been provided.

One of these comes from an extensive study of American mergers and acquisitions[5] which I and my colleagues have recently finished. Among other significant results we found that deliberate and systematic preplanning of acquisition strategy produces significantly better financial performance than an unplanned, opportunistic, adaptive approach. These results are valid under stringent tests of their statistical validity. The other result is the outcome of an independent study[6] by Professor Robert House who studied effectiveness of long-range planning on company performance. His conclusions in favour of planning are as strong as ours. Therefore, I feel reasonably confident in advancing the conclusion that strategic planning is a preferred alternative to growth through fully decentralised adaptation without the benefit of an explicit strategy.

The third question we must ask is under what conditions does recourse to strategy become essential. One condition is when very rapid or even discontinuous changes occur in the environment of the organisation. For a business firm this may be due to saturation of traditional markets; drastic changes in technology; sudden influx of new competitors; an unusually productive R and D department within the firm. Under these conditions, established organisational traditions and experience lose much of their validity for coping with the new opportunities and new threats. Without the benefit of a unifying strategy, the chances are high that different parts of the organisation will develop different and contradictory responses. The chances are therefore high that readjustment to the new conditions may be prolonged, turbulent, and inefficient. Chances are equally high that recognition of need to readjust will come too late to guarantee survival of the firm in its present form. A recent takeover wave in parts of the American industry is an example of a possible outcome.

Under these conditions, the firm is confronted with two very difficult problems: (1) how to choose the right directions for further growth from among many and imperfectly perceived alternatives; and (2) how to harness the energies of a large number of people in the chosen direction. Answers to these questions are the essence of strategy formulation and implementation. At this point strategy becomes an essential and badly needed managerial tool.

Such conditions were, in fact, the cause of interest in explicit strategy formulation in the US during the mid-fifties, when pent-up wartime demand began to reach saturation; when technology began to make obsolete some industries and to proliferate new ones; and when restructuring of international markets presented both new threats and new opportunities for business firms.

Another condition which makes recourse to strategy highly desirable occurs when the objectives of an organisation undergo a drastic change, either because of a shift in the objectives of its participants, or because of new demands imposed on it by society. This, it seems to me, is precisely what is happening today in many non-business purposive organisations: the Church, the university, the government. And this is the reason why we are seeking efforts to introduce PPBS, which is a variety of strategic planning, into most of these institutions. We are also observing how difficult it is to implant the concept of strategy and strategic planning into these organisations. The process is much more difficult in non-business institutions for reasons which I have no time to elaborate. But, by way of summary, I would like to mention several difficulties which are common to all purposive organisations.

One major source of difficulty comes from the fact that in most organisations the pre-strategy decision-making processes are heavily political in nature. Strategy introduces elements of rationality which are disruptive and threatening to the political processes. A natural organizational reaction is to engage in a fight against the environment rather than against the challenges posed by the environment. We have seen much of this during introduction of Planning, Programming and Budgeting Strategy (PPBS) in the US government. A no less important difficulty is that organisational structures of most purposive organisations are not suited to the introduction of strategic planning. A conflict arises between previous activities and the innovative activities. Organisations typically do not have the capacity to handle both nor motivational systems to encourage the use of strategy. Finally, organisations generally lack information about both themselves and their environment which is needed for effective strategic planning; nor do they have the managerial talents capable of formulating and implementing strategy.

In summary, strategy is a complex and potentially very powerful tool for coping with conditions of change which surround us today. But it is complex, costly to introduce, and costly to use. We have definite, though partial, evidence that it more than pays for itself. In many instances today it appears to be a tool which offers significant help for coping with takeovers of business firms, breakdown in law enforcement, student rebellions, breakdown in health delivery systems, urban congestion. Therefore I think that it merits serious attention as a managerial tool for a broad spectrum of social organisations. But it must be used with an awareness that it is neither a natural, nor a welcome addition to political behavioural processes within human organisations.

References

1. H. I. ANSOFF, *Corporate Strategy*, McGraw-Hill, 1965.

2. ALFRED P. SLOAN, *My Years with General Motors*, Doubleday, 1963.

3. A. D. CHANDLER, *Strategy and Structure*, Massachusetts Institute of Technology Press, 1962.

4. H. I. ANSOFF, 'Toward a strategic theory of the firm', *Economies et Société*, II, no. 3, Paris, 1968.

5. H. I. ANSOFF, J. L. AVNER, R. G. BRANDENBURG, F. E. PORTNER and H. R. RADOSEVICH, 'A study of acquisition behaviour of US manufacturing firms during the period 1946–65', to be published.

6. ROBERT J. HOUSE and STANLEY THUNE, 'Where long range planning pays off'. See pp. 77–87.

2

The choice of corporate objectives

M. F. CANTLEY

Once a firm has accepted the need for a strategic approach to managerial decision making and is aware of the factors it must consider in formulating the strategy, top management must address itself to the problem of developing objectives. Cantley argues that a formulation and statement of objectives is an integral part of corporate planning. He points out that objectives have three main purposes. First, they are used to rank alternative courses of action. Second, they are used as yardsticks against which corporate performance may be measured. Third, they provide a common framework of reference to ensure operational consistency within the firm. He concludes by suggesting how the formulation of objectives should be tackled and what it might usefully contain.

This article seeks to be academic, practical and eclectic. Academic, in so far as it seeks to develop a general understanding of the subject, to which to relate systematically its different aspects, and to compare some of the different writings on it; practical, because business science is an applied science; and eclectic, because in order to derive practical objectives from a general picture, we must be selective, just as each individual firm must perforce concentrate on a limited set of objectives chosen from the whole field.

The 'classical entrepreneur', central figure of business mythology, might be surprised by today's development of the management sciences; but perhaps above all by the space and thought devoted to 'objectives' – a subject at once so central and obvious to him as barely to require enunciation. If enunciation were required, had not Adam Smith convincingly shown that for every desirable result to follow, no other objectives were required than that each man should unstintingly pursue his own self-interest?

The present complexity of the subject derives, in the different social and economic conditions and purposes of today, not only from the erosion of the classical tradition based on the simple and readily defined aims of the entrepreneur, but from the diversity of purposes empirically observable in the practices of different undertakings.

Definitions and dimensions

Objectives in the modern corporation – Drucker's 'survival needs'

The concept of purpose in human activity is not a simple one. Our own century has found it an increasingly difficult philosophical question – as compared, for instance, with the relatively simple theocentric, single-purpose view of the universe which characterised European culture in the Middle Ages. The subsequent economic development of Europe, and the history of the resulting overt and implicit conflicts with the older, hierarchical social order are described by Tawney in *Religion and the Rise of Capitalism*. Adam Smith's view of the Providential coincidence of private self-interest and social good represents in some ways a last attempt at synthesis of a single, consistent system of values and objectives. Changes in the material aspects and the value systems of society as a whole are reflected in the changes in the nature and aims of our organisations, social, governmental and commercial, including in particular, in this context, the development of the joint stock company or corporation and within it, of its objectives. From being a small unit with a precisely defined range of activities serving the purposes of a small group, it had evolved to become a major economic and even social unit in society, increasingly detached in personal terms from its owners, and concerned with its own continuity and self-perpetuation. The point is exemplified in the specific feature of the memorandum and articles of association of a company. Originally related to the immediate circumstances of its origin and the aims of its founders, the statement of its incorporation was a restricted and restrictive definition of its aims and scope, comparable today to the precise terms of commodities and areas of operation to be specified by a transport operator to obtain a B-licence. Today the pattern is to avoid any restriction of the company management's freedom of action by specifying terms as widely as possible (the trend is well described by Gower).[1] This reflects an increasing recognition of a company's right to pursue its own survival as a legitimate objective; such survival generally demanding adaptive capability. Few companies have long-range plans encompassing a date for their own extinction – even in the extractive industries. One can readily foresee the continuing existence of a chemical corporation known as the 'Coal Board' long after the last pit has closed.

In his 1958 paper on 'Business Objectives and Survival Needs',[2] Drucker describes the following five 'survival objectives':

1 The enterprise needs a *human organisation designed for joint performance* and capable of perpetuating itself.
2 The enterprise exists in *society and economy* and hence needs objectives enabling the business to adapt, and at the same time aim at creating the most favourable conditions.

3 Its purpose is to *supply an economic good and service*; the only reason why business exists.
4 It exists in a *changing* economy and a *changing* technology, and is unique among all historic human institutions in having innovation and the pursuit of change as purpose characteristics.
5 Finally, *profitability* is an absolute requirement of survival.

Drucker states that this 'approach to a discipline of business enterprise through an analysis of survival objectives . . . twenty years hence (1958) might well have become the *central* concept around which we can organise the mixture of knowledge, ignorance, and experience, of prejudices, insights, and skills, which we call "management" today'.

The operational roles of objectives

Drucker's five survival objectives certainly characterise the modern corporation. They centre round a concept of adaptive survival, and indeed points (2), (3) and (4) are virtually three ways of stating the same requirement. This article, however, moves closer to the practical needs of the firm, and given the 'essential' objectives of Drucker, adds (rather than substitutes) the following 'operational' definition of the nature and purposes of objectives, and how they are used:

1 Objectives are used to *rank alternatives*. This is their central function in decision-making, i.e. in choosing between the forecast outcomes of alternative courses of action.
2 Objectives are used as *measures* – for targets, and for subsequent assessment of the satisfactoriness of performance, i.e. for control.
3 Objectives provide a common *framework of reference* to ensure the consistency of decisions and measures in different parts of the organisation.

In discussing specific objectives below, it will be clear that these operational characteristics in no way conflict with Drucker's five essential ones. Rather, they are more general. Even if the modern corporation were to change in form and merge into Galbraith's all-embracing 'technostructure',[3] and even in the public sector (or for that matter in the communist countries), these three operational roles of objectives must remain.

However, our present concern is with the choice of objectives in the corporation. In considering this, it will become evident how each item fulfils one or more of the three roles above; and which forms are specifically suitable for the corporation, according to the requirements spelt out by Drucker.

Basic classification of objectives

Each aspect of planning – objectives, forecasts, plans themselves – can be classified as follows:

1 By the *time-span* they relate to – e.g. 3 months, 1 year, 5 years, 20 years ahead

2 By *organisational level* – e.g. the world, the nation, the industry, the corporation, the division, the department.
3 By *function* – e.g. purchasing, capital investment, finance, production, distribution, marketing, service.

In speaking of corporate planning and corporate objectives we are concerned with the corporation as the highest organisational level, and are covering (or providing a common background for) the plans for all functions. Within the corporation, the higher the organisational level, the longer the time-span planned for; so that 'corporate' and 'long-range' planning tend to become synonymous.

'Corporate' objectives hence by implication become 'long-range' objectives. In considering them, however, we are obliged to examine how the shorter-term targets, and the targets for the lower organisational and functional levels are to be derived. A useful distinction is drawn in Ackoff[4] between 'objectives' as perennial, undated aspirations of the firm; and 'targets' or 'goals' as dated, scheduled manifestations of these objectives.

The problem of multi-dimensionality

The above multi-dimensional structure of objectives apparently conflicts with the first operational role, i.e. the ranking of alternatives. The process of ranking alternatives demands a single scale of measurement, which is why many authors repeatedly insist that to speak of more than one objective is inherently ridiculous. It is like Bentham's famous (or notorious) 'greatest good of the greatest number' – the trade-off is undefined. The central problem in attempting to specify consistent corporate objectives is that of making this many-to-one transformation. For on the one hand, the second and third operational roles demand, in practice, a multiplicity of objectives for the various organisational and functional centres within the firm, and for different time periods. But on the other, a firm confronted with any range of alternative present actions must make some choice (including in the 'actions' that of deferring a decision), and this implies the existence of some single measure of corporate 'utility' to which all other aspects of each alternative can be reduced. Whether this process of reduction is made explicit, and whether it remains consistent over time, are questions to which we shall return.

At each decision-making level there must be this means of trading off different objectives to give a simple ranking. The natural answer to this is the hierarchy structure, most ably expounded by Ansoff[5] in chapters 3 and 4 of *Corporate Strategy*. These hierarchies (Figs 4.1 to 4.4 of *Corporate Strategy*) are a useful method of laying out the goals in a way which distinguishes which are more basic ends, which are means, and how they support one another. They do, however, over-simplify the interdependencies which may well exist. For instance, a structural objective on independence and an earnings growth target may be incompatible, because given the financial structure of the firm and the nature of its business, the capital required for such growth may inevitably outstrip internally generated funds. More fundamental is the problem that merely listing objectives in a hierarchy does not define how they are in fact reconciled at each level; particularly at the top. Ansoff (chapter 4, last para.) says: 'This problem of selecting opportunities which are measured by a number of incommensurate components of an objectives vector does not have a satisfactory solution at present. . . . A specific method for evaluating incommensurate components of objectives will be developed in chapter 9', and in chapter 9:

> (priorities are assigned) to the respective objectives, since these can be used as 'weights' to compute an overall weighted rank for each of the remaining alternatives. . . . It must be recognized, however, that different numerical weights may lead to different choices . . . several alternative 'best' choices will emerge depending on the weights. Mathematical manipulation stops here and the full range of results and assumptions should be presented to the responsible executive for his final decision. Thus, while management science can offer help in clarifying choices, the final decision and the responsibility for it remain with the executive.

It might appear that these trade-offs are where analysis stops, and the corporation defines its character by its choices; these effectively show what its corporate utility function comprises. Further research can attempt to relate these choices to managers' value systems and such work is being undertaken by W. D. Guth at Columbia. Guth[6] specifies the manager's values in terms of a 'profile' based on six 'prototypes': economic; social; political; aesthetic; religious; theoretical, derived from Spranger's work.[7] For such work to move from descriptive to prescriptive would obviously involve the prescriber in specifying what our socio-economic objectives should be; an ambitious task.

Human and organisational aspects

We have seen already how the pursuit of rational decision-making, the first operational role of objectives, leads to psychological questions about managerial value systems. In private, family-dominated businesses it is usually evident that individual drives inform the firm's strategic choices. It is, however, no less true that any group of managers or long-range planners will have different priorities, for reasons such as these:

1 The members have different retirement dates.
2 If the company is taken over or goes bankrupt, through pursuing risky strategies, members' reemployment prospects will vary. They therefore worry to different extents about their own job security.
3 Members have different understandings of what the shareholders want, or should be told or given.

It is therefore valuable for the management to discuss and formulate objectives, so that their actions are better coordinated. Just how they will resolve their differences to achieve rational decisions is less clear, but a satisfactory basis is likely to incorporate some use of cardinal measures rather than simply voting on preferences.

In many small firms it seems unnecessary to spell out a 'common frame of reference'. The stock clerk, confronted with two identical products at different prices, will presumably order the cheaper without needing to refer to higher authority or a written policy statement. However, at more senior levels in the organisation, the alternatives are not generally so clearcut, so the need increases for explicit objectives. Again, in the short term, a company usually has little freedom of action. But the further ahead one plans, the greater the possible changes that may be planned for; and hence the greater the freedom of choice, and consequent need for a fuller statement of the objectives which direct choice. The long-range planner needs a fuller statement of objectives than the man responsible for next year's budget.

These reasons for making an explicit framework of objectives are reinforced by the growth in scale and complexity of modern corporations. Scale produces complexity, as the business becomes multinational, multidivisional and multi-product. Complex organisations need greater attention to their systems of information flow, and to the common 'language' of basic assumptions and objectives.

In any organisation containing a large number of people there are problems of maintaining motivation and control. It is useless and unjust to fire the ware-house superintendent because the dividend had to be cut. He is demonstrably at fault only if there is a clear relationship between the overall results and the items under his control – such as inventory level, reordering and stockholding costs. It must be made clear to him what is required of his area before he can be effectively assessed on his performance. On the 'no taxation without representation' principle, it also seems fair that he should be involved in setting his own objectives. In fact, as well as being 'fair', such consultation with the local functional expert is an essential part of the planning feedback cycle, to ensure the feasibility of the plan's targets. These points underlie the concept of 'management by objectives' – for a fuller description see Humble[8] and his references. Once the second and third 'operational roles' of objectives are recognised, it becomes clear that organisational structure and the elaboration of local targets and objectives are two ways of viewing the same problems – effective communication, coordination and control.

The field of choice

In this section we examine some of the measures and qualities which commonly figure or have been proposed as corporate objectives. Their relation to the operational roles and survival needs described above is discussed. The final section then discusses how the corporate planner will compile his own firm's portfolio from the boundless field of plausible objectives.

Profit maximisation

Maximising profits is the complete and sole objective of the firm in classical economic theory. It has been argued that in the long run any firms *not* maximising profit will be eliminated, bankrupt or taken over by a profit-maximising conglomerate. This conflicts with the view of *adequate* profitability as a requirement for survival, see Drucker's fifth objective above. The empirical evidence at least is clear that there exists living-space between the profit adequate for survival, and the maximum. The 'long run' may narrow the gap between adequate and maximum profits, but this theory is rather difficult to validate.

The objections to profit maximisation as an operational objective are as follows:

1 Classical economics is *static* – maximising this year's profit is assumed to be identical to maximising future years' profits. It therefore gives no indication of how short- and long-term returns are compared.
2 'Maximise' = 'select greatest possible'. The theory ignores uncertainty; since we don't know which actions give the greatest profit – probably some not even considered – we cannot identify the profit-maximising action.

The development of large comprehensive models of the company's operations and markets – such as the linear programming models used by some oil companies[9] – might appear to offer scope for 'maximisation'. But such models are essentially static, or at most cover only a short timespan because of computational limitations. 'Maximising' the profits via the model is conditional on the validity of the model as a representation of reality. The model is never comprehensive enough to specify all the uncertainties of change and possibilities of diversification and new strategies. There is only one fully accurate, comprehensive and implemented 'model' of firms and their environment – and we live in it.

The firm's response to the impossibility of profit maximisation, to uncertainty and to the limited scope of any model, is to hedge its bets. The concept of 'flexibility' is treated by Ansoff as a strategic objective – he defines it as the ability to safeguard profitability under *unforeseen* contingencies. Similarly Ackoff describes the model-maximising 'optimiser' as one ideal type of planner, but is forced to go beyond this and introduces 'adaptivising' – the building of initiative and responsiveness into every aspect of the firm – to meet the shortcomings of modelling. A model of the universe is implicit in profit maximisation.

Numerical economic measures

Profit maximisation, even if feasible, would fulfil only the first operational role – a single-dimensional method of ranking alternatives. The second rule demands specification of numerical targets. These will be the result of some iterative planning process in which their feasibility has been examined, and their satisfactoriness as targets will be assessed by comparison with prevailing opinion and the performance of other firms in terms of the same measures. The third operational requirement will be to derive for the other functional and organisational decision centres of the firm meaningful numerical targets consistent with the overall goals.

The idea of profit – an excess of receipts over costs – is central to any commercial operation, and it forms a basic measure of the efficiency of the resource conversion process. 'Profit' as an accountant's quantity requires careful definition of the treatment of depreciation and other 'allocated' quantities (as opposed to cash flows), but there are no insuperable problems provided the definition is consistently adhered to. In order to move from the absolute profit to a measure by which to compare different time periods and different projects or companies, it is necessary to define some dimensionless ratio.

The profit in any year can be defined, and a target set for it. A trade-off function is then required for profit in future years. Customarily, the 'time preference for money' is expressed by discounting. This demands definition of a rate (a problem raising several technical questions) and clarification of whether it is being applied to the profit (as defined, for instance, by the accountants) or the cash flows (which gives a more rational treatment of capital expenditures, but requires estimation of the time-lags for credit given and received).

We must clarify whether we are speaking of before or after tax profit. Both terms are used; it depends on the functional and organisational level we are speaking with. In multinational firms with sophisticated financial management, the figure used should be after loan interest and tax, since these are items capable of being influenced and improved. For the local national management, the gross trading profit is a more directly meaningful measure of efficiency.

In normalising these measures into ratio form, the commonest measure is

$$\text{'return on capital employed'} = \frac{\text{profit}}{\text{capital employed.}}$$

Various versions are widely used: profit before or after tax and loan interest; gross capital, depreciated capital, revalued capital, etc. If we want a measure of efficiency in the management of capital, uninfluenced by its source, then the profit should be gross, since the after tax profit is affected by the debt/equity structure of the capital. Historical capital cost, or historical cost less accumulated depreciation proves unsatisfactory for interfirm or interdivisional comparisons. It seems preferable to base the figure on an up-to-date valuation at the lower of current market value or replacement cost.

The return on capital can be conveniently disaggregated in the 'pyramid' or 'Dupont' ratio system, starting with:

$$\frac{\text{Profit}}{\text{Capital}} = \frac{\text{Profit}}{\text{Sales}} \times \frac{\text{Sales}}{\text{Capital}}$$

and proceeding to many further ratios. This simple hierarchical structure has the advantages of simplicity, and of unambiguous consolidation to the one measure at the top. It is therefore quite widely used in various forms – e.g. by Weinstock[10] of GEC–AEI–English Electric.

Since the shareholders are the legal owners of the business, their earnings as a proportion of their equity capital are a more fundamental objective than the return on capital, the rate of loan interest, the debt–equity ratio, and the rate of taxation. The debt-equity ratio is an interesting figure of strategic implications, since it reflects the firm's attitude to risk, or the adventurousness of its financial management. (An upper limit will naturally be imposed by the firm's creditors.) The gearing question was well explored in an empirical study by Donaldson,[11] who shows how its level can be related to calculable probabilities of bankruptcy or any other specified level of cash flow.

The advocates of discounted cash flow (DCF) may be unhappy with the use of return on capital, based as it is on an arbitrary definition of profit and valuation of capital, and ignoring the dynamics of several years ahead. The dynamics are implicitly handled by stating the ROC target as 'long-run average'. DCF is a tool appropriate to comparing alternative projects with finite life-spans. For a whole firm, hoping to survive indefinitely, there is an intractable problem either of horizon year valuation or of forecasting cash flows to infinity. With these major difficulties, it is unlikely that an 'internal rate of return' or 'present discounted value' calculated for a firm's whole activities could prove a widely used, understood, or popular measure – quite apart from its theoretical weaknesses.

The fact is that the latest published earnings are one of the figures of most interest to the investing community. They are, therefore, also of interest to the company management, who will be concerned to maintain their share price at a level sufficient to keep shareholders content with their performance, to deter takeover bidders, and to provide a strong 'currency' for any acquisitions they themselves wish to make. Discussion of the 'yield' of shares seems to be out of fashion, and financial journalists have now learnt to invert this and talk of price–earnings ratios. These figures reduce the need for fractions and percentages, but the old 'yield' had the advantage that it could still be meaningfully used for zero or very small values. As is well known, glamorous, fast-growth firms have high P/E ratios (low yields) and vice versa. The P/E ratio represents the ratio:

$$\frac{\text{share price}}{\text{earnings per share}} = \frac{\text{Total market capitalisation}}{\text{Total earnings (available for appropriation)}}$$

Suppose that the total market capitalisation represents a rational shareholder's valuation of the present discounted value of the company's earnings to infinity (ignoring the fact that 'share prices' are marginal prices). Then if his discount rate is i and he expects earnings per share to grow at rate g, the P/E ratio is $\frac{1 + i}{i - g}$.

Halford[12] develops this formula to make the obvious allowances for the dividend/retention policy and the shareholder's tax rate. It is a 'relative objective' that can certainly worry managements with poor performance.

As a strategic objective, it suffers from a number of technical problems – the treatment of inflation; the nonhomogeneity of shareholder's tax positions, psychology, and beliefs about the company's prospects; the fact that shareholders' cash flows are not just dividends, but sale of their shares; and above all, the fact that investors buy shares speculatively, valuing not on estimated earnings to infinity, but on their estimate of what some other investors may shortly believe the shares to be worth. Some of these effects can be mitigated by technical adjustments, but simplicity is sacrificed. However, if the management make an assumption about i, the shareholders' discount rate (e.g. treat it as an opportunity cost of capital, and find out the long-run average market return on equities – say, over the past five years) then they can deduce g. Thus they have a 'message' from the shareholders of what is expected as their growth rate of earnings per share. If they achieve this, they may, of course, find themselves in a positive feedback spiral.

This problem of setting growth rate objectives has been well treated by Marris,[13] who argues the following case very convincingly. Management can increase the growth rate by reducing current earnings, through investing in growth-creating areas such as R and D, marketing (long-range planning?) and the administrative costs of diversification. Growth can thus have a two-way effect: reducing current profits, but in the long run increasing the capacity to earn profits. There will, under certain assumptions, be a rate of growth which maximises the present value of future profits. Marris suggests that aggressive modern managements may have an interest in growth exceeding that required for shareholders' best interests, and that the only effective constraint on them is the fear of takeover which too low current earnings and share price might invite.

Another very significant constraint on managements, again directly related to shareholders, is the determination never to cut the dividend. This is very widely observed, unless and until prolonged decline or exceptional misfortune compels it. This objective imposes constraints on the stability required in current earnings (there is a trade-off problem here between liquidity of assets and acceptable limit of earnings fluctuations), and these impose stability requirements on sales volume and profit margin. A quantified objective on reducing sales fluctuation can provide a spur to search for new product lines or new geographical markets with independent or even complementary ups and downs.

The stability problem is also reflected in the need, particularly of large project, capital intensive industries such as chemicals, to achieve a balanced cash flow through the timing of major investments. To quote Lord Hill of Luton in his statement to the shareholders of Laporte Industries in 1968:

> Our industry is capital intensive and the investment per man employed is steadily increasing. . . . This means that in our forward planning we have to look further ahead each year. Not only have we to assess future profitability, we have to plan our investment programme so as to achieve the right mixture of short-term and long-term projects.

Stability also interacts with what managements may view as a safe limit to their gearing, or debt–equity ratio, as discussed above. The point, however, seems academic to the numerous companies which make comparatively little use of loan capital, although consistently earning returns substantially above market interest rates. The problem for them, well brought out by Galbraith,[3] is not that of obtaining fresh capital, but of finding satisfactory investment opportunities for the positive cash flows they are already generating internally.

In speaking of financial targets, it is important to define the money values because of the significant difference which inflation can make to projections more than a few months ahead. This is of particular significance to multi-national firms, who will wish to assess the stability and inflation of various currencies, and take operating decisions related to these on the form in which liquid assets are held, and the countries in which loan capital is raised. Technical difficulties can arise in long-term projections from differences in the rate of change of various prices and costs, and the admixture of some face value cash flows such as interest and debt repayments. These difficulties must be overcome by careful definition.

Structural objectives

Many firms have clearcut structural objectives for their future type and ownership. Family-owned firms may be keen to remain independent, or at least to retain a dominant interest in the equity. Others may be concerned to establish an image and product range that make them attractive takeover prospects for a suitably wealthy buyer. Many firms are determined to grow in order to remain economically viable, and to maintain their P/E ratio at a level which deters takeover. Such objectives may impose clear demands or constraints on growth rate and earnings. It is one of the advantages of systematic corporate planning routines that they help to demonstrate and quantify such implications.

Non-economic objectives, responsibilities and constraints

Modern corporations are increasingly willing, both for commercial self-interest and employee satisfactions, to align themselves with what they perceive to be the public interest. This is illustrated by the following quotation from Dupont's annual report (1968):

As public problems have grown more complex, there has been a redefinition of the traditional concepts of business leadership and ethics. As a result, the major industrial companies face intense pressure for direct involvement in the solution of wide-ranging social and environmental problems such as urban decay, air and water pollution, noise abatement, racial unrest, substandard housing, and inadequate educational, recreational and cultural facilities.

Specific requests and demands take many forms, and pose a difficult challenge to industry. Industrial know-how is often irrelevant to community problems, and industry's financial and technical resources are often inadequate. The essential fact, however, is that the need for action is great. There are sound commercial reasons, as well as legal and moral ones, why the business community must respond effectively.

Again, Honeywell's PATTERN system of scenarios and relevance trees (described by Jantsch[14]) requires the identification of social objectives, from which commercial opportunities and strategic R and D objectives are deduced.

Non-economic objectives and constraints are involved by many of the human and organisational factors referred to above. The attitude of a company's management to a declining town dependent on one of its less economic factories is often a complex mixture of public relations, philanthropy, and distaste for unpleasant and unpopular decisions. For whatever combination of reasons, the trend appears to be towards increasing acceptance of public responsibility; a trend encouraged in many cases by government policy. Voluntary acceptance of these 'burdens' may well be a partly instinctive response by corporations to Drucker's survival requirements – the phrase 'industries which are failing the nation' comes to mind.

Synthesis and conclusion

This paper has illustrated the many possible dimensions of corporate objectives. The trade-offs which may have to be made between these can vary from firm to firm, but typical problematical choices are:

● short-term or long-term profits
● profit and growth in current product-markets or increased flexibility
● independence or growth
● growth or current dividends.

Management science has no right answer to these choices. It can clarify them, but the actual choice made will often be based on the subjective values of the decision-makers. In its existence, a firm may never meet some of these problems, and may well not need a 'complete' statement of objectives. Where a firm meets such choices, but only rarely, it may make up its answers at the time, and hence its corporate style, character, utility function – what you will – evolves. Such decisions may well be apparently inconsistent over time – the 'mature corporation' acting differently from the entrepreneurial small firm from which it grew.

On those questions which in the nature of the firm's business are repeatedly encountered, explicitly or implicitly, it seems desirable that the firm should formulate its corporate objectives. They will presumably reflect Drucker's survival needs as seen in the particular firm; they must, to be practical, fulfil the three operational roles defined.

Notwithstanding what has been said above, the need for developing an explicit statement of strategic objectives is by no means widely accepted. This is illustrated by the recent BIM survey,[15] which found:

It is not normal British practice to set down overall statements of philosophy and purpose in transatlantic fashion. The companies participating in the survey are no exception in this respect. Only one company writes out in detail its overall purpose and aims, along with statements of policy in various matters, e.g. its relations with staff, labour and the trade unions, shareholders, suppliers and customers. One other company does this on similar lines, but in considerably less detail; a few companies indicate their overall purpose and general aims in their annual reports. Many companies do not consider it necessary to write anything down in this context. They believe that such things as the general purpose of the company and the kind of business it is in are clear enough by implication.

Some of the arguments against explicit formulation can be summarised as follows:

1 Formal objectives may hamper performance: they may act as a strait-jacket if too tightly defined, and if set too high, they are demoralising and/or disregarded.
2 Developing and updating a substantial system of objectives is expensive of top management time.
3 It's not worth setting comprehensively framed objectives when only a small number of strategic decisions have to be taken each year – just solve these current decisions, and don't worry about contingency plans for marketing on the moon.

Empirical evidence on the value of formulating objectives is mixed, but the most favourable views seem to come from the largest companies. This accords with the arguments advanced earlier on the increased need for common terms of reference in large organisations. The second point is certainly true. The first and third can only be answered by care in the setting of objectives, and in the selection of aspects for detailed consideration.

The statement of objectives is an integral part of an essential activity – planning. A labyrinth of analytical sophistication should not, however, be imposed abruptly on a company 'cold' to planning. Rather, elaboration of planning systems generally and of the objectives in particular should evolve gradually, by accretion and feedback, in response to perceived needs. Management's perception and understanding of these needs may, of course, be aided and accelerated by a (tactful) corporate planner.

References

1. L. GOWER, Modern Company Law, Stevens and Son, 1957.

2. P. F. DRUCKER, 'Business objectives and survival needs: notes on a discipline of business enterprise', Journal of Business, University of Chicago, no. 2, April 1958.

3. J. K. GALBRAITH, The New Industrial State, Hamilton, 1967.

4. R. L. ACKOFF and M. W. SASIENI, *Fundamentals of Operations Research*, Wiley, 1968, chap. 17

5. H. I. ANSOFF, *Corporate Strategy*, McGraw-Hill, 1967.

6. W. GUTH and R. TAGIURI, 'Personal values and corporate strategy,' *Harvard Business Review*, Sept.–Oct. 1965.

7. E. SPRANGER, *Types of Men*, New York, Springer-Verlag, 1928.

8. J. HUMBLE, 'Corporate planning and management by objectives', *Long Range Planning*, 1, no. 4, 1969.

9. See, for instance, B. WAGLE, 'The use of models for environmental forecasting and corporate planning', *Operational Research Quarterly*, 20, no. 3, Sept. 1969.

10. A. VICE, 'The Weinstock yardsticks of efficiency', *The Times*, 29 Nov. 1968.

11. G. DONALDSON, *Corporate Dept. Capacity*, Harvard Business School, 1961.

12. D. R. C. HALFORD, *Business Planning*, Pan Books, 1968.

13. R. L. MARRIS, 'Profitability and growth in the individual firm', *Business Ratios*, Spring 1967.

14. E. JANTSCH, *Technological Forecasting in Perspective*, HMSO, 1967.

15. BIM Information Summary 134, 'Is corporate planning necessary?' 1968.

3

Setting targets for profit and growth over the next decade

H. F. R. CATHERWOOD

Every corporate strategist must take into account the direction in which other firms, both in the same industry and elsewhere, are moving and are likely to move in the foreseeable future. A national organisation like NEDC attempts to set realistic growth targets for the economy as a whole, but its predictions may obviously have an important bearing on the strategy of the individual firm. In this article the author draws on his extensive experience of working with management groups in a wide variety of industries to illustrate the ways in which it is possible to set profit and growth targets appropriate to a specific firm or industry. He also discusses possible alterations in these targets which may in turn be the result of changes in the economic environment.

The relation of national growth to company growth

No one should be entitled to pontificate in this day and age without giving some credentials. The first credential of anyone from the NED office is that it is our business to look into the future to try to see the strategic issues over the next decade for the British economy in general and for all the major industries in particular. The office serves the council on which sit the six economic ministers and leaders of both sides of industry together with four rugged independents beholden to no particular interest. The office and council keep in touch with particular industries through twenty-three Economic Development Committees and the remit for the whole of the Neddy complex is first, the prospects for economic growth, and second, the methods of achieving it. To the government growth is a major political aim, to workers growth means higher wages and salaries and to industry it means higher profits.

At first Neddy attempted this process all on its own, but it was hard for an office outside the government machine to forecast government expenditure or to get government commitment. Then government took over the planning side of NED but industry was not sufficiently consulted, involved or committed. The present process of economic assessment is carried out in partnership between government, in the person of the Treasury, and the NED office. The government plays in national figures for three or four years ahead, and these are considered by the council and passed on to the Economic Development Committees to work out the implications for each industry. These detailed reports are then passed up to the council which passes them back to the government with its views. The reports are published together with government reaction and the whole process can then be rolled forward.

This conference has to deal with forecasting in yet more detail – at the company level. But many of the questions are the same and both at company and at national level it is necessary to look back before you look forward.

Analysis of past profitability

Each business has got a particular set of talents, connections with the market, with suppliers, with financiers and a particular set of physical assets, all of which together are more productive in some directions than they are in others. Over a ten-year period this particular mixture can be changed. But the change will require a cash flow and that cash flow has to be based on what the business does best today. Every business starts a ten-year forecast with its current earning power and its current earning power is usually based on its tried ability in certain fields over the past decade. To look forward for ten years you must first look back for ten years. So any company before it looks at the future should examine its product line, its markets and its management to see where its strengths and weaknesses have been.

Strong and weak products

Let us take products first. It is very necessary for any company to discover its bread-and-butter lines. These are the products which have made the major contribution to the company's cash flow over a ten-year period. It is necessary to dig this out of the past records because these will almost certainly not be the products on which top management's attention is concentrated. Management have to deal with problem areas and almost by definition with bread-and-butter lines these are not a problem. Management have to deal with product development for the future and almost by definition these are not the bread-and-butter lines. In addition, management tend to concentrate on the products which interest them and a product which is interesting is quite often uneconomic and again by definition will not be a bread-and-butter line.

Maybe a company's management ought to be sufficiently versatile to make every single product a bread-and-butter contributor. But the company which accepts that it can do some things better than others will get further faster than the company which is trying to do everything because its successes will not be so great, and even these successes will be weighted down and offset by its failures. The bane of British industry is the cross-subsidisation of failures by successes, so this exercise of examining the sources of profitability over a ten-year period is very necessary but will be highly contentious and, no doubt, bitterly resisted. But it is absolutely necessary for a firm ten-year look ahead.

Extrapolation of trends

The next necessary question is to ask ourselves what will happen if the trends of the last ten years continue into the next ten years. It is a fair guess that if we simply extrapolate trends we will find that the losses from the losers will swallow up the profits from the bread-and-butter lines. This is partly because losses tend to get worse and not better, and partly because over a ten-year period, the bread-and-butter line of yesterday will, if it is not overtaken by the process of change, almost certainly be challenged in the market by other companies who realise its potential. Of course extrapolation of trends is not an easy exercise. It must take into account trends in the market as well as trends within the company. For instance, with the general reduction in tariffs, imports are growing in most industries at a steady rate. A company must therefore reckon that if nothing else is done part of the growth of the UK market will be taken by imports and less will be available for the home producer. The other side of this coin is that the reductions of tariffs make export markets more profitable if the company can establish an increasing export business. If within the domestic market a company's market share tends to go steadily downwards then clearly something has to be done if the company proposes to expand at all. Another major trend is wage rates. If companies in the past decade had extrapolated their wage increases they would surely have made themselves much less dependent on labour than they have done and our investment per employee would have been much higher.

Breaks in the trend

It may be, however, that the trends look fairly good, but trends do not go on for ever. Unfavourable trends may level off, but so will favourable trends. Even if we establish our bread-and-butter items, even if we cut out the losers, we still have to consider whether the trends which have made the business successful in the past are likely to continue into the future and, more positively, what are the trends in the future which we can use to carry the business from the successes of one decade on to even greater success in the next decade.

The customer

The first point of reference obviously is the customer. The customer creates the cash flow which is the lifeblood of the business. What is the customer going to demand in the years ahead which he has not wanted in the past, and what has he wanted in the past which he will no longer need? These predictions are not quite so difficult as they might seem. The heavy investment now required by industry make it rather less flexible and decisions by industrial customers can often be predicted by the long-term commitments they have already made. Anyone investing in an enormous chemical plant is going to be a customer for feedstock and raw materials needed by that plant for quite some time to come. Government commitments to public expenditure programmes cannot be reversed quickly and are fairly inflexible over a number of years. We are now heavily committed to the use of containers in transport, to clean air and all its consequences, to a motorised society, and all this is likely to affect our customers' demands over the decade.

Industrial customers

This still, of course, leaves great areas of doubt. And these areas of doubt are the field for market research. Market research is the key to any ten-year look. It requires a lot of hard work but it also needs a great deal of imagination. It is terribly difficult for most people to imagine themselves into a decision-making position in five years' time, let alone ten years' time, to assume what will be assumed then and to feel the pressures which can only really be felt when the crunch comes. Yet if you are looking at industrial customers it is not perhaps quite so difficult since many of the decisions are economic decisions and will depend on the economic forces operating on the company in five or ten years' time. For instance, it can be predicted that some customers who now subcontract work because the production run is not long enough for them to make the product themselves will achieve a volume in the next ten years which makes it more economic for them to manufacture than to buy out. It can also be predicted that with the lowering of tariffs and the increase in international specialisation companies will reduce their British suppliers and expand their foreign suppliers.

The consumer

The consumer market is more difficult because much of the decision-making is irrational and yet it is more predictable because a great many individual needs remain basically the same. Rising income produces a larger and larger area of discretionary expenditure not spent on basic needs and this discretionary expenditure could go off in a lot of different directions. It could be spent on clothes, on holidays overseas, on savings, on stereo systems and television, on second cars, or on second houses. Even so, we have other economies with higher per capita incomes and larger discretionary expenditure to which we can look for guidance, especially those of Canada and the United States.

Foreign markets

This brings us round to the foreign market which will inevitably be much more important in the next decade than it has been in the last. The lowering of tariffs and the creation of large free-trade markets has already created a world market in industrial goods and this market will get into top gear in the 1970s. Industrial countries will shop around in Western Europe, North America and Japan and will buy only where they can get the best value. Britain, which has hitherto made everything for everyone, will have to adapt fairly fast and sell a lot more of a narrower range of products if it is not to be outclassed. Therefore, for every single company except those selling products with a very low price to weight ratio (such as cement) foreign markets will become even more important than they are now.

This will greatly alter the trends of the last decade. World trade is going far faster than the UK trade and the rate of change in the 'seventies is likely, therefore, to be much greater than the rate of change in the 'sixties. The limitation imposed by the slow growth of the UK market will no longer be overriding, and whereas in the 'sixties it has paid to be cautious, the cautious man in the 'seventies is likely to find himself trampled underfoot and left behind in the rush. This internationalisation of trade, therefore, is likely to produce a sharp upward bend in output, and the companies which are geared to take advantage of it will be successful. Those who are not geared to take advantage of it will find themselves much more swiftly overtaken and, if they do not adapt rapidly, will find themselves finally left behind.

In the 'sixties we have had the development of EEC and the successive reductions of tariffs and the General Agreement on Tariffs and Trade. The 'seventies are likely to see a further widening of international markets. This will probably not be by a general reduction of tariffs but by major moves such as the entry of the UK into the EEC or an equivalent move if this is not on, the increased operation of international companies, the removal of some remaining barriers in those countries such as Japan which are now so prosperous that these barriers can no longer be justified.

Political trends

It is not enough to look at markets. Any business lives in society and is part of society. So we must examine the likely trends in society. Business is just as subject to political trends as any other institution. But business is a fairly new institution and it has to fight slightly harder for a legitimate place in society than some older and more accepted institutions. Also, because business is competitive and because human nature places a higher value on cooperation than competition, business is still regarded with some suspicion in many societies. All these are factors which the businessman has to take into account. The question in the next decade is whether there will be a major attack from the rising generation on the institution of business or whether privately owned business will continue to be steadily accepted as an essential part of industrial society. It would be a bold man who would predict that business will escape unscathed through the 'seventies in every major country in which it operates. However, business does have very real economic power and the majority of people in most societies

c

recognise that this power is a power for good and want to accommodate political and economic power rather than engineer a confrontation. There is, however, a minority now becoming more active who want this confrontation, and this is another trend which business will have to predict and allow for.

At present this hostility to private business is no longer expressed so much at a political level but by pressure groups on the shop floors in individual companies. This shift is likely to be a major change in the trend of labour relations in the 'seventies and evidence of this change is already in view.

Technical innovation

Another major source of change is the increase in technical knowledge and the rate of application of that knowledge. The rate of technical knowledge has speeded up enormously and the rate of technical innovation, although it has come with disappointing slowness especially in Britain, is also speeding up. Each business will have to examine the processes which saw it through the 'sixties and decide whether those processes are adequate for the 'seventies. Somewhere, even now, the process which will make the existing methods and plant of every business obsolete is already known. The question big business has to ask is which new process is going to become economic in the 'seventies and how long it can afford to delay the changeover. Sometimes the new process will be much more expensive in development and in equipment. Sometimes it will be far cheaper. If it is more expensive then the businesses with the cash-flow adequate to launch themselves into the new era will be more likely to succeed. If it is cheaper then a whole host of new competitors will come in and the company's past resources will not help.

Marketing innovation

A less tangible innovation is a change in marketing technique. Yet it can be just as successful for those who cash in on it and just as disastrous for those who do not, as a change in the method of manufacture. A great deal of industrialised selling has become international and companies have been forced to treat the major industrial countries as part of their home market. Each business has to spot the trend in selling in the 'seventies and decide whether or not this is going to be a major factor and, if so, how it should be exploited and adapt to it.

Financial innovation

It is likely, too, that the 'seventies will see considerable innovations in company financing. It is a long time since interest rates have been so high and the shortage of money, the pressure for change and the cost of holding unproductive money will no doubt greatly increase the velocity of circulation and put considerable demands on all our financial mechanisms. The 'sixties were the decade of the Eurodollar, a method of putting to use United States funds in Europe. The 'seventies will no doubt see similar financial innovations and businesses which are dependent on money either for high-cost plant or for selling goods on credit will have to see that their own financial mechanism is in first-class trim.

Product innovation

I have left perhaps the most important break in trend until the last. That is the changes in products. All the other kinds of innovations will lead up to the actual product or service to be sold.

Probably the seeds of the new products which will take existing markets over the next ten years have already been sown. Probably the first products have appeared somewhere, even if only on an experimental basis. The problem is to connect the product innovation of the decade with your own business. What is necessary is not second sight, but a grasp of reality and a willingness to face the truth however unpleasant it may be. It is easier to go on flogging the old products. It requires less money and less skill. But over the decade today's products are not going to keep the business in being.

Competitors

No ten-year look is complete without an examination of competitors and an estimate of their likely strategy. In few industries will the competition of the 'seventies be the competition of the 'sixties. First of all there will probably be competition from companies outside the industry. Diversification is a continuous process. No company can keep quite strictly to the line of business and many companies are gradually spreading their interests along logical lines which lead them into competition in other fields. Some diversification is just plain stupid, but even a stupid diversification can cause a lot of trouble. However, it is the shrewd diversification which causes most trouble. Big companies wanting outlets will integrate forwards. Big companies wanting to secure their supplies will integrate back. They will then find themselves engaged in a different business and will apply their minds and their money to making it a success. The only safe course is to be sufficiently on top of your business to deal with these moves when they come and to be so competitive that the business does not look too attractive to the outsider.

Foreign competition

But the biggest challenge to the 'seventies will come from overseas. As the tariffs have gone down, as air freight and the container have made goods easier and faster to move, as the jets have made selling around the world so much easier, we have developed among the advanced industrial countries of the free world a world market in manufactured goods. In every industrial country the percentage of business accounted for by imports and exports has crept up and up. A few years ago a third of our manufactured goods were exported, now it is a half and in the 'seventies two-thirds of our manufactures will go to markets abroad and over half will be imported. So it will be more important to keep an eye on our competitors in Japan, California, Switzerland and Sweden than to keep an eye on our competitors down the road.

In the 'sixties our overseas competitors invested in new plant and equipment at a far faster rate than we did. This gave them a tremendous competitive advantage. Wage inflation harmed them less as their capital invested per man rose and their unit costs fell. New plant helped to improve the specification of their product, their equipment was more versatile, their product range wider as they incorporated the latest technical improvements. And as their capacity went up, their delivery dates shortened and they were able to take business which we could not touch. All this is a matter of record. Our share of world trade went down from 18 per cent in 1958 to 11 per cent in 1969. But during the whole of that time we were still protected by pretty high tariffs. We had, on average, higher tariffs than both EEC and USA and many of them were at deterrent levels. All that will have changed in the 'seventies. Tariffs have now come down to threshold level. They are a step not a wall and the big home markets in Europe, America and now Japan give those countries very low marginal costs for the end of the production run which they sell in world markets. So in the 'seventies, our competitors are world competitors and they will take some watching.

International specialisation

The great protection against any competition is the ability to hit right back. Specialisation in international trade means that everyone will find his product range cut down to size and will be forced to step up the sales of those products in which he is still competitive. If the range of profitable products is halved, then the sales of the other half must be doubled. But they cannot be doubled in Britain. They can only be doubled by taking that amount of business away from international competitors. That is tough – very tough – for it forces us to treat export markets as we treat home markets, to give them the same sales and advertising coverage, the same backing of services and spares. I have no doubt whatever that we will do it, but some companies will do it better than others and the process will sort the men from the boys.

Synthesis

So much for the analysis, now for the synthesis. It is hard enough to forecast the ten-year trends but even harder to find the best way to turn those trends to advantage in your own business. Fortunately we don't have to have all the answers right. Fortunately others, too, can make mistakes, and some options can remain open. But the nearer we get to the right answer, the better we will do. There is a difference between the man who, knowing his options, deliberately keeps them open and the man whose options are forced on him by a constant succession of unforeseen crises.

What is our business?

In looking at the assembled data, the first question to ask is, 'What is our business?' What is the mix of skills and knowledge, that ability to meet a particular demand with a particular supply, that spot in the customer's needs which is peculiar to us? What are we good at? The answer lies in our analysis of past profitability – when we outmatched the competition – the likely changes in the next decade and the competitive line-up to meet those changes. Somewhere there must be the optimum slot for the exploitation of the company's skill.

What does our customer want?

The next question, once we have narrowed down the range of markets and products is what the potential customer in those markets is going to want from his supplier. Customer needs do not remain the same from one decade to another. We have to ask what, in the decade to come, can I do for him that he cannot do more cheaply for himself? What skill do I contribute to his end-product, to his satisfaction as a customer? It is not enough to say that a customer wants steel rod or a motor car. He is seldom interested in the product itself. He is interested in what the product can do for him. If I buy an air ticket from London to Harrogate it is not because I want an air journey. I want to be in London the previous night and also to be in Harrogate in good condition by ten o'clock on 7 July. I am not especially interested in a hairbrush – I want the end-product, which is straight and tidy hair. A ten-year look will need to take into account all the ways in which this customer demand could express itself. It will then need to decide on the product or service the customer is most likely to want to buy and then and only then should some estimate be made of quantities.

Industry forecasts

It is at this point that NEDC makes its contribution through the little Neddy economic assessments of the medium-term prospects for particular industries. It tries first of all to make some qualitative forecast of the kinds of goods and services which the industry's customers will want, then it tries to put some numbers to this forecast, giving a range of potential demand for the industry for up to five years ahead, together with the resources required to meet it. It then considers the obstacles to higher growth and to the achievement of identified national or industry objectives and the action required to overcome them. Some of the more capital-intensive industries are suggesting that at the next economic assessment they should be provided with a ten-year long-range forecast.

The economic assessment is a new and, I think, useful tool in providing consistent and firmly based input on the economic environment to the company planning process. It also provides an opportunity for industrialists to influence the decisions made by government and unions which affect the economic environment. I hope, too, that we will be able to make an increasingly important contribution on the likely development of export markets and international competition. If international trade and competition are going to matter more and more then it is no longer right to treat export markets and international competitors as marginal factors in any economic assessment.

Competitive strategy

The overall assessment of demand does not, of course, deal with the individual company's competitive position. The next stage in synthesis is to determine the best strategy to exploit the company's potential strength and optimise its competitive position. It has to work out price elasticity of demand, to decide whether to trade volume for price or price for volume. Too few businesses accept that you can make more money at a lower price. Yet it has for many companies been the classic instrument of expansion and with higher capitalisation in the more lively international markets of the 'seventies it is likely to come into its own again. In any case, the company reckoning on high prices covering high production costs is more likely to be in trouble than the company adapting a competitive strategy.

Competitive investment

But, above all, companies must reckon on a competitive investment strategy. The company must not find that it has failed to match the investment and innovation of its key competitors. The company which out of a false sense of caution will not gear itself up to finance a competitive rate of capital expenditure is likely to find that this is the most reckless decision it ever made. In a rapidly changing competitive environment a company must have the resources needed to hold its own. Most companies are going to need more profits not less, but they will have to earn them in the face of high interest rates and high wages, so the ten-year look will have to incorporate the product and production strategy which will maximise profits and minimise costs.

A company will not only need investment, it will need management, the scarcest commodity in today's industrial world. The real lack in Britain today is a well-trained professional middle management. It is this resource which gives a company its flexibility and adaptability, which enables it to pursue a hard competitive strategy to spot and cash in on the winners.

Flexible response

Faced with all the possible combinations of opportunity and risk over a ten-year haul, companies have to put themselves into a position to develop a flexible response. Some decisions have to be taken, some commitments have to be made, but the wise company strategist will develop methods of spreading the risk of calling on resources only when they are needed, of keeping a mass of manœuvre so that he has the wherewithal to deal with an unexpected opportunity or challenge.

Spreading the risk

Risks have to be assessed before they can spread. No company can insure against all risks, but it can assess probabilities. It is probable that foreign companies will challenge it in the UK market. It is probable that labour relations will get more difficult, it is probable that plant will be more necessary and more expensive and that money will be dearer. All this may indicate the need to join forces with other British companies, to joint-venture instead of going it alone, to specialise instead of covering the waterfront, to lease and not to buy, to subcontract rather than do it yourself, to use and fight with international specialisation by shopping around in the world market in industrial goods, so that your supplies are at least as good as your competitors'. And if tariffs are coming down it may not be necessary to invest overseas behind tariff barriers. It may be best to concentrate resources, using surplus knowhow in patent licensing and franchising arrangements. Good management will have half a dozen options and will not rely on one alone.

Need for feedback and adjustment

Having sketched out the alternative corporate strategies, it should then be possible to fill them out with matching cash flows to see the hard resources the company will need on various alternatives and which will buy the optimum return with the minimum risk. But no diagnosis and prescriptions are for ever. Market technologies, economics, human relations are a changing and evolving kaleidoscope. Corporate strategy must be reviewed, amended, updated. At Neddy we do not believe in rigid targets locked up for five years in the pious hope that everyone will obediently carry them out regardless. We believe in a rolling plan, updated every year together with an evolving strategy which cuts back on losses and reinforces success. This kind of joint planning process, using all the resources of government and industry, is put forward by industrialists and I have no hesitation in commending it to you.

4

Setting up corporate planning

ERWIN VON ALLMEN

The field of corporate strategy is all-inclusive and the problems of actually devising a planning system and making it operate successfully may seem daunting to managers with no previous experience of this technique. Von Allmen provides a valuable blueprint for the corporate planner who is faced with the task of introducing the concept and the machinery of strategic planning to a firm. He emphasises the importance of defining priorities, assessing the organisational climate and aiming to produce tangible results as soon as possible. He suggests specific approaches to setting objectives, appraising the environment, developing planning systems and planning for acquisition and growth.

This article endeavours to identify the major problem areas in the introduction of corporate planning, explore their sources in a typical company and suggest to the planner some specific modes of behaviour to adapt to them. In spite of remarkable similarities among responsibility descriptions of the planning roles in various companies, the actual requirements of the individual differ widely. Further, these differences are a fairly simple function of corporate risk-taking character, and it is the planner who must select the priorities of his tasks. Lastly, no matter what planning tasks are undertaken, there are available a limited number of practical ways to start. Although these may not be theoretically elegant, they may serve to break the ice on the primary planning problem – the indifference of operating people.

A frame of reference

The observations which follow have been developed from several years in management consulting, as well as in the planner role of major representative American industrial companies. Hence they are more the product of personal experience and mixed success in a variety of circumstances, than a research paper. *The basic problem of every planner is that of trying to persuade otherwise distracted people not only to buy his product, but to help him fabricate it.*

No matter how astute his grasp of theory, and theoretical planning has been perhaps overdeveloped, if he does not effectively command an audience, he will realise little effectiveness or satisfaction. This single problem area now overshadows all others combined in the evolution of professional planning as a business discipline. Because of this most planners have to compromise the best interests of an ideal planning scheme for their company in order to obtain a lasting foothold. The matters cited are characteristic of the planning efforts of fairly sizeable American companies. Usually planning does not become the sole responsibility of one individual at turnover levels below $50–100 million. Interestingly, it seems that size is more determinant than the nature of the business, although from one business to another, actual planning techniques may differ. There is no surefire way to start a planning department which will yield comprehensive success. Approaches which operate in some companies fail in others. The commonest experience of the planner is high risk of failure with ultimate partial success, and this may be the criterion of satisfaction required to be a planner. Individuals who gravitate to planning too frequently find this unacceptable and their work loses momentum.

The planner's role

Experienced planners are becoming somewhat more available in the United States, but there is still a great influx each year into planning as more companies start or expand. This means that people from other disciplines are being 'converted' to planners because there is yet very little academic work available specific to the development of professional planners. Most new planners diligently prepare from available literature, seminars and society associations, and these are valuable beyond question because there is such a paucity of source data. When they ultimately phase into the role of planning practitioner in their companies, they must look to a position description. Almost irrespective of the company it will contain the following elements:

1 *Set objectives.* These are usually corporate objectives, but may further subdivide to operating division objectives. They may also be concerned with corporate functions such as marketing or production objectives.
2 *Maintain intelligence on the business environment.* This may take the form of special management advisories from monitoring the current environment, or forecasting the future environment. Often it will be concerned with a specific critical area to the business such as technological change or price of a basic commodity.
3 *Develop planning systems.* This will appear as coordination of division planning or consolidation of subsidiary plans. It may also emerge in terms of scheduling, format or updating of plans.
4 *Handle acquisition activities.* Usually described inaccurately in terms of seeking growth areas of diversification opportunities, there is usually provision for investigation and occasionally negotiation of acquisitions.

5 *Make organisation recommendations.* This area is usually tied to achievement objectives, presumed to be related to 'management by objective'.
6 *Organise budgeting.* This appears in various forms such as development of return on investment criteria and mechanics, preparation of short-term profit (or cash) plans.

Of course, there is an infinite variety of special tasks peculiar to the company and the planner of any given circumstance, but the most striking feature of planner position descriptions is their similarity from company to company. Any given planner is usually immediately struck by the fact that no single human could do all these things, much less do them well. Not too long thereafter he will learn that the enlistment of aid from other quarters in the company is even more formidable. It therefore becomes obvious that in starting a planning department the best compromise is to set priorities in the mix. From these he would then attempt to pursue, or at least emphasise, his duties consecutively. But before reviewing this process, why is the planning role characteristically so ill-defined? It is the first unpleasant axiom of planning that no matter how important the tasks, the planner tends to fall heir to those for which nobody else has time, but everybody feels should be done. It is common for planners to be solicited by management recruiting firms and operating companies for copies of planner position descriptions. The very obvious reason is that the role is not as yet clear cut in a company, although it is felt that there should be 'someone'. Every available 'laundry list' is being borrowed to be sure that nothing is overlooked! On the one hand, this lack of focus tends to exasperate the new planner, while on the other, it gives him wide range to select that which he believes might best be done. Note carefully, it is not suggested that he can do what he wants, but it does provide that he can (and must) decide what the organisation really wants.

From this typical breadth of choice the planner must answer the key question of his start-up: '*What is the real level of risk acceptance in my company?*' It may not be readily obvious why this question is the first which needs to be answered. Some reflection on the nature of decisions to be derived from the plans suggests pointedly that no other position in the company goes more directly to the heart of management aggressiveness or conservatism. This is not to propose a value judgement on either aggressiveness or conservatism *per se*. Experience dictates that irrespective of what is planned, the real long-range effectiveness of the planner's contribution is what is done. Although plans *say* much, the resulting activity is determined by the *willingness to act* of the decision makers, and this is a function of their propensity to take risks.

The intellectually honest managing director will make his decisions in ways which he feels will best represent the interests of his shareholders as he perceives these interests to be. With any visible history at all, the decision-making patterns of individuals or management groups is much more predictable than is generally acknowledged. In fact, public ownership of modern corporations is backed by the implied assumption that the risk-taking character of the management and its decisions will not be subject to abrupt changes.

Ultimately, the question reduces to the unchanging character of individual human behaviour. Without changing a management it is not really safe to assume that significant changes can be made in the action pattern of the company. The history of planners' frustration is written in the rigid, inflexible management structure crying for 'diversification!' and the very fast-moving company traders trying to organise reporting systems and long-range planning for individual companies of tenuous lifespan and unstable management team leadership. Frequently a company is simply talking out of character in the emphasis it would impose on its planner. At the very start, the planner should attempt to operate in the known range of what is *possible* with the people involved. Eventually, a well done planning job will begin to suggest greater flexibility of action to the conservative, without increasing risk, or higher orders of control without inhibiting the aggressive.

The planner's policy

No matter where the planner decides his efforts can first best be spent in the mix of choices in his job description, there are some important guidelines he must observe from the outset.

1 *His programme must be 'positive' in nature.* That is, it cannot assume significant contributions of effort or internal moral support from outside the department in the early stages. There are two reasons: (a) everyone is busy with his own problems, and (b) the function is regarded as so much black art; many will be genuinely seeking direction.
2 *He must immediately produce a tangible product.* This may not necessarily be a dramatic acquisition or other profound event, but there must be some token product.
3 *The new planning manager, especially if he is from outside the company, must be extremely wary of proposed internal political alliances to advance his programme.* The very first office guests are going to be heavily represented by the chronically frustrated organisationally side-tracked and crusaders for remote causes in corporate affairs.
4 *He should quickly determine where the real power of the company lies, and direct the planning programme to the probable needs of these individual(s).* Is the board of directors a figurehead? Is the chairman or the managing director the real source of impetus in the company, or is it an outside shareholder, an heir apparent now at lower level, or a more remote arrangement such as a sales director who has a personal rapport with a key account? These questions cannot be over-emphasised. With all the inherent handicaps the planner has, especially starting in a new business environment, his access to the sources of power in the company can help to neutralise them because he has been invited to participate in some of the most important problem-solving. Even a badly subordinated organisational spot can be dealt with if the planner knows the structure of the overburden, especially if he can enhance the prospects of his immediate superior.

5 *The planning manager and his supporting staff must assume the attitude of good staff.* They are purveyors of a service, the nature of which is to enhance the activities of others. This requires a high frustration tolerance level, an ability to communicate persuasively, and unbounded patience.

6 *Every modern company has a committee of some kind which moves its operations.* This committee is frequently the seat of power mentioned above, or is its direct instrument. The planner should make every effort to obtain membership in this group if he is not, as he should be, an *ex officio* member. This representation can be the point at which the gap is closed between the pious, well-intended talk about objectives and what the company actually does. In the structure of the group, there is great benefit to be derived in having a member whose principal responsibility is watchdogging the longer-range consequences of weekly or monthly decision-making. Even as an observer, the planner in this group can improve his future chances of success.

Many of the guidelines are Machiavellian in character, but if we are to be brutally realistic, they are extremely practical, irrespective of the personal ambitions of the planner. It is most critical in all these areas that the planner should know how to adapt to the environment quickly. The reason is simple – it is going to become clear early that he cannot achieve all that is on the position description, and his long-term effectiveness is going to be determined by minimising the early disappointment he conveys. Also, he is usually a novelty in the management and his function is going to be under very special scrutiny. If he is new to the company, this even has personal ramifications. There is no prescription for avoiding these rigours.

The organisational climate

As the planner becomes involved with line management of his company, with what kind of attitudes will he be confronted? These usually range from cordially uninterested to unfriendly. With all of the profound, rational and important reasons to the company as an incentive for active, enthusiastic participation and support from the line management, it is often unclear to many new planners why disinterest happens. The answer is that everyone from the managing director to the porter interprets the relationship between his own good and the company's differently. This occurs most dramatically at the manager/planner interface. Let us look at the manager's reaction to planning in more detail.

Actually, most line managers know only the incentives provided by short-term profit performance. There is invariably little or no lasting recognition, or monetary compensation, contingent on contribution to the planning process. Indeed, quality of planning is difficult to evaluate under the characteristic time pressure of daily operations. The average line manager will seem to be ill-advised to sacrifice energy or time from activities which can directly contribute to the more superficial elements of success, such as the current monthly profit or turnover figures.

Furthermore, the planning review consists too frequently of a single annual face-to-face presentation of a line operation's plan to a top management governing body of some sort. The line manager then orients his response to providing the maximum punch for a few hours at most, knowing that there will be little likelihood of follow-up. Performance is dealt with in terms other than plan and execution. To put it in other words, the line middle manager sees his fate tied to something other than this looseleaf book marked 'Long Range Plan', so why plan? Verification of this in actual experience is that sales trained or orientated managers generally attain higher grades for planning than their production or research counterparts, usually because of their general capacity for persuasiveness in a short presentation.

More subtle is the effect of short manager life cycle. It is common in industry today for manager turnover in a given middle management position to be in two to three years. In fact, it is acknowledged policy in many large concerns that individuals should not 'stagnate' in a spot. Two things happen: the manager recognises that there is little chance that he will truly have to live with the long-range consequences of what he plans, he lacks the perspective skilfully to translate the history of his role into its future since he is only temporarily its tenant.

While most of the aforementioned remarks are concerned with middle managers, there are counterpart problems with top managers. At this time, few top managers have come to their positions through the planning discipline. Likewise, the subject is not a matter of formal business study such as accounting, or, in general, a matter of common business experience. Thus, many of the senior top managers in industry like the idea of corporate planning, but simply do not know its mechanics. As a result, we have all the common errors: belief that entire business can be delegated like so many other facilitating management functions, improper delegation of time to it either in quantity or continuity, organisational misalignment of the planning group below some other function, improper selection of personnel or definition of responsibilities, and lack of ability to properly budget the function or evaluate its manager.

The theory of corporate planning holds out much to those who would put it to work and work at it. Unfortunately, it also beguiles the unwary into believing that there can result a dramatic, recognisable immediate effect from inauguration of a planning programme. The idea seems to have its origins in some of the effects that can be temporarily attained in sales as a result of a massive advertising campaign, production cost savings from temporary elimination of maintenance, and the like. Again, many companies decide that some formal corporate planning will give them a 'shot in the arm', when a little reflection would indicate that the start-up investment of time and energy will result in just the opposite. More sinister, the launching of a major effort into corporate planning is often the signal of a panic reaction to impending serious problems which are already in so advanced a stage that only some outside miracle could successfully intervene.

Some specific approaches

When the new planner is sufficiently well grounded in fundamentals, has set his opening priorities, and sized up the organisational climate, he must quickly set sail to produce the recommended tangible product(s) as soon as possible. Looking slightly beyond his start, it must represent a point of departure and be so conducted that it will point to the subsequent necessary involvement of others who will make his work increasingly meaningful. In short, he must lead people to pick up the threads of his starting efforts.

His programme must always operate with him in control of all phases at the start. Any line of activity should be planned so that failure of a line management colleague to participate adequately can be at least tentatively substituted for or bypassed. He should set a schedule and sacrifice planning quality or quantity to meet it. It is critical at the start that he convey credibility that the planning job will be done.

The following sections are dedicated to some specific devices from the points of the position description outline given earlier. Some reflect personal experiences; many the experiences of others. They have realized various degrees of success in individual cases. Hopefully they will suggest ideas which might be of possible use to planner readers.

Setting objectives

Setting corporate objectives has some very early tangible advantages as a planner's starting point. Most important, there is great public relations value, and a newly defined set of objectives can be made the theme of an annual report, trade publicity and shareholder support solicitation. In these hazardous times of the ready takeover and the vulnerable management, an even superficial approach to defining a predetermined destiny for the company has a stabilising influence.

The first establishment of these objectives is not as difficult as it seems, because, in truth, they are only intended to be tentative. It is usually possible for an individual to identify a single or limited number of business elements which determine the future of the enterprise, such as significant markets, products, manufacturing or service skills, and by speculating on these into the future come up with a pattern of objectives. This task can be made as detailed and comprehensive or superficial and quick as one would care to make it. In single-product, single-market businesses it becomes simpler to construct mathematical models and project goals in terms of related economic parameters. Nevertheless, there are superb examples of corporate objectives written for the fast-moving, successful, acquisition-minded company. The objectives are meaningful because they describe the future in terms of an enterprise whose business it is to buy and sell companies. This is a worthwhile distinction for the planner to recognise; it can help bypass the frustration of never being able to nail down the future of a shifting business base, and can be adapted to the flexibility of the organisation in varying degrees. A tentative slate of objectives then becomes the point of departure for meaningful debate towards refinement by the responsible authorities in the company. One may see this done in the most formal management committee meeting and in shirtsleeve sessions in the small hours of the morning. Properly done, the 'tentative objectives' are a major contribution the planner can make quickly, and obtain recognition for it.

In setting tentative starting objectives, it is not necessary to fall into the trap of being 'for God and Motherhood' in order to fill the page. Try to keep stated objectives meaningful in terms of other relatively determinable facts. 'We will maximise our return on investment consistent with risk expectations of our shareholders', means essentially nothing. Much more effective might be, 'We will remain competitive in our field(s) of business by maintaining our market share and our return on investment at no less than others in the same field(s)'. With a little market and investment research, plus intuition, most companies could verify their future performance in these terms. Thus, the terms are meaningful, understandable, and leave some flexibility for the effects of sizeable swings in the economic environment, even if the objective is not perfect in all respects. Actually, even the most highly developed corporate objectives contain a realistic margin of flexibility that gives them vitality.

The environment

Monitoring the business environment is a catch phrase which does not mean much until it is put into the context of the business involved and who wants it monitored. Far too much time is wasted in this area by planners at the outset. Operating people in their various responsibility roles are much more conversant with the characteristics and daily gossip of their immediate commercial environment. Nearly everybody reads the same sources of business news. In one company a planner took over an existing planning department, spending about $20 000 annually supporting a continuing survey of the competition in its industry. About twenty top managers of the company had a looseleaf book with each of the competitors indexed, and they would continuously circulate new pages with the latest financial reports, product data, management changes, etc., from publicly available sources. The planner organised an internal anonymous survey among the recipients and found that most had the books maintained by their secretaries and never or rarely referred to them. It was dropped without complaint.

A good way to honour this responsibility is to publish a periodic planning department newsletter which must be crisp, terse, and interesting. Everybody already has too much to read. Try to include items concerning things about the future which are not likely to have been read by everyone elsewhere. Make pertinent interpretive comments. Occasionally slip in something about planning as a function, such as a unique use of a computer for model work, or a well-defined set of objectives of some other company.

Attempting to monitor the entire environment for that which is newsworthy and meaningful to everybody is hopeless. Start by keeping a file of clippings or notes from other sources as you learn interesting items, and once monthly dictate a newsletter. After a few months, look for responses to this project, ways to make it more useful or frequent, or drop it. A worthwhile departure might be a quarterly or annual review system of the most significant environmental phenomena. A point of editorial focus for inclusion and interpretation of newsletter material would be relevance to objectives of the corporation, especially those of non-financial nature which would not be covered by more conventional reports.

Planning systems

Development of planning systems and all the related activities which are concerned with the suggestion of planning mechanics is the most difficult area in which to make a start. This is because it is awkward to conceive of something less than the classical 'upward pyramid plan, review, and revise' process. The reader may be familiar with several variations. The surest guarantee of failure is to attempt to start with this most comprehensive planning system. Instead, the planner should attempt to start by turning the process around and make the planning system originate from his personal efforts. While a busy pressured line manager might be completely indifferent to writing a long detailed plan, he can usually be persuaded to at least discuss it in an informal conversation.

Probably the least productive planning systems are the rigid format type where the operating manager is required to 'fill in the squares' for future years' sales, profits, return on investment, etc. A start of this type is a powerful temptation among planners, because it then appears so easy to summarise, statistically analyse and sum up to a total plan. It readily defeats its own validity because it is not possible to devise a format which will arrange the 'squares' in a way which accurately describes the thinking process of the operating line manager. A flagrant example in actual experience was a consultant-designed planning system for a large, diverse American company. At the heart of this system was the requirement for a turnover forecast by each operating division. A major portion of company volume was done in its grain trading operation, where the truly critical operating factor was the 'spread' between purchase and selling price. Elaborate futures trading was engaged in and a staff of highly skilled traders employed to project the spread in literally split-second buy-and-sell transactions. A true turnover forecast was almost meaningless. The entire planning system collapsed and had to be reconstituted, with the loss of nearly a year, following a corporate insurrection against its rigidity and lack of significance.

Using the proposed approach, the planner can originate a plan for each of the important subdivisions of his company's business. Let the operating manager provide the main line of thinking and the planner do the interpretive writing. Leave a well-defined time for a review by the line manager involved but keep the initiative for the generation of the comprehensive plan with the planner. Several important advantages are realised:

1 The planner controls the schedule, and since it is at least tentatively his plan, he can see that it finishes by a scheduled date.
2 The planner controls the format. He can experiment or introduce necessary changes as the first plan emerges, devising methods for accommodating contingencies, for example.
3 The planner can improvise compromises in areas of sensitivity by serving as a lightning rod between potential disputants. This can be advantageous (if dangerous), for example, when two operating managers might rationally have at least a fragmentary claim on the growth of the company into a new area of business. The planner can preclude from becoming the registry where new claims are staked which subvert the overall company interests in close-quarters fighting.

Lack of ability to deal with alternative action courses, contingent events, and technical innovation factors are main handicaps of the 'square-filling system'. By starting, at least, with the planner interview-and-transcribe planning approach there can be developed on a working basis those characteristics of the format and the system which will put it on the fullest participating basis among the line managers as soon as possible. Further, a plan tends to reflect greater unity of approach and delivery if it is channelled through a single integrative 'think through'.

The first plan will probably be too abbreviated to appear authoritative. There will always be time to develop participation in something more elaborate. The commonest failure is an opening plan which is both encyclopedic and exhausting to the creators. Subsequent years see its shrinkage at almost negative exponential rate, and the onset of general planning disinterest and neglect.

Acquisitions

Attempting to organise approaches to grafting on new acquisitions, unlike objectives or planning systems work, is something with questionable applicability in all situations. Thus, while it is fashionable to think that a clever planner can in some way create a capacity for acquisitions in a company, the heart of the matter is really the capacity to take risks, mentioned earlier. Here, the starting planner's best approach is to send up a trial balloon. By a quick survey of the company's history it will be readily evident whether there has been any risk-taking capacity in this area. If there have been no acquisitions of consequence, the best move is to start conservatively.

The planner should draw up a list of those companies or types of companies which would be acquisition targets by the most straightforward type of integration with current company operations. Usually the simplest common sense will suggest these. He then estimates the price ranges which might be affixed to these, using price–earnings ratios for known deals in the industry involved, public share values, or any other evidence which might be available and useful. Next, a summary of the company's financial position and its capacity to issue shares (of whatever type), debt, or cash is drawn up. This will suggest crudely what size or number of acquisitions can be sought. A list of several 'deals' using an intuitive order of priority and proposed purchase prices is hypothesised. Clearance is sought from the top management of the subject company to make contact with top management in the target companies to open discussions on the matter.

The risk-taking capacity of the planner's top management can then be determined as inversely proportional to the requirement for additional detailed data, need for consultants, reviews by the executive committee (or board of directors), postponements until other developments are clearer, etc. etc.

This is only a starting point; more information will probably be in order, and committees will need reviews. As soon as it becomes excessive, the planner may count this as an interesting exercise but not be further distracted by it.

Where there is a solid background of acquisition performance in a company, the planner stands ready to plough more fertile ground. These situations are rare. In them, the top man in the company is invariably the source of impetus in the acquisition programme, and the planner's role is frequently one of scout and analyst. In this situation, there is usually little need for the planner to generate initiative, and his task then becomes one of merely picking up the thread of ongoing events.

The investigation and negotiation of acquisitions is a subject area which has filled volumes. Further, since it is not generally a matter of concern when *starting* a planning department, one need not dwell on it extensively here. Let us only summarise from some practical experience what the planner will learn in this area as soon as he does become active in it:

1 The rule is *caveat emptor*, and the corollary is that the seller will always know more about the merchandise than the buyer.
2 It is important to know why one is buying a company, and what the ideal purchase would be for that purpose. The ideal purchase will never be found, but it is useful to know by how much the buyer can afford to compromise, as well as when the entire purpose has been lost.
3 In recent years, almost anywhere in the world there has been a seller's market. Be prepared to talk humbly and bid high. The best companies are not out begging.
4 The deal is not completed until the papers are signed.
5 The deal is not a success until it has accomplished its original purpose.

Organisation

In the area of organisation planning, the safest and most productive position for a new planner is to avoid the issue. Obviously the plans anticipate people capable of their execution, but the planner cannot be limited by their immediate availability in the organisation. If he is drawn too rapidly and into too much detail into long-range organisational planning he will compromise his own presumed neutrality. Further, until he has a solid basis for knowing who presently does what, he can hardly contribute meaningfully. The best attitude in this area is one of total professional aloofness, defining roles but remaining as remote as possible from putting people in them.

Financial considerations

In the areas of budgeting, return on investment analysis, and related fiscal matters, the beginning planner will be confronted with what will be his most sensitive internal relationship among fellow 'staff' management. The financial officer of a company, because of his classical responsibility to make the projections which will keep it solvent, can regard the planning function as competitive in a narrow sense. A sound planner–financial officer relationship is basic to making both roles work. One has seen the planning department of a major company totally undermined by a vindictive financial vice-president who withheld critical data, and, on the other hand, have seen a planner–treasurer combination meaningfully advance the interests of another company.

Some companies have attempted to avoid problems in these areas by giving both functions to the same individual or, all too frequently, subordinating the planner to the financial officer. This latter arrangement is perhaps productive of the least friction, but often the least useful data. It is extremely dangerous to generalise in view of the emerging number of excellent financial people with a keen sense of broad business responsibility, but too often the entire planning process is reduced to pro forma profit statements and balance sheets.

Return on investment analysis is a particularly difficult area of rapport between financial and planning people. There is a growing enchantment with some of the more highly sophisticated techniques such as discounted cash flow, usually in the financial community. While these can become important for a treasurer because they are such helpful decision-making instruments with his stock in trade (cash), their value to a planner is usually more remote. His purpose is to encourage good decisions among the line operations people, and invariably they do not understand such approaches as DCF. Surely most appreciate the meaning of a cash payout period; one in three can calculate some sort of return on average investment, and one in a thousand can interpret DCF. In fact, too few financial people are aware of the subtle potential sources of distortion which can be introduced by DCF.

In summary, the starting planner should aim for a working arrangement with his financial counterpart, and keep the planning mechanics on a financial technical plane which will do the job the planner wants. It is uncommon to see an operating man make a 'wrong' decision using the traditional financial analytical tools with understanding. As a starting planner, keep the financial analyses simple. There is always time to escalate the sophistication.

Growth areas

The identification of growth areas is an especially nebulous task, made all the more so because the basic cause and effect phenomenon has all too frequently dropped from view. To an unrecognised degree, growth is the product of enterprising management, and the ability and willingness to throw resources behind satisfying a particular need. In short, it is less a matter of 'growth areas' than growth companies. When an area is demonstrating itself as one of dramatic growth, the corporate participants at that point have already realised the premium returns of the entering risk takers. At that point, subsequent entrants assume the usually formidable costs of starting up and overtaking the leaders. Usually their arrival is in time to collide with masses of competitors at the price-cutting over-supply stage. We have seen this in the United States in transistors and big-volume petrochemicals, for example.

Yet the United States is confronted with enormous unsatisfied needs, and the companies who find ways to meet the needs are going to grow. This can hardly be less true for other companies and other countries. In visits to the Soviet Union one is awed at the accomplishments resulting from the focusing of centrally controlled wealth, in the space programme, for example. One is also depressed by the continuing relative backwardness of the consumer world. The same phenomena operate in free societies, and the planner must look at growth as occurring where resources are sent. Thus the popular 'growth areas' in America are urban development, undersea research, rapid transit, molecular biology, leisure-time activities and a host of service and technical businesses of increasing sophistication.

Where any company puts its resources is as much an act of faith as a planner's cleverness, however, and we are thrown back on the capacity for risk-taking. Perhaps the best experience for the beginning planner is to summarise (perhaps only for himself) the strengths of his company. Thereafter he could attempt to list, however speculatively, ways in which these strengths could be brought to bear on the opportunities of the future as they seem to present themselves. This might be done on a regularly scheduled basis, say every six months, in a special report. Unless there is extraordinary internal company pressure for major departures, a mere listing of growth opportunity areas is useless. One has seen too frequently such misfits as highly consumer marketing orientated company managements pondering long lists of esoteric technological possibilities. In these there was not a real possibility that they could either contribute meaningfully or judge the commercial performance of those whom they might bring on to do so.

Other considerations

Starting a planning activity has many common problems with all the other departments of a company. There must be space, budgets, personnel, job adjustments, etc., and it is almost impossible to particularise for every case. The following are a few additional suggestions:

1 When requesting budget funding, it is usually to the planner's advantage to demonstrate his needs in terms of a percentage of company turnover. It does not take too much insight on the part of a managing director to grasp the implication of an excessively penurious allowance on his stated importance of the function. If the planner could perform completely on all the points of his description, he would justify a budget one hundredfold that which most receive.
2 The most effective planners do not spend excessive time in the office. A substantial departmental travel budget and a patient family are necessary.
3 Make a point of establishing early contacts with counterparts in other companies. There is great mutuality among planners. This can be invaluable in opening channels of communications between companies which would be impractical or unlikely by other methods.
4 Seek variations on the basic planner theme where contributions are possible. In one company where my principal responsibility was originally diversification, the most significant ultimate contributions were quickly obvious in disposition of operating units whose continuance would be a non-profitable distraction. Other opportunity areas might be licensing, international activities, or joint ventures.

Conclusion

To summarise, the major problems of starting a formal planning effort are basic in company psychology. It is important that the new planner establish himself by selecting his first areas of concentration where action should come quickest. These are established by an evaluation of the company's risk-taking characteristics. Thereafter, the planner originates projects which are controlled by himself in such a way that they cannot lose their momentum if proposed participants fail to perform. In this way, work can be completed which is used as the point of departure for further refinements. From some of the simple starts suggested, the planner's experience will essentially have to dictate subsequent moves. In general these would be towards the full development of a comprehensive planning scheme as the needs of his company direct. There is a variety of good, workable forms the end-product might take, even for a single company, and the planning literature is heavy with discussions in this area. In any reasonable company environment, a good planning beginning will probably ensure some degree of success. The degree will probably never be more complete than a director of production accepting that he has been given a perfect plan. Nevertheless, there is the potential for continuous challenge with matching satisfaction and, occasionally, a success of genuine breakthrough stature.

5

How to evaluate
corporate strategy*

SEYMOUR TILLES

One of the difficulties involved in adopting a corporate strategy is that top management must to some extent be influenced in their thinking by the experience of other companies with long-range planning. Are they in error in believing that strategic planning is just as applicable to one company as to another? Is it possible to devise a body of criteria which can be applied to all long-range corporate plans in order to evaluate their relevance and likely success? Dr Tilles suggests six points which top management can use to evaluate their corporate strategy and concludes that if all these criteria are met, though success cannot be guaranteed, they will at least be valuable in so far as management gains 'both the time and the room to manœuvre'.

No good military officer would undertake even a small-scale attack on a limited objective without a clear concept of his strategy. No seasoned politician would undertake a campaign for a major office without an equally clear concept of his strategy. In the field of business management, however, we frequently find men deploying resources on a large scale without any clear notion of what their strategy is. And yet a company's strategy is a vital ingredient in determining its future. A valid strategy will yield growth, profit, or whatever other objectives the managers have established. An inappropriate strategy not only will fail to yield benefits, but also may result in disaster.

In this article I will try to demonstrate the truth of these contentions by examining the experiences of a number of companies. I shall discuss what strategy is, how it can be evaluated, and how, by evaluating its strategy, a management can do much to assure the future of the enterprise.

Decisive impact

The influence of strategy can be seen in every age and in every area of industry. Here are some examples:

- from the time it was started in 1911 as the Computing-Tabulating-Recording Co., International Business Machines Corporation has demonstrated the significance of a soundly conceived strategy. Seeing itself in the data-system business at a time when most manufacturers were still preoccupied with individual pieces of equipment, IBM developed a set of policies which resulted in its dominating the office equipment industry
- by contrast, Packard in the 1930s was to the automobile industry everything that IBM is today to the office machinery industry. In 1937, it sold over 109 000 cars, compared with about 11 000 for Cadillac. By 1954 it had disappeared as an independent producer.

Strategy is, of course, not the only factor determining a company's success or failure. The competence of its managerial leadership is significant as well. Luck can be a factor, too (although often what people call good luck is really the product of good strategy). But a valid strategy can gain extraordinary results for the company whose general level of competence is only average. And, conversely, the most inspiring leaders who are locked into an inappropriate strategy will have to exert their full competence and energy merely in order to keep from losing ground.

When Hannibal inflicted the humiliating defeat on the Roman army at Cannae in 216 BC, he led a ragged band against soldiers who were in possession of superior arms, better training, and competent 'noncoms'. His strategy, however, was so superior that all of those advantages proved to be relatively insignificant. Similarly, when Jacob Borowsky made Lestoil the hottest-selling detergent in New England some years ago, he was performing a similar feat – relying on strategy to battle competition with superior resources.

Strategy is important not only for aspiring Davids who need an offensive device to combat corporate Goliaths. It is significant also for the large organisation faced with a wide range of choice in domestic and international operations.

Dynamic concept

A strategy is a set of goals and major policies. The definition is as simple as that. But while the notion of a strategy is extremely easy to grasp, working out an agreed statement for a given company can be a fundamental contribution to the organisation's future success.

In order to develop such a statement, managers must be able to identify precisely what is meant by a goal and what is meant by a major policy. Otherwise, the process of strategy determination may degenerate into what it so often becomes – the solemn recording of platitudes, useless for either the clarification of direction or the achievement of consensus.

Identifying goals

Corporate goals are an indication of what the company as a whole is trying to

achieve and to *become*. Both parts – the achieving and the becoming – are important
for a full understanding of what a company hopes to attain. For example:

● under the leadership of Alfred Sloan, General Motors achieved a considerable
  degree of external success; this was accomplished because Sloan worked out a
  pattern for the kind of company he wanted it to be internally
● similarly, the remarkable record of Du Pont in the twentieth century and the
  growth of Sears, Roebuck under Julius Rosenwald were as much a tribute to
  their modified structure as to their external strategy[1].

Achieving. In order to state what a company expects to achieve, it is important to
state what it hopes to do with respect to its environment. For instance, Ernest
Breech, chairman of the board of the Ford Motor Company, said that the strategy
formulated by his company in 1946 was based on a desire 'to hold our own in
what we foresaw would be a rich but hotly competitive market'.[2] The view of
the environment implicit in this statement is unmistakable: an expanding overall demand, increasing competition, and emphasis on market share as a measure
of performance against competitors.

Clearly, a statement of what a company hopes to achieve may be much more
varied and complex than can be contained in a single sentence. This will be
especially true for those managers who are sophisticated enough to perceive that
a company operates in more external 'systems' than the market. The firm is part
not only of a market but also of an industry, the community, the economy, and
other systems. In each case there are unique relationships to observe (e.g. with
competitors, municipal leaders, Congress, and so on). A more complete discussion of this point is contained in a previous *Harvard Business Review* article.[3]

Becoming. If you ask young men what they want to accomplish by the time they are
forty, the answers you get fall into two distinct categories. There are those – the
great majority – who will respond in terms of what they want to *have*. This is
especially true of graduate students of business administration. There are some
men, however, who will answer in terms of the kind of men they hope to *be*.
These are the only ones who have a clear idea of where they are going.

The same is true of companies. For far too many companies, what little thinking goes on about the future is done primarily in money terms. There is nothing
wrong with financial planning. Most companies should do more of it. But there
is a basic fallacy in confusing a financial plan with thinking about the kind of
company you want yours to become. It is like saying, 'When I'm forty, I'm going
to be rich.' It leaves too many basic questions unanswered. Rich in what way?
Rich doing what?

The other major fallacy in stating what you want to become is to say it only
in terms of a product. The number of companies who have got themselves into
trouble by falling in love with a particular product is distressingly great.[4]
Perhaps the saddest examples are those giants of American industry who defined
their future in terms of continuing to be the major suppliers of steam loco-
motives to the nation's railroads. In fact, these companies were so wedded to

this concept of their future that they formed a cartel in order to keep General Motors out of the steam locomotive business. When the diesel locomotive proved its superiority to steam, these companies all but disappeared.

The lesson of these experiences is that a key element of setting goals is the ability to see them in terms of more than a single dimension. Both money and product policy are part of a statement of objectives; but it is essential that these be viewed as the concrete expressions of a more abstract set of goals – the satisfaction of the needs of significant groups which cooperate to ensure the company's continued existence.

Who are these groups? There are many – customers, managers, employees, stockholders, to mention just the major ones. The key to corporate success is the company's ability to identify the important needs of each of these groups, to establish some balance among them, and to work out a set of operating policies which permits their satisfaction. This set of policies, as a pattern, identifies what the company is trying to be.

The growth fad

Many managers have a view of their company's future which is strikingly analogous to the child's view of himself. When asked what they want their companies to become over the next few years, they reply, 'bigger'.

There are a great many rationalisations for this preoccupation with growth. Probably the one most frequently voiced is that which says, 'You have to grow or die'. What must be appreciated, however, is that 'bigger' for a company has enormous implications for management. It involves a different way of life, and one which many managers may not be suited for – either in terms of temperament or skills.

Moreover, whether for a large company or a small one, 'bigger', by itself, may not make economic sense. Companies which are highly profitable at their present size may grow into bankruptcy very easily; witness the case of Grayson-Robinson Stores, Inc., a chain of retail stores. Starting out as a small but profitable chain, it grew rapidly into receivership. Conversely, a company which is not now profitable may more successfully seek its survival in cost reduction than in sales growth. Chrysler is a striking example of this approach.

There is, in the United States, a business philosophy which reflects the frontier heritage of the country. It is one which places a high value on growth, in physical terms. The manager whose corporate sales are not increasing, the number of whose subordinates is not growing, whose plants are not expanding, feels that he is not successful. But there is a dangerous trap in this kind of thinking. More of the same is not necessarily progress. In addition, few managers are capable of running units several times larger than the one they now head. The great danger of wholehearted consumer acceptance or an astute programme of corporate acquisition is that it frequently propels managers into situations that are beyond their present competence. Such cases – and they are legion – emphasise that in stating corporate objectives, bigger is not always better.

A dramatic example is that of the Ampex Corporation. From 1950 to 1960, Ampex's annual sales went from less than $1 000 000 to more than $73 000 000. Its earnings went from $115 000 to nearly $4 000 000. The following year, the company reported a decline in sales to $70 000 000, and a net loss of $3 900 000. The *Wall Street Journal* reported: 'As one source close to the company put it, Ampex's former management "was intelligent and well-educated, but simply lacked the experience necessary to control" the company's rapid development.'[5]

Role of policy

A policy says something about how goals will be attained. It is what statisticians would call a 'decision rule', and what systems engineers would call a 'standing plan'. It tells people what they should and should not do in order to contribute to achievement of corporate goals.

A policy should be more than just a platitude. It should be a helpful guide to making strategy explicit, and providing direction to subordinates. Consequently, the more definite it is, the more helpful it can be. 'We will provide our stockholders with a fair return', is a policy no one could possibly disagree with – or be helped by. What is a fair return? This is the type of question that must be answered before the company's intentions become clear.

The job of management is not merely the preparation of valid policies for a standard set of activities; it is the much more challenging one of first deciding what activities are so strategically significant that explicit decision rules in that area are mandatory. No standard set of policies can be considered major for all companies. Each company is a unique situation. It must decide for itself which aspects of corporate life are most relevant to its own aspirations and work out policy statements for them. For example, advertising may be insignificant to a company which provides research services to the Defense Department, but critical to a firm trying to mass-merchandise luxury goods.

It is difficult to generalise about which policies are major, even within a particular industry, because a number of extraordinarily successful companies appear to violate all the rules. To illustrate:

● in the candy industry it would seem safe to generalise that advertising should be a major policy area. However, the Hershey Company, which is so successful that its name is practically the generic term for the product, has persistently followed a policy of no advertising. Similarly, in the field of high-fidelity components, one would expect that dealer relations would be a critical policy area. But Acoustics Research, Inc., has built an enviable record of sales growth and of profitability by relying entirely on consumer pull.

Need to be explicit

The first thing to be said about corporate strategy is that having one is a step forward. Any strategy, once made explicit, can quickly be evaluated and improved. But if no attempt is ever made to commit it to paper, there is always the danger that the strategy is either incomplete or misunderstood.

Many successful companies are not aware of the strategy that underlies their success. It is quite possible for a company to achieve initial success without real awareness of its causes. However, it is much more difficult to successfully branch out into new ventures without a precise appreciation of their strategic significance. This is why many established companies fail miserably when they attempt a programme of corporate acquisition, product diversification, or market expansion. One illustration of this is cited by Myles L. Mace and George G. Montgomery in their recent study of corporate acquisitions:

> A basic resin company . . . bought a plastic boat manufacturer because this seemed to present a controlled market for a portion of the resin it produced. It soon found that the boat business was considerably different from the manufacture and sale of basic chemicals. After a short but unpleasant experience in manufacturing and trying to market what was essentially a consumer's item, the management concluded that its experience and abilities lay essentially in industrial rather than consumer-type products.[6]

Another reason for making strategy explicit is the assistance it provides for delegation and for coordination. To an ever-increasing extent, management is a team activity, whereby groups of executives contribute to corporate success. Making strategy explicit makes it far easier for each executive to appreciate what the over-all goals are, and what his own contribution to them must be.

Making an evaluation

Is your strategy right for you? There are six criteria on which to base an answer. These are:

1 Internal consistency.
2 Consistency with the environment.
3 Appropriateness in the light of available resources.
4 Satisfactory degree of risk.
5 Appropriate time horizon.
6 Workability.

If all these criteria are met, you have a strategy that is right for you. This is as much as can be asked. There is no such thing as a good strategy in any absolute, objective sense. In the remainder of this article I shall discuss the criteria in some detail.

1 Is the strategy internally consistent?

Internal consistency refers to the cumulative impact of individual policies on corporate goals. In a well-worked-out strategy, each policy fits into an integrated pattern. It should be judged not only in terms of itself, but also in terms of how it relates to other policies which the company has established and to the goals it is pursuing.

In a dynamic company consistency can never be taken for granted. For example, many family-owned organisations pursue a pair of policies which soon become inconsistent: rapid expansion and retention of exclusive family control of the firm. If they are successful in expanding, the need for additional financing soon raises major problems concerning the extent to which exclusive family control can be maintained. While this pair of policies is especially prevalent among smaller firms, it is by no means limited to them. The Ford Motor Company after World War II and the *New York Times* today are examples of quite large, family-controlled organisations that have had to reconcile the two conflicting aims.

The criterion of internal consistency is an especially important one for evaluating strategies because it identifies those areas where strategic choices will eventually have to be made. An inconsistent strategy does *not* necessarily mean that the company is currently in difficulty. But it does mean that unless management keeps its eye on a particular area of operation, it may well find itself forced to make a choice without enough time either to search for or to prepare attractive alternatives.

2   Is the strategy consistent with the environment?

A firm which has a certain product policy, price policy, or advertising policy is saying that it has chosen to relate itself to its customers – actual and potential – in a certain way. Similarly, its policies with respect to government contracts, collective bargaining, foreign investment, and so forth are expressions of relationship with other groups and forces. Hence an important test of strategy is whether the chosen policies are consistent with the environment – whether they really make sense with respect to what is going on outside.

Consistency with the environment has both a static and a dynamic aspect. In a static sense, it implies judging the efficacy of policies with respect to the environment as it exists *now*. In a dynamic sense, it means judging the efficacy of policies with respect to the environment *as it appears to be changing*. One purpose of a viable strategy is to ensure the long-run success of an organisation. Since the environment of a company is constantly changing, ensuring success over the long run means that management must constantly be assessing the degree to which policies previously established are consistent with the environment as it exists now; and whether current policies take into account the environment as it will be in the future. In one sense, therefore, establishing a strategy is like aiming at a moving target: you have to be concerned not only with present position but also with the speed and direction of movement.

Failure to have a strategy consistent with the environment can be costly to the organisation. Ford's sad experience with the Edsel is by now a textbook example of such failure. Certainly, had Ford pushed the Falcon at the time when it was pushing the Edsel, and with the same resources, it would have a far stronger position in the world automobile market today.

Illustrations of strategies that have not been consistent with the environment are easy to find by using hindsight. But the reason that such examples are plentiful is not that foresight is difficult to apply. It is because even today few companies are seriously engaged in analysing environmental trends and using this intelligence as a basis for managing their own future.

3 Is the strategy appropriate in view of the available resources?

Resources are those things that a company is or has and that help it to achieve its corporate objectives. Included are money, competence, and facilities; but these by no means complete the list. In companies selling consumer goods, for example, the major resource may be the name of the product. In any case, there are two basic issues which management must decide in relating strategy and resources. These are:

● what are our critical resources?
● is the proposed strategy appropriate for available resources?

Let us look now at what is meant by a 'critical resource' and at how the criterion of resource utilisation can be used as a basis for evaluating strategy.

CRITICAL RESOURCES

The essential strategic attribute of resources is that they represent action potential. Taken together, a company's resources represent its capacity to respond to threats and opportunities that may be perceived in the environment. In other words, resources are the bundle of chips that the company has to play with in the serious game of business.

From an action-potential point of view, a resource may be critical in two senses: (a) as the factor limiting the achievement of corporate goals; and (b) as that which the company will exploit as the basis for its strategy. Thus, critical resources are both what the company has most of and what it has least of.

The three resources most frequently identified as critical are money, competence, and physical facilities. Let us look at the strategic significance of each.

Money. Money is a particularly valuable resource because it provides the greatest flexibility of response to events as they arise. It may be considered the 'safest' resource, in that safety may be equated with the freedom to choose from among the widest variety of future alternatives. Companies that wish to reduce their short-run risk will therefore attempt to accumulate the greatest reservoir of funds they can.

However, it is important to remember that while the accumulation of funds may offer short-run security, it may place the company at a serious competitive disadvantage with respect to other companies which are following a higher-risk course.

The classical illustration of this kind of outcome is the strategy pursued by Montgomery Ward under the late Sewell Avery. As reported in *Fortune*:

> While Sears confidently bet on a new and expanding America, Avery developed an *idée fixe* that post-war inflation would end in a crash no less serious than that of 1929. Following this idea, he opened no new stores but rather piled up cash to the ceiling in preparation for an economic debacle that never came. In these years, Ward's balance sheet gave a somewhat misleading picture of its prospects. Net earnings remained respectably high, and were generally higher than those of Sears as a percentage of sales. In 1946, earnings after taxes were $52 million. They rose to $74 million in 1950, and then declined to $35 million in 1954. Meanwhile, however, sales remained static, and in Avery's administration profits and liquidity were maintained at the expense of growth. In 1954, Ward had $327 million in cash and securities, $147 million in receivables, and $216 million in inventory, giving it a total current-asset position of $690 million and net worth of $639 million. It was liquid, all right, but it was also the shell of a once great company.[7]

Competence. Organisations survive because they are good at doing those things which are necessary to keep them alive. However, the degree of competence of a given organisation is by no means uniform across the broad range of skills necessary to stay in business. Some companies are particularly good at marketing, others especially good at engineering, still others depend primarily on their financial sophistication. Philip Selznick refers to that which a company is particularly good at as its 'distinctive competence'.[8]

In determining a strategy, management must carefully appraise its own skill profile in order to determine where its strengths and weaknesses lie. It must then adopt a strategy which makes the greatest use of its strengths. To illustrate:

- the competence of the *New York Times* lies primarily in giving extensive and insightful coverage of events – the ability to report 'all the news that's fit to print'. It is neither highly profitable (earning only 1·5 per cent of revenues in 1960 – far less than, say, the *Wall Street Journal*), nor aggressively sold. Its decision to publish a West Coast and an international edition is a gamble that the strength of its 'distinctive competence' will make it accepted even outside of New York.
- because of a declining demand for soft coal, many producers of soft coal are diversifying into other fields. All of them, however, are remaining true to some central skill that they have developed over the years. For instance: Consolidation Coal is moving from simply the mining of soft coal to the mining *and transportation* of soft coal. It is planning with Texas Eastern Transmission Corporation to build a $100-million pipeline that would carry a mixture of powdered coal and water from West Virginia to the East Coast. North American Coal Company, on the other hand, is moving towards becoming a

chemical company. It recently joined with Strategic Materials Corporation to perfect a process for extracting aluminum sulphate from the mine shale that North American produces in its coal-running operations.

James L. Hamilton, president of the Island Creek Coal Co., has summed up the concept of distinctive competence in a colourful way: 'We are a career company dedicated to coal, and we have some very definite ideas about growth and expansion within the industry. We're not thinking of buying a cotton mill and starting to make shirts.'[9]

Physical facilities. Physical facilities are the resources whose strategic influence is perhaps most frequently misunderstood. Managers seem to be divided among those, usually technical men, who are enamoured of physical facilities as the tangible symbol of the corporate entity; and those, usually financial men, who view physical facilities as an undesirable but necessary freezing of part of the company's funds. The latter group is dominant. In many companies return on investment has emerged as virtually the sole criterion for deciding whether or not a particular facility should be acquired.

Actually, this is putting the cart before the horse. Physical facilities have significance primarily in relationship to overall corporate strategy. It is, therefore, only in relationship to other aspects of corporate strategy that the acquisition or disposition of physical facilities can be determined. The total investment required and the projected return on it have a place in this determination – but only as an indication of the financial implications of a particular strategic decision and not as an exclusive criterion for its own sake.

Any appraisal of a company's physical facilities as a strategic resource must consider the relationship of the company to its environment. Facilities have no intrinsic value for their own sake. Their value to the company is either in their location relative to markets, to sources of labour, or to materials; or in their efficiency relative to existing or impending competitive installations. Thus, the essential considerations in any decision regarding physical facilities are a projection of changes likely to occur in the environment and a prediction about what the company's responses to these are likely to be.

Here are two example of the necessity for relating an evaluation of facilities to environmental changes:

● following the end of World War II, all domestic producers of typewriters in the United States invested heavily in plant facilities in this country. They hypothesised a rapid increase of sales throughout the world. This indeed took place, but it was shortlived. The rise of vigorous overseas competitors, especially Olivetti and Olympia, went hand in hand with a booming overseas market. At home, IBM's electric typewriter took more and more of the domestic market. Squeezed between these two pressures, the rest of the US typewriter industry found itself with a great deal of excess capacity following the Korean conflict. Excess capacity is today still a major problem in this field.

- the steady decline in the number of farms in the United States and the emergence of vigorous overseas competition have forced most domestic full-line manufacturers of farm equipment to sharply curtail total plant area. For example, in less than four years, International Harvester eliminated more than a third of its capacity (as measured in square feet of plant space) for the production of farm machinery.

The close relationship between physical facilities and environmental trends emphasises one of the most significant attributes of axed assets – their temporary utility. Accounting practice recognises this in its treatment of depreciation allowances. But even when the tax laws permit generous write-offs, they should not be used as the sole basis for setting the time period over which the investment must be justified. Environmental considerations may reveal that a different time horizon is more relevant for strategy determination. To illustrate again:

- as Armstrong Cork Company moved away from natural cork to synthetic materials during the early 1950s, management considered buying facilities for the production of its raw materials – particularly polyvinyl chloride. However, before doing so, it surveyed the chemical industry and concluded that producers were overbuilding. It therefore decided not to invest in facilities for the manufacture of this material.   The projections were valid; since 1956 polyvinyl chloride has dropped 50 per cent in price.

A strategic approach to facilities may not only change the time horizon; it may also change the whole basis of asset valuation:

- recently a substantial portion of Loew's theatres was acquired by the Tisch brothers, owners and operators of a number of successful hotels, including the Americana in Florida.[10] As long as the assets of Loew's theatres were viewed only as places for the projection of films, its theatres, however conservatively valued, seemed to be not much of a bargain. But to a keen appraiser of hotel properties the theatre sites, on rather expensive real estate in downtown city areas, had considerable appeal. Whether this appraisal will be borne out is as yet unknown. At any rate, the stock, which was originally purchased at $14 (with a book value of $22), was selling at $23 in October 1962.

ACHIEVING THE RIGHT BALANCE

One of the most difficult issues in strategy determination is that of achieving a balance between strategic goals and available resources. This requires a set of necessarily empirical, but critical, estimates of the total resources required to achieve particular objectives, the rate at which they will have to be committed, and the likelihood that they will be available. The most common errors are either to fail to make these estimates at all or to be excessively optimistic about them.

One example of the unfortunate results of being wrong on these estimates is the case of Royal McBee and the computer market:

- in January 1956 Royal McBee and the General Precision Equipment Corporation formed a jointly owned company – the Royal Precision Corporation – to enter the market for electronic data-processing equipment. This joint operation was a logical pooling of complementary talents. General Precision had a great deal of experience in developing and producing computers. Its Librascope Division had been selling them to the government for years. However, it lacked a commercial distribution system. Royal McBee, on the other hand, had a great deal of experience in marketing data-processing equipment, but lacked the technical competence to develop and produce a computer.

The joint venture was eminently successful, and within a short time the Royal Precision LPG-30 was the leader in the small-computer field. However, the very success of the computer venture caused Royal McBee some serious problems. The success of the Royal Precision subsidiary demanded that the partners put more and more money into it. This was no problem for General Precision, but it became an ever more serious problem for Royal McBee, which found itself in an increasingly critical cash bind. In March 1962 it sold its interest in Royal Precision to General Precision for $5 million – a price which represented a reported $6·9 million loss on the investment. Concluding that it simply did not have sufficient resources to stay with the new venture, it decided to return to its traditional strengths: typewriters and simple data-processing systems.

Another place where optimistic estimates of resources frequently cause problems is in small businesses. Surveys of the causes of small-business failure reveal that a most frequent cause of bankruptcy is inadequate resources to weather either the early period of establishment or unforeseen downturns in business conditions.

It is apparent from the preceding discussion that a critical strategic decision involves deciding: (a) how much of the company's resources to commit to opportunities currently perceived, and (b) how much to keep uncommitted as a reserve against the appearance of unanticipated demands. This decision is closely related to two other criteria for the evaluation of strategy: risk and timing. I shall now discuss these.

4   Does the strategy involve an acceptable degree of risk?

Strategy and resources, taken together, determine the degree of risk which the company is undertaking. This is a critical managerial choice. For example, when the old Underwood Corporation decided to enter the computer field, it was making what might have been an extremely astute strategic choice. However, the fact that it ran out of money before it could accomplish anything in that field turned its pursuit of opportunity into the prelude to disaster. This is not to say that the strategy was 'bad'. However, the course of action pursued *was* a high-risk strategy. Had it been successful, the payoff would have been lush. The fact that it was a stupendous failure instead does not mean that it was senseless to take the gamble.

Each company must decide for itself how much risk it wants to live with. In attempting to assess the degree of risk associated with a particular strategy, management may use a variety of techniques. For example, mathematicians have developed an elegant set of techniques for choosing among a variety of strategies where you are willing to estimate the payoffs and the probabilities associated with them. However, our concern here is not with these quantitative aspects but with the identification of some qualitative factors which may serve as a rough basis for evaluating the degree of risk inherent in a strategy. These factors are:

1 The amount of resources (on which the strategy is based) whose continued existence or value is not assured.
2 The length of the time periods to which resources are committed.
3 The proportion of resources committed to a single venture.

The greater these quantities, the greater the degree of risk that is involved.

UNCERTAIN TERM OF EXISTENCE

Since a strategy is based on resources, any resource which may disappear before the payoff has been obtained may constitute a danger to the organisation. Resources may disappear for various reasons. For example, they may lose their value. This frequently happens to such resources as physical facilities and product features. Again, they may be accidentally destroyed. The most vulnerable resource here is competence. The possible crash of the company plane or the blip on the president's electrocardiogram is what makes many organisations essentially speculative ventures. In fact, one of the critical attributes of highly centralised organisations is that the more centralised they are, the more speculative they are. The disappearance of the top executive, or the disruption of communication with him, may wreak havoc at subordinate levels.

However, for many companies, the possibility that critical resources may lose their value stems not so much from internal developments as from shifts in the environment. Take specialised production knowhow, for example. It has value only because of demand for the product by customers — and customers may change their minds. This is cause for acute concern among the increasing number of companies whose futures depend so heavily on their ability to participate in defence contracts. A familiar case is the plight of the airframe industry following World War II. Some of the companies succeeded in making the shift from aircraft to missiles, but this has only resulted in their being faced with the same problem on a larger scale.

DURATION OF COMMITMENT

Financial analysts often look at the ratio of fixed assets to current assets in order to assess the extent to which resources are committed to long-term programmes. This may or may not give a satisfactory answer. How important are the assets? When will they be paid for?

The reasons for the risk increasing as the time for payoff increases is, of course, the inherent uncertainty in any venture. Resources committed over long time spans make the company vulnerable to changes in the environment. Since the difficulty of predicting such changes increases as the time span increases, long-term projects are basically more risky than are short ones. This is especially true of companies whose environments are unstable. And today, either because of technological, political, or economic shifts, most companies are decidedly in the category of those that face major upheaval in their corporate environments. The company building its future around technological equipment, the company selling primarily to the government, the company investing in underdeveloped nations, the company selling to the Common Market, the company with a plant in the South – all these have this prospect in common.

The harsh dilemma of modern management is that the time-span of decision is increasing at the same time as the corporate environment is becoming increasingly unstable. It is this dilemma which places such a premium on the manager's sensitivity to external trends today. Much has been written about his role as a commander and administrator. But it is no less important that he be a *strategist*.

SIZE OF THE STAKES

The more of its resources a company commits to a particular strategy, the more pronounced the consequences. If the strategy is successful, the payoff will be great – both to managers and investors. If the strategy fails, the consequences will be dire – both to managers and investors. Thus, a critical decision for the executive group is: What proportion of available resources should be committed to a particular course of action?

This decision may be handled in a variety of ways. For example, faced with a project that requires more of its resources than it is willing to commit, a company either may choose to refrain from undertaking the project or, alternatively, may seek to reduce the total resources required by undertaking a joint venture or by going the route of merger or acquisition in order to broaden the resource base.

The amount of resources management stands ready to commit is of particular significance where there is some likelihood that larger competitors, having greater resources, may choose to enter the company's field. Thus, those companies which entered the small-computer field in the past few years are now faced with the penetration into this area of the data-processing giants. (Both IBM and Remington Rand have recently introduced new small computers.)

I do not mean to imply that the 'best' strategy is the one with the least risk. High payoffs are frequently associated with high-risk strategies. Moreover, it is a frequent but dangerous assumption to think that inaction, or lack of change, is a low-risk strategy. Failure to exploit its resources to the fullest may well be the riskiest strategy of all that an organisation may pursue, as Montgomery Ward and other companies have amply demonstrated.

5   Does the strategy have an appropriate time horizon?

A significant part of every strategy is the time horizon on which it is based. A viable strategy not only reveals what goals are to be accomplished; it says something about *when* the aims are to be achieved.

Goals, like resources, have time-based utility. A new product developed, a plant put on stream, a degree of market penetration, become significant strategic objectives only if accomplished by a certain time. Delay may deprive them of all strategic significance. A perfect example of this in the military sphere is the Sinai campaign of 1956. The strategic objective of the Israelis was not only to conquer the entire Sinai peninsula; it also was to do it in seven days. By contrast, the lethargic movement of the British troops made the operation a futile one for both England and France.

In choosing an appropriate time horizon, we must pay careful attention to the goals being pursued, and to the particular organisation involved. Goals must be established far enough in advance to allow the organisation to adjust to them. Organisations, like ships, cannot be 'spun on a dime'. Consequently, the larger the organisation, the further its strategic time horizon must extend, since its adjustment time is longer. It is no mere managerial whim that the major contributions to long-range planning have emerged from the larger organisations – especially those large organisations, such as Lockheed, North American Aviation, and RCA that traditionally have had to deal with highly unstable environments.

The observation that large corporations plan far ahead while small ones can get away without doing so has frequently been made. However, the significance of planning for the small but growing company has frequently been overlooked. As a company gets bigger, it must not only change the way it operates; it must also steadily push ahead its time horizon – and this is a difficult thing to do. The manager who has built a successful enterprise by his skill at 'putting out fires' or the wheeler-dealer whose firm has grown by a quick succession of financial coups is seldom able to make the transition to the long look ahead.

In many cases, even if the executive were inclined to take a longer range of events, the formal reward system seriously militates against doing so. In most companies the system of management rewards is closely related to currently reported profits. Where this is the case, executives may understandably be so preoccupied with reporting a profit year by year that they fail to spend as much time as they should in managing the company's long-term future. But if we seriously accept the thesis that the essence of managerial responsibility is the extended time lapse between decision and result, currently reported profits are hardly a reasonable basis on which to compensate top executives. Such a basis simply serves to shorten the time horizon with which the executive is concerned.

The importance of an extended time horizon derives not only from the fact that an organisation changes slowly and needs time to work through basic modifications in its strategy; it derives also from the fact that there is a considerable advantage in a certain consistency of strategy maintained over long periods of time. The great danger to companies which do not carefully formulate strategies well in advance is that they are prone to fling themselves towards chaos by drastic changes in policy – and in personnel – at frequent intervals. A parade of presidents is a clear indication of a board that has not really decided what its strategy should be. It is a common harbinger of serious corporate difficulty as well.

The time horizon is also important because of its impact on the selection of policies. The greater the time horizon, the greater the range in choice of tactics. If, for instance, the goals desired must be achieved in a relatively short time, steps like acquisition and merger may become virtually mandatory. An interesting illustration is the decision of National Cash Register to enter the market for electronic data-processing equipment. As reported in *Forbes*:

> Once committed to EDP, NCR wasted no time. To buy talent and experience in 1953 it acquired Computer Research Corp. of Hawthorne, California. . . . For speed's sake, the manufacture of the 304s central units was turned over to GE. . . . NCR's research and development outlays also began curving steeply upwards.[11]

6 Is the strategy workable ?

At first glance, it would seem that the simplest way to evaluate a corporate strategy is the completely pragmatic one of asking: Does it work? However, further reflection should reveal that if we try to answer that question, we are immediately faced with a quest for criteria. What is the evidence of a strategy 'working'?

Quantitative indices of performance are a good start, but they really measure the influence of two critical factors combined: the strategy selected and the skill with which it is being executed. Faced with the failure to achieve anticipated results, both of these influences must be critically examined. One interesting illustration of this is a recent survey of the Chrysler Corporation after it suffered a period of serious loss: 'In 1959, during one of the frequent reorganisations at Chrysler Corp., aimed at halting the company's slide, a management consultant concluded: "The only thing wrong with Chrysler is people. The corporation needs some good top executives." '[12]

By contrast, when Olivetti acquired the Underwood Corporation, it was able to reduce the cost of producing typewriters by one-third. And it did it without changing any of the top people in the promotion group. However, it did introduce a drastically revised set of policies.

If a strategy cannot be evaluated by results alone, there are some other indications that may be used to assess its contribution to corporate progress:

- the degree of consensus which exists among executives concerning corporate goals and policies
- the extent to which major areas of managerial choice are identified in advance, while there is still time to explore a variety of alternatives
- the extent to which resource requirements are discovered well before the last minute, necessitating neither crash programmes of cost reduction nor the elimination of planned programmes. The widespread popularity of the

meataxe approach to cost reduction is a clear indication of the frequent failure of corporate strategic planning.

Conclusion

The modern organisation must deploy expensive and complex resources in the pursuit of transitory opportunities. The time required to develop resources is so extended, and the time-scale of opportunities is so brief and fleeting, that a company which has not carefully delineated and appraised its strategy is adrift in white water.

In short, while a set of goals and major policies that meets the criteria listed above does not guarantee success, it can be of considerable value in giving management both the time and the room to manœuvre.

References

1. For an interesting discussion of this relationship, see A. D. CHANDLER, jr., *Strategy and Structure*, Massachusetts Institute of Technology Press, 1962, pp. 1–17.

2. See EDWARD C. BURSK and DAN H. FENN, jr., *Planning the Future Strategy of Your Business*, McGraw-Hill, 1956, p. 8.

3. SEYMOUR TILLES, 'The manager's job – a systems approach', *Harvard Business Review*, Jan.–Feb. 1963, p. 73.

4. See THEODORE LEVITT, 'Marketing myopia', *Harvard Business Review*, July–Aug. 1960, p. 45.

5. 'I? for Ampex: drastic changes help solve big headache of fast corporate growth', *Wall Street Journal*, 17 Sept. 1962, p. 1.

6. MYLES L. MACE and G. G. MONTGOMERY, *Management Problems of Corporate Acquisitions*, Boston, Division of Research, Harvard Business School, 1962, p. 60.

7. MONTGOMERY WARD, 'Prosperity is still around the corner', *Fortune*, Nov. 1960, p. 140.

8. PHILIP SELZNICK, *Leadership in Administration*, Row, Peterson & Company, 1957, p. 42.

9. JAMES L. HAMILTON, *Wall Street Journal*, 11 Sept. 1962, p. 30.

10. See 'The Tisches eye their next $65 million', *Fortune*, Jan. 1960, p. 140.

11. 'NCR and the computer sweepstakes', *Forbes*, 15 Oct. 1962, p. 21.

12. 'How Chrysler hopes to rebound', *Business Week*, 6 Oct. 1962, p. 45.

6

Corporate strategic planning - the American experience

SEYMOUR TILLES

Corporate strategy is such a relatively new addition to modern management practice that there is at present little empirical evidence which might either validate or refute many of the claims being made on behalf of long-term planning. In this article Dr Tilles points out the lessons which may be drawn from the experience of United States companies with strategic planning and pays particular attention to its costs as well as its benefits. In the main, his analysis suggests that many American companies have tended to reduce planning to a rigidly structured mechanical exercise which bears little relationship to the real world of business and fails to take account of so many unquantifiable factors which will ultimately help to determine its success. He concludes by suggesting certain steps which top management should take when instituting a system of corporate planning so as to avoid these pitfalls.

Strategic or long-range planning started as a formal activity in the United States before it began in other countries. Since at this point, many European companies are now beginning to be seriously interested in the establishment of such a formal activity, it is worth reviewing the US experience to see what may be learned from it that may be valuable to companies about to create a formal planning activity, or which have recently done so.

Among the more valuable aspects of US experience for such companies to review are the errors which have been made. Having been among the first to try to do long-range planning, companies in the US have been the first to make the classical mistakes that tend to be made in this field because of lack of experience. These mistakes should be carefully considered by others about to begin such an activity, for there is now no real justification for repeating them.

The first major error that many US companies have made has been to view long-range planning as the imposition of a checklist procedure, rather than as an attempt to deal with the major concerns of senior management. There is, unfortunately, in the long-range planning field, a great preoccupation among its staff practitioners with format and technique. When planners gather, the subject of conversation is frequently the content and format of planning manuals. But the major purpose of planning is not to go through the motions for the sake of creating a document, it is to help the senior corporate management deal with some real problem which concerns them. As an illustration of the kind of situation that preoccupation with technique may create, let me relate the recent experience of a major US corporation. In a meeting of executives convened to discuss planning procedures, the corporate controller proudly announced that for improved validity in considering the return on investment for major projects, they would henceforth use a discounted cash flow method of calculating returns over an eight-year period, rather than an eight-year average return. He was followed by the marketing manager, who said that due to the unsettled conditions in the market, there was very little confidence in their ability to predict prices even as much as three months in advance. Since return on investment is a direct function of the price level, the controller's new concept is not only not much help − it is misleading. It implies a degree of accuracy which the other facets of the procedure clearly do not warrant.

Unfortunately, the tradition already established among planners in the UK is that planning is a compilation of standardised routines which one goes through in order to produce a document. As the distance between such procedures and the real concerns of senior management either remains wide, or indeed broadens, there is generally a growing frustration with the futility of the process.

Rejecting the value of intuition

If we consider how many companies have been well managed, and produced consistently high profitability for many years, before planning as a formal process existed, then one of the conclusions that we are forced to consider is that many operating executives are able to make far better decisions than they can explain. Unfortunately, many planners in US companies have got off to a poor start by rejecting the validity of intuition. They viewed the planning process as a substitute for the judgement of the operating executive, rather than seeing it as a way of making such considerations explicit, and exploring its implications. Planning cannot be a substitute for experience-based judgement. It just isn't well enough developed to fulfil that task.

One illustration of that concerns the president of a glass company in the US who convened a task force in 1947 and asked them to consider what new product opportunities the company ought to consider. Looking at the growth in consumer demand, and the heavy increases in apparel sales, they recommended that the company consider the manufacture of glass buttons. He thanked them for their efforts, but said that the company would produce television tubes as its next product, because it seemed to him that was a greater opportunity. Of course, he was right.

Planning is a learning process

One of the difficulties that has been created in US companies, through lack of experience, has been the disappointment and the frustration that comes from continuing to make mistakes, even though a planning activity has been begun. However, the basic justification for a planning activity is not that it will avoid errors; it is, instead, that it will enhance the amount of learning that takes place from the errors that are made.

Despite the value which is placed on experience in the corporate world, it is by no means true that learning automatically takes place. A colleague and I recently did a historical analysis of the electronics industry – looking at the introduction of radio, television, computers, and semi-conductors. One of our conclusions was that the electronics industry apparently does not learn from its experience, because the companies involved seemed to behave with surprising consistency, ignoring the lessons which might have been learned from the earlier transitions.

The great contribution of planning to learning is that it is a way of inducing operating executives to state in advance what they think will happen at some point in the future; and to then go back and honestly appraise how close they come to being right – and what things they missed that should be considered more carefully in making subsequent estimates. This is the kind of systematic review that helps executives to learn, but which frequently does not occur without having a formal planning activity. Of course, if such review is to result in learning, it has to take place in a non-threatening context. Learning requires that the team's attention be focused on 'What was not considered?', rather than 'Whose fault was it that our estimate was off?'

Future and present responsibility

One of the common organisational errors that have been made in the US with respect to planning has been the attempt to separate responsibility for the present from the responsibility for the future. Indeed, in many US companies the line executives get along very well with the planning group, because the line executives run the company as it exists today, and the planning group looks at the company five years out. Each year, as the cycle rolls forward, the planning group is pushed out another year. Relationships are amicable, because the planning group is banished to the perpetual future, and has no effect at all on current operating decisions.

Ideally, of course, what the planning activity should help to accomplish is the acceptance on the part of the line management that it has a responsibility for assuring the future profitability of the company; and that the amount of time into the future that this responsibility extends is related to organisational position. Theoretically, the higher up in the organisation one is, the longer into the future he must spend part of his time trying to see. Unfortunately, this is not the case in many companies. Indeed, the widespread installation of computers frequently causes a reverse effect. It is now technically feasible for senior management to have an enormous amount of information about current operations, which tends to draw their attention into the present. It is not until the senior management learns to content itself with more aggregate reporting, leaving the middle management to cope with the details, that effective planning can be considered. It is for this reason that some companies have seriously considered coding their data banks so that upon inquiry from a senior executive on a question of detail, it would point out: 'You are above the level in this company authorised to have this information.'

Planning is as much a political as a rational exercise

The late Lyman Bryson, a distinguished American political scientist, once described the essential problem of the consultant as that of putting knowledge at the service of power. I believe this is also an extremely valid description of the problem of planning within a company. In many companies, the planning group tends to be staffed with bright young men who are very highly trained, but who are completely devoid of political power. In some US companies these young men have been left to themselves to wallow about intellectually exciting pursuits which are neither understood by the rest of the company, nor perceived by it as relevant to their concerns. This gives rise to what may be described as the gap between insight and influence. As an indication of how great this gap may become, one executive recently said about the planning group in his company: 'In the midst of all our grimy political problems, they are engaged in immaculate conception.'

Rigidity and flexibility

Many chief executives oppose long-range planning because they are concerned about the possibility of important opportunities being missed, simply because they were not included in the original plan. This is a real hazard, the US experience would indicate. Once a plan becomes part of the managerial programme of a company, and represents a large investment of management time and effort, it is difficult to change. But even if it is a large, thick book, it may not yet contain some of the most promising alternatives that the company might consider. This aspect of planning is illustrated by the fact that in many US companies, some of the ideas that eventually prove to be the most successful are 'bootlegged' in their early developmental phases. Indeed, one researcher in a large American company told me that since some of the best ideas in the lab seemed to come from bootlegged research, the researchers were encouraged to spend part of their time on such activities. When it is no longer possible for middle-level executives to do anything except that which is contained in the plan, the benefit of these activities is lost.

Treating planning as long-term budgeting

One of the most common, and most serious, errors that have been committed by US companies in launching their planning activities has been to think about planning as synonymous with long-term budgeting. Their feeling in getting started was that since the budgeting process was already in operation, what they would do was to simply extend the budgetary considerations for several more years, and that this would then become the planning activity.

Actually, although they are related, planning and budgeting are two distinctly different activities. The essential purpose of budgeting is a narrowing down of alternatives – selecting those few which are consistent with the company's resources and which represent the highest return. The essential purpose of planning is a widening out – attempting to assure that there is an adequate range of alternatives from which to make a selection. The importance of such an activity can be seen from the fact that many companies do not use their assets aggressively, because they lack the ideas to pursue. Indeed, there are probably about as many companies whose growth is limited by their ability to generate attractive growth ideas, as there are companies whose ability to grow is limited by their ability to mobilise additional investment funds. One of the purposes of planning is to attempt to assume that the company remains funds-limited, in the sense of actively employing all of its available capital in the pursuit of promising opportunities.

Trying to plan in the context of no financial dicipline

In a number of US companies, despite the popularity of the profit motive as a description of executive behaviour, there is no financial discipline. In these companies, executives do not fully accept their responsibility for assuring future corporate profitability, and missed profit targets are not cause for searching examination of the contributing causes.

In such a context, planning is likely to be simply an idle exercise, because an essential motivating force for taking it seriously is absent.

Getting a planning activity started

So much for the errors which have been made. Suppose, however, that having carefully considered each of these mistakes, you felt they could be avoided in your organisation, and that a formal planning activity was desirable. What should you do in order to get it started? The first issue to be resolved, and one of the most important, is the question of sponsorship – who wants planning to be done? Who is going to take upon himself the responsibility for saying 'I want this activity started, because I think it will help me'.

An important conclusion to be remembered – based on the US experience –

is that no progress is made until sponsorship is undertaken by a line executive having the responsibility for a significant part of the company. It need not be the president or chairman. In many US companies, effective planning has been done by the manager of a single division deciding to act as a guinea-pig, and to try to see what benefit such activity might produce. Frequently, the results have been so impressive that they led to the adoption of planning in other divisions as well, and eventually also at the corporate level. Effective planning practised in any major part of a large organisation, frequently leads to its adoption throughout the company. The request by President Johnson that other departments in the US government attempt to use some of the planning processes developed by Secretary MacNamara within the Department of Defence is a case in point.

It should be stressed that until a senior line executive is willing to accept sponsorship responsibility for planning, little progress – if any – can be anticipated. Until that occurs, the planners are really engaged in a selling programme, or perhaps a missionary activity. With luck and faith they can be successful, but the role of missionary is characteristically one involving high risks.

Once the sponsor has come to the fore, the next question must be: what specific purpose does the sponsor have in mind? Why does he want planning? What results does he hope to get from it? The answers to these questions are an immediate indication of how much benefit the sponsor can anticipate from this activity. The clearer the purpose that the sponsor has in mind, the better chance of having some contribution from planning. This may be increasing the rate of growth of earnings, or developing more earnings from the US market, or finding diversification opportunities, or any other specific objective that is a valid one in the light of current considerations. However, it is not valid to want a planning activity 'because it would probably be a good thing to have one', or because 'others in our industry are doing this, maybe we should do it, too'.

Once a statement of purpose has been decided upon, the sponsor must communicate this to his subordinates. He must ask them to participate in the accomplishment of this objective, through their part of the planning effort. It is critical that the sponsor shares his concept of purpose, and his commitment to sponsorship, with his subordinates. If he does not do this, they have no reliable way of appreciating his intent, and of knowing what may be expected of them. At this point, the company is ready to consider which additional staff positions may be needed in order to carry out its planning activities. These additional staff may now be viewed as positions which are created in order to help the senior corporate executives do planning as they feel it should be done.

As an illustration of the importance of this sequence, some time ago the Boston Consulting Group convened a small group of chief executives in order to discuss various aspects of corporate planning. One of the topics discussed was 'are planners necessary?' One segment argued vehemently that they were. Another segment argued with equal vehemence that they were not. After considerable debate, the difference of opinion was resolved by both groups agreeing that while planners may be necessary, planning should not be begun by designating a corporate planner.

What can a planning group contribute?

If a planning group is created, the US experience would suggest that considerable benefit may be derived from such a group by having it accept the following tasks:

1 Providing more environmental perspective.
2 Developing a better understanding of important relationships.
3 Gaining a better understanding of the company from a corporate perspective.
4 Getting more value from the budgetary process.
5 Obtaining a greater degree of communication and consensus among senior corporate executives.

Let us look at each of these:

Providing more environmental perspective

One of the important problems in any company is to gain a better understanding of its position, viewed from the outside. Most executives receive a great deal of information about what goes on within their own activities and within their own company. These executives, however, frequently receive very little information about what goes on that is of importance to them, but outside their own company. And yet, some of the factors which influence the future profitability of the company stem from outside the company, rather than from within it. Examples of this are competitor's activities, technological changes, changes in distribution channels, and governmental actions. As these change, they affect directly the opportunities and threats which the company must consider, and the choices it should make. An important potential contribution of a planning group is to periodically review these factors, producing an environmental audit of the company's position.

As an illustration of such an effort, one company president took a group of bright young men in his organisation, and assigned each of them the task of finding out as much as he could about one of his major competitors. At the time of the annual presentation of divisional plans, a simulated case was distributed, in which the group representing the company outlined what it intended to do, and the 'competitors' responded. After having these responses, the company's executives were forced to conclude that if their competitors' executives were as capable as their own young men, the company would have a difficult time indeed if the conditions indicated in the simulation really occurred.

Better understanding of important relationships

One of the basic problems in doing valid future planning is gaining a better understanding of the key relationships which characterise the operation of the business. In a petroleum company, some of the key relationships are the impact of increased petroleum consumption on tanker requirements, of changes in product mix on refinery design, and of growth in overall sales, and the number of senior executives required. In selling toothpaste in a new market, some of the important relationships are those between sample size and number of customers produced; between promotional expense and additional sales revenue, and between advertising emphasis and market segmentation. One of the important missions of a planning group is to help identify what some of the key relationships are, and to try to establish their quantitative characteristics. This is one of the important applications of mathematical modelling, and one reason why models are being used to an increasing degree in planning activities.

Corporate perspective

One of the common ways in which planning begins in large companies is with a concern for having the executives who have divisional responsibility develop better plans for their own activities. As these divisional plans begin to take shape, and to acquire credibility, a more serious question is posed for those who bear the responsibility for the overall activity: 'Is the overall company anything more than simply the sum of the individual divisions?' For those companies who believe that this should be true, the essential question is then in what ways may the overall organisation use its combined capabilities to pursue opportunities beyond those which the divisions might undertake individually. Important contributions which a planning activity can make to the deliberations on this question are the determination of the particular strengths and weaknesses which are revealed by the overall pattern of activity, the identification of those areas of opportunity which seem particularly appropriate in the light of existing commitments, and outlining the implications for the current portfolio of operations of major trends which are currently perceptible. Another activity which some companies are asking their planning groups to become engaged in is participation in the development of a 'target company' concept.

The concept of a target company is particularly useful, because it makes specific a whole set of relationships at a future date, and is therefore a much more meaningful statement of intentions than a single number, or a few numbers, which are supposed to encompass the corporate objectives. Developing a target company concept, which is both internally consistent and externally valid, takes a great deal of work and judgement. In this process, a corporate planning group can make a particularly useful contribution.

Getting value from budgeting

In its application within the US government, one of the most important purposes of planning is to improve the value of budgetary process. This can also be the case within companies.

The budgetary process can be improved in each of the following ways:

- developing more and better alternatives from which to make a choice
- developing more common and more valid assumptions about external conditions as a basis for allocation
- providing the capability to have more iterations in the process, and thus achieve a greater measure of internal consistency.

Earlier, we mentioned the importance of improved alternatives as an aspect of budgeting. Clearly, a budget can be no better than the quality of the alternatives presented for choice. Hemingway once said that the test of a novel was how much good material was left out. Similarly, one test of a good budget would be how many exciting ideas had to be omitted, because there just was not money enough to pursue all of them.

One of the curious aspects of budgeting is that as it is practised in some companies, it seems designed to keep basic assumptions implicit, while giving a good deal of attention to their quantitative implications. Thus, many budget reviews focus almost entirely on numbers, and rarely on an examination of the basic assumptions which produced the numbers. One of the significant contributions of the planning process to budgeting is that it focuses attention on the assumptions themselves, and thus frequently narrows considerably the range of opinion which must be reconciled in the budget review.

As it is practised in a number of US companies, budgetary reviews are a somewhat truncated process. Large amounts of information are carefully built up from one level of the organisation to the next during the months preceding the budget review. Finally, at the annual budget review, the essential aggregate conclusions are presented – and there may be substantial sums lopped off in order to keep the over-all sum within bounds which are felt to be appropriate. However, there is rarely time to go back and redo the whole process under the new guidelines, and to develop another internally consistent presentation. As a result, the budget tends to be a patched-up version of a carefully developed effort.

In order to be able to have more than a single pass at their budget, a number of companies have gone to a greater degree of automation in their budgeting process, and have developed financial models which permit a much greater degree of experimentation in the establishment of budgetary constraints. These companies can ask a broad range of 'what if?' types of questions, and see the impact of changing assumptions on their initial budgetary decisions. Among the companies that have such procedures are Xerox, IBM and General Electric.

Communication and consensus among senior executives

If a company is to be dynamic and aggressive, it must have an executive group capable of easy communications, and in substantial agreement on matters of basic policy, so that its members can pursue their own interests and yet reinforce each other's initiatives. These conditions do not automatically come about –

they have to be worked at. One of the ways in which it can be worked at is to have the executive group heavily involved in the development of corporate plans. This permits the range of opinions to be gauged and open deliberations to occur with respect to these. In some companies, the degree of communication developed this way, has been sufficiently great so that it permitted the objective examination of other aspects of the company's operation as well – including such delicate issues as organisation structure and office arrangements.

Conclusions

While many US companies have been able to derive a great deal of benefit from skilful application of planning procedures, we must be careful not to give the impression that planning can help solve all problems under any circumstances. As an illustration of the kind of context in which its application may be of limited value, the president of a large US company, who had earlier been its corporate planner, told an audience recently: 'When I was in the planner's position, I frequently felt that we either had to change our plans or to change our senior executive group. Now that I am president, it is much easier to make that choice.'

7

Where long-range planning pays off
Findings of a survey of formal, informal planners

STANLEY S. THUNE and ROBERT J. HOUSE

How does the adoption of formal long-range planning procedures affect a firm's economic performance? The authors have studied firms in six industrial groups and have summarised their findings. Company comparisons, which make up the first phase of the study, show that formal planners significantly outperform informal planners with respect to five economic measures. In addition, they bettered the records they achieved before formal planning was adopted. The second phase of the study is an industry-by-industry analysis. Formal planning firms in the drug, chemical and machinery industries consistently outperform informal planners: no clear associations can be established in the food, oil, and steel industries. Positive economic performance and formal planning are most strongly related among the medium-size companies in rapidly changing markets.

This article reports the results of a study of the changes in economic performance associated with formal long-range planning in US firms with annual sales of $75 million or more. To determine whether changes in performance are associated with long-range planning it is necessary to make two comparisons: first, the performances of a group of companies over two equal periods of time before and after they initiated planning, and, second, the performances, during a comparable period of time, of companies that use formal planning with a group of comparable companies that do not. Further, it is necessary to discount any differences found in the above comparisons that may have resulted from such factors as inertia prior to the initiation of long-range planning, historical factors such as patent advantages, or historically superior managerial performance.

In order to make the above comparisons, a sample of thirty-six firms representing six industrial groups were carefully selected from ninety-two companies that responded to a questionnaire submitted by the authors. (All firms in nine industries with sales of $75 million for 1965 were sent the questionnaire. Of the 145 firms contacted, 92 responded.) The purpose of the questionnaire was to identify those companies actively engaged in formal long-range planning.

Table 7.1 Summary of questionnaire response

Industry	Number mailed	Companies responding	Formal planners	Informal planners
Drug	14	8	6	2
Food	21	9	6	3
Chemical	22	19	16	3
Steel	16	7	4	3
Oil	22	17	14	3
Machinery	14	8	3	5
Communications	4	3	2	1
Electronics	23	16	16	0
Aircraft	9	5	4	1
Total	145	92	71	21

Table 7.2 Composition of sample*

Industry group		Sales as of base-line date		
		Formal planners	Informal planners	
Drug	A	180	A'	160
	B	200	B'	200
	C	220	C'	270
	Ave.	200	Ave.	210
Chemical	A	105	A'	160
	B	115	B'	175
	C	225	C'	235
	Ave.	143	Ave.	190
Machinery	A	110	A'	155
	B	160	B'	160
	C	180	C'	200
	Ave.	150	Ave.	173
Oil	A	370	A'	310
	B	1,200	B'	560
	C	1,760	C'	1,100
			D'	775
	Ave.	1,100	Ave.	686
Food	A	350	A'	300
	B	500	B'	315
			C'	415
	Ave.	425	Ave.	380
Steel	A	75	A'	100
	B	700	B'	110
	C	1,100	C'	710
	Ave.	625	Ave.	307

* A and A', B and B', ... = matched pairs.

Responding companies were classified as formal planners if their questionnaire responses indicated that they determined corporate strategy and goals for at least three years ahead, and if they established specific action programmes, projects, and procedures for achieving the goals. Companies that did not meet these requirements were classified as informal planners.

Table 7.1 presents a breakdown of the respondents by planning approach and industry. From the ninety-two responding companies, seventeen formal and nineteen informal planners were selected in a manner permitting reasonable comparisons over at least seven years. Table 7.2 describes these companies by industry, and by sales as of the base-line date, that is, the date they initiated formal planning. As the table shows, the pairs of firms (formal–informal) are well matched.

Company performances

The performances of formal and informal planners were computed over periods of seven to fifteen years, depending on their industry. In some industries (steel, for example) it was possible to make comparisons over a period as long as eleven years because of the early date at which long-range planning was introduced in that industry. The specific periods studied varied by industry as follows: drugs, 1960–5; food, 1958–65; chemicals, 1958–65; steel, 1955–65; oil, 1959–65; and machinery, 1959–65.

Fig. 7.1 Performances of formal and informal planners during planning period

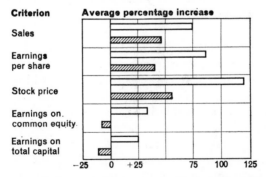

The performances of the companies were then analysed in terms of five economic measures: sales, stock prices, earnings per common share, return on common equity, and return on total capital employed.* A statistical analysis comparing all formal versus informal planners during the above periods (see Fig. 7.1) shows that the planners significantly outperformed the informal

* All indexes are adjusted for changes in the number of common shares outstanding. Changes in accounting procedures were taken into account in the calculations and analysis.

planners on three of the five measures: earnings per share (44 per cent), earnings on common equity (38 per cent), and earnings on total capital employed (32 per cent). Because these results are statistically significant, average data can be used for comparison.* Although the results for average sales and stock price appreciation were also substantially greater for the planners, a company-by-company comparison showed that these averages were greatly influenced by a single company. The average data, therefore, could not be used.

A second way to analyse the data is to compare the performance of the formal planners from the time they initiated planning through 1965 with their own performance over an equal period of time prior to the start of formal planning. Fig. 7.2 presents such a comparison for five of the six industries based on data

Fig. 7.2 Performances of companies before and after formal planning.*

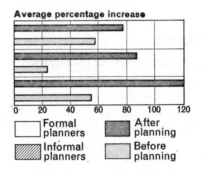

Average percentage increase

Formal planners
Informal planners
After planning
Before planning

* Data used for five industries. Steel was excluded because the preplanning period for this industry was atypical. Data on earnings on common equity and total capital were not available for the preplanning period.

available for that period of time. (The steel companies were omitted because the preplanning period for this industry was atypical; the eleven-year period prior to 1955, the year in which the companies initiated formal long-range planning, would have required consideration of performance during World War II.)

Here again, we find a remarkable association between economic performance and long-range planning; planners outperformed themselves on all three available measures of economic performance. The increases are impressive: 38 per cent in sales, 64 per cent in earnings per share, and 56 per cent in stock price appreciation. Data on earnings on common equity and total capital are not available for the preplanning period.

Although the preceding comparisons make an impressive case for long-range planning, they could have resulted from other factors: generally superior

* The statistical method used was a two-way analysis of variance, using industrial grouping and formal planners versus informal planners as the independent variables, and changes in sales, stock prices, earnings on common equity, earnings per share, and earnings on total capital as the dependent variables. Five analyses of variance were computed, one for each measure of economic performance.

management, an early product monopoly position, or some other earlier advantage that resulted in continuing superior performance. To determine whether such forces did, indeed, account for our findings, the performance of the informal planners was compared to the performance of the formal planners during a period of time prior to the date formal planning was adopted. The length of time over which this comparison was made was equal to the period during which formal and informal planners were compared in Figs. 7.1 and 7.2. This comparison showed no significant difference between the two types of planners.

Thus, the first major conclusion of the study is quite clear: formal planners, from the time they initiated long-range planning through 1965, significantly outperformed informal planners with respect to earnings per share, earnings on common equity, and earnings on total capital employed. Furthermore, these companies outperformed their own records based on an equal period of time before they began formal planning. Finally, informal planners did not surpass formal planners on any of the measures of economic performance after long-range planning was introduced.

Industry-by-industry comparisons

The second phase of the study consisted of an industry-by-industry analysis. In this phase, the informal planners were compared to the formal planners within each industry; their performance during the planning period was compared with their own performance during an equal period of time prior to the adoption of formal plans. Fig. 7.3 presents comparisons of the average changes in economic performance for both types of planners, by industry, during the planning period.

The long-range planning firms in the drug, chemical, and machinery industries consistently outperformed the informal planners on all five criteria of business success. It can also be seen that the planners in the food industry did better with respect to earnings per common share, stock price appreciation, and earnings on common equity; were approximately equal to informal planners with respect to sales increases; and were slightly lower with respect to earnings on total capital.

However, from 1950 through 1957, prior to the adoption of formal planning by the food industry, the planners performed slightly better than the informal planners in all categories. This earlier advantage suggests that their higher performance after the initiation of long-range planning may well be a result of their performance during the previous planning period. Thus, these findings should be discounted since no clear association can be established between economic performance in the food industry and long-range planning.

The same phenomenon occurred prior to the adoption of formal planning in the oil industry; for the period from 1952 through 1958, companies that began formal planning in 1959 outperformed informal planners in all five

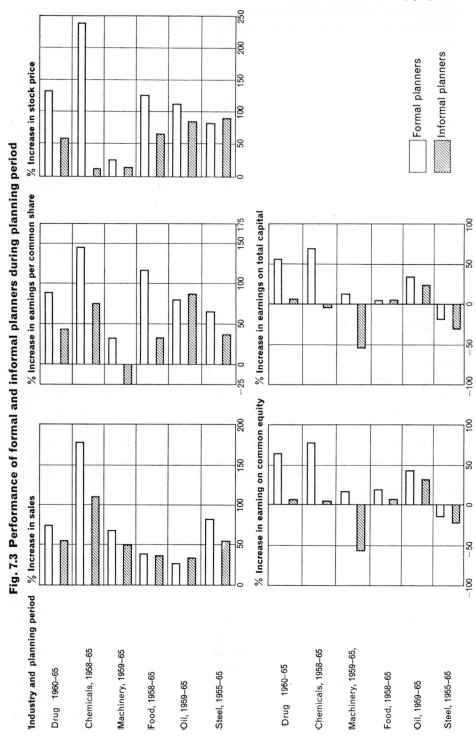

Fig. 7.3 Performance of formal and informal planners during planning period

measures of economic performance. Thus, the slightly superior economic performance of the planners in the oil industry during the planning period is not only associated with the initiation of long-range planning but also with earlier competitive performance. With respect to the steel industry, no comparisons were possible for an equal period prior to the adoption of long-range planning because of the early date at which planning was initiated in this industry.

Why industrial differences?

It is clear that companies that initiated formalised long-range planning in the drug, chemical, and machinery industries have significant competitive advantages over those that did not, beginning with the time they started planning through 1965. These findings raise the question as to why formal long-range planning is more closely associated with economic performance in certain industries. For example, we might ask why the food, oil, and steel companies did not enjoy the same economic advantages after initiating planning, even though their pre-planning performance had been better than that of the informal planners.

Several factors may account for these findings. First, political or governmental factors may have a bearing on firm performance; for example, the production and distribution of oil are known to be highly dependent on international political forces and of steel on defence plans. However, we find this explanation does not hold in the food industry where production and distribution are not related to such factors.

Another factor that may account for industry differences concerning the association between planning and performance may be the size of the companies within the industry. To test this possibility correlations were computed between the sales of the company as of the initiation of planning and changes in the five indexes of business success. As can be seen from Table 7.3 consistent negative

Table 7.3 Correlations between sales at beginning of planning period and changes in measures of economic performance

Increase	Formal planners	Informal planners
Sales	−·404	·278
Earnings per share	−·301	·204
Stock price	−·210	·081
Earnings on total capital	−·302	·326
Earnings on common equity	−·296	·427

correlations were found between sales and economic performance for the long-range planners; the opposite was found for informal planners. Thus, among the informal planners the rich got richer; among the formal planners, the poor got richer.

Differences in the performance of planners from industry to industry might also be attributed to the degree of competitiveness in the market place. All three industries in which formal planners had the least impressive results operate in markets characterised by a lower rate of technological innovation and new product introduction. On the face of it, this appears to be a plausible explanation. One indication of technological innovation within an industry is the amount of expenditure for research and development. Table 7.4 presents data on R and D expenditures in the six industries studied from 1960 to 1965. It is clear that the advantages associated with formal long-range planning are primarily concentrated in the more rapidly changing industries, and that positive economic performance and formal planning are most strongly related among the medium-size companies in the rapidly changing markets.

Table 7.4 R and O funds in manufacturing companies (as % of net sales, 1960–5)

Industry	1960	1961	1962	1963	1964	1965
Food and kindred products	0·4	0·4	0·4	0·4	0·4	0·4
Chemicals and allied products	4·5	4·3	4·2	4·3	4·5	4·2
Industrial chemicals	5·7	5·2	4·9	5·1	5·0	4·6
Drugs and medicines	4·6	4·3	4·3	4·7	5·9	5·9
Petroleum refining and extraction	1·0	1·0	1·0	1·0	1·2	1·2
Primary metals	0·8	0·8	0·8	0·8	0·8	0·8
Primary ferrous products	0·6	0·7	0·6	0·7	0·7	0·7
Machinery	4·7	4·2	4·0	4·2	4·3	4·1

Source: *Basic Research, Applied Research and Development in Industry*, 1962 and 1965 (Survey of Science Resources Series; National Science Foundation, NSF 65–68).

In this study, companies that engage in formal long-range planning, when considered as a group, have historically outperformed a comparable group of informal planners. Further, it was found that the successful economic results associated with long-range planning tend to take place in the rapidly changing industries and among the companies of medium size. These findings are consistent with what we would expect intuitively; it would be expected that changes in managerial practices in smaller firms are less likely to be offset by inertia and more likely to exert leverage.

However, it would probably be naïve to conclude that formal planning is the sole cause of the successful performance of the firms studied. It is more likely that these companies are using other analytically oriented and modern management practices in other decision areas as well. For example, we have speculated that firms engaged in formal planning also use more sophisticated methods for organisation design and analysis; managerial selection, development, and compensation; and administrative control. Thus, it is most likely that formal planning is a characteristic of a well-managed firm rather than the single cause of successful economic performance.

Although the data make an impressive case for long-range planning by firms in the medium-size, rapidly changing category, the results should be considered suggestive rather than conclusive. Because serious efforts were made to isolate critical variables by matching companies by size and industry, the sample was necessarily small, and the matched groups were still less than perfectly comparable.

Corporate strategy and the environment

A. Planning and the business environment

8

A strategic merger policy

GERALD D. NEWBOULD

Although most companies have some kind of policy for mergers, a more specific or 'strategic' policy is necessary during periods of intense merger activity. The author argues that the merger boom in British industry of 1967 and 1968 tended to be self-generating. Most mergers of this period were of the 'horizontal' variety, affecting established market positions and shares. In this situation companies were compelled to anticipate and indeed initiate future mergers simply in order to re-establish their former positions. The author concludes by suggesting a way of formulating a strategic merger policy.

The underlying trend in merger activity is an upward one. This necessitates the construction of a corporate merger policy, and most companies, certainly those of any size, already have a corporate merger policy.

Distinct from the underlying trend, there occurred a huge boom in merger activity in 1967 and 1968. The purpose of this paper is to demonstrate that the experience of this merger boom necessitates the construction of a new kind of corporate merger policy – a strategic merger policy, which will exist alongside the normal merger policy, but at any one time the strategic would take precedence over the other.

The normal type of merger policy would operate for most of the time (it is this type which already exists in many companies) and, in general, it will indicate the procedure to be adopted when a merger opportunity exists,* and has been adopted at varying levels of informality or sophistication. It will be at its most informal when the company does not actually seek potential merger opportunities[1]; in this company the merger policy will be a procedure for vetting those opportunities which present themselves to the company through casual contacts, or visits from merger brokers. The policy would indicate criteria by which a merger would be regarded as acceptable. The criteria would normally cover product and market specifications, personnel requirements, etc., as well as some financial criteria. At more sophisticated stages, the normal merger policy may be part of a corporate plan and mergers are undertaken to conform with the

* 'Merger' here covers merger, takeover, deal, acquisition, etc.

growth paths laid down in the current plan. Or the merger policy may have been formulated because investment opportunities and market growth in the company's existing fields of activity are no longer sufficient to satisfy an unspecified, or only partly specified, growth objective. In these companies the merger opportunities not only present themselves, but are actively sought and, in each case, the list of criteria will be applied as a vetting before final appraisal and decision.

The other type of policy, designated a strategic merger policy, would operate in specified circumstances; normally this would be in the course of a general merger boom, or whenever a merger had been enacted involving one (or more) of the company's competitors. Section 1 looks at the last merger boom and derives therefrom the necessity for a strategic merger policy; section 2 examines the general nature of such a policy and details how a policy might be constructed.

1. The last merger boom

The necessity of a strategic merger policy

The last merger boom coincided almost exactly with the twenty-four months of 1967 and 1968. Activity earlier and since has been on an upward trend, but always at 'normal' levels. However, in the two years, about 10 per cent of the UK's non-nationalised assets were the subject of some form of achieved or intended takeover. Over £5200 million was paid for shares carrying votes in other firms, and over 2500 firms were taken over. Looking at large firms, 70 per cent of the UK's top 100 firms were involved as bidders or victims* and 25 per cent of firms with a value in excess of £10 million were taken over.[2]

Since this scale of activity occurred within two years, it is already possible to see that involvement in merger activity is not necessarily that which can be related to the normal merger policy; that type of policy presupposes an orderliness of involvement which may be impossible in a merger boom, and a speed of involvement possibly far below that necessary for continued existence.

There are two main features of the merger activity of 1967 and 1968 which form the basis for proposing the desirability and necessity of a strategic merger policy. The first relates to the predominance of horizontal mergers, and the second to the concentration of the activity to a few industries. Some other features are presented after these two basic ones have been discussed.

Mergers can be defined by reference to the market-product relationship between the bidding firm and the victim firm. Where the firms operate in the same market the merger is referred to as 'horizontal'. Apart from 'vertical' (where one firm is a supplier or customer of the other), there is no clear consensus of

---

* While maintaining the description 'merger' to cover all types of situation, there was defined in each situation a bidding firm and a victim firm. The bidding firm is not that which *legally* bids (e.g. firm C, which has been formed by A and B, to take over each), but that which is the prime mover in the situation (e.g. A or B, depending upon which is the prime mover), and the other (e.g. B or A) is the 'victim'.

opinion on labelling other market–product relationships, but for present purposes 'horizontal' and 'other' is sufficient. The numbers and values of horizontal and other mergers in the 1967–8 boom are shown in Table 8.1.

Table 8.1 The predominance of horizontal mergers in 1967–8

Market type	Number of mergers	Value of mergers (£m)
Horizontal	337 (83%)	3713·890 (85%)
Other	70	651·621
	407	4365·511

While there were over 2500 completed mergers, the table is confined to those in which £1 million or more was paid for the victim firm. £1 million was chosen, somewhat arbitrarily, as the cut-off point to distinguish 'important' from 'unimportant' mergers. Here a merger is 'important' if it effects a change in established market positions. Clearly, the value of the acquired firm is not the most satisfactory way of determining whether such a change has occurred; the most satisfactory would be its market share relative to that of the bidding firm, but as these figures are not universally available the other measure had to be adopted. With this as a rider, Table 8.1 shows that over 80 per cent of the mergers by number or value were within a given market, and that there were over 300 shocks of some magnitude delivered to existing market positions.

In 1966 it was likely that there were many markets in which there were only a few firms operating, and even more markets in which the current positions on market shares had not changed for some time. In these markets, there would have been established an equilibrium level of competition and a code of interfirm behaviour which each firm had come to accept as part of its operating environment. Then in two years many such environments were altered, in some cases radically, by a merger between two of the firms.

Faced with a position where there are new market positions, what is the rational policy? If the change was a minor one, then it may have been ignored in many instances. If the change could be regarded as important then it is unlikely to be ignored. Importance, as above, will depend upon whether the established rankings in market share have been altered; especially if numbers 2 and 3 in the market have merged, and their combined market share exceeds that of the firm previously ranked as number 1, that firm has suffered a relative diminution in size, and it might anticipate both a higher level of competition and a different code of interfirm behaviour.

With such anticipation it becomes rational for the firm to merge to restore its former position, and prevent any further diminution if other firms have the same anticipation. In the same way, mergers between firms at lower rankings affect those firms previously near to them in size and effectiveness, and eventually affect those previously above them.

　　Therefore, merger activity can become self-generating, each merger leading to an increased desire from other firms within that market to merge; and so a spiral of merging can take place, because it has become rational corporate policy to merge.

　　The other main feature referred to on p. 88 can now be given to support this view. It is possible that the horizontal mergers, noted above as the typical type in 1967 and 1968, occurred in the pattern of one merger per market. If this were true, the self-generating view of merger activity would be defeated; but, if the merger were not only horizontal (as established) but also confined to a limited number of markets, it would be strong evidence for the view.

　　Academics and the Monopolies Commission always have found difficulty in defining a market: here, a merger is allocated to the 'market' represented by the Minimum List Heading in the Standard Industrial Classification in which the victim firm lies. There are 179 Minimum List Headings,[3] the 407 'important' mergers (in Table 8.1) occurred in only 103 of them – since all the mergers occurred in only 58 per cent of the Minimum List Headings, it is a preliminary indication of the relative concentration of the merger activity.

　　Some other data are summarised in Table 8.2. There were nine Minimum List

Table 8.2 The industrial concentration of mergers in 1967–8

	No. of MLH*	Percentage of MLH	No. of mergers	Percentage of mergers
Overall total	179	100	407	100
Total in which merger occurred	103	58	407	100
Total in which number of mergers exceeded ten	9	5	131	32
Total in which number of mergers was five to nine	16	9	104	26
Total in which number of mergers was five or over	25	14	235	58
			Value of mergers (£m)	
Overall total	179	100	4365·511	100
Total in which consideration exceeded 1·1% (£50m)	17	9	3113·890	71

* MLH = Minimum List Headings, see text.

Headings in which the number of mergers exceeded ten, and there were between five and nine mergers in a further sixteen Minimum List Headings. These twenty-five Minimum List Headings represent only 14 per cent of the total Headings in the Standard Industrial Classification, but 58 per cent of all mergers occurred in these twenty-five industries. In value terms there is even greater concentration of activity. Taking 1·1 per cent of the total value of the mergers as a cutoff point (this represents about £50 million paid for firms within one industry), this level of activity occurred in only seventeen Minimum List Headings, but the value involved in these seventeen was 71 per cent of the total.

Therefore, the evidence for the self-generating view of merger activity is clear. Horizontal mergers (those within one market) were predominant and mergers were confined to a relatively small range of industries.

The above are the two main bases upon which stands the proposal for adopting a strategic merger policy, but there are other facts which support the proposal and suggest that in the 1967–8 boom strategic considerations were then already important.

There was an absence of serious attempts at valuing the worth of the victim firm; many potential bidding firms accepted some current market indicator (for example, the share price, the PE ratio) as the value of the potential victim and went ahead with the bid. The whole financial, economic and strategic analysis of a merger situation and preliminary negotiation with the victim firm and/or merchant bankers was compressed into eight weeks or less for half of a sample of thirty-eight firms investigated. In fifteen cases the time period was four weeks or less.

Only one firm formally considered whether it was an alternative to merger to expand internally (organically), and often very high prices were paid to acquire victim firms. Direct questioning of executives in bidding firms revealed that market dominance and defensive/strategic considerations were the main reasons for their own merger activity.

On conventional economic and financial grounds, it would be difficult to understand many facts about the merger activity which took place in the UK in 1967 and 1968. On strategic grounds, however, much of the merger activity can be understood. If the management of a firm sees its market position being threatened by a merger between two of its competitors, it will know if life is going to be more difficult because of the merger, whether the existing market position needs to be defended and whether the relative *status quo* needs to be restored. In this general type of situation, merger is the obvious, even unique, solution. Merger is fast and certain in securing an increased market share and an increased absolute size. As a strategic consideration, merger becomes a rational policy for the firm.

2. The nature of a strategic merger policy

In connection with merging for strategic reasons, one requirement may be vital, if the objective for the bidding firm (firm A) has arisen because of another merger in the market. The requirement is to stop the enlarged firm or other firms acquiring more market control, and this can be met only by buying a firm with a significant share of the market. In a number of cases there will be no choice, for there may be only one firm which has the necessary share. In this case, speed may be essential, and two sets of discussion (and decisions) by the management of firm A will be necessary.

First, to what extent are conditions going to be more difficult for firm A if no more mergers take place, and what is the likelihood of further mergers in either case of firm A making a bid, or not so doing? This will depend upon a knowledge of the market situation (the number of firms remaining and their shares of the market will be the main data) and of the personalities involved. If the decision is that conditions are going to be too difficult for firm A, even if no more mergers take place, or further mergers are likely with or without any move by firm A, then this firm must merge with another.

Hence, the second discussion is on what premium over the existing share price should be bid (and here the experience of merchant bankers will be invaluable), or what price the owners of a non-quoted company will accept. While it may be virtually impossible to calculate what price could be afforded to avoid the costs involved in future difficult trading conditions (that is, a fundamental rather than a tactical analysis), 'desk-top' estimates on a discounted cash flow basis[4] will give some indication of the task implied in the prices being offered to the shareholders of the victim firm. This is necessary because the (enlarged) firm A will still have to show over time improvements in those performance indicators viewed by the press and by its shareholders.

If there is a choice of firms left in the market, speed is less likely to be necessary. The newly merged firm may be fully occupied in integration and it, too, may be awaiting further moves from the remaining firms in the market. If the firm is not involved in integration, it may pay firm A to wait before launching a bid until the other firm is so involved, and, hence, more fully occupied. Equally, if other bids are expected from elsewhere, then it may pay to wait, so that a better analysis of the situation may be built up. Given a choice of victim firms, two analyses can be carried out, both primarily industrial: which firm is most suitable for firm A to acquire, and which firms are most likely to be bid for by other firms. Only if there is a choice of suitable firms is extensive financial analysis likely to be required, but even if one firm is eminently suitable, it may be wise to have a contingency bid for the second most suitable.

Where there are potential bidding firms other than firm A involved, the situation can become quite complicated and a long-term view should be taken to work out the net result of a series of mergers, commencing with a different one being taken over first – first by firm A and then by other bidding firms.

The aim in this serious game of plotting future positions of market power is for firm A to know what to do when another firm makes a bid (that is, make a counterbid or bid for a different firm given that the other bidding firm is temporarily at a disadvantage), or to know what counter-moves are likely if firm A makes a bid.

So far, it has been assumed that firm A is bidproof by virtue of its size and efficiency (either – even both – would appear insufficient in the experience of 1967 and 1968), but if this is not the case further strategic analysis is necessary. Speed may be even more urgent than in any of the situations cited above. If the merger has shifted the prevailing balance of power, especially between the top two or three firms in the market, and firm A is not one of these, it is likely to be one of the intended acquisitions of the major firms. Two choices are present if firm A believes that it is an intended acquisition sooner or later.

One choice is to take over the largest firm it can manage, and smaller ones also if possible, to build up its own market share to that of the market leaders. There are two dangers. One is that of counterbids for such firms from the market leaders to restore the relative positions prevailing before an earlier merger, or to prevent the relative rise of firm A. The other is that of weakening the management structure of firm A and market performance in the merging period, making it less defensible from a bid by the market leaders. Industrial analysis of the intended victims of firm A will lower the chances of weaknesses or serious diversion arising in firm A as the victim firms are integrated, but financial analysis, as before, may be restricted to checking on the extent of the task being set to maintain 'normal' growth in financial performance indicators. The other choice is the market leaders by which it would prefer to be taken over. There may be personal or industrial reasons why one is preferable, and contact could be made by firm A with this market leader, so that that firm will be at an advantage should a bid for firm A arise from elsewhere. Equally, of course, as happened frequently in 1967 and 1968, firm A could simply approach the market leader of its choice and lose its identity sooner rather than later.

A possibility which has been omitted so far is that of bids by firms outside the market. A competitor of firm A (or firm A itself!) may be bid for by a firm which has not previously operated in this market. This not only extends the number of moves and countermoves, but is likely also to push up the price to be paid. This price effect is possible for two reasons. The first is that the outsider may be prepared to pay a substantial premium (for a market share, for a management with direct experience, etc.) to get into the market. The second effect is that the firm may be substantially larger than those already in the market, and hence can afford to go beyond the prices offered by smaller firms, because it can 'hide' more easily an expensive acquisition in its consolidated accounts until it reaches normal profitability levels. The potential entry of a large outsider is, of course, also a possibly serious situation. If the potential entrant is large relative to the existing competitors it may be able, in the future, if it desired, to switch resources (men, advertising or profits) from its outside activities to this single market, in order to exert pressure on the remaining competitors.

Table 8.3 gives some examples of situations in which strategic considerations may have been important in 1967–8. The examples have been chosen not on the best-example criterion, but on the criterion that in these examples it was easier than usual to measure the market shares as they existed early in 1967.

Much will be apparent from this section about the nature of a possible form of strategic merger policy, but in terms of a generalised 'desk-top' approach such a policy could be constructed in the following way:

Table 8.3 Examples of strategic influences in markets in 1967 and 1968

(a) Market 'W'

Firms	A	B	C	D	E	F	Rest (5)
Existing state	24	22	18	13	11	5	7
Bid 1 (S)	24	22	18	24'	—'	5	7
Bid 2 (U)	42'	22	—'	24	—	5	7
Bid 3 (S)	29'	22	18	24	—	—'	7

(b) Market 'X'

Firms	A	B	C	D	E	F	G	(Rest 11)
Existing state	19	13	12	12	9	9	8	18
Bid 1 (S)	19	13	12	12	11'	9	8	16'
Bid 2 (S)	19	13	12	12	11	9	9'	15'
Bid 3 (U)	19	13	12	14'	11	9	9	13'
Bid 4 (S)	19	13	14'	12	11	9	9	13'
Bid 5 (S)	19	13	14	16'	11	9	9	9'
Bid 6 (S)	19	27'	—'	16	11	9	9	9
Bid 7 (S)	19	27	—	16	12'	9	9	8'
Bid 8 (S)	19	28'	—	16	12	9	9	7'
Bid 8 (S)	19	28'	—	16	12	9	9	7'
Bid 9 (S)	19	29'	—	16	12	9	9	6'
Bid 10 (S)	21'	29	—	16	12	9	9	4'
Bid 11 (U)	Firm A attempted to merge with a firm outside of this market far larger than any firm within the market.							

(c) Market 'Y'

Firms	A	B	C	D	Rest (16)	'Outside'
Existing state	16	12	10	7	55	—
Bid 1 (S)	26'	12	—'	7	55	—
Bid 2 (U)	26	—'	—	7	55	12'
Bid 3 (U)	26	—'	—	19'	55	—
Bid 4 (S)	38'	—'	—	7	55	—

(d) Market 'Z'

Firms	A	B	C	D	E	F	G	Rest (17)
Existing state	21	12	10	9	9	5	5	29
Bid 1 (S)	21	12	12'	9	9	5	5	27'
Bid 2 (S)	21	12	12	9	9	10'	—'	27
Bid 3 (S)	21	21'	12	—'	9	10	—	27

Notes: Figures show market shares; S or U in parentheses indicate successful or unsuccessful bids; ' indicates changes due to current bid.

1 Delimit each market in which the firm operates, and then for each market:
2 name each competitor (and name any firm waiting to enter the market);
3 calculate or estimate the market share of each firm (including own firm);
4 simulate changes in market shares.[5]

On the basis of this simulation:

5 define steps to be taken (for example, counterbid, or merge elsewhere) on the basis of a bid being announced in reality;[6]
6 investigate and value each potential victim named in 5 above;
7 review 3 to 5 from time to time to take account of internal growth, product developments, etc., or unsimulated events;
8 review 6 from time to time;

Though this procedure can be simple, it may nevertheless be a worthwhile investment of some managerial time. There is increased value in any action which has been the subject of forethought; and, since a merger will involve the whole structure and future course of the firm, it is an action which needs forethought – possibly more than appeared to exist in many mergers in 1967 and 1968.

Summary

There is much to be gained from studying mergers, for it is a field in which there is a comparative lack of rigorous empirical knowledge and investigation. This is true whether merger activity is at a normal level or at boom heights, such as in the UK in 1967 and 1968. For corporate merger policy, it is suggested that the policy might be different according to the level of merger activity, a normal policy being appropriate to normal levels and a strategic policy appropriate to boom levels. A strategic merger policy would seem necessary on the basis of evidence of the last merger boom.

The date at which such a policy will become necessary requires a forecast of the next merger boom. For a boom to develop, the self-generating nature of mergers discussed in this article needs to be ignited. Perhaps the uncertainty of entering the Common Market and competing more openly with European-scale firms may be a sufficient ignition. Hence the need for a strategic merger policy would arise when entry into the Common Market is widely anticipated, but the time to prepare a strategic merger policy is before it is needed, so that preemptive bids can be made or countered on the basis of planned anticipation.

Notes and references

1. See, for example, A. R. WYATT and D. E. KIESO, *Business Combinations: Planning and Action*, International Textbook, 1969; G. R. YOUNG et al., *Mergers and Acquisitions Planning and Action*, Routledge & Kegan Paul, 1965; H. I. ANSOFF, *Corporate Strategy*, McGraw-Hill, 1965. A brief summary of the experiences of the 1967 and 1968 merger boom relevant to the normal type of corporate policy is in G. D. NEWBOULD, *Management and Merger Activity*, Guthstead, 1970.

2. These data and others presented in Section 1 are taken from Newbould, op. cit.

3. In the Standard Industrial Classification there are 181, but an inability to distinguish the major activities for individual firms of spinning and doubling in the

cotton and flax systems (412); weaving of cotton, linen and manmade fibres (413); and woollen and worsted (414) has led to these three being treated as one Minimum List Heading in this article.

4. See, for example, Newbould, op. cit., pp. 59–62.

5. The easiest way to do this is to use pieces of card to represent each firm, the length of each card being directly proportional to the market share of the firm it represents. 'Simulation' then consists of placing two cards together to represent a merger, and placing further cards together to represent strategic and defensive mergers in response to previous mergers. A re-run of the simulation consists of commencing with a different initial merger.

6. The outcome of the simulation, of course, could be for this firm to make the first move to preempt another merger which is regarded as possible and likely.

9

Corporate strategy, marketing and diversification*

HARRY HENRY

In order to understand the relationship between corporate strategy and the marketing concept Professor Henry postulates a number of questions which top management should ask themselves. A company should first of all decide what its objectives actually are; secondly it should assess its existing product mix and market position and the probable shape of the future; thirdly, in the light of these assessments, it should then formulate its long-term corporate objectives. This process of rigorous self-appraisal is a necessary prerequisite of successful strategic planning and as a conceptual framework may be applied to all companies in all situations.

The corporate strategy concept, being only about five years old, is currently extremely fashionable: the marketing concept, now almost twenty years old, has lost a good deal of its glamour. Since it is characteristic of most of us to seek for new management techniques which will give us better results without actually requiring us to modify in any substantial degree the way in which we conduct our businesses, we are naturally inclined to turn our enthusiasm to concepts which have not yet come to the crunch, in the hope that this will enable us to sweep under the carpet earlier concepts, the later stages of implementation of which are beginning to cause us some embarrassment. But the introduction of the corporate strategy concept in no way supersedes or vitiates the marketing concept. Indeed, it is largely meaningless without it, while a good deal of the difficulty involved in the implementation of the marketing concept arises from the fact that this latter needs to be viewed against the background provided by the corporate strategy concept itself.

Despite its relative novelty, the subject of corporate strategy has already accumulated a pretty massive literature, though it is difficult to avoid the impression that many of the contributions are saying the same thing in slightly different words. This is not because of any lack of insight or integrity on the part of their authors: it arises from the fact that there are relatively few main components of the concept, and that once they have been listed out it is virtually impossible

* This paper is a condensed version of Professor Henry's book, *Perspectives in Management, Marketing and Research*, Crosby Lockwood & Son, London, 1971.

97

to think of any others. But the complexity of the subject, and hence the opportunity it offers for re-exposition, arises from the fact that most of its components can be seen as interacting with each other in almost any sequence or combination you care to select, and that one particular sequence and combination will attach different significance than another to a specific component.

What is meant by this will perhaps become rather clearer if we look at the very simplified hierarchical diagram of the corporate planning process, consisting merely of four questions:

1 What are our corporate objectives?
2 What business are we in?
3 What are our relevant strengths and weaknesses (internal and external)?
4 So where do we go from here?

The fourth question, of course, will automatically break down further into sets of options and plans, and the first three questions will prove on examination to be nothing like as simple as they might seem at first sight. They will be discussed at a later stage: what we are concerned with at the moment is to indicate that we cannot answer the first three questions (and hence put ourselves in a position to tackle question 4) simply in the order 1, 2, 3; other orders could be just as relevant, or even more so.

Suppose, for example, one of the corporate objectives is set as a materially increased return on capital employed and the company is engaged in an industry where (a) capital employed consists largely of fixed plant, and (b) the market in which the industry operates provides only a low return. Unless the company can find some much more efficient method of operating, unknown to its competitors (which may be possible, but is improbable), such an objective might be unattainable until question 2 has been answered by saying 'some other business than our present one'. But before you can say this, you have to answer question 3, which covers not only the skills inherent in the business but also such things as the nature of the assets. Even if you decide to get out of the business, how do you do so? If you sell the assets on their earnings performance, you are no better off, and you can probably sell them on their capital value only if you are lucky enough to find some megalomaniac competitor obsessed with growth.

This is only one example: it is not too difficult to think of others which will equally well serve to illustrate that these three questions cannot meaningfully be answered in any fixed hierarchical sequence. And, obviously, if we run into this sort of difficulty in so simplified a model, the complications that arise when we start treating the concept more realistically, and therefore in greater detail, will increase exponentially.

Corporate objectives

I have mentioned corporate objectives without so far attempting to indicate what these may be. I am not here suggesting what they should be: let us at this stage simply look at some of the areas which have been advanced as appropriate objectives for corporate strategy, starting off with what may be called the 'economic' ones, which are listed below. In most cases the word 'growth' may be assumed as being attached. What that means we can come to later.

Areas of possible economic objectives:

- return on equity
- return on assets (variously defined)
- price/earnings ratio
- volume of business
- size of operation
- liquidity
- flexibility
- risk reduction
- share of market

Not all of these necessarily belong in this list, but before we deal with them we might consider other objectives which, though non-economic and frequently not made explicit, can be just as significant to the management or the shareholders of a company. In practice they loom largest when the management are the controlling shareholders, but that is another matter.

Areas of possible non-economic objectives:

- survival of the business
- security for management
- security for personnel
- size of operation
- company prestige
- social responsibility.

It may seem a little surprising that 'survival of the business' should be listed among the non-economic objectives, and that 'size of operation' should appear on both lists. But before these paradoxes are explained it would be as well for us to consider what we mean by 'growth' and also to make reference to the question of time.

The investor who puts his money into equities, as against fixed-interest stocks, does so today for two reasons. One reason is as old as investment itself: he is putting his money at risk in the expectation that his foresight and judgement will be suitably rewarded, by a higher rate of return than he could hope for if he sought greater security – say in government bonds. The second reason, resulting from the general acceptance of the fact that we shall live for ever in conditions of regular inflation, is his desire to maintain his return at least constant in real terms.

Under present conditions in the money market the average investor does not attempt to separate in his mind these two components of his expectation: it is not at all certain that even the institutional investors do. But it is important that corporate managements should, in order that they may determine what degree of 'growth' they feel obliged to provide. Clearly they are required to furnish sufficient growth in return on equity to counter inflation: equally clearly they are required to provide some special return on equity to remunerate the share-holder for his risk. But whether that special return should itself be subject to growth – inflation apart – is by no means so obvious, particularly if such growth involves any increase in the size of risk.

Inflation underlines the time element involved in corporate objectives. But, even without this, corporate objectives must necessarily be long-range, taking into account not only likely changes in market needs and the probability of developments in production technology, both within the firm itself and outside, but also other external circumstances subject to change, and the consequences of the company's long-range strategy itself.

Indeed, at any particular moment of time corporate objectives must be determined by the nature, structure and situation of the company in question, and the criteria may differ not only quantitatively but also qualitatively. What is appropriate for a giant corporation with equity widely distributed in public hands may not be acceptable to the middle-sized company still basically in family hands: in the latter case particularly non-economic objectives may be of major significance. Further, such operating objectives as increased return on invest-ment, growth in scale of operations, and reduction of risk, may often be incom-patible one with another: how the company will choose among these must depend upon its current position and the requirements of its owners.

At this point we return to a more detailed consideration of the areas of possible objectives, beginning with the economic objectives. Growth in return on equity has already been discussed: an alternative objective might be growth in return on assets though there is vigorous controversy about which criterion is the better, and, indeed, about how 'assets' are going to be defined and I do not want to get involved in this.

It is unusual to list growth in price/earnings ratio as a possible corporate objective, but I think it legitimate at least to consider it in this context. Since a high P/E ratio reflects the judgement of the money market that a particular com-pany has considerable growth potential still to be developed, it cannot be expected to be maintained for ever, but in the short term it may be of major importance to a company planning growth by acquisition and intending to use shares rather than cash for that purpose, or indeed, to a company planning to go to the market for more equity. Whether what is thus essentially a tool of growth may legitimately be regarded as an objective in its own right is an interesting philosophical point, but in practice it is difficult to separate the two, certainly over the sort of time-span we are considering. At the same time, a high P/E ratio is some defence against being taken over, and if the avoidance of takeover is a legitimate objective of the business – something we shall examine among the non-economic objectives – then the same considerations apply.

I have listed growth in the volume of business, along with growth in the size of the operation, as among the possible corporate objectives, because a number of people regard them in this light. I do not: growth for its own sake seems fairly pointless. It may, of course, provide the necessary mechanism for growth in profitability, but in this case it becomes a tactical manœuvre, not a strategic objective. It may inhibit the growth of a competitor to a position of market dominance, but before such inhibition is accepted as a necessary corporate objective it is as well to be sure that the threat of competitive market dominance is real and not merely emotional or superstitious. Unless there is some reason to suppose the threat actually does exist, then growth in the size of the operation unrelated to growth in profitability ought really to be included among the non-economic objectives. And the same considerations apply to growth in market share, which is simply another aspect of the same subject.

It may be added that growth in volume of business, even if it does not result directly in any increase in the return on equity, could be conceived as likely to have beneficial side-effects, resulting from an increase in the over-all scale of operations. But this is looking at the matter through the wrong end of the telescope: if the over-all corporate objectives of the company entail a higher level of activity, then that higher level might be considered a means rather than an end in itself, as indeed might the effect of being in an expanding business on the morale of the executive staff and on the company's success in staff recruitment.

Liquidity and flexibility should perhaps be considered together. Whether or not a change in either or both is an appropriate corporate objective must depend entirely on the nature of the business, the industries in which it is operating, its existing capital structure, and the requirements of its owners in terms of both economic and non-economic objectives.

Let us now consider the examples listed of non-economic objectives, of which the first is survival of the business. Here we must define our terms: clearly it is no part of anybody's corporate objectives to run a company into bankruptcy. The economic objectives concerned with return on equity or assets look after this, however, and when we talk about the survival of the business otherwise we mean its survival as a separate entity, which is quite another thing.

It may well be to the economic advantage of the owners of a company – that is, the shareholders – that the company should be taken over at a good price and submerged in some other company. Indeed, a very considerable number of shareholders live in hopes that this will happen to some of their investments. In these circumstances the fight which managements put up to fend off takeover bids may sometimes be viewed with a jaundiced eye by at least a substantial minority of shareholders. On the other hand, the ultimate decision rests in the hands of the shareholders as a whole, and the question of the right of a board of directors to run a company in such a way that it is not particularly attractive to a potential takeover bidder, so that the shareholders are not led into temptation, raises questions about the duties and responsibilities of directors which it would be out of place to discuss here. And while it is true that non-economic objectives of the type listed may sometimes be held by a mass of outside share-holders it is equally true that they are more usually found to exist in companies where the management holds equity control, and more particularly in family businesses.

In this context, the objective of security for management may simply mean that the family would rather have a given level of profit, and jobs, than a higher level of profit and no jobs. This is their right, as is their right to choose the other objectives listed. Size of operations and company prestige, in so far as they are not implicit in the company's economic objectives, fall into this same general category of decisions which it is the right of managements to take as a matter of personal preference when they are also the owners of the business but which are possibly beyond their proper powers when they are not. On the other hand, the questions of security for personnel and social responsibility are nothing like so easy to deal with in these terms, and open up major issues well beyond the orbit of corporate planning. All that can really be said here is that if these are regarded by the management of the company as legitimate objectives then the corporate planning procedure has no option but to accept them as constraints on the economic objectives.

The second question we asked in our simplified model of the corporate planning process was 'what business are we in'. This is the question on which the most popular attention has been focused in the recent literature of management, and it has produced some very odd answers, the basic philosophy underlying many of them being enshrined in Theodore Levitt's now classic article on 'Marketing myopia' in the *Harvard Business Review* of July–August 1960, and encapsulated in his observation on the buggy whip industry, which read: 'No amount of product improvement could stave off its death sentence. But had the industry defined itself as being in the transportation business rather than the buggy whip business it might have survived. It would have done what survival always entails, that is, changing.'

This particular example has so tickled the fancy of management enthusiasts that it is almost heresy to ask just what it means, or what is understood by 'the transportation business', or who defined buggy whips as being part of it, or what the buggy whip makers were in a position to change to. Another example from the same article unconsciously underlines the difficulty even more strongly:

> The railroads did not stop growing because the need for passengers and freight transportation declined. That grew. The railroads are in trouble today not because the need was filled by others . . . but because . . . they assumed themselves to be in the railroad business rather than in the transportation business. The reason they defined their industry wrongly was because they were railroad-oriented instead of transportation-oriented; they were product-oriented instead of customer-oriented.

Now I yield to no man in my contempt for excessive product-orientation, but a market cannot really be defined except in relation to the products serving it, and the hard fact remains that railways are in the busines of providing rail transportation, not transportation in general. If the market for their category of product is declining, so that they wish to invest elsewhere, then obviously it makes sense whether their existing railway operations and experience would give them a competitive edge in the airline business. If this is not the case, then there is no particular reason for them to choose airlines as a diversification.

Skills and resources

Indeed, there is some case for suggesting that the business a company is in can only be defined as the business of meeting its corporate objectives. How it ought to go about this is something which derives, not from Cartesian definition-mongering, but from a meticulous appraisal of what means it has to that end: in current Corporate Planning terminology, what are its strengths and weaknesses.

These means fall into three main categories:

1 Production resources and skills.
2 Marketing structures and skills.
3 Financial resources and availabilities.

Production resources and skills include, of course, R and D facilities, and the financial resources and availabilities will naturally condition the two other categories. (It may be noticed that I have not included in this list anything that can be identified as 'general management skills'. This is because I personally do not believe that such generalised skills exist independently of the specialised skills already listed. General management has skills, of course, but these represent a mix, in various proportions, of the major business skills in production, marketing and finance. The thinking that sometimes leads companies into enterprises they do not know how to operate, that 'we understand the art of management' is perhaps on a par with that of those of us who came out of the services after the last war having as our only qualification 'I know how to control men'.)

The means and resources existing within the company, or available to it, must then be measured against the markets to which these are appropriate, and against likely developments in those markets. In fact, the appraisal of the company's strengths and weaknesses, though it is likely to be time-consuming and to entail a lot of work, is conceptually the simplest part of the task. Where the real difficulty is encountered is in delimiting the relevant markets.

Here, as in so much else in management theory, we run straight into problems of definition. In the first place, we have to decide whether the word 'market' is defined by use or by geography: the question of geography is not unimportant, and we shall return to it later, but at this stage it is desirable to confine our definition to that of use.

But even at that we can find ourselves in some confusion, since whatever definitions are selected are likely to be either too narrow or too wide. What is the market for breakfast cereals? If we define it in terms of the present volume of consumption of the product category we have something which at least is clearcut, but which is liable to have a very restrictive effect on our thinking. If, on the other hand, we try to define it in terms of the potential market, then there is no breakfast cereal market at all – merely a breakfast market, in which each brand of cereal battles for market share not only against all other brands but also against grapefruit, porridge, eggs, bacon, sausages and kippers – and, indeed, against nothing at all, an option always open to the commuter in a hurry. Similarly, should not the market for frozen vegetables be defined in terms of the total market for vegetables – frozen, canned and fresh alike? We are back here, in effect, with the problem of whether the railways are in the transportation business or in the rail transportation business, and it is probably true to say that most manufacturers are inclined to take the narrower definition. On the other hand, some service industries adopt the much wider definition, and declare, for example, 'we are in the entertainment business' or even more widely, 'we are in the leisure business'.

The conceptual framework which has been put forward as providing a basis for decision in the light of corporate objectives and the company's resources, the product/market matrix, does not help a great deal with this problem. This, like so much else in corporate planning theory, is Professor Ansoff's, and takes, under his title of 'Growth Vector Components', the form shown in Fig. 9.1,

Fig. 9.1

Product Market	Present	New
Present	Market penetration	Market development
New	Product development	Diversification

though he uses the word 'mission' instead of 'market' for classification purposes, in order to make a distinction between the need being served and the actual customer.

This is possibly not the most useful breakdown. A market can only be defined as the market for a product, and in this case the product itself defines the market. Thus a present product cannot be said to have the potential of a new market – that is, if we are ignoring the geographical sense of the term. A new market otherwise is only open to a new product. At the same time, however, there could sometimes be a case for considering a market as being defined by a certain type of distribution structure: we shall see an example of this later.

We might consider here an alternative matrix, based on the classification of present markets as 'saturated' or 'extensible'. Saturated markets are those where the total volume of sales is unlikely now to increase very rapidly whatever the industry does about it, such as toilet soap, or cigarettes, or toothpaste, so that a new product can only gain a foothold at the expense of existing products: extensible markets are those which can be regarded as capable of being expanded either through an increase in the number of consumers or an increase in the average per capita consumption. This is rather more in line with the realities of modern markets, and produces the schedule of growth vectors shown in Fig. 9.2.

At this point it is necessary to consider what difference is made if we take into our thinking the definition of markets in geographical terms. This approach

Fig. 9.2

Product Market	Existing	New
Saturated	Market penetration	Product development
Extensible	Market development	Product/market diversification
New		diversification

is, of course, far more common in the United States than here, because of the much more regionalised nature of the US economy, and when we ourselves adopt it we normally do so in terms of export markets. Conceptually, however, it makes remarkably little difference: though the product may be an existing one so far as our production processes are concerned, it is a new product in marketing terms for the market in question, and though the particular vector thus involved might perhaps be better described as 'market extension' rather than 'diversification' yet the fact that we are probably going outside our established marketing structures and skills could well justify our continuing to regard the operation as a diversification.

The precise point at which a particular market ceases to be 'extensible' and becomes 'saturated' is, of course, likely to be very much a matter of degree and of judgement. Nor is the distinction always clear between 'existing' and 'new' products: indeed, the difficulties here are likely to be not only conceptual but also practical. Continuous product improvement is the rule rather than the exception for most industries today, and the point at which such improvement turns an existing product into a new one is not easy to identify. Yet this can be of considerable importance in leading a company to decide which growth vector offers the greatest potential for the effort and resources likely to be involved. For an existing product in a saturated market, for example, market penetration can only come from more skilful marketing (broadly defined): a clear product improvement, however, could shift the operation over towards the product development vector, where the return might be materially greater. This problem becomes even more intractable when we turn to those industries which are in the habit of producing new models at reasonably frequent intervals, and possibly most intractable of all in connection with cars.

Selecting vectors of operation

It now remains to review briefly how we go about selecting which are the vectors in which we are going to operate, in the light of our corporate objectives and the production, marketing and financial resources and skills of which we dispose. The growth vectors are, as we have seen, identified by the interrelation between alternative product conditions along one dimension and alternative market conditions along the other. To a major extent the product conditions may be regarded as being under our control, in so far as we can lay down specifications and, according to our skill, have those specifications met at one price or another. But market conditions are largely outside the control of the firm, and have therefore to be taken as externally determined. It therefore follows that in any market/product interaction it is, with rare exceptions, the market which calls the tune, and it is to this fact that I refer when I point out that the corporate strategy concept in no way vitiates the marketing concept, but needs to take it in.

But in making it clear that the marketing concept should be subordinate to the corporate strategy concept we must not overlook the fact, already pointed out, that marketing considerations must always be important, and may well be dominant, in any implementation of corporate strategy. For product development requires that the product thus developed shall be acceptable to the consumer, by meeting a consumer need; market development assumes that the market for an existing product is extensible, because latent needs exist which can be exploited; diversification presupposes that a market/product organism can be found in an area of which the firm has no direct knowledge.

We have described the market/product vectors as growth vectors, but one at least of them need not be so unless we wish so to identify it. Market penetration, the vector made up of an existing product in a saturated market, does not necessarily imply growth. If the corporate strategy is simply to jog along as heretofore, in line with corporate objectives which are probably mainly non-economic, then no growth is called for. A considerable number of small and middle-sized firms remain quite happy with this situation and abstention from growth is equally possible in extensible markets, where market development potential exists but is regarded as of no particular interest. By the same token, product development in either saturated or extensible markets may not necessarily subsume growth for the firm as a whole: it may simply involve the updating or replacement of models which are becoming obsolescent.

If, however, the corporate strategy calls for growth, then growth potential can be found in any of the vectors we have considered, the size of this growth being a function of the external market conditions and of the production, marketing and financial resources and skill available.

Growth in market penetration, for example, will require in particular the application of marketing skills and of financial resources: the volume of these required may well need to be considerable, since within a saturated market increased market share can only be obtained at the expense of competitors, who will probably fight back. Market development, though it may involve less need to counter competition from other producers, may equally involve a heavy investment of marketing skills and financial resources to create the increased demand from consumers. In both these vectors, however, the enterprise will normally understand something about the dominant variable, the nature of the market, and it may sometimes be felt that companies are too prone to wander off into the more uncharted forms of expansion, and even into outright diversification, before there has been adequate exploration of the growth potential immediately to hand. Product development will call most heavily upon production skills, while product/market development calls upon all three of production, marketing and financial resources, and though the payoff may be correspondingly greater so may the risks.

In considering which growth vector to go for, therefore, the firm has to examine what resources it has available which may be appropriate and how far their allocation is likely to be justified by the likely outcome, having regard to the long-term corporate objectives of the company. Leaving aside the question of financial resources, the decision frequently boils down to a choice between expansion along the production channel and expansion along the marketing channel.

A company which is making cars, for example, may decide to start making fire-engines. So far as production techniques are concerned, this is a logical development. But difficulties might arise because cars are sold to private individuals through car-dealers, whereas fire-engines are for the most part sold to public authorities direct, and the two sets of marketing skills required may have little connection. On the other hand, a firm which manufactures certain types of foods and sells them to grocers may decide that its most relevant skills lie not in its existing food-production technology but in its marketing structures, so that its expansion strategy lies in selling to those same grocers other foods of which it previously had no direct knowledge.

Integration

Within expansion vectors there is another sort of approach to the problem – that of integration, either horizontal or vertical. Both can be fitted into the corporate strategy mode, but they complicate it considerably and really form a subject of their own. I would say about vertical integration only that the judgement that it will serve the company's corporate objectives is frequently based upon an assessment of its appropriateness to the company's resources which is emotional rather than realistic.

Diversification

We have so far not dealt with the last of the growth vectors – diversification. The word itself is often used in a rather slipshod fashion and is frequently applied to activities which, in strict Ansoff terminology, are more accurately defined as expansion. But in the conceptual structure we are considering here 'diversification' is limited to the combination of new products with new markets, which in its purest form represents the entry of the firm into a market unrelated to its existing markets with a product unrelated to its existing products. It will be obvious that here in particular the appraisal of the company's strengths and weaknesses, and consideration of the appropriateness of its skills and resources, are of supreme importance. If my doubts as to the meaningfulness of the concept of generalised management skills (independent of the special skills which go to form the management mix) are accepted, it follows that the resources which a company can put into such a new venture must be viewed in specific rather than in general terms. Though the corporate objectives of the company may seem to call for diversification, very little purpose will be served by a diversification exercise which falls flat on its face because the company is unable to make success of it.

Of course, the possibility always exists that the special skills required may be brought in. This assumes in the first place that the company understands enough about its new business to know what to buy, which is by no means always the case, but even if it is reasonably successful in this the difficulty still remains that corporate management, with whom lies the ultimate responsibility, may not possess the skills necessary to manage the operation, and may not be able to acquire them in the necessary time-span.

This leads on, in fact, to that special form of multiple diversification which is the conglomerate. The problems of conglomerates are far too large a subject to be entered into here, but they do bring into focus the major distinction between 'control' and 'management'. Conglomerates control, rather than manage, and they do so by the application of their financial skills and resources rather than through the application of production and marketing skills, and the question which is beginning to nag is whether the warning financial signals arrive too late after the non-managed production and marketing errors have been committed for the damage to be easily repairable. In considering diversification of this order as a growth vector, therefore, the company whose corporate objectives call for growth will need to give very detailed attention to the question of whether it is not likely to run less risk by a policy of expansion in those areas with which its existing production and marketing skills have some sort of relationship.

Two points may be made in conclusion. The first is that corporate planning is *ad hoc*, of indefinite time-span, and involving top corporate management: this must be distinguished from long-range planning at the operating unit level, which is routine, of limited time-span, and decentralised to operating managements. The second point is that the conceptual framework is helpful and, indeed, probably indispensable as a background to any corporate planning operation. But the way in which any particular company chooses to go about the job in practice is likely to be unique, because that company's situation is unique: there is no system or routine which can be adopted as a general standard.

Fig. 9.3

Corporate Planning	Long-range planning
Ad hoc	Routine
Indefinite time-span	Limited time-span
Corporate management	Operating managements

10

The impact of supply markets on corporate planning

DAVID FARMER

Many writers have commented on the difficulties associated with the reduction of the myriad of functional objectives within the company to a consistent corporate objective. It is the contention of the writer that the mechanisms which exist within many companies to attempt this task are out of balance because insufficient attention is paid to source planning. This article illustrates some of the consequences of omitting sourcing data from the base from which the corporate plan is evolved. The author suggests that the interdependence of corporations necessitates careful consideration of external strengths in supply markets as well as in relation to the company's own.

An examination of the literature associated with corporate planning reveals a surprising deficiency: little or nothing has been written about materials/component source planning vis-à-vis corporate plans.

The importance of major sourcing decisions to the success of many corporate plans is clear to see. One aspect of this, for instance, is clearly illustrated by the effect on UK car production of the various strikes at component manufacturers during 1969 and 1970. The publicity given to these stoppages resulted in a number of interviews with relevant senior executives of the major car manufacturers which were published in the national press. Each of these is illustrative of the critical importance for the future of major source decision-making.

A Ford spokesman said: 'In areas where there is the greatest risk we have moved towards alternative suppliers. This is obviously more costly but in existing circumstances a more realistic approach.' A British Leyland executive said: 'What was historically a correct buying strategy has become, with hindsight, the wrong one. The harvest is coming home to us.' Vauxhall and Rootes spokesmen each agreed that they too had turned to a policy of increasing the proportion of business given to a secondary source. In all these cases corporate plans and objectives were adversely affected as a direct result of supply failure. Among other things, quite apart from the direct imposition on fixed costs of the stoppages, foreign manufacturers gained larger shares of the British domestic market. As a result, there seems little doubt that the car manufacturers – who are among the most sophisticated purchasers on the British scene – will pay greater attention to this aspect of their planning in the future. Or more correctly, perhaps, that they will place greater emphasis on the strategic aspects of their source decision-making than they have hitherto.

So far as the car makers are concerned, the current change is really one of emphasis, although the European implications of component sourcing as well as design commonality have added a further dimension. No longer is the emphasis upon meeting market needs alone, it is now seen to be necessary to plan the sourcing of components from the strategic point of view just as any aspect of market planning and strategy for the vehicles themselves. In the event, multi-national sourcing makes sense from the logistics viewpoint as well as in respect of strategy, although it would appear that the car manufacturers have based their plans largely upon the premise that supply failure in one country may be alleviated by delivering parts from component suppliers based in another. As a BLMC spokesman put it: 'If British makers cannot supply us with parts, then it must become an increasing trend for us to utilise our European facilities.' Whatever the cost of this second sourcing (duplicate tooling, etc.) it would seem to be a relatively small insurance when set against a production loss of 125 000 units, which was the recent BLMC experience.

Why is it that it has taken a crisis situation to focus the car makers' attention on the real extent of the critical nature of source planning? Is it, as at least one of the quotations suggests, that they considered short-term advantages rather than long-term gain? Certainly, it is easy to be wise after the event, but it is the thesis of this paper that in general a great deal more attention needs to be paid to source planning and its relevant risks than has traditionally been the case. And since, as we have already indicated, the car makers are among the most sophisticated purchasers, it will be seen how this places source planning in industry in general.

It is the belief of the writer that in the current business environment effective source planning is vital to success. Among the reasons for this we might list:

1 Faster developing technology.
2 Fewer sources as a result of takeover, merger or large unit domination.
3 More highly capital intensive processes.
4 Faster new product transfer from US/European associates in the case of multinational businesses.
5 Increased worldwide political risks.
6 A greater awareness by previously cheap markets of their commercial strengths.
7 A trend towards tighter quality control requirements in the more sophisticated industries.
8 Tighter specification control by governments.
9 The requirement of larger volumes by the mass production industries.
10 Increased industrial unrest.
11 Ever-increasing development costs in the technological industries.
12 Inflation.

At least two other factors may be added to this list: (*a*) over 50 per cent of the revenue of manufacturers in all the developed countries (taken as a whole) is disposed of in purchasing materials and services, thus underlining the importance of effective source planning (see Fig. 10.1). Because of the proportion of this

Fig. 10.1 Percentage distribution of the sales £ in a typical British manufacturing concern.

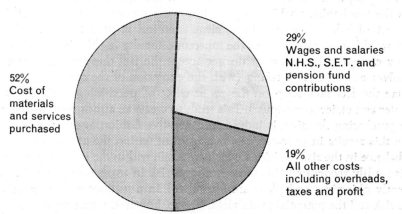

52%
Cost of
materials
and services
purchased

29%
Wages and salaries
N.H.S., S.E.T. and
pension fund
contributions

19%
All other costs
including overheads,
taxes and profit

Since such a large proportion of a company's income is disposed of in this way, the importance of managing the spend is clear to see. Strategic planning is a key factor in this management. Corporate plans and strategies may well be affected by activities in a company's supply markets as much as in its own. Effective planning will take both into account.

expenditure in relation to the revenue of most manufacturing companies, it is possible through a 5 per cent saving in material costs to produce a contribution equal to that which could be produced by a 25 per cent increase in turnover. Every pound saved is a pound additional contribution. Since cost is to a great degree a function of the performance of the source (delivery, quality, service as well as price), sound major sourcing may well be regarded as a critical management decision; (*b*) an awareness of the futurity of source decision-making is important, for it can be shown that in most manufacturing companies the major sources have been supplying goods to the organisation for more than four years. An unpublished survey carried out by the writer showed this to be true in 85 per cent of responding British companies in manufacturing industries with sales revenues of £1 million and above. The trend is confirmed by the work of Robinson, Faris and Wind[1] in the United States, where they show (*inter alia*) that the more established a supplier the less likelihood of a new supplier gaining access!

In isolation, each of these factors can critically affect corporate plans. In total they illustrate in some degree the complexity of the sourcing risks which an enterprise faces. Yet, if we were to make a general statement with regard to sourcing decisions, we would state that: (*a*) they are often highly intuitive; (*b*) the manpower resources which are allocated to the procurement function in many companies are extremely limited; (c) of those companies which practise long-range planning, there is little evidence of the inclusion of any aspect of supply.

One effect of this state of affairs is that in many companies imbalance exists in the development of corporate plans. Many writers have commented on the difficulties associated with the reduction of the myriad of functional objectives within the company to a consistent corporate objective. It is the contention of the writer that the mechanisms which exist within many companies to attempt this task are out of balance because insufficient attention is paid to source planning.

It would appear that part of the inherent difficulty in this situation is that, in many cases, top management do not accept the fact that the supplies activity involves conscious risk taking (with the exception of the commodity markets, where the feedback loop on the profit effect of purchasing decisions is both shorter and easier to compute). This tends to create an atmosphere within which the purchasing function is judged in a negative fashion against its failures. In turn this results in over-cautious management within the supplies activity and imbalance in the risk decisions which are made within the company as a whole. It is readily recognised that there is always risk in marketing products. Consequently objectives and plans are formulated in a manner commensurate with this risk and the potential profit yield. Not so, however, with supplies, where the inference is that decisions have to be made which eliminate risk and where the company's developing needs will be met from an unchanging supply market. As we have seen, the decisions which are taken by supplies executives do involve considerable risk. Risk which requires adequate consideration in the formulation of corporate plans; conscious policy-making in stating profit motivating risk parameters; effective forecasting and planning and creative input from the company's supply management.

It seems that the pendulum has swung away from the attitude of the traditional European entrepreneurs, who 'displayed a tendency towards backward integration . . . in other words there was a concern for safeguarding the supply of raw materials by controlling its source through ownership'.[2] The marketing approach of recent years with its movement towards controlling outlets either through ownership or through some other means, has captured the attention of managers and planners alike. Few, it would appear, have retained the balance which is illustrated by the approach of the increasingly successful Marks & Spencer in the UK.

Relating source planning to the Ansoff checklist

Ansoff in *Corporate Strategy*[3] makes little reference to the importance of sourcing decisions, slotting them in his classification under the generic title 'administrative'. We may, however, draw inference from the relationship between aspects of source planning and his basic checklist. The following section is illustrative of this relevance.

1 Include all four, rather than the last two steps of the generalised problem-solving sequence. Emphasis should be on the first two steps, monitoring the environment for changes and searching for attractive product opportunities.

Because of the tendency to relegate supply function decision-making to the last of Simon's four phases, there is little tradition of action in the first two areas as far as formal source decision-making and planning are concerned. However, such decisions *are* taken informally and most often in an *ad hoc* manner as part of research or design processes. Particularly in the technological industries, routes taken at these early stages may well have long-term effects on company profitability when the item comes into production (affecting ROI).

This is particularly true of such decisions in multinational companies. The need for perceiving the variety of opportunities in the source decision-making area in relation to ROI is thus important to success. As Ansoff suggests: 'a method which fails to provide for the choice between continuing concern with the operating problem as against attention to the strategic leaves a key part of the problem to intuition and judgment'.

At the *perception* stage we should take these factors into consideration along with key data relating to our markets, investment, etc., fast-developing materials, new processes in the supplying industries, and economic and political movement affecting traditional supply markets, being among the variables which relate from the supply viewpoint. W. L. Swager[4] has stated that 'specific forecasts for designers, materials scientists and engineers are essential to enable decisions to be taken regarding the materials technology in some future period, say five to twenty years hence'. It is important to strategic decision-making that such input is also available as it affects the commercial prospects of the company. A company's decision whether to make or buy, diversify or lay down new plant might well be coloured by such intelligence.

Formulation

As in every other aspect of business, a company can never be sure that its key materials and sources are the best available. Apart from any other factor, the very conservatism of the business approach to suppliers (i.e. risk avoidance) suggests a propensity to avoid alternatives. Relating to this tendency towards risk avoidance at the buying point, Robinson and Faris state: 'This avoidance of uncertainty is achieved by using decision rules that emphasise short run reaction to short run feedback.'[5] Following from their research they further state that buyers' action can be expected to result in the following decisions:

1 To split every order between two or more suppliers.
2 To be loyal to reliable sources.
3 To avoid using new sources unless no risk is involved.

There are overtones here of the Cyert and March theory that 'when an organisation discovers a solution to a problem by searching in a particular way, it is more likely to search in that way in future problems of the same type'.[6] Again, we may draw inference from Ansoff regarding these tendencies when he writes: 'The firm can take a completely passive attitude and wait for the opportunities to come to it. However, . . . for most firms this leads to uncoordinated, insufficient and potentially costly management practices.'

The dangers are as apparent in the source decision-making area as in any other. The largest single cost centre of the majority of manufacturing companies relates to materials purchases, and since sources are so important in this respect, they ought to receive attention commensurate with their importance.

Among the alternatives open to a company at this formulation stage we might include, for example: make or buy; development of new sources either through the medium of their own resources or as a direct result of financial or technological aid from the buying company itself; consideration of alternative materials or potential materials as they might affect the company's own processes; consideration of fuel sourcing policies particularly in relation to the type of capital plant to be purchased; and the many implications of reciprocal or barter trading with eastern European markets.

Evaluation

At first glance the evaluation of a variety of sourcing routes might appear to be deceptively simple. A typical generalised statement might read that the objective of such an exercise should be, to obtain the materials required by the company to meet its market needs at the lowest possible price. Unfortunately, apart from any of the other points raised, 'price' and 'cost' of materials to a company are two different things. The computation of cost in manufacturing or processing is as complex as it is relatively simple in the buy/sell situation. Delays in supply, quality failure and the necessity to maintain inventory all add to material cost and all are affected in a variety of ways by the source decision.

The comparatively recent moves towards supplier quality assurance schemes and 'bonded' stockholding by the supplier are themselves manifestations of action by the more sophisticated purchasers to limit the impact of these variables. Delays in delivery which result in company plant shutdown may well be computable in terms of lost production hours. What is not as easily calculated is the true cost of the root cause of that delay.

While it may be argued that such matters are operational and not within the scope of planning, they are symptomatic in many cases of the imbalance at the planning stage which we have already discussed.

There are implications here, too, of the basic source decision, 'make or buy'; decisions which in the experience of the writer are frequently made in less than an objective manner and even then against questionable data. Vanderhaas's[7] comment on one aspect of this is enlightening.

To make an item instead of purchasing it (or vice versa) is a far more complex decision than would appear to be generally recognised. Manufacturing involves decisions to commit capital for lengthy periods, not only with regard to a particular process or operation, but also in periferal activities. Because of greater sophistication in processes, and inflation (*inter alia*), it will also involve increasing capital commitment as time goes on. Further, it suggests utilisation of management and other resources on an increasing scale. Since the basis of any strategy must be to utilise company strengths against competitive weaknesses, such dissipation of resources (financial, facility and management) needs to be very carefully considered. Such decisions must certainly affect the 'particular flows which will reflect the unique competitive advantages of product market opportunity'.[8]

Clearly, at the planning stage the decision must be to utilise available resources in the most effective way towards the achievement of company objectives. When we source outside the company we seek to allow it to concentrate on those things which it is best placed to do whilst using outside resources where they will prove to be economically attractive.

The crux of the matter is where to concentrate company effort. The variables involved in this aspect of decision-making are wide-ranging and complex, in some respects even more so than those which apply in the company's own markets. Such complexity should attract adequate planning effort.

We have already mentioned many of the factors which go to make up this complex situation. Among the more crucial is the increasing sophistication and polarisation of supply markets, the companies which make up those markets and the activities of competitors in those markets. The financial, technical and political characteristics of these markets now and in looking to the future, necessitates careful evaluation of the company's own situation and needs in parallel with the likely activities of competitors and the influence of substitute processes or materials. The inference here is that the input from the supplies executive to the data bank upon which a corporate plan is established involves him in a skilful appraisal of changes in the future external environment. In terms of the overall corporate plan it ought to be a significant contribution.

Other aspects of evaluation as it relates to the materials sourcing segment of planning might include consideration of development of minor sources to obviate monopolistic strategies of major suppliers; market search intelligence as to the continued viability of existing sources of geographical areas and the possibilities of developing new sources of areas (this is particularly relevant to crop and derivative sourcing), and, when relevant, sourcing considerations in relation to the location of a new factory.

With regard to the latter point, it is not unusual for the location of supply sources to be a key factor in the decision where to locate a factory. When a factory is to be sited in another country this could well be even more crucial. As many US companies found when establishing themselves in Europe, the development of indigenous sources can be a long and expensive process. Thus, when planning a new facility consideration should include (a) the location of possible currently viable supply sources, and (b) other sources which while not currently viable show potential for development.

Source implications and renewal

In Ansoff's discussion on long-term objectives he places considerable emphasis on *renewal*. In his Fig. 4.1[9] he includes what he terms 'proxy measurements' which have been selected to make use of data which are commonly generated for systematic diagnostic analysis of a company's performance. It is noticeable that he omits any mention of source considerations. This may be in line with his inclusion of sourcing under his 'administrative' classification. However, his inclusion of the words 'which are commonly generated for systematic diagnostic analysis' is a further indication of the imbalance which we have already discussed. Steiner's[10] research would appear to support this lack of consideration. He shows (*inter alia*) that executives in a wide range of industries rate materials matters very lowly when listing what they consider to be key strategic factors in their own environment. Yet the influence of supply markets on many aspects of renewal in today's commercial environment necessitates careful consideration by planners (see Fig. 10.2). No company is an island, and to achieve renewal requires that we pay close attention to planned development with key sources. The Rolls-Royce/Lockheed situation illustrates the interrelationship of such renewal patterns in the technological industries. Similar patterns may be observed in many other situations.

The external competitive strengths of a company may be considerably affected by its relationship with its sources; with their technological ability; with their financial stability and with their R and D, etc. Thus, in attempting to analyse a company's performance we should consider its strengths in establishing and developing these external relationships. These relationships may well have considerable bearing on the selection of the product mix which the firm will produce. For example, ICI and Courtaulds manmade fibre developments were key factors in the planning of many clothing and carpet manufacturers in the UK in the early 'sixties. Shell Chemicals and their developments had a similar effect on plastic bottle manufacturers (and others) at the same time.

In their current planning, car manufacturers must take note of potential development by outside sources regarding, for instance, the question of a battery-powered auto unit. And the oil companies must consider their source planning in a different light following the recent activities of the Gulf States. So too must power users (and governments) consider their fuel policies in the light of these happenings.

In construction, the advent of packaged prepared timber coming into the UK from Canada has considerably affected the traditional patterns of a very conservative industry. An example of this change relating to the activities of a timber importer is included in a survey recently undertaken by the writer.

In 1965 most of the softwood imported by the company was in random lengths. Mechanical handling equipment at that time was limited to a crane and the company did not fabricate timber. In 1969 more than 50 per cent of

Fig. 10.2 External appraisal: some of the factors which affect a company's supply markets

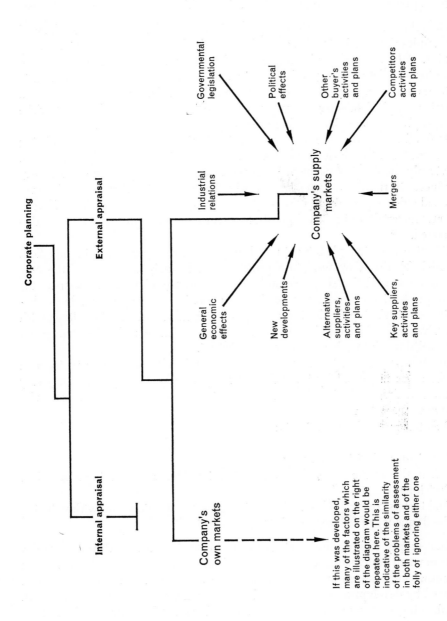

the softwood imported by the company was in the form of close stacked packages . . . and over 30 per cent of the company's turnover was accounted for through the manufacture of roof trusses and infill panels [manufactured from prepared timber imported from Canada].[11]

Here the product mix of the company, as well as its basic policy, was changed as a result of external stimulus at the least partly from their raw material supply market. This company and many others like it reacted to change rather than planning to take advantage of it. Yet in retrospect there were many economic pointers in this supply market which suggested that a change would come about. Effective supply data generated as part of those used for the establishment of the company's corporate plan would have proved extremely beneficial.

In the food industry the onset of containerisation has resulted in beans being imported from the Great Lakes area of North America virtually all year round. Previously the freezing of the St Lawrence made it necessary for the baked bean producers in the UK to carry large stocks. The change in what we might term external efficiency resulted in the producing company reducing stock levels both for raw materials and finished goods. Stockturn and thus profitability were also increased.

Effective sourcing planning in at least one of the companies in this field ensured (a) that they were in a position to take early advantage of the new arrangements; (b) that they were able to plan and use released storage space for more productive purposes at an early date; and (c) that they were able to plan their own marketing (including pricing, special offers and own branding) with the advantage of knowledge of lower real costs. These and other connected factors did much to enhance the company's ROI.

In each of these cases the competitive strength of the company in its own markets was improved by input from its key sources. Clearly there are many overtones of renewal with external sources stimulus in these and other examples known to the writer.

Ackoff suggests that planning is:

1 Anticipatory decision-making;
2 When the future state, that we desire, involves a set of interdependent decisions;
3 And is thus concerned both with avoiding incorrect actions and with reducing the frequency of failure to exploit opportunities.[12]

Our supply markets and their many technologies present a more complex picture when anticipating the future than does our own (if only that we ought to know our business better than that of the next man). We cannot fail to be affected by developments in our supply markets as we strive towards our needs. In planning to exploit opportunities and reduce the frequency of failure, we must consider our supply market and its developments and its likely effect upon our future product mix. This is clearly anticipatory decision-making; the decisions we make vis-à-vis our supply market are interrelated with both our internal decisions and those we make with relation to our own markets; adequate consideration may well enable us to obviate errors and take advantage of opportunities.

One approach to corporate planning embracing source considerations

Materials costs represent approximately 80 per cent of the works cost in certain instances in the chemical/pharmaceutical industry. As a result, some companies have developed much of their planning around the core of their raw material supply data. The following outline is illustrative of the approach taken by a medium-sized European based multinational company in this industry, who develop their planning cycle around a five-year base (two years dynamic, three years projected). The process which is illustrated here is the operation-plan for a twelve-month period, which is derived from the twenty-four month section of the long-range plan.

1 The international corporate planning group make world economic forecasts. From these forecasts they derive a series of economic assumptions which are sent to the national company planning teams in the various countries in which the company is represented.
2 From the supply viewpoint, the next stage is for the national planning team to refine these assumptions in relation to their own environment. They add data on new plant, processes, materials and suppliers which have become available or are projected to be available in the period relating to the plan. These data are produced as a result of their own research.
3 An international purchasing planning meeting is then structured which is attended by representatives of each of the national companies. Here the data which each has produced are exchanged with a view to creating a consolidated plan towards lowest overall cost.
4 Following this meeting each national company issues a planning report to other meeting members. Subsequently a final plan is evolved for the coming year with a projection into year two and beyond.
5 This plan is then used as a basis by the national companies upon which to establish standard prices following consideration of any new data.
6 These standard prices are then passed to marketing who assess the data in line with their own research and plans.
7 Production work closely with marketing in planning their future loading and break down the marketing estimate into volume requirement.
8 The production volume breakdown; marketing estimates and the standard prices are then used by the company controller in the preparation of his budgets.

In the broader context, such action as to support a minor source in its struggles against a giant are stated from the plan as objectives, as are make or buy:

product/market surveys and product R and D projects. Other strategies, defensive or offensive, as will result in the achievement of stated objectives in the plan are also laid down in this way.

In this instance effective contribution from supply in drawing up the corporate plan has been recognised as a necessity by the company. It would appear to be reasonable to infer that this recognition has resulted from the crucial relationship between materials cost, total works cost and contribution (and thus ROI). Yet while the proportion of materials in this case is considerably higher than the norm for all industries, most producing companies recognise materials as their largest single cost centre. In all such cases, a company plan which pays little attention to key sourcing considerations must surely be in a state of imbalance.

Ackoff's illustration of planning a house is pertinent to this argument. We may paraphrase it by stating that the decision to source at X for key material Y has an effect on performance of the company as a whole, the examples quoted in this paper being indicative of the relevant consequences.

> Effective planning requires close collaboration of creative experts and managers in efforts to solve the many difficult problems involved.[13]

Such creative input from the supply area may well prove to be a key factor in successful planning in most companies, particularly in the cost-sensitive days of the 'seventies.

References

1. P. J. ROBINSON, C. W. FARIS and G. WIND, *Industrial Buying and Creative Marketing*, Allyn & Bacon, 1967.

2. H. VANDERHAAS, *The Enterprise in Transition*, Tavistock, 1967.

3. H. IGOR ANSOFF, *Corporate Strategy*, Pelican, 1970.

4. W. L. SWAGER, 'Materials', *The Science Journal*, Oct. 1967.

5. P. J. ROBINSON, C. W. FARIS, see ref. 1.

6. R. M. CYERT and J. G. MARCH, *A Behavioural Theory of the Firm*, Prentice-Hall, 1963.

7. VANDERHAAS. See ref. 2.

8. ANSOFF. See ref. 3.

9. Ibid.

10. GEORGE STEINER, *Strategic Factors in Business Success*, Financial Executives Research Foundation, 1969.

11. D. H. FARMER, *The Impact Upon Traditional Construction of Packaging Methods and the Use of Components*, University of Manchester Institute of Science and Technology, 1970.

12. RUSSELL L. ACKOFF, *A Concept of Corporate Planning*, Wiley, 1970.

13. Ibid.

11

The changing relationship between management and shareholders

H. REDWOOD

The 1969 Fisons' Stockholder Survey is the most sophisticated attempt so far made in the UK to bridge the gap that is commonly thought to exist between a large company and its shareholders. Shareholder satisfaction is regarded as a prime objective by many corporate strategists, yet current research points to the invalidity of the traditional view that so long as a company maximises earnings or net present value, this will automatically be reflected in the share price. Moreover, as the author points out, the results of the Stockholder Survey indicated that shareholders did not accord exclusive priority to financial returns. Looking ahead, the author anticipates that financial institutions will become even more important as shareholders and will thus take a more active part in company affairs. As a result management will have to develop a much closer relationship with shareholders, both institutional and individual, than in the past.

This paper is about the ordinary, normal, year-by-year relationship between managers and shareholders; a relationship that is not often discussed, either because it is not news or because it does not exist, or is believed not to exist.

In the 1970s there may well have to be a more active relationship between management and shareholders than there has been for many years. Management will no doubt adapt itself and form new ties with shareholders just as it has seen the need for doing so with government and with employees: gradually, sometimes reluctantly, but in the end quite positively and often very successfully.

Ownership and management

The gulf between managers and shareholders has for years been part of the industrial landscape – at least for those who are employed by the 'Fortune 500' or by the top hundred companies in Britain. The gulf, however, is really a gap: an interval between the two very different periods of the first and second Industrial Revolutions which may have little in common except that in each of them ownership has a voice and is heard. In between – from say 1929 to perhaps as late as the late 'sixties – shareholders lapsed into silence, either willingly or under duress.

It was not always so. Originally, managers were owners who knew how to manage what they owned. Most of the leading industrial firms of today have their roots in the entrepreneurial era of the nineteenth century and early twentieth, when owner-managers and their families built the foundations for what have since become the stamping-grounds of professional managers. The tradition of ownership survives, often in name only, but sometimes with continued family leadership or participation. This ranges all the way from the dynastic traditions of Ford and Du Pont to the large impersonally named corporations whose origins are often no less entrepreneurial.

The Standard Oil Company of Ohio was incorporated by John D. Rockefeller and his associates in 1870 as the forerunner of the huge Standard Oil Trust which was later broken up. The descriptively styled United States Steel Company was put together by Andrew Carnegie in 1901. Nearer home, the memory of owner-managers is still preserved in the composite title of Unilever, the 'Mond Division' of Imperial Chemical Industries, the brief partnership of Rolls and Royce, and incidentally the name of my own company. On the continent, one of Germany's foremost chemical firms, Farbwerke Hoechst, carries in small print the legend 'formerly Meister Lucius & Brüning', while in France nationalised factories produce cars named after Monsieur Renault. The list could be extended indefinitely without illustrating anything more than a truism: that the growth of most of the great companies with household names and indeed of whole industries, was catalysed by men who owned what they managed. There was no conflict between the two because they were one and the same.

When conflict arose, it was between ownership and society. Enormous power, ruthlessly exploited as in the days of the great monopolies, had to be challenged and curbed by government on both sides of the Atlantic. It was anti-trust legislation which first clipped the wings of the owner-manager who had once been free to manœuvre at will. In doing so, government set in motion a sequence of events that opened the doors of industry to the professional manager. This era dates essentially from the 1920s and '30s. There had, of course, long been professional managers, working without benefit of ownership in the shadow of the great captains and their families. But the professional had been subservient to the proprietor. From the 1920s onwards, their roles were reversed, gradually but decisively.

There were many reasons for this, nearly all of them connected with the breaking-up of the monolithic blocks of power which had ruled industry during its roughest, literally most 'golden' years. Apart from government, growing pressure from the unions and the passing of time itself weakened the aggressive instincts of many of the founding families. With a few notable exceptions, the second and third generations were not possessed by the forces that had driven their predecessors towards property and power; they owned too much already and were big spenders. They had no option but to employ professional managers. Moreover, the dispersal of private fortunes as a result of rising taxation and death duties contributed to the dilution of ownership.

More important than these, however, in hastening the decline of the industrial emperors was the growth of industry itself: very few companies (among whom Du Pont are perhaps the most celebrated example) were capable of financing their growth without recourse to external loans. These forced them sooner or later to go public and so to broaden the base of share ownership in a series of money-raising cycles.

As the owner-manager bowed out, so the professional stepped in. That was natural enough; but what made him supreme in industry was the advent of some twenty years of almost unbroken world crisis. From the Wall Street crash of 1929 and the Great Depression of the early 1930s to World War II, and the postwar period of reconstruction, events moved in favour of the professional manager and against shareholders. In the 1930s, shareholders had to be thankful if their companies managed to survive at all. For their shares to retain some recovery value, good management was essential. Moreover, the crash had demonstrated that equity was a form of risk investment after all. Shares could fall as well as rise, and when the bottom dropped out of the stock market, many an investor was ruined. During the years that followed, it was no use complaining. If the investor chose to 'speculate', he was playing with fire; and if he burnt his fingers, there was no point in blaming management: he had only himself to blame.

Paradoxically the seller's market of the 1940s and '50s which followed the depression and the war, again favoured management rather than shareholders. True, management had to be moderately effective in order to produce the badly needed goods; but under conditions of perpetual shortage, there was relatively little competitive pressure. All-round 'scientific' management was still a dream – a slightly absurd luxury sported by a few pioneers. In fact, wartime controls and the seller's market of the postwar decade brought management closer to government and left the shareholder out in the cold. Badly shaken by the depression, shareholders of the forties were not in a position to make demands which, everyone agreed, were hardly relevant to the national interest. The manager had to produce. Costs and profits were not unimportant, but they were secondary issues. Dividends were low on the list of priorities.

The mid-1950s at last brought a bonanza to the long-suffering shareholder. The postwar boom still continued, but controls were relaxed, management and government drifted apart, and the shareholder was rewarded with steadily rising dividends and spectacular capital appreciation. He had waited long enough, for it was not until 1954 that the *Financial Times* and Dow Jones Indices of share prices went beyond the levels which they had originally reached in 1929. The share boom continued with only brief cyclical interruptions throughout the remainder of the 1950s, but slowed down in the 1960s. It is, however, probably true to say that the still prevalent attitudes of management towards shareholders, and vice versa, were conditioned by this comparatively brief interlude of lush profits in the 'fifties. Shareholders tended to assume, not entirely without justification, that management was easy. One sometimes has the impression that they still think so today. Conversely, management came to regard the shareholder as something of a parasite: uninvolved, uncommitted, and sitting pretty on a magic formula of

F

enrichment without risk. This erroneous impression, too, needs to be dispelled in relation to today's cooler industrial climate.

In effect, during the 'fifties, the relationship between management and shareholders was not really being tested. Conditions were such that the power of the professional manager in the industrial company rose to its zenith. He had saved the firm from the depression, brought it safely and usefully through the war, and was now riding high. He regarded the company as his company. Dividends and lip service had to be paid to shareholders once or twice every twelve months, but for the rest of the year management, often fiercely loyal to the concept of 'Our Company', preferred to ignore shareholders and to get on with the job.

The advent of the affluent society in the late 'fifties and 'sixties began to outmode these attitudes and the 'seventies can be expected to complete the process. Whether we like it or not, the era of almost unchallenged supremacy for the professional manager in the private enterprise sector of industry in the United States, in Europe and perhaps in Japan is drawing to its close if it is not already over. The professional manager will remain the key to a company's success or failure. In this sense he is indispensable. But he will become accountable to an extent that he has not experienced since the days when the owner-entrepreneur was there to make him fetch and carry.

Two of the many factors that distinguish the affluent consumer society from its predecessors are the apparently contrary trends towards wider share ownership on the one hand, and an increasingly powerful concentration of holdings on the other. Both have their origin in the rising tide of funds flowing into investment, through direct as well as indirect channels. Although the number of individual investors is growing, the proportion of all industrial shares held by individuals is falling. This tendency favours indirect investment through four principal types of institutions: the insurance companies, pension funds, investment trusts, and unit trusts.

The insurance companies and pension funds receive routine savings from most of the working population and reinvest a notable proportion in industrial ordinary shares. By contrast, investment trusts and unit trusts receive funds for investment both from individual savers and from other institutions. A survey conducted for the London Stock Exchange in 1965 and published under the title 'How does Britain save?' demonstrated that 93 per cent of the adult population of Great Britain had money saved or invested in one form or another. Only 7 per cent were themselves share-owners (and this included those holding unit and investment trusts), whereas 63 per cent invested indirectly through insurance policies alone, and a higher proportion still through the combined range of institutional channels. The increasing concentration of share ownership through the medium of the institutions is gradually organising shareholders into a potentially cohesive movement. This movement is forming reluctantly, almost involuntarily. The more traditional institutions do not particularly want to exercise an active voice in industry but the pressure of competition and the responsibilities which institutional management carries on behalf of its own prime investors, are propelling the movement inexorably towards the use of its growing power to influence management.

Indeed, the pressure on management is growing from all directions: shareholders, government, labour and not least from the market place. The buyer's market, typical of a consumer society, is making it more difficult to achieve the very results which shareholders are demanding. Such demands are spurred by professional analysts who are subjecting management performance to extensive and often very penetrating scrutiny, either in public through the medium of the financial press, or in the city and institutions. Managers can no longer afford to ignore shareholders who have always been the ultimate arbiters of managerial performance. But in the past shareholders have tended to avoid independent judgement unless and until some event occurred that compelled them to speak or vote: bankruptcy, bids, fraud, major boardroom disputes and other apocalyptic circumstances. This reticence is less extreme today. In the 1970s, it may well come to be regarded as quaint.

Objectives

Management must therefore clarify its own attitude towards shareholders, not for the day of reckoning but for every day. It must make the efforts to define corporate objectives: that set of principles which will pinpoint why the company is in business, and set out criteria to direct its conduct and measure its progress.

If the company is publicly quoted, the degree to which management will run it for the benefit of shareholders is a question that demands to be answered. It is certainly not the only way of running a business. Managers can put their effort into sales volume rather than profit; into absolute profit growth in preference to a high return on capital employed; and into less tangible objectives such as market leadership, technical innovation, the balance of payments, or service to the community. All these have their place in the wide spectrum of business objectives, but none focuses the manager's attention as sharply on the efficient use of the investment funds entrusted to him as the overriding aim of *growth in earnings per share*.

In this context, earnings are the profits attributable to shareholders after interest and taxation. They are therefore a suitable measure of managerial performance not only in the market place, but in relation to the use of various forms of finance, from overdraft to equity. The aim of growth in earnings *per share* means that the earnings attributable to each share must grow which may not be the case if too many rights issues are made to finance too little growth. Put another way, growth in earnings per share will benefit shareholders by way of higher dividends or in terms of capital appreciation, but neither of these benefits can accrue over the years unless earnings grow. All sources of capital fit into the concept: fixed interest loans have a gearing effect on earnings per share, whereas convertible issues delay the broadening of the share base for some years whilst laying the foundations for new earnings.

The earnings per share concept has the unique advantage of satisfying professional managers, institutional lenders and shareholders. It fulfils the manager's need to measure his own performance and his company's rate of growth, and at the same time enables shareholders to judge whether their expectations of higher income and capital appreciation are likely to be met. This creates between managers and shareholders a link in the area of business strategy which can be translated down the line into straight industrial targets for production, sales, and all those management functions which are related to earnings.

Of course, growth in earnings per share is not, and cannot be, the sole objective of the modern industrial company. The uninhibited, all-out pursuit of earnings growth by management and shareholders is neither feasible nor desirable in today's society. There are constraints, some of which (for example anti-trust legislation) date back to the era of the owner-manager, whilst others (such as safety or avoidance of pollution) have become particularly prominent in recent years. Society rightly has an array of watchdogs to ensure that industry does not dedicate itself exclusively to the cause of soulless efficiency in the pursuit of profit.

Managers may get the impression, from time to time, that society is perhaps too worried about their souls and not sufficiently bothered about their efficiency. Management must comply with the law and will also take public opinion into account when taking decisions. But, operating within society's ordinary constraints, it is perhaps not unreasonable to suggest that managers of publicly quoted companies who set themselves the basic objective of growth in earnings per share are also setting the tone for a sane relationship with shareholders during the 1970s.

Fisons' shareholder surveys

So much for theory. It was when we had defined a composite set of long-term objectives in our strategic deliberations in Fisons, that we had to ask ourselves: 'Are we certain that this is, in fact, what shareholders want? We assume that certain objectives will appeal to them because they make sense to us. We also assume a great many other things about shareholders: are these assumptions correct?'

The fact was: to Us (management), They (shareholders) were an entirely anonymous group – 33000 of them to be precise, in Fisons. That much was known from the stock register. There were plenty of names and addresses, but a lack of identity. Confused mental pictures suggested a range of shareholder personalities, from the speculator moving in and out of the company's shares with a skill that was to be admired and deprecated in equal measure, to one's retired uncle and aunt bravely struggling with inflation on a minute so-called 'unearned' income. And then there was the institutional investor: faceless, tucked away somewhere in the city and rarely seen as a living presence.

Perhaps managers also have a tendency to assume that shareholders know little and care less about the company's activities – the very aspects of the business in which the manager is most closely involved. It might be invigorating to challenge some of these stereotypes with a few facts; hence the decision in 1969 to carry out an attitude survey among Fisons' shareholders. It may be of interest to explain briefly how this was done, some aspects of what it revealed, and what influence it has had on management thinking.

The first step was to clarify the purpose of the surveys. This was defined as:

Firstly; to find out who shareholders are and whether they have changed over time and with changes in the business. Secondly; to find out how much they know of Fisons. Thirdly; to ascertain their attitude towards the company. Lastly; to determine what shareholders expect from management.

It was decided to seek this information from three separate pieces of research, namely:

(a) A full analysis of the shareholders' register;
(b) An attitude survey of private shareholders, i.e. individuals;
(c) A similar survey among institutional shareholders.

The surveys were designed by Fisons' own market research company (Product Surveys Ltd) which is experienced in the area of opinion surveys. The methods and techniques normally used for consumer research were successfully adapted to the rather different style of approach required for interviews with shareholders. Indeed, it was decided to engage an outside agency for the actual field work because the atmosphere during all personal interviews with shareholders had to be neutral, so as to avoid any possible bias that might have arisen from direct contact between shareholders and Fisons' employees.

Product Surveys Ltd therefore devised the questionnaires, organised the surveys and supervised the field work which was commissioned externally. The completed questionnaires were analysed by computer and then tabulated with a full commentary. Next, the implications were considered and the findings presented with visual aids to two separate meetings: the first was addressed mainly to directors and the second to a broad cross-section of senior managers including a number from Fisons' companies abroad.

One of the more original aspects of this work was the decision to conduct separate surveys, of private and institutional shareholders, with different questionnaires. Altogether, 239 private shareholders and 66 institutions were interviewed, the institutional questionnaires being couched in professional terms whilst the questions put to private stockholders were more colloquial. Bearing in mind the comparative novelty of the exercise – an approach to one's own shareholders through external interviewers in a normal business context when the company was in no way in the news – a gratifying response was achieved. Only a very few shareholders declined to be interviewed and, whereas there had been some slight apprehension about causing annoyance, the reaction to the survey itself tended more towards pleasure (tinged, perhaps, with surprise) that management should have gone to the trouble. Only one small shareholder commented *en passant* 'They ought to get on with the business instead of wasting my money!' The vast majority did not seem to think it a waste of time or money.

Some features of these studies, presented here in broad outline, will perhaps give an impression of the coverage and of the results obtained.

The analysis of the share register, set in historical context, showed that the number of shareholders had risen from 500 in 1931, when the company was only just beginning to emerge from family control, to over 33 000 in 1969. Throughout this period of nearly forty years, the number of holders had grown at a faster rate than the number of shares. During the same period, there was a basic trend away from holdings by 'sole individuals' who had held nearly 90 per cent of all shares in 1931 but only 45 per cent in 1969. Steadily and progressively, a growing proportion of the company's shares had passed into institutional hands.

An interesting subsidiary trend showing that, among private shareholders, women had acquired a larger proportion of stock than men by the early 1960s, prompted a comparison between Fisons' ownership pattern and that of the market as a whole, as shown by the 1965 Survey (*How does Britain save?*) carried out on behalf of the London Stock Exchange. It emerged that Fisons' ownership pattern (women 52 per cent, men 48 per cent) was the reverse of the national pattern (men 60 per cent, women 40 per cent). Information published in recent years by other companies tended to confirm this finding.

The indication that Fisons' shareholders were not necessarily typical of British shareholders as a whole prompted further comparison with published data. As a result, it was confirmed that the profile of our private holders was also untypical in other respects, such as age groups, socio-economic groups, and methods of share acquisition which include purchase, gift, inheritance, and employment. It seemed, therefore, that a company may attract, hold, fail to hold, or repel various types of investors whose composite characteristics will build up to a distinct and fairly clearcut shareholder profile. Further evidence from the surveys also suggested that this profile can change over the years or as a result of changes in the business. It may be surmised that a company's 'shareholder personality' is as individual as its 'management personality', and that the two are probably interrelated.

The division between institutional and private holdings of Fisons' shares in 1969 was fully analysed. It was demonstrated that the institutions representing $7\frac{1}{2}$ per cent of all holders, between them held 45 per cent of all the shares. Separate analysis revealed that the average institutional holding was ten times larger than the average private holding. Although the dearth of comparable published information precludes exact comparison, this result was in line with expectations and probably with the general stock market pattern, in trend if not in magnitude.

In view of the large and growing number of shares held by the institutions, the study was extended to analyse present holders according to the date of their first purchase of Fisons' shares. It was discovered that 31 per cent of institutional holders who made their first purchase of Fisons' shares more than five years ago, held 68 per cent of the total stock that was in institutional hands in 1969. Their average holding was over five times larger than that of institutions who first bought Fisons less than three years ago.

The analysis suggests, though it does not prove, that the institutions, once in, tend to be long-term holders of shares in companies which they judge to be appropriate investments. The study covered only existing holders and did not indicate the extent to which past institutional holders may have sold out during the 1960s. Nor can it be excluded that some holders who first bought more than five years ago have been in and out several times since then. Nevertheless, other aspects of the survey tended to confirm the impression that the institutions regard themselves as long-term investors once they have committed themselves to a sizeable holding in the context of their overall portfolio policy. The analysis of average size of present holdings against date of first purchase reveals a stepwise building up of positions by long-term institutional shareholders, probably stimulated by recurrent opportunities over the years to take up new issues or to convert from loan stock into equity. By contrast, the newcomers may well be testing the temperature for some time before deciding to take a deep plunge.

An important question connected with the buying and selling of shares is that of investment advice. The surveys investigated the sources of advice used by private and institutional holders, respectively. It was evident that stockbrokers and the financial press formed the predominant channels of advice to both classes of holders. Private shareholders also used other professional advisers such as bankers, solicitors and accountants; but it is likely that these generally turn to stockbrokers and to the financial columns of the press for primary advice. The only major third source of primary opinion was represented by studies or personal contacts established by the institutions themselves, either at executive level or through their own research departments.

Particular attention was given in the course of these surveys to the exploration of shareholders' knowledge and attitudes. First, they were asked: 'What industries come to mind when you think about Fisons?' The replies indicated clearly that institutional respondents were generally more knowledgeable about the company's spectrum of activities than private shareholders. Not surprisingly, nearly all holders who knew anything at all about Fisons, identified fertilisers (or agriculture) as one of its activities. It was interesting to find, however, that the pharmaceutical field in which much of the company's growth has occurred in recent years, was mentioned by as many as two-thirds of the institutions, but only by a quarter of private shareholders. The exception to the general conclusion that professional investors were more knowledgeable, as one would expect, was on the subject of horticulture or amateur gardening where the private investor scored a higher level of awareness. This was clearly due to familiarity with the company's brand and product range in home gardening.

The most interesting finding in this part of the survey was that the rate of awareness of various activities on the part of the institutions was broadly in line with the relative contributions to Fisons' profit made by each activity in recent years and published in annual reports to shareholders. It could therefore hardly be argued that the institutional investor was either ignorant or indifferent. The depth of his knowledge may have been uncertain and probably varied a great deal, but bearing in mind that investment in Fisons was only one item in large and diverse portfolios of shares, it could be said that the institutions knew what they most needed to know.

From knowledge of activities, the interviewers went on to ask institutional shareholders: 'How would you score the industries you have just mentioned for profit growth potential using a scale of 1 to 5?' The question was carefully phrased to relate to the industrial sector as such, and not to the company's position in it. The results showed that pharmaceuticals were given the highest score and fertilisers the lowest, although the spread between them was rather less than might have been expected in the light of what was then known about market conditions. At all events, the views of shareholders generally reflected the development policies which were being pursued by management.

Finally, the questionnaire turned to the criteria by which institutional and private shareholders judge management performance. This was a 'prompted' question in that respondents were asked to pick and grade the four criteria which they regarded as the most important, from a list presented to them. The lists shown to institutional and private holders differed somewhat but gave similar emphasis to the balance between financial and non-financial criteria.

The results showed the following preferences, graded in order of their importance to each type of shareholder:

Institutions	*Private*
1 Growth in earnings per share	1 Management capability
2 Management capability	2 Increasing sales
3 Return on capital	3 A safe investment
4 Widening international interests	4 Widening international interests

The highest rating was given by the institutions to 'growth in earnings per share'. By contrast, neither of the main financial criteria submitted to private holders, i.e. 'net profits' or 'appreciation in the share price', reached the leading scores. Nor did 'appreciation in the share price' receive a particularly high score with institutional respondents. This is not perhaps quite as surprising as it seems at first sight. Discounting the unlikely explanation that the professional investor could be bashful about admitting to a desire for capital gain, a more probable reason is that he regards 'growth in earnings per share' and 'management capability' as pre-requisites which, in turn, can be expected to lead to 'appreciation in the share price'. Indeed, the high rating given by both classes of shareholders to the concept of 'management capability' will be noted. It was also interesting to find 'a safe investment' gaining a high score with private but not with institutional holders, whereas both showed a significant desire for international expansion.

Conclusions

Among the many conclusions drawn from this survey of Fisons' shareholders the following may be relevant here:

1 The individuality of the company and its shareholders stood out clearly. There were fairly strong indications that the two are interrelated and that changes in the one will, over a period of time, bring about changes in the other. Shareholders are segmented groups, not a formless mass.

2 It was no surprise that earnings growth emerged as management's top priority in its relationship with shareholders; but there were, in addition, various other indicators suggesting that:

3 Shareholders are not totally preoccupied with financial growth in their attitude towards management. Although there is no substitute for good results, shareholders value the company's overall reputation. Their expectations of growth are tempered with a certain amount of realism. They expect management to manage for results, but shareholders are concerned with means as well as ends.

4 Institutional shareholders, with a steadily growing stake, appear to be essentially committed to long-term holdings. The pressure of inflowing funds, the limited choice of acceptable outlets, and the difficulty of disposing of massive blocks of shares are all contributory factors to a growing sense of commitment.

Looking ahead to the 1970s, one may expect an intensification in the trends that have been apparent in the relationship between shareholders and management since the end of the postwar seller's market. Some of the main features in the coming decade could be:

● a continued rise in the proportion of total shares held by institutional investors

● a demand for the disclosure of more detailed, and more easily comprehensible information to shareholders, involving more frequent communication with management

● pressure from and on the institutions to take a more active part in company affairs and, if necessary, to intervene in order to safeguard the interests of their own prime investors

● more scope for the function of independent analysts and commentators who will have to combine financial knowledge with practical experience of industry to a much greater extent than hitherto. The demand for investment advice will give a more professional accent to the art without, however, turning art into science

● increasing interest by employees in becoming shareholders, and by management in sponsoring appropriate schemes. It is nevertheless unlikely that these can have more than a marginal impact on the basic trend away from individual holdings and towards the preponderance of institutional ownership of quoted companies.

Finally, and perhaps most important for management, the pressure to improve performance in all respects will continue and probably gather pace. On the other hand, a growing sense of realism on the part of the investor can also be anticipated. Shareholders are well aware of society's demands on industrial management. The response to such demands must often cut across the straight profit considerations that are normally applied to management decisions.

Exaggerated expectations of profit growth are out of place in an environment where the intervention of constraints and social priorities will increasingly become the order of the day. That is no alibi for managers who will continue to strive for ambitious targets; but it will involve some restraint and the renunciation of fanciful dreams on the part of shareholders and professional commentators. To foster realistic attitudes, management must encourage the flow of information and promote understanding of genuine problems. If this can be achieved, communications between management and shareholders in the 1970s will – perhaps for the first time – take the form of a dialogue.

PART II

B. Planning and the social environment

12

The role of business in society

THOMAS KEMPNER, KEVIN HAWKINS and KEITH MacMILLAN

Public concern with the social responsibilities of business has grown enormously in recent years as the social and environmental costs of industrial growth have become more and more manifest. Pollution is only the best known and most conspicuous example of the failure of top managers, both in the past and at the present time, to appreciate the interdependence of business and society as a whole. In this article the authors point out the practical difficulties that companies are likely to encounter in attempting to reconcile their conventional objectives of profit and growth with new and often nebulous ideas about social responsibility. They trace the historical evolution of the relationship between public welfare and private business interests and point out the dangers involved in permitting governments too free a hand in setting down the rules to control business behaviour. They conclude that it would be far more desirable for the business community to develop its own code of behavioural norms which would meet the growing demand for companies to incorporate 'wider' objectives into their strategic plans.

Business policy is the study of the functions and responsibilities of senior management and the problems which affect the character and success of the total enterprise. Organisations choose strategies which fit their objectives. These strategies stem from management's understanding of the changing environment – cultural, social and economic. Objectives are often expressed in economic (or profit) terms, although for non-profit organisations other criteria will apply.

In the simplest terms the organisation monitors the environment (this may be an intuitive rather than a conscious process) and formulates or reformulates its objectives. Strategies and planning processes then follow to translate the objectives into desired outcomes.

The process described in the last paragraph is subject to constraints which may change over time. For example, they include various aspects of government policy, some of which may be embodied in law. Others are determined by pressure groups such as trade unions or consumer councils. A more general area includes the changes induced by new beliefs about tolerable behaviour – for instance on pollution.

The nature of the social responsibilities of organisations is a changing and often nebulous concept. Nevertheless, it is a matter of rapidly increasing importance. It is our contention that these issues may replace economic growth as the major area of discussion in the next decade. For the societies of advanced countries can now afford the luxury of concern over quality rather than quantity – a point to which we shall refer again below.

The task of the chief executive in a large modern company has never been more difficult than it is at the moment. It is on the chief executive – the corporate leader – that the ultimate responsibility for the performance of the organisation under his control rests. Yet the criteria for evaluating business performance are increasingly open to question just as the character of business organisation itself is currently undergoing rapid change. *A priori* one can see that the performance of a business firm is a direct function of its organisational structure.

Performance criteria

There have been few periods in history in which business, broadly defined, has not been scrutinised by individuals and interest groups fundamentally out of sympathy with the conventional objectives of commercial enterprise. Hostile criticism of this kind has always sprung from a realisation that there is an apparent dichotomy between the objectives and methods of business. Let us assume that the objectives of business enterprise are primarily economic in the sense that they are concerned with the allocation of resources. In any industrial society the firm is the primary allocative agent, whether it operates through the price system or under central bureaucratic direction. Dissatisfaction has arisen because the practical working of this system inevitably involves certain consequences for social relationships as between, on the one hand, the ownership of a firm and its management and on the other hand, between the firm itself and its employees, suppliers, customers and the community as a whole. The ancient controversy over the 'just price' illustrates this dichotomy between economic decisions and their wider social impact. The phrase itself crystallises the inconsistency since the word 'just' has obvious ethical connotations while 'price' clearly relates to the bidding for resources.

This traditional conflict of economic ends and social means is now acquiring a new dimension as public concern with the environment reaches explosive proportions. In advanced industrial societies the growth in real incomes over the past two decades has enabled almost all basic physical and subsistence needs to be met. But by the same token these rising standards of comfort and education have also enabled a growing number of people to observe and contemplate the social costs of their own material enrichment, or what an economist would call the 'external diseconomies' involved.[1] Similarly the function of the business firm itself is now to *create* wants as well as to satisfy them.[2] But these wants are themselves becoming more and more intangible, as their satisfaction is to an increasing extent psychologically induced. One consequence of this change in economic and social priorities is that people are now coming to express their rising expectations in non-material terms. The prospect of a 'leisured society' appears to conflict with the tangible costs, in both real and human terms, of the present-day acquisitive society. To take an obvious example, the spread of motor car ownership is a direct result of rising real incomes. But now the point appears to have been reached when the benefits of additional car ownership are outweighed by its cost – measured in terms of atmospheric pollution, urban traffic congestion, loss of life and the effect of noise on the human nervous system. The producers of cars, however, continue to evaluate their performance in purely commercial terms, i.e. in terms of profit and corporate growth or in H. Igor Ansoff's words: 'The return to the firm, or profit, is optimised in some sense in relation to the resources employed to produce it.'[3]

This implies that in so far as the objectives of the firm are still primarily economic, the unrestrained pursuit of growth must inevitably be called into question, which means that the fundamental purpose of business itself is under attack. It follows from this, therefore, that the traditional criteria for evaluating business performance are increasingly open to doubt, just as the organisation of business is itself becoming more complex.

One cannot blame the firm for its emphasis on both total growth and growth in profits. The former has been a major objective of every government in the world for a long time. Presumably also it was accepted as a proper aim by the electorate. Progress, however defined, was seen as depending on economic growth. Change was accepted, perhaps reluctantly, as the consequence of the striving for greater material wealth. The firms of the past and present responded magnificently to this primary aim. In advanced societies millions of people were able to choose a way of life unlimited by the constraints of bare subsistence. Whether the choice was always exercised wisely is another matter, but it is not a consequence for which firms can be blamed. Society accepted then things about which it now has regrets – pollution, noise, the danger and the unpleasantness of many occupations.

Growth in profits as a measure of success fitted admirably with the general objectives of economic growth. Increasing profits attracted resources to the growing and away from static or declining industries. Profitability was linked to the success the firm had in winning customers for new or improved products. Thus a correct assessment of consumer choice by the firm led to greater profits and growth for itself, the economy and general welfare. Yet the very success of this system as a method of allocating resources has made it possible to question some of its assumptions. So that one can now afford the luxury of asking whether growth is always worth the consequences. The trend is bound to increase. Once basic necessities cease to dominate, concern shifts to semi- or non-material objectives – to the environment, the background for a satisfactory life or simply greater leisure.

Organizational development – the multinational corporation

One of the most remarkable developments in business organisation over the past few decades has been the growth of the large corporation; a process observed first in the USA and now to an increasing extent in Great Britain and Europe. Small and medium-size firms still exist in large numbers but it is the absolute size and behaviour of the *biggest* that has become a major problem both for the managers concerned and for the rest of the community. This growth in the size of the major corporations has been accompanied by a corresponding development in their geographical and commercial areas of activity.[4] The business policy-maker must now focus his attention on the multinational corporation which operates in a wide range of diverse product markets. The multinational corporation is no longer subject to the same constraints as its purely national or parochial predecessor. These constraints operated largely through the medium of the national government (e.g. taxation, anti-monopoly legislation) and the local social environment (deriving from the historical position of the large firm as the major wealth-creating and socially unifying agency in a particular locality).

Technological change

Current trends in technology, far from alleviating these policy problems, are on the contrary tending to aggravate them. As we have suggested above the social costs of technological change that are *external* to the firm are rarely immediately apparent either to the firm's own policy makers or to anyone else. But in addition we must consider the *internal* social costs generated by the firm's technological maturity and, in particular, the effects of the latter on the employees concerned. This is not, of course, a new problem for management, and has indeed been present since the first days of the industrial revolution. But in recent years the problem has begun to have direct repercussions on managers themselves in the form of increasing managerial redundancy, as automation develops from mechanisation and machines tend to duplicate mental as well as manual processes. Two examples may illustrate the immediate relevance of this problem. First, we have the increasingly familiar case of the middle-aged, 'experienced' but innumerate manager who cannot adapt to the computer-based management techniques of today. Second, mergers arising from the search for technological economies may lead to numerous redundancies at *all* levels of management, as well as of the labour force.

Ownership and control

These problems are made even more complex by the fact that a firm's policy-makers are frequently themselves employees, as the divorce of corporate owner-ship from control has marched in step with the growth of the firm itself.[5] Thus the internal legitimacy of the chief executive is increasingly precarious. Not only must he make decisions on all the above policy problems but he must also justify his own leadership by making the right decisions.

In this situation it is perhaps inevitable that the intelligent policy-maker should consult and seek to draw inspiration from the literature of business policy and corporate strategy. In doing so, he finds himself confronted by a multitude of objectives and performance criteria, many of which are mutually incompatible and represent little more than a platitudinous declaration of intent. Objectives such as maximum long-term profits, or maximum earnings per share, or a specified rate of growth in assets, or simply 'survival' to name but a few, are all subject to a wide variety of interpretations.[6] The more enlightened texts tacitly admit this weakness by conceding that corporate objectives are primarily a function of the particular firm.[7] What is an appropriate objective for one firm may be completely irrelevant for another. It may be, of course, that most managers still regard 'business policy' as a mere rationalization and formaliza-tion of existing business practice. One leading authority has remarked: 'On occasions when more urgent but less important operating problems permit, policy is what the president of a country or a corporation is likely to think about at night.'[8]

The classical entrepreneur

These problems were, of course, much simpler when the functions of policy-maker, owner and manager were fused together in the person of the entre-preneur. In the so-called classical age of entrepreneurship – the nineteenth century – the objectives of the businessman were in accord with those of society as a whole to an extent that had never been experienced before. In the early stages of industrialisation, when the role of the state was one of relative abstention and indifference, there were strong and obvious incentives for the individual employer to restructure local patterns of life and work to suit his own require-ments. It is true that the nineteenth-century entrepreneur is popularly regarded as the reactionary foe of trade unionism and the ruthless exploiter of child labour. But to adhere to this view is to judge the industrial revolution according to the criteria of modern humanitarianism. Many employers provided com-munity facilities such as housing and education. They also regulated employee behaviour both inside and outside the factory, by, for example, stimulating religious fervour and temperance.[9] Although this kind of action was very much in their own interests it still constituted an entrepreneurial preoccupation with 'social responsibility' which has since been much weakened by the growth of the welfare state. A striking analogy is the comparable role of the business leader in more newly industrialised societies, such as Italy, Japan or Nigeria.

Business legitimacy

Not surprisingly, therefore, the nineteenth century saw much less questioning of the legitimacy of the objectives and methods of business. The success of commercial enterprise was generally deemed to be an essential pre-requisite of social progress. It was not, in fact, until the early part of the present century that the business ethic in Britain came under attack. The credibility of the Victorian rationale of universal improvement through individual enterprise, so avidly propagated by Smiles, was severely shaken by two increasingly apparent failures on the part of the business community. Firstly, British businessmen were criticised for failing to hold their predominant position in the world markets, i.e. they were not *efficient* enough. Secondly, the rising trend of industrial violence and strikes seemed to indicate a failure on the part of some employers to recognise and come to terms with the divergent aspirations of their employees, i.e. they were not *socially responsible*. These two lines of attack were developed during the interwar period by critics such as the Guild Socialists and the Quaker employers.[10] British industrialists were alleged to be too tough on their employees but not tough enough on their foreign competitors.

Participative leadership

In response to this rising volume of criticism, apologies for the traditional structure of power in industry developed a new theory of reconciliation. This asserted that a democratic participatory style of business leadership could reconcile all the apparent conflict of interest both within the firm and between the firm and society. This restates traditional managerial ideology that the industrial enterprise is a unitary organisation, and all groups within it are, or should be, dedicated to the same objectives – success, measured in terms of profits, minimum costs and growth. Thus the function of persuasive leadership backed up by a policy of good human relations, is to convince both employees and the rest of the community that the achievement of these objectives is in the best interests of all. It is assumed that once people are made aware of this 'self-evident truth' they will naturally accept it, and industrial conflict will largely disappear – hence the importance which exponents of this view place on good communications.[11] Does this emphasis on consultative participative leadership mark a genuine change of purpose in the community to a different, not necessarily better, set of objectives? Or is it nothing more than a polished façade behind which power continues to be exercised and 'participation' is a weapon of control?

A new professionalism?

If business is changing to different ranges of responsibilities does this not constitute an effective solution to the dichotomy between the commercial objectives and the social responsibilities of business discussed earlier in this paper? Is there a new professionalisation of management deriving out of 'participative' leadership on the one hand, and the separation of ownership and control on the other, which will tend to move along an evolutionary path towards an adequate solution?[12] A priori, such a development of a professional 'esprit de corps' seems unlikely for as Selekman has said:

> In well-developed professions, such as medicine or law, ethical codes are formulated and enforced; the penalty is expulsion. Moreover, entrance into the profession is by examination. The examination leads to a licensing procedure. Thus violation of the ethical codes means not only expulsion for the wrongdoer, but inability to continue in practice.
>
> Such procedures are not open to business. Anyone can enter into business; anyone can start his own firm. Expulsion from a trade organisation is no serious penalty; it is known only to the insiders, and it has little effect on the consumers whom the business serves.[13]

There is thus no fixed body of enforceable norms and ethical sanctions governing the practice of management, which implies that management is incapable of self-regulation and that behavioural constraints must be externally applied. Or, again in Selekman's words:

> If the tensions of conscience were not constantly at play, the forces of competition would tend to degrade standards to the lowest common denominator, it is in the interest of the community that management be checked by the power of unions and government. For conscience needs an ally in the form of costs – possible losses through strikes or government regulations to serve as a counterweight to the costs based on the self-interest of profitability. Without counter power, the necessity to be practical as a way of ensuring survival in a competitive world would win out in the debate of the 'ethical ought versus the technical must.'[14]

Having said all this, therefore, we must now consider the problem of reconciling the policy of the autocratic corporation with that of elected government.

Self-help or legislation?

As we see it, there are two fundamental choices facing the makers of public policy. On the one hand they can put their faith in the ability of business leaders to discipline themselves and develop their own code of professional norms, spurred on by exhortation and the power of public opinion. This approach may, however, be found wanting in so far as there is no guarantee that the accumulated legacy of environmental problems associated with economic growth, such as pollution or technological redundancy, will be tackled in a coordinated and systematic way – if indeed they are tackled at all.

Moreover, it may be unreasonable to expect current organisations to take the blame and costs of the actions of their predecessors who acted in a very different social and political climate.

On the other hand, they can put the onus of regulating business behaviour in the hands of an external statutory authority, and enforce a predetermined code of norms by legal sanctions. Though this kind of strategy would probably achieve some tangible results in the short term, there is an obvious danger that an enforceable code of norms on these lines would become arbitrary, inflexible and unresponsive to changing economic conditions. It would also give rise to a degree of uncertainty with regard to the precise objectives to be pursued by the statutory body concerned. The apparent conflict between the aims of the Industrial Reorganisation Corporation and the Monopolies Commission illustrates the dangers involved in conferring this kind of power on external agencies. And, of course, the activities of all such bodies are usually viewed with suspicion and scepticism by the business community itself.

Few people would deny that it would be preferable for business to regulate itself. The problem centres on the criteria which individual businessmen can use in the day-to-day running of their company, where conflicts arise between purely commercial priorities and other social values, where the former has an objective measurement of its importance – profit – and the latter has not.

We believe that this is a crucial matter for the survival of a private enterprise business system, and yet in all the armoury of scientific management there is no technique that will ensure that the chief executive gets the right balance between the 'ethical ought' and the 'technical must'. Is it not after all impossible to programme a computer with ethical values? Perhaps it is, but an increased awareness of possible criteria may evolve if an attempt is made to make the full implications of values explicit. If, for example, some of the social costs which we have mentioned can be measured, it may be possible to have prolonged and detailed debate on such issues as the rights of private shareholders in the giant corporations, or the attitude of national governments to multinational enterprise. There can also be extensive discussion on whether there should be more legal categories of firms, to take account of differences in size, structure or range of markets.

Any such debate must be an informed one however, which takes place against a background of accessible empirical data. At present there are unfortunately very few research studies undertaken at business policy level. Those that there are suffer from serious methodological handicaps. They are, in the main, based either on published accounts, questionnaires or, more rarely, case studies, and they all suffer from the obvious difficulty that they can report only what management chooses to reveal. There are nevertheless an increasing number of most illuminating empirical studies,[15] and, of course, some managements are more forthcoming than others, but on the whole, businessmen are still very unwilling to expose themselves to the public eye.

The reasons for such reluctance are not too difficult to understand. In the first place, there is the problem of property rights. If a business is classed as private enterprise then should it not be allowed to stay 'private'? Should the owner of a firm be forced to disclose what he is doing with his own property? But as we have noted, the ownership of many firms is so dispersed, the attitude of shareholders so difficult to elicit, and the interests of employees, customers and the community so pressing, that management's role as trustee is now diffuse.

The second argument often used against greater disclosure is that it would affect the long-term security of a company by informing competitors of its activities, or encouraging speculation. But is it not a desirable precondition for the efficient allocation of resources within competitive markets that as much knowledge as possible is available to the controller of resources?

We do not intend to discuss the validity of such arguments any further in this paper. It is, of course, more relevant to any discussion of business policy but has been discussed competently elsewhere.[16] Our purpose is simply to suggest that statutory intervention either to establish criteria or in the first instance to elicit data, is in no way as desirable as business taking the initiative itself.

In this respect the universities, and particularly those concerned with business education, can probably be of great assistance. They are in the most favourable position to develop closer links with business. They have the expertise to undertake research into the social costs and benefits of business success and their impartiality may be accepted by business and government alike.

The new business schools in Britain are often accused of being too technique-orientated. This may or may not be true, but they are educating a new generation of business leaders, and are therefore an obvious platform for the debate on the future of business. It is in the interest of business itself that this new generation appreciates all the main issues of business policy. It is only in this way that there is hope for a true professionalisation of top management.

References

1. For a straightforward exposition, see E. J. MISHAN, *The Costs of Economic Growth*, Staples Press, 1967.

2. *Ibid.* Also J. K. GALBRAITH, *The New Industrial State*, H. Hamilton, 1967.

3. H. IGOR ANSOFF, *Corporate Strategy*, McGraw-Hill, 1965; Penguin Books, 1968, p. 44.

4. L. TURNER, *Politics and the Multi-National Company*, Fabian Research, Series 279, 1969.

5. See, for example, A. A. BERLE and GARDINER C. MEANS, *The Modern Corporation and Private Property*, Harcourt-Brace and World, 1968.
   P. SARGENT FLORENCE, *Ownership, Control and Success of Large Companies*, Sweet & Maxwell, 1961.
   B. HINDLEY, 'Capitalism and the corporation', *Economica*, Nov. 1969.

6. For a discussion of such problems, see J. ARGENTI, 'Defining corporate objectives', *Long Range Planning*, March 1969.

7. JOHN CHILD, *British Management Thought*, Allen & Unwin, 1969.

8. E. P. LEARNED, C. R. CHRISTENSEN, K. R. ANDREWS and W. D. GUTH, *Business Policy, Text and Cases*, rev. edn., Richard D. Irwin, 1969, p. 3.

9. For a discussion of factory discipline and labour problems in the early Industrial Revolution, see S. POLLARD, *The Genesis of Modern Management*, Edward Arnold, 1965.

10. CHILD, op. cit.

11. See, for e.g., J. A. C. BROWN, *Social Psychology of Industry*, Penguin 1954.

12. For a discussion of such possibilities, see P. DERRICK and J. F. PHIPPS, *Co-ownership Co-operation, and Control: An Industrial Objective*, Longmans, 1969.

13. B. M. SELEKMAN, *A Moral Philosophy for Management*, McGraw-Hill, 1959, p. 109.

14. Ibid., pp. 104–5.

15. See, e.g., T. NICHOLLS, *Ownership, Control and Ideology*, Allen & Unwin, 1969; A. SINGH and G. WHITTINGTON, in collaboration with H. T. BURLEY, *Growth, Profitability and Valuation: A Study of United Kingdom quoted companies*, Cambridge, Dept. of Applied Economics, Occasional Paper 7, 1968; R. J. MOUSEN, J. S. CHIN and D. E. COOLEY, 'The effect on the separation of ownership and control on the performance of the large firm', *Quarterly Journal of Economics*, 1968.

16. See, e.g., H. ROSE, *Disclosure in Company Accounts*, Institute of Economic Affairs, 2nd edn., 1968.

13

Should government and company planners influence each other?

H. F. R. CATHERWOOD

In this article the author argues the case for closer cooperation between planners in government and planners in business along the lines of the planning dialogue which occurs in NEDC. He answers critics who complain of government pressure on industry and the undue influence of business on government, and suggests that 'consultative planning is essential if national plans are to be made flexible and realistic, and if company plans are to be made with the national interest in mind'.

It would seem at first sight that there should be no need to debate the advisability of a planning exercise aimed at increasing the accuracy and efficiency of forecasting trends in economic movement and industrial and government policies. Businessmen may not be expert in running the economy but they do know more about business than economists, civil servants and politicians, and some way has to be found of translating this experience and tapping it for the management of the economy. Yet there is no open and shut case for two-way pressure and influence between government and company planners. Those who would keep government pure from industrial influence and industry free from government influence have a case and we should not brush it off with slogans of enlightenment.

Political pressure

Let us look first at the case for company planners keeping themselves free from government influence. Here governments have a case to press or, to put it as the advocates of this view would put it, a line to shoot, a line which is allegedly well on the optimistic side of the probable outcome. It is pointed out that they want to get re-elected, to justify their policies to the electorate and to argue, therefore, that they will give the magic touch the economy needs. But, less contentiously, they have to deal not only with the electorate, but also with a great many other people with whom successive governments have entered into commitments of one kind or another. Any comprehensive published plan must either be optimistic on the imponderables such as the balance of payments and productivity or leave the reconciliation of international commitments with the growth rate vague, making the plan less credible. Alternatively, it must spell out this reconciliation well in advance and so give prior notice to all kinds of lobbies that their interests are for the chopper. It can be said, therefore, that the pressure is to pitch the figuring on the optimistic side of the given policies, with the half-implied intention that harder but unspecified policies will be forthcoming as the need arises.

Inconsistency of government policy

However, the company planner is entitled to observe that policies to which there is no firm commitment are not to be relied on and he is entitled – on the past record – to decide that they will be adopted according to the pressures at the time and to make his main judgement on the likely force of those pressures and not at all on what is said in a published plan. This kind of scepticism covers the levels of government expenditure, the parity of sterling, the operation of the capital account and military commitments. The figuring of the 1965 plan assumed that other policies would give way and that growth would be given priority. Changes of policy did come, on sterling in November 1967 and on military expenditure East of Suez early in 1968, and on the sterling area in the Basle agreements in the summer of 1968. But in July 1966 it was clear that the timing of the 1965 projections was at least a year out, and probably more, and the major changes in policy had not been made.

Lack of financial reserves

The lack of first-line reserves at the disposal of government also tempts the company planner to ask whether the government is, in fact, in a financial position to carry out its plan, whether it does not depend on external factors such as the growth of world trade, whether the company planner should not have his eye on these rather than on government's published intentions.

Obsolete plans

Finally, the company planner is entitled to observe that a five-year plan soon becomes out of date – if it is credible for a year it is lucky, for the remaining four it becomes increasingly incredible.

Some of these criticisms apply to one particular kind of plan – a fixed five-year plan with a one-line projection from year one to year five. I doubt very much if we will see that kind of plan again. Plans in future are likely to have more than one line of projection for gross national product and are likely to be rolled forward every two years, if not annually. In other words, they are likely to be less brittle, more flexible and therefore more realistic than the National Plan Mark I.

The early months of 1969 saw the rebirth of this newer planning concept and the publication of the British Government's Green Paper, *The Task Ahead.* Until then no central assessment had been forthcoming from government to replace the 1965 Plan – partly because of economic uncertainties leading up to devaluation and, later, the need to see how devaluation was working out.

There has been, of course, an overriding need to establish a continuous two-way traffic between government and particular industries in the information which both need to make rational and necessary economic decisions. There has been a realisation and an acceptance that this new planning process, in which both government and industry pool knowledge and ask questions, should be a more successful interchange than those which have gone before.

The difficulties of governments in making firm commitments ahead of time is a more formidable objection to consultative planning because it cannot be changed by altering the technique of planning. The original idea when NEDC was set up in 1962 was that it should be a body in touch with government through the ministers who sat on it, but visibly separate from government who would not, therefore, bear full responsibility for the plans which it issued. The disadvantage of this method was that the planners at NEDC could only get the government expenditure plans on an 'under the counter' basis and even if they got the right set of plans they could not advertise them as such. It was also thought to be too close to government to produce any policies which were too openly in conflict with government policies, though in answer to this I should add that my predecessor, Sir Robert Shone, was the first person to point out in the 1963 NEDC Plan that exports would not rise at the required rate unless they were 'made more profitable'. At the time this was a pretty bold departure from official policy as were other suggestions in the so-called Orange Book, *Conditions Favourable to Faster Growth.* However, it could be argued that NEDC fell between the two stools and was neither one thing nor the other – not so much a donkey as a mule.

In 1964 the incoming government accepted this criticism and took over full responsibility for the planning process, but the 1965 National Plan which was the result has been the object of much of the criticism of government planning since then. It is, however, only fair to say that though the government did not immediately take all the measures necessary to achieve the rate of growth in the plan, it has, during the last three years, taken a great many of them and some of them have been of a very fundamental character. It is not, therefore, fair to be completely cynical about government's ability to back up a plan with policies. It even committed itself to the East of Suez withdrawal well ahead of the point at which public commitment was operationally necessary. Furthermore, this kind of decision, a decision to change a foreign policy which has lasted for a century or more, does not recur with every five-year plan. So the case against a major macroeconomic plan issued and endorsed by government is not proven.

Just as industry can make a case for closing its ears to government planning, so government can make a case for ignoring the voice of industry. But, while the industry case has certain well-known spokesmen, the government case, for obvious reasons, is only made within the confines of Whitehall itself. It is not usually made by ministers, who are ideologically committed to planning, but has been made pretty forcefully by some of their advisers.

The narrow view

The essence of this case is that very few companies have any need to look at the economy as a whole. Their effort and energy are concentrated on a very narrow sector. Even ICI accounts for less than 1 per cent of the national product. Experience in companies of those parts of the economy outside their sector is minimal and yet it is very hard for businessmen who are asked by government for their general advice, not to extrapolate from the particular which they know to the general which they do not know. It is hard, for instance, for the head of a large and successful business – just the kind of man who usually gets the ear of government – to realise that maybe three-quarters of the economy is made up of businesses a good deal less efficient than his own. The management members of the original NEDC have often been criticised by government advisers for putting the view that productivity could be stepped up fairly quickly to support a 4 per cent growth rate provided only that government allowed domestic demand to go ahead to sustain 4 per cent growth. The businessman is accustomed to setting sales and profit objectives which will keep his staff on their toes. He is in direct control and can take immediate action if a division does not perform well. But government is not in direct control, it can only influence and its actions tend to be subject to lengthy time-lags. And if growth is not backed up by productivity, the inflationary pressures can trigger off a run on sterling which has the most disastrous consequences.

There is a quick answer to this particular argument. It is that the businessmen on NEDC have taken all this to heart even more acutely than the government. In fact, in the period leading up to the squeeze of 1966, their great watchword was 'steady as you go'. My present fear would be the other way round, that they have become altogether too pessimistic about the possibility of higher productivity. No doubt their natural interest in higher growth will reassert itself.

Problems of size

The second problem is rather more subtle and, because of that, gives rise to some terrible misunderstandings. The businessman is trained to go for the big issues, to hit the high spots. The details, the routine, will be delegated down the line while the top brass are doing the big deal, the takeover, the new project, the joint venture, the closure. Maybe some do fuss about the details, but most of them know they should not. But government cannot work like that. The economy is far too unwieldy, the scale is utterly different and therefore it can only operate on the margin. You can close a plant in six months but not an industry. A company can grow at 20 per cent p.a. but not the whole economy. Government thinks of a productivity increase of 0·3 per cent over the annual trend as enormous. A company would scarcely notice it. So when government proposes a policy like the Regional Employment Premium to make a marginal shift of employment from the south to the north, industry howls it down as derisive. 'It will only make one firm in twenty put down a plant in the north instead of the south,' they say. 'But,' say government, 'that 5 per cent shift is exactly what we want.' The figures are illustrative of the general drift of the argument, not, of course, exact magnitudes. It has been very much the same with devaluation. 'It is only an 8 per cent advantage,' says industry, 'it will only make a marginal difference.' 'But,' says government, 'we only need a marginal difference. We need a 2 per cent to 3 per cent shift of resources, that is all, to produce a £500m surplus.' 'In any case,' says industry, 'there is scarcely any price-elasticity of demand, it all depends on competitive delivery dates, good design, good distribution arrangements, availability of credit and, above all, on marketing.' 'You tell that to the IMF,' says the government, 'tell the international bankers that wage increases and price increases do not affect the balance of trade, tell them that they have their correlations all wrong; tell it to the OECD, tell it to Working Party Three, tell it to the Group of Ten and listen while they split their sides laughing – oh, and while you are at it, ask them for another £500m and as you are collecting it, tell them why our share of world trade has gone down as our unit costs have gone up.'

The trouble with these imaginary dialogues on broad principles is that they are imaginary. They very seldom take place outside NEDC and even then there is a limit to what you can get in one morning a month. But while it is my job to promote such a dialogue, standard form for a minister's adviser is to encourage the minister to be polite, to commit himself to nothing and to remember that businessmen are unlikely to give sound economic advice!

The answer to these objections is that you ignore business opinion at your peril and that if there are gaps in their economic outlook then the joint planning process will help to fill them and meantime some allowances have to be made. I have come to the solemn conclusion after all my traumatic experiences in industry and in public service that it never pays when people ignore another point of view. The planning dialogue in EDCs and NEDC is, in my view, the best way of tapping this business experience because it brings both sides together to look at something concrete in which both are interested and this exercises a very considerable discipline on the discussion so that it does not degenerate into dinner-table dogma. The more thoroughly this dialogue is understood and the more times both sides go through the process, the more support it is to all parties. That is why the first tentative offers should not be written off.

Business as an interested party

The third objection from Whitehall is that the company man is an interested party in the dialogue. His avowed aim and object is to maximise profits for the particular company which pays his salary and he will, therefore, tend to lobby that particular interest. This is both unfair and untrue. It is certainly not true of the national representative bodies who sit on NEDC. There one is dealing with people who are national figures in their own right and whose position does – and should – matter more to them than trying to exert leverage on behalf of the particular set of companies which happens at that moment to pay their salary. There is a long tradition of public service in Britain, not confined to the Civil Service, and if there is any legitimate complaint of those in the top echelon it is the other way round, that they spend too much time in the public interest and too little in their company's. But coming on down the line to the professional company planners, to the experts, I do not think that the charge of interest can be applied at all. Where the experts get together they do so as experts, whether they are in government service or private industry and, in my experience, they are motivated entirely by professional skill. In any case, the constitution of NEDC and the EDCs is so framed that the body does not represent any one interest, but the skill and expertise of all are available to it.

Government, too, is, as we have seen, subject to the charge that it has other interests, its interest in getting re-elected. Politicians would, no doubt, reply that this interest coincides with the general interest. If they run the economy well in the general interest, they will get re-elected and if they do not they will not, therefore it is in their interests to run the economy well. There is more truth in this than most businessmen will allow, but suspicion exists on both sides. That is why it is better, in my view, that if businessmen need to have their attention drawn to wider interests it should be done in the framework of NEDC and the EDCs on which they are represented. Planning should not be a unilateral act of government but should be conducted in partnership, with each side pressing on the other the hard facts of life which both sides must take into account if their own detailed plans are not to be futile.

Government's influence on industry

Coming from the general to the particular, it is easier to say what influence industry should exert on government than the other way round, because industry is so varied and so complex that it is hard to generalise. My only general point would be that industry does not invest enough. It has plenty to complain of, high interest rates, low growth, sharp fluctuation in demand. But even in a gloomy situation you can be too gloomy. The European Free Trade Area, the tariff reductions under the Kennedy Round and the net benefit of devaluation add up to a considerable inducement to invest for world markets which industry generally has not yet taken.

Recently I met a most distinguished Japanese economist who told me that Japan's growth was investment-based. I said that I had always thought expansion was usually demand-based because business would not invest unless it could see profitable demand ahead. He said that there seemed to him to be good reasons for making investment well ahead of demand:

1 It had been necessary to invest in order to restore Japan's place in world trade.
2 You could not create the demand without having the investment to meet it.
3 In order to keep competitive in new techniques you had to have a high rate of new investment.

All of these reasons apply in Britain, too, and yet we are at the bottom of the investment league. The real answer to the IMF is that our drop in share of world trade is due to our drop in share of world industrial investment, that our high unit costs came not from high wages but from low output and that you cannot have high output unless you have high investment. Recently there have been signs that, at last, we may be recovering some of the lost ground.

Out-dated economic theories

But company planners also have facts of life which must be brought home to government planners. The chief of these is that the production model on which government operates is old-fashioned. There are two reasons for this.

The first reason is that economic theory takes time to establish itself. One famous government economist concluded an argument by telling me that my point was quite contrary to an established economic theory which denied that capital intensive industries had certain characteristics which I maintained they did. I hastily looked up the theory. I then discovered that it was propounded in the 1940s and was based on data at least a quarter of a century old. And that is relatively recent. Keynesian theories are based on the patterns of industry and world trade forty years ago. And as for Adam Smith he is 200 years old. Now, of course, not all that Adam Smith, Keynes or Leontieff have said is wrong. But it needs to be interpreted against the background of industry today. An academic economist may well be right to withhold judgement for twenty years to see how a theory works out in practice. But he cannot advise business or government to wait too. Government needs advice from people who are accustomed to making up their minds in good time and whose information is firsthand even if it would not qualify for an academic thesis.

The second reason is that, because of the balance of payments constraint, the rate of economic growth in the UK has been less than the growth in all other advanced industrial countries. So the model of the British economy on which the economists work is subject to an overriding governor which makes it faulty as a basis for policy. We do not know from looking at the past what would happen without this particular governor. Nor do we know what can happen when new technology is applied on a scale never experienced in the past.

Britain has available to it the same skills as other advanced industrial countries, the same fund of technical expertise, a much better capital market, a higher than average record of industrial discipline (though this has been put under such strain that our record is not what it was) and, whatever the moralists may say, just about the same will to work. From experience of industry, therefore, one is inclined to argue that if the governing constraint were removed, the economy could go ahead at the same rate as that of Germany, France, Italy, Japan or America. On the other hand, it is argued with some force by economists without direct industrial experience that there the balance of payments constraint is not crucial, that what is good for our creditors is good for the British economy and British industry, that the overriding constraint is the growth of productive potential. It was thought at one time that devaluation would put this argument to the test, and if it had removed the balance of payments constraint, this might have been so; but I think it is likely that the argument will go on, that the one side will argue for the progressive removal of the balance of payments constraint to enable the underlying dynamism of new technology to emerge, while the others will argue on the basis of a 'steady state' economy continuing to apply the economic thesis of the 'thirties, believing us incapable of going faster if the governor is removed until we fall so far behind that consistent application of the wrong theory will eventually prove it to be right. The object of industrial planning which I cherish most is to see that this argument is conducted on even terms.

14

Meeting social responsibilities: the cost and the implications

R. A. LONG

In a highly industrialised and urbanised country such as Britain, the planning of transport facilities involves the problem of preserving the environment and the quality of life. In this article Mr Long explains how British Rail has attempted to reconcile its financial priorities with wider 'social' objectives. He argues that the role of the railways has become that of environmental conservator, while road and air transport 'devour and pollute land and airspace with increasing social impact'. He discusses the role of cost-benefit studies, their possibilities, and present limitations. He suggests that hitherto project planning has emphasised technological engineering at the expense of social engineering and argues that 'the balance must be redressed within this decade'.

The management of change is ever more difficult than the design of change. This stems from a tendency to engineer the future mainly in technological and economic terms, leaving the social engineering as a secondary, or even a separate, objective. As a result, the social 'bugs' of change linger long after the other 'bugs' have gone.

No large organisation in this day can make a simple choice between economic and social objectives. The position is well summed up in a recent speech by Henry Ford II. Having first noted that 'hardly anyone disputes the proposition that service to society requires at least a short-run sacrifice of business profit', Ford proceeds:

> As long as public expectations with respect to the social responsibilities of business were relatively narrow and modest, business could pass muster by sacrificing only a little of its short-run earnings. Now that public expectations are exploding in all directions we can no longer regard profit and service to society as separate and competing goals, even in the short-run. The company that sacrifices more and more short-run profit to keep up with constantly rising public expectations will soon find itself with no long-run to worry about. On the other hand, the company that seeks to conserve its profit by minimising its response to changing expectations will soon find itself in conflict with all the publics on which its profits depend.

The decisions to be made in these circumstances are for later discussion, but the points to emphasise here are, first, that no organisation can today make a choice to go specifically to one or other of the two extreme objectives, and secondly, that this position holds equally for all types of organisation – whether nationalised or not. Indeed, in the recent past many privately controlled organisations have been at great pains to indicate that they are inspired by social considerations and a number of nationalised industries have emphasised their commercial motivation.

Management's responsibility

In practice, we are all involved in the same issues and it must be accepted that the management of any industrial undertaking – whether it is owned by the state or by shareholders – has four broad types of responsibility: to its owners; to its employees; to its consumers; and finally to those whose health, peace and happiness are affected by the activities of the undertaking, and by the efficiency and sense of responsibility with which it conducts these activities. This last group is the emerging fourth estate of industrial life. To a large extent, there is overlapping between these four categories. Employees are often direct consumers of the goods or services they produce; in the case of a state-owned undertaking they are also in the owner category; and above all they are also members of the local community who are affected in a non-material way by the activities of the undertaking. For example a worker in a chemical plant may also be a keen angler whose weekend enjoyment is spoiled by the discharge of waste products from that same plant into the local river, killing off the fish.

Environment and the quality of life

This inevitably leads to the subject of the quality of life – the environment in which we live – since this is of the utmost concern to the community. All thinking people are becoming acutely aware of the deplorable effects which the activities of certain undertakings, and the use, collectively or individually, of certain means of transport, can have on the environment in which we and our families live our lives – effects on the air we breathe, on the safety of our children, on the enjoyment of our rivers, beaches and countryside and perhaps most of all on the peace and quiet of our homes. I suggest that industry must address itself to minimising these effects, and to improving the environment and thus the overall quality of life in this ever more crowded island. Managements of large undertakings, and managers as leading citizens, must seek to assess the cost of meeting their responsibilities in this sphere.

This whole question of the environment, of reconciling technological progress with the quality of life, has become one of the current explosive issues in the USA. This concern is exemplified in the fortieth anniversary issue of the magazine *Fortune*, which is a special issue on the environment. The subtitle of the lead article includes the sentence: 'Unless we invent means of dealing with technology's side-effects, they will bury us.' And the editorial includes the following:

Within the last year an immense transformation has occurred in public concern about the environment. One scientist describes the shift with a metaphor drawn from geology: 'First, islands of anxiety about specific environmental ills – like the redwoods, the rivers, or the slums – rose from a sea of apathy; when they rose further, land appeared between them; we became aware that all those separate environmental issues were connected, all part of a single challenge to our civilisation.' Now that environmental anxieties have coalesced, they will be a permanent part of the American awareness, part of the set of beliefs, values, and goals within which US business operates.

The new awareness brings a danger of its own, stepping up the urgency of our situation. Unless we demonstrate, quite soon, that we can improve our environmental record, US society will become paralysed with shame and self-doubt.

Already we hear voices – and not merely from noisy rebels among the young – exploiting our environmental anxieties as part of an indictment against the basic characteristics and trends of Western civilisation.

We know that isolated societies with very low levels of technology do not greatly damage their natural environments. We also know that our high-technology society is handling our environment in a way that will be lethal for us. What we don't know – and had better make haste to test – is whether a high-technology society can achieve a safe, durable, and improving relationship with its environment. This – and not a return to the pre-technological womb – is the only possibility worth investigating. During the next fifty years we will replace, anyway, nearly all of our manmade environment. Will it cost more – or less – to do it right? Will it cost more – or less – to deal carefully with nature? The cost of a decent environment might be enormous by conventional accounting standards while its true social cost would be zero.

These issues are also of pressing concern in this country. Indeed, because of our special problems of space and congestion, they must loom larger in our minds. We have not the space, coastline and landscape to permit us to be profligate with our resources. We have not the room to rebuild and renew our main cities to fit a 'non-returnable container' society and we have too much capital – financial, historical and aesthetic – tied up in our existing infrastructures.

It will be noticed that I have already ceased to use the phrase 'the community'. I am using the words 'us', and 'we', and 'our'. To too many people the community is 'them', but the problems we are discussing affect all of us. It is too facile to speak of car-owners, for example, as a separate and underprivileged group. We are effectively already all car-owners, and certainly will be by the end of the 1970s when there will be two cars for every one on the road today. The problem is to devise means of using our cars in a sensible manner which does not destroy our environment.

Transportation and the environment

Mention of cars leads me to my main theme, which is the relationship between various modes of transportation and the environment. How is the environment and the quality of life in this crowded island, where space is so precious, affected by the ways in which we move ourselves and our goods around? And what has rail transportation to offer society in this connection? I suggest that a modern railway can play a major role in the improvement of the quality of life in this country and that the British Rail contribution in the area of social responsibility is possibly more lively than that of many other undertakings for historical, technological and statutory reasons.

The railway record in the past is certainly not beyond reproach: in the last century steam railways were massive violators of the environment. In these days of bitter opposition to the building of urban motorways in London, it is interesting to read, in Alan Jackson's book *London Termini* (David and Charles Ltd, 1969), how many acres of land were cleared of housing to make way for such termini as St Pancras and Liverpool Street, with little or no compensation to the thousands of tenants who were evicted. Of the building of St Pancras, for instance, we read that 'during the first half of 1866, several thousand houses in Agars Town and Somers Town, almost all of them mean and squalid, were demolished to make way for the railway. Evicted without compensation of any kind, some 10 000 people crowded on to adjacent areas, making new slums and breeding ground for epidemic disease.' A few years later, the Great Eastern Railway paid between 30s and 50s to evicted tenants. But, as Jackson goes on to say 'they spent the few shillings compensation on a bottle or two of gin and the hire of a cart and squeezed themselves in to adjacent streets, increasing the already pitiable overcrowding of the Shoreditch area'. That was how land was cleared for the railways a century ago. Not much thought of 'meeting social responsibilities' in that bustling age when the railway system was being built!

Today the railway role has become that of environmental conservator, mainly because it now seeks to exploit through automation the potential capacity of its guided system within its existing infrastructure. Road and air, on the other hand, now devour and pollute land and air-space with increasing social impact. Also, the Transport Act of 1968, for the first time in our history, made British Rail the servant of national and regional economic planning.

The railway now has a clearer relationship between social and financial aims than existed under the Transport Act of 1962 when the first Beeching plan was bringing financial success to the railway but colliding with the social values of society. Society reacted and the Transport Act of 1968 established not only the area of British Rail's social responsibility but also the terms of financial compensation. The whole of the rail freight and interurban passenger services are now strictly commercial in that they live or die according to the willingness of their users to pay the costs of the services. There is another group of services – notably commuter lines – where the social value is deemed to be greater than the commercial value. In these cases BR is paid the difference between the commercial revenue and the costs: it is, therefore, now compensated for running these services and can no longer claim to be financially out of pocket because it accepts these social responsibilities. This grant is, in reality, not a railway subsidy but a means of encouraging the potential motorist to use rail and so avoid increased costs in urban 'gluepot' areas. Another beneficiary is the motorist with no reasonable alternative to using his car, who finds the congestion level less intolerable. To bring the social responsibility choice nearer to the local community, the decision to make these grants for services within their areas will increasingly be transferred from central government to the recently created Passenger Transport Authorities in four major provincial conurbations.

The conflict between social and financial aims in the field of freight transport suggests less mature development. One example involves the question of where to get the material for forming the causeway to carry the M4 motorway across the low-lying area south of Reading. No less than $3\frac{1}{2}$ million cubic yards of fill is required for this purpose. More than half of this fill could have been brought by rail from South Wales – coal spoil, which the Welsh mining valleys have good reason to see moved. But the scheme has been rejected by the road authorities, which means that all the fill is to consist of clay excavated from nine sites close to the line of the motorway. As John Barr wrote in *New Society*:

> By the end of the year nearly 500 acres near the motorway line could be a wilderness of holes in the ground. . . . The Welsh spoil scheme would have been dearer than digging holes adjacent to the motorway. But in the long term the central government and the taxpayer – not only the Berkshire ratepayer – will be paying in one way or another for the Berkshire diggings. There will be the immediate costs of squalor and disruption, of lost agricultural land; the ultimate costs of reclamation. Perhaps a cost-benefit study would have shown the South Wales scheme to be impracticable; but the study should have been made, and in time. If, say, it appeared that the scheme would cost £1 million, what benefits could have been set against these costs? What value would reclamation in the Welsh valleys have had? Could the government's subsidy to British Rail's Western Region have been cut during the period of the scheme? Would the government have been able to spend less on improving the Berkshire roads if a lot of the fill were moved by rail not road? What value would hundreds of Berkshire acres kept in agricultural production have had?

They are questions which I think all of us would like to see answered. Unless transport and land use problems are considered jointly we shall be without the organisational 'integrators' of our environment.

Before considering other areas of conflict between social aims and financial criteria, it would be more helpful to consider some of the implications of this sort of situation. I referred earlier to the assertion by Henry Ford II that no organisation would choose between the extremes of plain profit-making and attempting to keep up with social expectations. Ford recommended not a middle course but an entirely different approach. Instead of regarding profits as competing with public expectations, such as environmental demands, he argued that business should look upon the rising public standards as opportunities for profit. 'We have to ask ourselves what do people want that they didn't want before, and how can we get a competitive edge by giving them more of what they really want?'

In the transportation field, what they clearly want is a fast, clean, comfortable and reliable service, and what they appear not to want – up with which they will not put – are noise, congestion and pollution. Pollution, incidentally, is not confined to the state of the air we breathe; it applied equally to visual pollution and intrusion. As Tom Davies wrote in the *Sunday Times* when referring to the £3400m plan to improve England's roads: 'The luckier ones will have their houses knocked down: they will be compensated. But the motorway fringe dwellers who will find the value of their property dropping, their gardens sprayed with smoke and their sunshine exchanged for darkness will be unable to claim a penny.'

I would not deny the need to spend money on new roads – plus compensation to the fringe dwellers – but it is clear that the current generation of Inter-City rail passenger services is increasingly supplying these neeeds and avoiding the quality disbenefits about which we are becoming increasingly concerned whether in land use or air space intrusion. The great advantage to us as the community is that in this case we can both have our cake and eat it – in the sense that the Inter-City rail services are fully viable and get no external financial support. It is in everyone's interest that this happy situation should be preserved. I must say bluntly that the suggestion heard in the more enthusiastic aeronautical circles that there would be great advantages to be derived from even more vigorous financial support for ailing domestic air services flying over our heads and paralleling surface routes is not one which commends itself to me as either attractive or socially responsible. Also, I find the recent proposals to spend up to £3400m on interurban roads somewhat lacking in relevance to problems of land use. Indeed, for two White Papers to appear within one week, one recommending the pouring of still more acres of concrete and one advocating the protection of the environment, gives a particular piquancy to our discussions.

The sensible way out of this problem is I think admirably put in a *Report on Transportation Requirements* prepared for the New England Regional Commission in July 1968. The summary of the report concludes as follows:

One of the findings of this report is that an ultra-high-speed rail service between Boston and New York is the most promising method of alleviating a pressing transportation problem of the region. The problem is intermodal, arising from the already serious and increasing congestion of highways and airways. The solution involves making use of the outstanding characteristic of rail transportation, namely high capacity. If rail speed can be sufficiently raised to permit a schedule attractive to air passengers, and fares kept low enough to attract highway passengers, the problem will be materially alleviated. Congestion in the other modes will be lessened, leaving them free to develop their capacities in meeting other transport problems. The airways are needed for further development of longer-distance markets, where their speed capabilities are much more effective. The highways are needed for the development of shorter and more dispersed markets, where the automobile's flexibility is most effective.

Unless the rail solution can be developed, expenditures measured in billions of dollars must be faced for increasing airway and highway capacity. Even beyond such cost, a serious question exists as to the social acceptance of the voracious use of land and other such destructive side-effects as noise and air pollution which might well result. For these reasons it is imperative that a careful examination of the possibilities of immediate establishment of improved rail service be undertaken.

An even more serious criticism which can be levelled at some of the 'concrete and jet' solutions to interurban transportation problems is that even after the expenditure of hundreds of millions of pounds the means will, after a few years, have been found to be self-defeating. We shall then have met the enormous cost, both financial and environmental, and find ourselves back in the same position.

Urban transportation problems

The interurban problems of the 1970s are complex and serious, but they pale into insignificance as compared with the problems of the conurbations – and this is of desperate importance because the conurbations are where more of us are going to live. Here again the concrete and high-technology enthusiasts are busy. Not that I have anything against either concrete or high technology: it is the misplaced enthusiasm which is inimical to social responsibility.

The essence of one of the most important problems in this field – the journey to work in Central London – is that some one and a quarter million workers move into Central London each morning and move out again each evening. No more than 10 per cent of these can physically be accommodated in private transport and – here is the rub – no expenditure on concrete, computer controlled traffic systems, moving pavements, or electric city-cars will enable this 10 per cent to be materially increased unless we move towards a Los Angeles solution which would effectively move the outskirts of London close to Hadrian's Wall. Our problem therefore is essentially how to convey the 90 per cent in civilised conditions which will meet the demands for quality of the seventies. The problem cannot be solved by drastically reducing the demand. If the work of Central London is materially reduced, London as such will die and the whole country will suffer.

These civilised conditions postulated for public transport cannot be secured on the cheap. Nor can the environmental disbenefits of the alternatives be avoided without some sacrifice. But the cost, while large, is not insupportable. Some £350m investment, for example, would suffice over the years to 1981 to provide a complete railway commuter system into London which would transform rail services throughout the London and South-East area. A formidable sum – but only a fraction of what some enthusiasts would like to spend on roads alone in the area. Clearly, much will have to be spent on roads in the area in the years ahead, but a judicious rearrangement of priorities would provide a much better transportation future for the twenty million inhabitants of the area.

The problems of London and the South-East are there now for all to see. What is not yet seen by everyone is that each of the other major conurbations in the country is inevitably going the same way, and we must take account of this in planning strategies for the 'seventies. The Buchanan Report on *Traffic in Towns* (1963) showed this with brutal clarity. I quote from the final paragraph of the Report of the Steering Group, chaired by Sir Geoffrey Crowther. They noted that a vigorous programme of urban road building would be required in any case, but that they could not 'hold out any hope that this by itself will go very far towards solving the problem'. They finished the Report by saying:

> We are nourishing at immense cost a monster of great potential destructiveness. And yet we love him dearly. Regarded in its collective aspect as 'the traffic problem' the motor car is clearly a menace which can spoil our civilisation. But translated into terms of the particular vehicle that stands in our garage (or more often nowadays, is parked outside our door, or someone else's door), we regard it as one of our most treasured possessions or dearest ambitions, an immense convenience, an expander of the dimensions of life, an instrument of emancipation, a symbol of the modern age. To refuse to accept the challenge it presents would be an act of defeatism. The task it sets us is no greater, and perhaps less, than was presented to the rural England of two centuries ago by the Industrial Revolution followed by the railway. If we are to meet our challenge with a greater balance of gain over loss than our great-grandfathers met theirs, we must meet it without confusion over purpose, without timidity over means, and above all without delay.

There is a heartening, if gradual, change of thought. Already in Glasgow and Merseyside it is beginning to be accepted that the future of mass urban transportation must lie with a full development of rail services, although we sometimes find them under the newer phrases of 'rapid-transit' or 'duo-rail'. On Merseyside, indeed, we are moving already towards new line construction with the active help and encouragement of the local authorities. In other countries more than sixty cities are currently developing new rail systems.

Costs and benefits

If we cannot afford to be profligate in meeting our social aspirations, we have to be as careful in devising cost-effectiveness in the achievement of social aims as we are in planning for profit. This means that we have to measure as accurately as possible the social benefits and disbenefits of alternative strategies and choose accordingly. I must add that 'the wreckers' are already at work, waving beckoning lights in murky scenes, so that we could well come on to the rocks. I mention only two distinct dangers – first, of overestimating benefits of a doubtful kind, and second, of understating disbenefits.

The overestimation of benefits leads to what has been called the pursuit of 'fairy gold' and in this category I put the estimates on value-of-time savings which have been used in a number of recent assessments. Time certainly has a value, but it is very doubtful whether an aggregation of a large number of minute time-savings of sometimes as little as thirty seconds each has any real meaning at all. If it is applied at rates approaching those quoted as the value per hour of air-business time to the Roskill Commission it is leaving the world of reality altogether.

On the other hand, there is a distinct danger that some of the disadvantages with which the community is so greatly concerned may be understated. Here the problem is that where a money value has to be put on something that is not normally bought and sold (and a money valuation has to be made because this is the only way the 'sums' can be done), the nearest equivalent valuation may be taken whether this is appropriate or not. Thus in putting a value on noise disturbance, the tendency has been to try to assess the fall in the value of property subject to profound noise change. This may or may not be an adequate method where noise affects are localised, but it is certainly not applicable to a situation of serious and pervasive noise intrusion where the luckless householder has nowhere to run. The impact of the supersonic jet and the VTOL aircraft could come into this category. The valuation of Norman churches on the basis of fire insurance premiums, and the contents of the 'church expenses' boxes in St Paul's as a measure of its worth may be a ready, but an unconscionably rough basis of measuring the cost of losing them. Indeed on this basis (as has been said elsewhere), if a way up the steps could be found, it might be possible to show a total social benefit from turning our national monuments into car parks.

Conclusions

I have been able to deal in a summary manner with only a few of the considerations involved in this very wide field. I finish by drawing together some of the threads:

1 Any enterprise following a course which conflicts with the values of society

will not in the long term be tolerated, however commercially successful it may be in the shorter term.

2 The cause of conflict stems partly from the greater emphasis placed on technological engineering than on social engineering. The balance must be redressed within this decade.

3 We must get right away from the position in which environment is regarded as something 'they' pay for, something 'they' give up and concentrate on better methods by which 'we' can evaluate a corporate problem. This will (a) require improved disciplines in estimating costs and benefits; (b) involve organisational controls which must be effective and flexible but not so autocratic as to be unacceptable. One promising development is the Passenger Transport Authority which is responsible for using road and rail as its servants in building mobility into its area without destroying the other elements of good living. These measures will be expensive and| lengthen decision-making. The long-term planner will be under even greater pressure.

4 The process of participatory democracy will reach new levels. We may have to face an explosion of commissions, hearings and inquiries. There is a real danger that our environment will be talked away from us, rather than just stolen. The end result could be just as disastrous.

5 There will be new slants on technological advance. It may be necessary to divert research and development effort into areas where the social pay-off is particularly high. For example, I suggest that a research priority should be to exploit the potential of existing road and rail transport infrastructures in this country rather than to other developments, surface or air, which offer technological promise but seriously threaten the environment.

6 The cost of meeting our social responsibilities may be heavy: the penalties of not meeting them will be heavier. In practice much can probably be achieved by a judicious amendment of priorities at the margin.

7 No one will be impressed by being told that his environment is now worsening at only 5 per cent per annum, when it might have been 10 per cent. We require a positive improvement.

8 Ignorance, misdirected enthusiasm, inadequate social benefit evaluation and apathy are far more serious dangers than malice. The man who once carved a railway through workers' houses or now plans to put an airport at the bottom of our garden, or a motorway through the spires of Oxford, or chemical effluent in our rivers is not a Philistine. He thinks he is dragging us technologically into the next century. It is up to us to decide the type of next century we want. The responsibility for the brief is ours and adds a new dimension to the task of planning in the 'seventies.

15

Business and consumerism

GEORGE A. STEINER

In an age of increasing industrial concentration the protection of the ordinary consumer from the abuses of monopoly power is likely to become more and more important as a priority for public policy. The author reviews American experience in the field of consumer protection and discusses a number of related problems of strategic importance. Is the consumer a mere pawn in the hands of sophisticated advertising executives? How far should the government go in discouraging social habits it believes to be undesirable? The author concludes with a statement of principles which business may follow in order to respond more effectively to the demands of 'consumerism'.

In 1962 President Kennedy sent a special message to the Congress on the protection of consumer interests. This was the first message of its kind and marked the beginning of a wave of 'consumerism' which has since picked up momentum.

The concern of many businessmen for the consumer has not been one of the more glorious chapters in business history. Until recent years the consumer has been patient with only intermittent efforts to protect his interests. Today, however, consumers, and spokesmen for them, are increasingly aggressive in demanding better treatment.

It is the purpose of this article to examine the underlying reasons for the growth of consumerism; to review briefly past history of consumer protections; and then to discuss some major issues of today, such as the independence of the consumer, the morality of product obsolescence, automobile safety, manufacturer liability for defective products, cigarette advertising, and the response which businessmen should make to consumerism.

Consumerism

President Nixon began his special message to the Congress about consumer rights (on 30 October 1969) with these words: 'Consumerism – Upton Sinclair and Rachel Carson would be glad to know – is a healthy development that is here to stay.' He was referring to a broad and increasingly aggressive movement, supported by government and the population in general, to protect consumers from a wide range of dangers connected with the products and services they buy and use. The protection sought is not only against outright fraud and physical harm but against more subtle injuries from such practices as deceptive advertising and fine print in warranties which void seller guarantees.

The beginning of what today we call consumerism is not clear, but may be marked in President Kennedy's special message to the Congress on 15 March 1962. Momentum picked up a little with a few new pieces of legislation in 1964 and 1965. An important boost was given to the movement by the publicity associated with the publication in 1965 of Ralph Nader's book *Unsafe at Any Speed*. It probably was not so much the book itself that spurred the movement at this time, but the fact that a General Motors official began an investigation of the personal life of Ralph Nader which was interpreted by the press as being a search for something to discredit Nader and his report. Publicity given to this investigation led to a public apology by the President of General Motors before a Senate Committee which at the time was investigating automobile safety.

The American public, which for so long had been patient about product and service abuses, began to express itself in strident ways. Politicians heard: a flood of bills inundated the Congress and many were passed in the next three years. The movement for protection is still strong, as evidenced by the fact that during the first seven months of the 91st Congress, which began in January 1969, there were well over 100 bills introduced to protect consumers, and many of these were passed.

One characteristic of today's consumer revolt – and that probably is not too harsh a term for what is happening – is a rising expectation for better product performance, more product safety and better information to permit consumers to make more informed choices. The threshold of acceptable performance is widening. Consumers are demanding and legislation is reflecting a new consumers' bill of rights. President Kennedy, in his special message noted above, spoke of certain rights which all consumers had. President Nixon picked up these rights and said:

> Consumerism in the America of the 1970s means that we have adopted the concept of 'buyer's rights'.
> I believe that the buyer in America today has the right to make an intelligent choice among products and services.
> The buyer has the right to accurate information on which to make his free choice.
> The buyer has the right to register his dissatisfaction, and have his complaint heard and weighed, when his interests are badly served.
> This 'Buyer's Bill of Rights' will help provide greater personal freedom for individuals as well as better business for everyone engaged in trade.

Consumerism does not mean that *caveat emptor* – let the buyer beware – is replaced by *caveat venditor* – let the seller beware. It does mean, however, that protecting the consumer is politically acceptable and the government increasingly will survey consumer demands for better treatment and respond to them with new guidelines for and regulations over business.

What is behind consumerism?

It seemed paradoxical that the American consumer is at one and the same time the envy of the world for the quality and abundance of the products and services he consumes, and at the same time is dissatisfied with the products and services he consumes. Why the paradox?

General discontent

This is the age of discontent, of scepticism and challenge to established authority. Begun by the young, these attitudes have extended into other areas of American life, including consumer reactions. Today's consumers are much better educated than those of the past and now challenge older practices which they once bore in silence. They question the authority of the uncontrolled market place. This is an age, too, of vocal expression of discontent; and consumers, fed up with bad treatment at the hands of manufacturers, advertisers, merchants and repairmen, are voicing their complaints.

Are the complaints justified? Every consumer would say 'yes', because every consumer has been frustrated with a variety of consumption problems. Furthermore, consumers are bombarded almost daily in the press with illustrations of product and service deficiencies, recalls and deceptions. Businessmen claim that dissatisfied consumers represent only a small fraction of the total. This may be so, but the rising tide of consumer complaints is based upon solid, and often painful, causes. I do not want to dwell at length on sources of consumer complaints, but some illustrations are in order.

Unsafe, impure and defective products

Late in 1968 the National Highway Safety Bureau reported that one out of every eleven tyres it tested failed to meet federal safety standards. This report was widely publicised and resulted in recall campaigns by tyre manufacturers. Consumers were not impressed by complaints of the manufacturers that the tests were extreme and that rarely is an automobile accident caused by a defective new tyre. The issue of automobile safety is a major one today, and will be treated in some detail later in this article. Less spectacular but highly lethal defects are found in other products, such as the imported eyeglass frames made of a highly inflammable cellulose nitrate; the infant's rattle that easily comes apart to expose three-inch spikes; toys with electrical, mechanical or excessive heat hazards; and TV sets with radiation danger. Consumers will not soon forget the consequences of thalidomide, and wonder how many of today's drugs contain dangerous side-effects.

Deceptive promotion

In 1969 the National Academy of Sciences' National Research Council reviewed almost 4000 drug preparations for the Food and Drug Administration (FDA), and concluded that most were effective in the claims made for their use. However, 7 per cent, or close to 300, were not. Included in this list were mouthwashes, the sales of which total over $200 million each year, which when used as a part of a daily hygiene regimen were found to have no therapeutic advantage as a germ-killer over salt water, or even water. In another area are deceptions connected with packaging of products. One study asked housewives to find the best buy in supermarkets among fourteen products, and they made the wrong choice 40 per cent of the time because of problems in comparing products. Packages come in so many different sizes, weights and designations that matching them with price is virtually impossible. Which contains most toothpaste: a 'medium' tube of Colgate, a 'large' container of Crest or a 'giant' tube of Pepsodent? The answer is that they all contain 3·25 ounces of toothpaste!

Who has not received through the mail, or at his local gasoline station, a chance to win riches? The Federal Trade Commission (FTC) has concluded that in some of these games the chance of winning is something like 3·4 in 1000 for a $3·87 prize, and 1 in 1·2 million for those 'plentiful' $1000 prizes. Furthermore, the FTC has discovered that prizes are planted in designated regions, stores and sometimes on specific individuals.[1] Following hearings on games before the Subcommittee on Investigation of Sweepstakes Promotion, House Small Business Committee, Chairman Dingell concluded: '. . . our accumulated data show than an average of only about 10 per cent of the prizes advertised and ostensibly "offered" are ever, in fact, actually awarded – and, even worse, that 90 per cent of the few prizes that are awarded are of the least expensive variety, more being mere trifles worth perhaps a dime or a quarter. Seldom, indeed, are the first, second or third prizes – the large ones that enticed millions of people to enter the "contests" – prizes such as automobiles, vacations in Europe, yachts, colour television consoles, $10 000 in cash, $100 a week for life – ever awarded.'[2]

Illusive guarantees

In an examination of warranties and guarantees on major house appliances, the FTC concluded that 'it is fair to state that in some instances the exclusions, disclaimers and exceptions so diminished the obligations of the manufacturer that it was deceptive to designate the document as a warranty, because the remaining obligations were lacking in substance'.[3] Out of 200 warranties examined, thirty-four had some exceptions, disclaimers and exclusions. Several warranties contained all of these, and in some of them the same exceptions were stated more than once.

Failure to fulfil guarantees

Equally serious are the complaints of consumers that manufacturers and retailers fail to meet their warranties. A housewife who complained about the temperature of her refrigerator was told that 'the controls had not settled down' and she should continue to experiment with them. The cases are many where retailers, distributors and manufacturers use ingenuity and resourcefulness in avoiding fulfilling warranties, forcing costs for repairs on the consumer, and delaying action until the warranty period expires. In commenting on the unhappy lot of the consumer who gets no satisfaction from his local dealer and goes to the manufacturer, the FTC said:

> It is not uncommon for the manufacturer to ignore the appeal altogether and make no response. Some do respond and advise the consumer to contact the dealer about whose conduct she complained. Others recommend contact with a distributor or area service representative. This often leads to what is described as the 'run around' with a considerable exchange of correspondence, broken appointments and nothing being done, with the manufacturer, distributor and retailer, all disclaiming any blame or ability to solve the problem.[4]

Sloppy and excessively priced repair service

A survey was made of TV repair service in New York City. In twenty homes a tube was made inoperative by opening the filament, which is equivalent to a tube burning out. Of the twenty servicemen called to repair the sets, seventeen were reported to be dishonest or incompetent. Excessive costs ranged from $4 to $30 on what should have been a total cost of $8.93, including the charge for service and labour.[5] Independent repair services have deteriorated to such an extent that manufacturers are developing their own training programmes for mechanics.

No forum for complaint

A major problem of consumers is that when they are dissatisfied they literally have no place to complain. If the problem is one of clear fraud, redress might be made through Better Business Bureaux or the courts. For obvious reasons, however, the purchaser of an inoperable or defective home appliance is not likely to seek redress in a court of law for failure of the retailer, distributor or manufacturer to conform to the terms of a warranty.

Journalistic exposés

The flames of consumer discontent have been both lit and fanned by a number of writers whose books have become best sellers. Among the leaders are, in order of their appearance, Vance Packard's The Hidden Persuaders (1957) and The Waste Makers (1960). In the first volume Packard attacked the use of motivation research and what he called 'manipulation' of consumers by advertising. In the second volume he attacked planned obsolescence. In 1962 Rachel Carson published her *Silent Spring*, a devastating account of how our products are polluting our environment. Jessica Mitford's best-selling criticism of the undertaking industry was published in 1963 under the title *The American Way of Death*. Ralph Nader's *Unsafe at Any Speed* came in 1965 and John Galbraith's *The New Industrial State*, which among other things popularised the large company as a monster that held the consumer in its grip, appeared in 1967. There were many more, but these books all were highly critical of business, all were best sellers, and all gave consumers new information about products.

Other problems

This does not exhaust the list of problem areas for consumers. There is the area of hidden charges in the form of service costs. The complexity of new products is so great that manufacturers find it difficult to communicate to consumers adequate information about how to use a product. As President Kennedy observed in his special message to the Congress, noted above: 'The housewife is called upon to be an amateur electrician, mechanic, chemist, toxicologist, dietician and mathematician – but she is rarely furnished the information she needs to perform these tasks proficiently.' Manuals purporting to describe how products can be put together and used efficiently are sometimes models of incomprehensible English. Marketing is increasingly impersonal. Despite the Truth-in-Lending Act of 1968, many consumers still do not know just how much they pay for credit. Consumers wonder how many businessmen seek to sharpen their skills to obfuscate consumer information once a product and service are sold. All these problems are illustrative, for the list is far longer.

The business response

The response of businessmen in the past to the rising crescendo of consumer complaints has sometimes been rather unenlightened. Particular business interests have fought against just about every new piece of legislation designed to protect consumers. When they have lost the battle, they have sought to escape the regulations by weakening the bite of regulatory agencies, either by putting pressure on Congress to pass less rigorous laws, or by denying funds to enforce them. The business attitude generally is that 'present laws are adequate', and that the current furore is completely unjustified, since the number of genuine complaints is very few. In commenting on this issue, *Business Week* observed that this type of business response is fairly predictable. An automatic response is to deny everything; or to blame wrongdoing on the small, marginal company; or to discredit the critics; or to hire a public relations man to change public opinion; or work to make existing legislation less effective. But many businessmen may actually do something constructive.[6]

Is the consumer sovereign or captive?

Traditional economic theory presupposed 'consumer sovereignty' in the market place. In this view, the initiative for and choice of what is produced lie with the consumer. Goods and services are produced in response to his wants. It is the 'vote' of the consumer in the market place which spells financial success or loss for producers. In this theory, the consumer is considered to be well informed about costs, quality and other characteristics of products and services and is in a position to make a choice in conformity with his own self-interests. Here is the 'economic man' who, when duped by one producer or retailer, will take his business elsewhere and will, therefore, by such actions force producers and distributors to accede to the interests of consumers. Under such circumstances, complaints are few, and those producers who understand consumers and satisfy consumer wishes will be the most successful in making profits.

This **is** completely the reverse of the facts, says Galbraith. To Galbraith, the consumer is the pawn of business. The mature corporation is in a position to manage what the consumer buys at prices controlled by the corporation: 'The producing firm reaches forward to control its markets and on beyond to manage the market behaviour and shape the social attitudes of those, ostensibly, that it serves.'[7] This is the view that company managements lay plans to trap the consumer into doing what the company wants through sophisticated advertising, packaging, product design and other marketing and merchandising techniques. The consumer has so many different alternatives that he has trouble in making a choice and the right sort of appeal will determine his choice. That which survives on the market may not necessarily be the best product but the one that is most effectively 'sold'. Far from being a sovereign, the consumer is a puppet, a captive of business.

Which of these views is correct? Neither is, but both have a certain degree of validity. There is no question at all that advertising does have an important influence on the consumer, but there is reason to believe that it is not as great as asserted by Galbraith. In a thorough study of the subject, Bauer and Greyser conclude that 'the consumer is no helpless passive target of communication'.[8] No amount of company planning was able to save the Corvair automobile following adverse publicity about its safety. Much depends upon the consumer, the product, the time of purchase, information and other circumstances about his purchase to determine whether he is in control or is being controlled. It is probably fair to say, however, that the growing complexity of products, the paucity of information about them and uncertainties in the minds of consumers about many characteristics of products, make consumers more amenable to the blandishments and hoopla of advertising.

Product obsolescence

Critics claim that manufacturers' self-interests lead them to engage in what is called 'product obsolescence'. This can mean a deliberate under-engineering of a product to produce a shorter life-span to force consumers to make premature replacement purchases. It can also mean styling changes, or advertising, which persuade consumers to replace products before their usefulness is ended. Automobiles, household appliances, light bulbs and toys are often cited as products with built-in obsolescence. Is a producer acting responsibly when he makes a product that lasts for five years when it could be made to serve much longer?

Critics see built-in obsolescence as a waste. They say that expenditures for replacements could be used for other products, and purposely shortening the life of a product is a loss to consumers and society. On the other hand, the defenders of 'under-engineering' point out that the fickle consumer will turn away from the higher-priced product which lasts longer in favour of the lower-priced product with a shorter life. The consumer will also react favourably to styling because he wants change and newness. Critics assert that such consumer reactions are induced by manufacturers, but the defenders of product obsolescence say that this is the way consumers are and that manufacturers are doing no more than meeting consumer interests.

Product obsolescence results, partly, from the effort of manufacturers to induce mass consumption in order for them and society to reap the benefits of mass production. With mass production, producers can cut costs per unit, which in turn will increase demand for products having elastic demands. Under such circumstances there are opportunities for profits. All this is quite legitimate and morally responsible in our society.

Product obsolescence involves a question of trade-off. Electric light bulbs, for instance, can be made to last longer, and long-life bulbs are on the market and cost only a little more than ordinary bulbs. The informed purchaser knows, however, that the long-life bulbs have thicker filaments and use more power. Light bills are, therefore, higher for the same amount of illumination.

A watch can be made to last almost indefinitely, but would cost far more than the cheap watch which lasts but a few years. For most products there is a trade-off between length of life and such factors as cost, quality, safety and performance. Who is to make such decisions? In modern business they are made by managers and engineers, who must, in turn, base their conclusions on many forces, not the least of which is the response of customers.

It should be pointed out in this connection that consumer attitudes in the United States run more towards newness, innovation and style rather than towards sameness and utilitarianism which not only accepts but demands long life in products. There are those who assert that advertising is the cause of this consumer philosophy. There is some truth to this, but I think there are deeper values in society which lead generally to the preference of the new over the old product.

The social responsibilities of a manager are discharged if the consumer understands the facts about his product in sufficient degree to appraise the value of purchasing an alternative product that promises a longer life. It is a breach of morality, says Walton, with whom I agree, when '(a) obsolescence is deliberately engineered into a product that may be legitimately presumed by the ordinary reasonable man to have a longer period of service, and (b) this presupposition is deliberately exploited by the vendor'.[9]

Cigarette advertising

A major current issue between business and consumers concerns cigarette advertising. This issue stems from research findings that cigarettes are injurious to smokers' health and the decision of the federal government to take action to control advertising of cigarettes. A number of issues are bound up in cigarette advertising and will now be examined.

The surgeon general's report and industry response

First of all, it is important to begin with the Surgeon General's now famous report on cigarette smoking which was made public on 11 January 1964.[10] This was followed by other studies, all of which leave no doubt about the hazards to health and longevity which cigarette smoking entails. The tobacco industry founded a Tobacco Institute to study the effects of smoking on people and has persisted in its assertions that evidence linking smoking and disease is largely a statistical association which does not prove a causal relationship. The Institute says that smokers are different types of people from others and that they may be more susceptible to disease than others because of these different characteristics. Anyway, they say, no one knows the mechanisms by which smoking causes cancer.[11]

Both the statistical and clinical evidence is overwhelming that cigarette smoking is injurious to health and shortens life expectancy. The following are a few conclusions of extensive studies. A four-year study of tens of thousands of smokers and non-smokers, matched in many characteristics except that some smoked and some did not, resulted in this conclusion: 'Lung cancer death rates were eleven times as high among current cigarette smokers as among those who never smoked regularly and eighteen times as high among very heavy smokers as among men who never smoked regularly.'[12] Another study concluded that smoking even as few as one to nine cigarettes a day shortens life expectancy. 'Every regular cigarette smoker is injured, though not in the same degree. . . . Cigarette smoking is not a gamble; all regular cigarette smokers studied at autopsy show the effects.'[13] The Surgeon General has repeated many times his conviction that 'I think we have established cause and effect in lung cancer. I don't think there is any question about it.'[14]

Regulatory action

In quick response to the Surgeon General's Report, the FTC on 22 June 1964, issued a Trade Regulation Rule providing that all cigarette labelling and advertising must carry a health warning statement. The industry, together with influential senators and congressmen, was able to get enactment of the Federal Cigarette Labelling and Advertising Act of 1964 which provided that as of 1 January 1966 all cigarette packages and cartons sold in the US and its possessions must bear the following statement: 'Caution: Cigarette Smoking May Be Hazardous to Your Health.' This was a much more moderate warning than the FTC wanted to place on cigarette packages. Of considerable importance to the industry also was the fact that the Act prohibited until 1 July 1969 any requirement that cigarette advertising include a similar statement, or the imposition of any health labelling requirement other than that in the bill, by any governmental agency. These provisions, of course, stopped further action by the FTC. But the FTC moved in other directions.

On 2 June 1967, the FTC held that the 'fairness doctrine' applied to cigarette advertising on broadcast media. This was done, according to the FTC, 'to alleviate constant exposure to the one-sided blandishments of cigarette commercials and the health risks attendant thereto to the American public'.[15] Under this ruling, stations which have commercials that promote the use of cigarettes 'as being attractive or enjoyable' are required to provide 'a significant amount of time to the other side of this controversial issue'.

In its 1969 *Report to the Congress Pursuant to the Federal Cigarette Labelling and Advertising Act* (p. 35), a majority of the FTC commissioners recommended repeal of the Federal Cigarette Labelling and Advertising Act, and a requirement that cigarette packages and advertising carry the following warning: 'Cigarette Smoking Is Dangerous to Health and May Cause Death From Cancer, Coronary Heart Disease, Chronic Bronchitis, Pulmonary Emphysema and Other Diseases.' It recommended that packaging and advertising carry a statement of tar and nicotine content of cigarettes. It recommended that cigarette advertising be banned entirely on television and radio and that these broadcasters spend a significant part of their broadcast time, as a matter of social responsibility, 'for programmes and announcements on health hazards of cigarette smoking'. Finally, it recommended that additional funds be spent by the government to educate people about the hazards of cigarette smoking and to undertake research to find a cigarette not hazardous to health.

Congress allowed the provision of the Labelling Act of 1964 to lapse on 1 July 1969, but the FTC did not step into the act because of pending legislation in Congress on this subject. In March 1970 Congress passed legislation which strengthened the Labelling Act by banning all radio and television advertising after 1 January 1971. Six months following the President's signing the bill a stronger warning must be placed on cigarette packages as follows: 'Warning: The Surgeon General says cigarette smoking is dangerous to your health.'

Voluntary industry action

When Congress passed the Cigarette Labelling Act it was contemplated that the tobacco industry would impose voluntary limitations on cigarette advertising, and this, together with an educational programme warning of the hazards of smoking, would alert the public to the dangers. The cigarette producers established the Cigarette Advertising Code (CAC) and the Television and Radio Codes administered by the National Association of Broadcasters (NAB). All advertising copy must be submitted to the NAB for clearance before public dissemination.

Provisions of the code, which went into effect on 1 January 1965, included a ban in all advertisements of smokers who appeared to be under twenty-five, of known athletes depicted as smokers, of hospital or other related settings associated with health care, of medical claims that could not be substantiated by medical research and of scenes depicting seductive women and/or otherwise establishing a link between smoking and romance.

The code has not been effective, and little has changed in advertising. Indeed, said a former manager of the Code Authority's New York office before a Congressional investigating committee, the NAB strategy 'has been to avoid meaningful self-regulatory action as long as the possibility exists that Congress will enact legislation favourable to the broadcasting and tobacco industries'.[16] Smokers are pictured as 'fun' people, the 'in-group', and the adults of this society. Lung-searing smoke is still being sold by fresh country air commercials, health hazards by healthy hero-types and cough inducers by young love lyrics. The FTC sadly concluded that reviews of cigarette advertising themes in 1964, 1967 and 1968 'amply demonstrate the futility in relying upon voluntary regulation of cigarette advertising to achieve any significant changes in the content and meaning of cigarette advertising'.[17]

Why attack advertising and not production?

The fundamental aim of the FTC in its anti-smoking campaign is to protect the public health. Its frontal attack has been to force on cigarette packages a health warning, launch an educational campaign, restrict advertising and force broadcasters to give time to anti-cigarette 'commercials'.

Since the production of cigarettes is legal it cannot now be forbidden and it is unlikely that Congress will pass legislation authorising its stoppage. Not only are powerful business and agricultural interests against ceasing production, but large numbers of consumers would also oppose such a move. Furthermore, with the disastrous results of Prohibition still in memory, Congress is not likely to repeat that kind of blunder. In light of the legality of production it does not make much sense to place a complete ban on broadcast advertising. The government's attack on advertising, however, is based on the assumption that limiting or eliminating broadcast advertising will have a positive effect on reducing smoking and keeping people from starting to smoke.

Whether this will, in fact, occur remains to be seen. In the meantime, restricting the marketing of a legal product is a new precedent in regulation and opens up a Pandora's Box of potential problems. For example, does this precedent mean that advertising of guns, or of dairy products (a source of cholesterol) or alcohol, face similar restrictions?

Have government programmes cut smoking?

The FTC reported that in 1963 cigarette sales were 516 billion. The total declined in 1964 but gradually increased to 1968, when 540 billion were sold. Since the population grew much more rapidly than total cigarette sales there was a net drop in consumption per capita between the periods. The year 1969 saw a drop from 1968 of 2 per cent in total cigarette sales and, of course, a much greater decline in per capita consumption.

Educational campaigns and increased tobacco taxes (which were about 50 per cent in 1969) were partly responsible for these declining numbers. A greater decline was undoubtedly arrested by the build-up in military forces during this period, a factor that increases cigarette smoking. There is no evidence that the downturn in per capita consumption or total sales in 1969 was brought about in any significant way by changes in cigarette advertising.

This does not, of course, foretell what might happen if advertising were seriously regulated or stopped. We do know that a complete or partial ban on cigarette advertisements in effect in a number of European countries has not stopped smoking. In Great Britain, for example, cigarette advertising over TV was banned in 1965, and sales reached new highs. The US is not Great Britain, however, and an attack on the health menace of cigarettes from many fronts might be successful in achieving the basic government objective.

Basis for FTC advertising control

One basis for the FTC's action is the 1938 Wheeler-Lee Amendment to the 1914 Federal Trade Commission Act which 'prohibits unfair and deceptive trade practices, including false and misleading product advertising'. The FTC contends that cigarette advertising is particularly misleading, since it implies that smoking is not harmful. Indeed, as one Commissioner put it, 'the industry spends hundreds of millions of dollars each year on such advertising – and the rate of expenditure is increasing – to obscure the fact that cigarette smoking is a dangerous and harmful habit which each year shortens the lives of hundreds of thousands of people'.[18]

The industry reply is that advertising is neither false nor misleading. The industry does not deny the health hazard in its advertising. It says that the hazard is closely related to smoking habits and consumption of individuals over which it has no control. It is argued that all products have some harmful potential impact depending upon the situation, circumstance and use or misuse by the user.

The rights of state governments have also become involved, since the Labelling

Act provided uniform labelling among the states. There was no complaint, however, largely because those states usually most concerned about their rights are those where tobacco interests are the strongest.

The FTC Commissioners felt that they had the authority to lay a complete ban on broadcast advertising.

Book-burning FTC style?

Professor Milton Friedman, a non-smoker, objects to the FTC anti-cigarette-advertising approach because he believes that it is 'hostile to the maintenance of a free society'. Whenever we ride in an automobile, he says, we risk our lives. We do it, however, because the advantage is worth the risk. Similarly, a smoker may view the pleasure of smoking as justifying the cost to him in reduced length of life. Why not ban Marx's *Das Kapital* or Hitler's *Mein Kampf*? They have caused far more deaths than cigarettes. Or, why not require them to carry a label: 'Reading Is Dangerous to Mental Health and May Cause Death From Revolution and Other Disturbances'? 'In a free society,' he says, 'government has no business to propagandise for some views and to prevent the transmission of others. Freedom of speech includes the freedom to preach for or against communism, for or against fascism – and also for or against smoking.'[19]

This is a ringing call to freedom of speech with which no one can disagree, but it is not the whole of the issue. Does not the government have some responsibility to protect the public health? Constitutional guarantees of freedom of speech are also paralleled with rights of all the people, including protection of public health and welfare. Freedom of speech is not without some limits of responsibility. The government does have a right, authorised by the Wheeler–Lee Amendment, and the people have a right, to be protected from false and misleading advertising. Despite industry claims to the contrary, is cigarette advertising grossly misleading? Does not the government have a duty to assure that advertising is more truthful than untruthful?

There is a real question whether freedom of speech is bridged when powerful industries can saturate the communications media with strong messages favouring their interests when contrary views which favour the consumer rather than the producer interests cannot as forcefully be expressed. May this circumstance not be more harmful to freedom of speech than government regulation of advertising?

Beyond this point, however, there seems to me to be a basic implied obligation of government to act in such circumstances, because there seems to be a growing feeling among consumers that if the government does not react adversely to a product on the market it must be all right. As we have seen previously this is far from the case.

Finally, the implication in Friedman's statement that only the smoker is injured is contrary to the facts. In this day of publicly supported medical care, the better the health of the nation, the lower the cost to all taxpayers. Higher medical costs associated with diseases caused by cigarette smoking are charges which everyone must bear. Does not the public generally, therefore, have a right to take action which will in its judgement reduce the total medical costs which all society bears?

Achieving government's objectives

On the assumption that the basic objective of the government to protect the public health is a sound one, how best can this objective be achieved? Aside from current programmes to restrain advertising, and mass education about the hazards of cigarette smoking, taxes on cigarettes may be increased to discourage consumption, they may also be increased to finance research which seeks to make cigarettes with less or no health hazards; standards for tar and nicotine contents of cigarettes might be set; specification of tar and nicotine content may be required on all packages of cigarettes and in advertisements; existing purchase laws for minors can be enforced; and the current educational programme may be so intensified as to constitute a new programme.

How should business respond to consumerism?

'Consumerism' raises a major problem for manufacturers and distributors – the issues being whether they will try to stem the tide or take actions which will lower the demands for government legislation which in turn will increase business options in buyer–seller relations.

Businessmen are increasingly taking collective action to respond favourably to consumer complaints. For instance, the Grocery Manufacturers' Association earned a reputation for brass-knuckle intransigence in combating the Fair Packaging and Labelling Act of 1966, but sought to regain public favour by creating the Consumer Research Institute. This Institute, run by a professor and supported by the manufacturers that sell through supermarkets, several advertising agencies and national food associations, is responsible for studies about consumers' complaints. The US Chamber of Commerce is now trying to get its local affiliates to hold joint meetings with consumers to understand their dissatisfactions.

One corporation at least, RCA, has created a new corporate function – the Office of Consumer Affairs. It has wide-ranging responsibility for the quality and responsibility of RCA's products and services. The head of this office reports directly to the chief executive of the company.

Self-regulation is, of course, a potentially effective business response, but in the past it has not worked too well. One reason is that if members of an industry seriously get together to adopt standards and practices which are enforced, they run a risk of violating the anti-trust laws. If standards are to be meaningful, they must raise the level of practice, and to impose them on marginal producers might be construed as a method of putting them out of business.

A single manufacturer who seeks to improve the performance and quality of his product faces the possibility of having to do this at a cost which will force him to raise his price. If his competitor does not act in a corresponding way, the first manufacturer may be driven to the wall. It is for this reason that some producers welcome government standards, even though they would rather avoid government interference.

No one wants to drive a responsible businessman out of business, except possibly his competitors. So what can he do? The US Chamber of Commerce studied this question carefully and concluded that manufacturers, distributors and all businessmen concerned with consumer goods and services could do a number of things, such as the following: seek continuously to upgrade both product quality and marketing methods; simplify and modernise warranties; fulfil warranties and improve the quality and speed the performance of servicing; develop a system to provide consumer feedback on products and servicing under both warranty and non-warranty; improve training programmes with emphasis on product capabilities and limitations to avoid overselling; price on an objective unit basis, such as weight, volume, and standardised ingredients to permit consumer price comparisons; expand information regarding safety, performance, and durability of products and consider such systems as federal certification of voluntary standards as well as notification and recall systems for defective products in order to improve product safety. They could also take forthright positions against fraud and deception, especially that which is practised on low-income groups; help to recast Better Business Bureaux to become consumer ombudsmen; cooperate with local chambers of commerce and Better Business Bureaux in giving better information to customers who request assistance; and intensify efforts to foresee the social consequences of the use of their products in order to anticipate consumer complaints.

References

1. Time, 18 April 1969, pp. 86–7.

2. JOHN D. DINGELL, Subcommittee Hearings on Investigation of Sweepstake Promotions, House Small Business Committee, Press Release, Washington, DC, 12 Nov. 1969.

3. Presidential Task Force on Appliance Warranties, Washington, DC (mimeographed), 1969, p. 47.

4. Ibid., p. 61.

5. E. G. WEISS, 'The corporate deaf ear', Business Horizons, 11, Dec. 1968, pp. 5–15.

6. Business Week, 6 Sept. 1969, p. 96.

7. J. K. GALBRAITH, The New Industrial State, Hamish Hamilton, 1967, p. 212.

8. R. A. BAUER and S. A. GREYSER, Advertising in America: The Consumer View, Division of Research, Graduate School of Business, Harvard University, 1968.

9. CLARENCE W. WALTON, Ethos and the Executive: Value in Managerial Decision Making, Prentice-Hall, 1969, p. 200.

10 US Public Health Service, *Smoking and Health*, Public Health Service Publication, no. 1103, Washington, DC, Jan. 1964.

11. *Time*, 25 April 1969, p. 100.

12. *New York Times*, 10 Dec. 1963.

13. Medical Bulletin on Tobacco, in FTC Report to Congress, 1969, Appendix p. 1.

14. *Time*, 25 April 1969, p. 100.

15. FTC Report to Congress, 1968, p. 2.

16. FTC Report to Congress, 1969, p. 30.

17 Ibid.

18. ELMAN, in FTC Report to Congress, 1968, Appendix.

19. *Newsweek*, 16 June 1969, p. 53.

16

People and pollution: the challenge to planning
COLIN HUTCHINSON

Almost every day articles in the national press describe ways in which the quality of life is being adversely affected by a deteriorating environment. Population growth is the major cause of the increasing range of environmental problems. More people require that we make more use of our natural resources. A larger population also results in increasing intensity of pollution of land, air, and water. This article presents a brief outline of the dilemma which concerns us all, but especially those who are responsible for long-range planning in government, in industry, and in the community. An ecological approach is advocated, paying due attention to the balance of nature.

The issues raised in this article are primarily concerned with our standards and our values as individuals and as a community. The community with which we are concerned is not only the nation, but the world, because many of the problems are not contained within national boundaries. They need to be understood and faced at every level of community life from the individual, through industry and commerce, to local and national government, and finally to the international level. We are learning how to deal more effectively with problems that are concerned with clarifying objectives, improving standards of performance, and examining our values on the scale of the firm or the government department. This knowledge and the required skills of application need to be developed rapidly in order to grapple with the crisis of population growth and pollution. Let us examine the scope of the interrelated issues which concern us all.

We are all aware of the growing population, but we frequently lack appreciation of the speed of growth, and its consequences. Furthermore, the forecasts of world population in 1980 or the year 2000 seem to be regularly underestimated. The figure for 1980 was estimated within the range 2976 to 3636 million in 1951, but between 3850 and 4280 million in 1958.[1] The growth of world population, and current estimates for the future are shown in Fig. 16.1[2] and Table 16.1.[3]

A current estimate of world population in the year 2000 provides a range from 5400 million to 7000 million.[4] The higher figure is based on a projection of existing trends, while the lower figure assumes much greater success with population stabilisation than is currently in evidence.

Fig. 16.1 World population growth

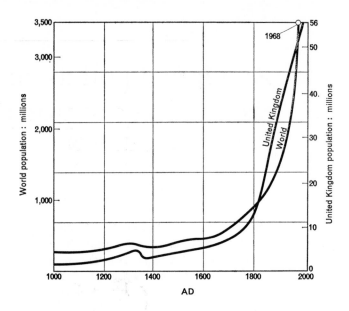

Table 16.1 Growth of world population

MILLIONS	YEAR (APPROX.)	YEARS TAKEN TO INCREASE WORLD POPULATION BY 1000 MILLION
1000	1830	200 000
2000	1930	100
3000	1960	30
4000	1975 (approx.)	15
5000	1985–1990	10–15
6000	1993–2000	8–10
7000	2000–2010	7–10

Clearly population is not growing at an even rate in all countries, but, generally speaking, those countries with high densities now (e.g. Europe) expect less growth than those with current lower densities. Asia is an exception since it experiences rapid growth with an existing high density. This is shown in Table 16.2.

The size of world population is controlled by only two variables – death rate and birth rate.[5] We have learned a great deal about the control of death rate, and this is by far the greater reason for the phenomenal growth that has occurred during the last thirty-five years and is still occurring. Several births were needed many years ago in order to have two or three surviving children. This is no longer the case, and yet our values and prejudices often prevent effective birth

Table. 16.2 Forecast of world population and density

AREA OR REGION	'ooo SQUARE MILES	1960 POPULA-TION (MILLIONS)	DENSITY PER SQ. MILE	1970 POPULA-TION (MILLIONS)	DENSITY PER SQ. MILE	2000 POPULA-TION (MILLIONS)	DENSITY PER SQ. MILE
More developed*	22 776	976	43	1082	48	1441	64
Less developed	34 392	2021	59	2510	73	4688	135
World total	57 168	2997	52	3592	63	6129	107
East Asia ...		794		910		1287	
...	10 891		152		185		318
South Asia ...		865		1107		2171	
Europe	1 903	425	223	454	240	527	277
USSR	8 645	214	25	246	29	353	41
Africa	11 806	273	23	346	29	768	65
North America	7 464	199	27	227	30	354	47
Latin America	8 860	212	24	283	32	638	72
Oceania	3 303	16	5	19	6	32	10
Antarctica	4 410						
World total	57 168	2998	52	3592	63	6130	107

* Europe, USSR, N. America, Japan, Temperate S. America, Australia, New Zealand.
Sources for the above table: E. J. Kormondy, *Concepts of Ecology*, p. 169; L. D. Stamp, *Our Developing World*, p. 38; *Reader's Digest Great World Atlas*, pp. 136 and 144 (mainly for the acreage split between North and South America).

and fertility control methods from being used. In many respects we are fortunate in the UK in that we would go a long way towards stabilising our population if unwanted pregnancies could be avoided. Asia is less fortunate, and more drastic, less popular measures may need to be taken if disaster is to be averted. It has been estimated that only 4 per cent of women in the world have access to the latest and best methods of birth control, and 30–40 million abortions are performed annually in the world.[6] Studies in the UK reveal that approximately half of all pregnancies are unwanted,[7] and for this reason the Family Planning Association has launched a current campaign with the slogan 'Every child a wanted child'. For those whose family is complete, the operation of male vasectomy seems to be the ideal choice, since side-effects are adverse in an insignificant number of cases, and it is entirely reliable as a means of fertility control. It provides health and sex life benefits to the majority of men and their wives.[8]

The consequences of population growth and high-density living are obvious in every major urban area of the world, and in South-East England, to quote one example, an additional 2 500 000 people are expected by 1991.[9] Already the tolerance level for adverse weather, or a minor human failing, is so fine that major disruption of traffic is caused by very small variances from normal standards. This is only one consequence; others will be examined in the following sections.

The horror of the consequences of unchecked population growth are described in detail in Professor Paul Ehrlich's book, *The Population Bomb*.[10] In three scenarios he describes possible international disasters which might arise if population continues to grow at its present rate. The first depicts another world war triggered by catastrophic floods in China leading to massive starvation and breakdown in communications. The second describes how food riots become anti-American riots, and ultimately result in a holocaust. The situation is greatly aggravated by excessive pollution resulting from short-term artificial aids to food production. In the third scenario a more cheerful future is described, but ultimate success is dependent on food rationing in the Western world, and universal birth control practices. It suggests that even this outcome cannot avoid millions dying of starvation before balance and sanity are restored.

Some people believe that the development of technology could enable the world's surplus population to settle on other planets. It would take only fifty years for Mercury, Venus and Mars to be inhabited to the density of that on earth, assuming that some way could be found to sustain life there. Furthermore, those who travelled to these planets would have to practise stringent birth control in order to ensure arrival at their destination. The journey would take many years, and the confined space of their craft would not permit unchecked population growth during the journey. It seems senseless to establish a human environment on another planet when we cannot manage our own on earth. Finally the cost of such a project would exceed our capabilities, for many years.

Educated people throughout the world, but especially in Europe and America, need to face the ecological problem now. It is our problem as a world community, but successful measures in the developed countries could be the starting point. Success depends on a genuine readiness to examine existing beliefs, values and standards, then to understand what needs to be done and to do it thoroughly and quickly. Time is short, action is needed now.

Environment

The basic elements of our environment in which this rapidly growing population exists is made up of land, air and water. Because of the increasing demands of the human population on our environment, we use more artificial aids to improve food production, and urban and industrial developments generate increasing quantities of toxic waste. Our efforts to deal with these problems concentrate so strongly on the immediate short-term benefits that we either remain oblivious to, or deliberately ignore, many dire long-term consequences.

Land

The first and greatest demand on our land surface is for food. In 1967 and 1968, food production rose by 5 per cent each year, but despite this, the Director-General of the FAO warned that the potential of new techniques would only be realised by strong government support, especially in the developing countries.[11] At the present time, the food position in many parts of the world is critical, and only North America has a significant surplus. (Europe has a surplus of dairy produce which it has difficulty in dealing with but this has little relevance to the world food problem.) Although increased food production is being achieved by high-yielding varieties of crops, such as wheat, fertilisers and pesticides are also used, and contribute to the improved production. Chemical substances have played a considerable part in improving short-term yields, but in recent years, there has developed a growing concern for the adverse consequences that often materialise later.

A crop which is fertilised chemically and sprayed with pesticides, both of which are safe to man and animal life, may, nevertheless, be poisonous if the quantity builds up through food chains. A chemical applied as an insecticide or as a fertiliser affects the whole life composition of the soil. The bacteria, grubs and insects play a vital part in the crop-bearing potential of the soil, as well as being eaten by birds and other animals. Birds especially can be deprived of their food supply, or they can eat grubs and insects which contain minute quantities of poison. Some poisons such as DDT exist in toxic form long after their initial use. They build up in food chains with some appalling long-term consequences.[12,13] Three examples illustrate how poison in a food chain builds up:

1 Clear Lake in California, a favoured resort for anglers, was inhabited by prolific numbers of gnats, which were a considerable nuisance. It was decided that the lake should be sprayed with DDD (similar to DDT), and this action proved successful. Five years later a second spraying proved necessary, and after another three years a third spraying led to the virtual extinction of the gnats. After the second and third sprayings, large numbers of western grebes (a swan-like bird) died. Analysis revealed that these birds had considerable quantities of DDD (1600 parts per million) in their fatty tissues. Later the food chain was traced. The DDD had been applied to the water as one part per 50 million, but had been absorbed by the plankton which contained 5 parts per million. Fish live off the plankton and they accumulated 40 to 300 parts per million. Finally the fish were eaten by the grebes and the concentration of 1600 parts per million was a lethal dose to the grebes.[14]

2 Brown pelicans have also been affected by DDT and its relatives, but in this case the poison affected the eggs. Eggs were laid but their shells were so delicate the birds could not sit on them to hatch them. Consequently, there are now no baby brown pelicans from Mexico to Alaska.[15]

3 DDT has been found in the body fat of Americans, and between 1954 and

1956, this amounted to 5·3 to 7·4 parts per million. There is some evidence that this has risen to a consistently high figure.[16]

DDT has been used here as an example but there are other more pernicious insecticides which have been brought under more careful control. Even DDT is the subject of controversy, but Norway, Sweden and Canada have banned its use and it seems likely that the USA and UK may do the same or at least bring it under much stricter control. The Consumers' Association stated in a report in *Which?*[17] that in the UK there was a voluntary Safety Precaution Scheme which was intended to apply to the use of insecticides both for agricultural and domestic purposes. Despite this, out of twenty aerosols tested, only six declared all their active ingredients, and eleven did not declare any ingredients. Four of the brands tested contained DDT.

Pesticides remain active for varying periods after their original use. Some lose their potency because resistances are developed by insects and this leads to the development of new varieties. The long-term consequences of their use cannot always be accurately foretold. The short-term benefits seem so positive and dramatic that the long-term risks often seem insignificant. Is there another way to deal effectively with insect pests?

We are concerned with one example of insect control, and how technology has been used for short-term benefits, sometimes leaving grave long-term problems. Recently, increased attention has been paid to the biological control of insects because the method can be specific, and effective, without leaving the countryside sprayed with poison. The starting point is a detailed understanding of the behaviour and feeding habits of the insect which needs to be controlled. This determines the insects' role in the ecology. Biological control can then be accomplished by several means such as the introduction of another insect, bird or animal which will devour the pest, or by controlling the breeding processes, or by influencing the food chain of which the insect forms a part. In one experiment, a massive quantity of sterile male insects was released in an area where this insect was a severe pest, and within months that breed was wiped out. In another experiment, a small mammal was introduced because of its known preference for eating an undesirable moth.[18] In England, the Soil Association at their Haughley Research Farms are conducting several experiments, one of which is designed to explore the natural control of insect pests.[19]

The concentration here has been on DDT and the biological control of insect pests. This is just one example of the contrast between the chemical and the ecological approach to farming and agriculture. Clearly the chemical approach has given many magnificent short-term benefits, but the long-term costs are only now becoming apparent. The ecological approach has an unrealised potential needing much wider understanding and support if it is to be developed to a scale that has economic and health benefits. The Soil Association in the UK is in the forefront of this movement, but its research projects only began in 1968.[20] More support could speed up some of this research, but time is also required to work through the findings and their significance. The dissemination of what is already known could be accomplished more quickly and effectively with better educational and promotional schemes, but this needs money as well as understanding.

While discussing the land, it is important to look at trees and forests, because of the vital part they play in the life cycle, and in weather and rainfall. Their importance is increased because of the time it takes for hard woods to reach maturity – about one hundred years for trees like the oak. Today in Britain, something like 90 per cent of our timber is imported, and even major timber producers like Finland, import hard wood. But who in today's world of short-term thinking and problem solving is looking at world timber requirements one hundred and one hundred and fifty years ahead, and at current timber usage? It has been estimated that every Sunday's issue of the *New York Times* requires the timber from 150 acres.[21] Is this a wise use of resources? Even if timber can be replaced by artificial products, we will still need trees for their role in nature.

The demands on land use are considerable, and lead to much controversy. The need for a third London Airport is a striking topical example. One estimate of air passenger traffic by the British Airport Authority gave figures of 16 million passengers in 1968, and an estimated 53 million in 1980.[22] If this additional air traffic is to be achieved, we need more airport space, but how can this demand on the land surface be evaluated against other demands? Alternatively, could vertical take-off passenger aircraft enable more air traffic to use the existing airports? How would the noise problem be overcome?

Redistribution of land use has been studied at some length, especially in Great Britain. Table 16.3 gives details of past and possible future land use.[23]

Table 16.3 Possible changes in land use in Great Britain

CATEGORY	PREWAR '000 ACRES	%	POSSIBLE NEW USE '000 ACRES	%
Arable – intensive	1 000·0	2	2 820·0	5
Arable – farm crops	11 069·4	20	15 500·0	27·5
Orchards and fruit	261·3	·5	845·0	1·5
Permanent grasslands	18 897·5	33	14 100·0	25
Rough grazing	18 775·2	33	8 450·0	15
Forest and woodland	3 219·2	6	9 000·0	16
Houses and gardens	1 719·9	3	3 380·0	6
Unproductive	1 399·2	2·5	2 246·7	4
Total	56 341·7	100	56 341·7	100

The biggest changes shown here are converting 6 000 000 acres of permanent grassland to arable farm crops, and a similar acreage to forest and woodland. The figures quoted were prepared when population estimates were far below the population we now have in Great Britain. The loss of agricultural land to other uses in Great Britain is estimated at 83 000 acres per annum.[24]

Our land in the UK is limited. We have about 1 acre per person, compared with $3\frac{1}{4}$ acres in France and $12\frac{1}{2}$ in the USA. The importance of making wise use of this very limited land surface cannot be overemphasised. If the quality of life in Britain is to be preserved and improved, we need to have a population policy and we need to ensure that nothing we do now causes deterioration of the land surface. This requires detailed re-examination of land usage, and careful consideration of long- and short-term issues.

Air

In 1954, the Beaver Committee reported on air pollution in Britain, and estimated the total cost to the nation of all forms of air pollution at £250 000 000 in that year, of which £10 000 000 was attributable to crop damage. In 1956, Parliament passed the Clean Air Act, but despite this, damage from air pollution was estimated as costing £350 000 000 per year in 1967.[25] Included in the causes of air pollution are industrial fumes, open fires in the home, and road traffic, and its effects are not confined to national boundaries. Sweden is affected by polluted air from Britain.[26]

In America, the problems are severe in many places, and the cost of controlling air and water pollution is expected to rise from $10 000 to $300 000 million by the year 2000, and it is also suggested that pollution may become an issue in the 1972 Presidential campaign.[27]

If we take a longer view, there is a growing concern for the effects of industrial fumes and dust suspended in the atmosphere and the possible effects on our climate. There is a difference of opinion here too – some say the filtration effect will reduce the sun's heat, thus increasing the amount of ice on earth, others, that the addition of carbon dioxide to the atmosphere will raise the temperature on earth, thus melting the polar ice-caps and flooding coastal cities.[28]

The effects of air pollution are widespread, and costs of controlling it increase steadily. More emphasis on dealing with it at source is needed, in order to reduce the consequences and the overall costs to the community.

Water

We are all familiar with the Freedom from Hunger Campaign, but warnings are with us now of the impending need for a Freedom from Thirst Campaign.[29] We use the sea, lakes, and rivers, as dumps for disposing of waste products. The most classic example of how this can lead to the destruction of life due to heavy pollution is Lake Erie, an area of 10 000 square miles, or a little less than the area of Wales. Table 16.4 shows the effects of this pollution on commercially and gastronomically important fish landed from this lake.

The cause of this change has been directly attributed to violation of ecological principles, resulting in the creation of conditions in which the fish cannot breed.[30]

Pollution of waterways also occurs in Europe, and one dramatic example

Table 16.4 Fish caught in Lake Erie[30]

	PEAK CATCH (lb)		POUNDS CAUGHT IN 1965
Lake herring	48 800 000	(1918)	1 000
Sanger	6 200 000	(1916)	500
Blue pike	26 800 000	(1936)	500
Whitefish	7 100 000	(1949)	6 000
Walleye	15 400 000	(1956)	783 000

resulting in the death of 40 million fish in the Rhine occurred in June 1969, when 250 miles of the river were poisoned. The cause is believed to have been pesticides, which leaked from drums carried in a barge.[31] In England, too, we have our problems, especially in the Trent. The Tame, which is a tributary of the Trent, receives 15 000 000 gallons of virtually untreated sewage daily from Birmingham and other West Midland boroughs.[32]

Water causes other problems too. In West Pakistan, 23 million acres (about two-thirds the size of England) are artificially watered by canals. This network of manmade waterways with water seeping over the land surface has raised the water table, i.e. the level at which the soil is permanently damp. The effect of this has been to waterlog the land in some places, thus drowning the roots of crops, or in other places to bring salts up through the soil to the land surface, thus poisoning the crops. It has been estimated that it will take twenty years and cost $2000 million to repair the damage.[33]

The building of dams to provide more water is also littered with its problems. The great potential for fish production above the Kariba dam in Rhodesia never materialised because of choking from weeds. Reservoirs in England present more severe problems as the demands on our land surface increase. Additional water supplies often mean that reservoirs have to be built thus flooding the land surface. Invariably, there is controversy over the location of reservoirs and the best use of the land in question. More forward thinking and more extensive research into water-bearing properties of soils and plants might lead to other means for increasing water supplies without flooding the land surface.

Even the sea does not escape massive pollution as was demonstrated by the *Torrey Canyon* disaster.[34] Initially it was easy to see how this oil destroyed bird life, when thousands of dead birds were washed ashore. The pressure to deal with the oil, in order to save the holiday beaches of Cornwall, and to save the birds, resulted in drastic remedies. Massive quantities of detergent were used to destroy the oil – with a good deal of success. Later, when the full effects could be examined, it was estimated that more damage to marine life was caused by the detergents than by the oil. If we pollute water with toxic chemicals, then use other toxic chemicals to neutralise the first, we cause twice the damage, or more, to the wild life, and to plants. There is an overwhelming need to understand and

H

apply methods that preserve the balance of nature, and do not violate ecological principles.

Ecology

The balance of nature is vital to our survival, and our fundamental resources of land, air and water, are limited. We have learned during the past fifty years to accomplish much that seemed impossible at one time. Much effort has been put into some remarkable achievements, but we now need a comparable or even greater effort to enable us to decide what it is relevant to do, both for short- and long-term results. We need to learn to choose not to do things that are within our capability, because of their adverse long-term effects, and we need to learn to allocate more resources to solving long-term problems. If we do not do this now, there may not be a long term.

An analogy can help to bring into sharper focus the dilemma that now confronts us all. The successful aquarium is a minute example of nature in balance. Most amateurs have great difficulty in establishing and maintaining this balance without additional air. Fish die and there seems to be no obvious cause, and more fish are purchased. They too, die in due course and periodically the whole tank goes green and slimy. Common faults of the unskilled amateur are too many fish, overfeeding, too few plants, and pollution from paint, detergents or fly-killers. In the same way as the amateur makes these mistakes in his aquarium, mankind makes similar errors in his world. The analogy cannot be extended too far, but if accepted as a means of illustrating the principles of ecology, it has served its purpose. In the world, we are all amateurs. It is a frightening thought, needing massive research and educational schemes. We not only need to understand the ecology of our environment much better than we do now, but in many cases, we fail to make use of the knowledge we have, because of prejudice, because of our values, and most of all, because of our failure to look beyond today and tomorrow. Those who are concerned with long-range planning in business and in government have a major role to play in bringing about a more mature approach to our problems.

Some groups of people in various organisations have tried to define certain principles regarding the protection of our environment. Definition of idealistic principles has value provided that we regard them as a long-term aim, and that interpretation and application in the short term requires that they be treated as a guide and not as rules. One example of a collected view of fundamental principles is given below.[35]

1 The conservation of the natural resources of the earth is a responsibility of man, both individual and collective.
2 The natural resources of the earth are not to be damaged, wasted or seriously diminished solely for short-term or local benefits.
3 Physical or ecological changes in the environment, which may, because they are of wide geographical extent, or intense, long-lasting or irreversible in their

effects, damage, waste or diminish the natural resources of the earth, should be prevented or controlled by international action.

4 Each state must be responsible for the prevention of damage, waste or diminution of natural resources, caused by activities, constructions or experiments in its territory or under its jurisdiction which:

(a) are designed to control life-span reproduction or growth of animals or plants;

(b) cause pollution of the air, the land, rivers or standing waters, or the sea;

(c) may induce modifications of the weather or climate.

Definition of general principles is a necessary starting point, but we now need the widespread understanding and application that follows from it.

Impact

Too often the action that is taken is fragmentary, stemming from some narrow view of a specific issue. Independent societies and organisations mount a campaign to prevent a road destroying an aspect of our environment, or to shift the intended location of an airport. A government department may be successful with a specific case of pollution, or irresponsible use of drugs. Specialisation on a particular theme is needed, and without it, much more damage may have been caused in the past, but it is no longer sufficient. Too many factors are interdependent, and we need much better integration of effort to achieve the necessary impact. We need, in particular, effective action to stabilise world population.

Some progress is being made – it needs to be understood and encouraged. The British Prime Minister expressed concern for the quality of life at the Labour Party Conference (September 1969), and Mr Crossland now has a brief to investigate our environment with particular regard to pollution. The Chief Medical Officer of the Department of Health and Social Security in his report for 1968[36] devoted one section to environmental health and the need to review the way in which current problems of air and water pollution are dealt with. Speedy review and more effective action are necessary. The results that follow from these intentions will be observed with interest.

The Council of Europe has announced that 1970 is to be European Conservation Year (ECY) and the United Nations plan for 1972 to be International Conservation Year. Each business firm, each government department, and each individual has the opportunity to consider their own attitudes to these issues, and to decide what contribution can be made to achieving improvement. How much time have we got? When will we act?

How can business contribute?

There are already some firms which recognise their responsibility and take action. For example, ICI have spent £28 million in the past ten years to combat pollution from its UK chemical plants, and plans to spend a further £60 million over the next ten years on capital equipment. Running costs will be £11 million annually. Alcan are spending £60 million on a new smelter of which £2 million is the cost of pollution safeguards.[37] The china clay industry in Cornwall plan to pump their inert waste direct to the bed of the English Channel. Shell have developed a wide range of books on nature. Much more could be done, and the review and development of long-range planning provide opportunities for improving existing practices.

The whole question of greater environmental awareness should not be viewed by business solely as a reason for defensive measures. All that can be done to prevent pollution at its source is very desirable, and in many cases will require expenditure not previously incurred. There are also going to be many opportunities for a wide range of businesses. Those with a positive approach will find much scope for new business growth. For example, there will be an increasing need for dealing with pollution problems at source, i.e. within the factory and the home. There is already a growing demand for food which has not been treated with chemicals of any kind. This development is likely to continue but is held up by lack of shops, and too little effective publicity. There may develop a demand for advice to farmers and gardeners on organic farming and biological pest control. Urban development, pollution-free traffic in towns, and relocation of industry all offer business opportunities to the perceptive entrepreneur. Waste disposal, including the conversion of much existing 'waste' into saleable products, such as compost, already occurs in a few isolated cases. Those concerned with marketing and advertising may find promotional opportunities in schemes associated with conservation. 1970 – European Conservation Year (ECY) – provides the starting point. Such schemes could popularise products whilst increasing awareness of environmental problems, and thereby providing a service to the community as well as good PR to the business. The rapidly growing education industry has a great scope for literature, films, and courses on all aspects of ecology, environmental change, pollution control, and many related subjects. How can long-range planners build this into their company plans for the mutual benefit of the community and the firm? Large business organisations have a great potential for making a major contribution towards environmental problems, and their resources and organising ability somehow need to be applied to these increasingly severe dilemmas.

Most of the existing effort, such as that of the Conservation Society, which is concerned with the triple issues of Population, Environment and Resources, relies on private subscriptions and voluntary help. Its scope and effectiveness could be greatly enhanced with additional support.

Conclusion

Central to all environmental problems is stabilisation of population. Our responsibility in this generation is firstly towards the population we already have in Britain, in Europe and throughout the world. What we do in the next ten or twenty years will have a very great impact on the quality of life for those who are alive now and those who are yet to be born. All other issues concerning pollution in all its forms, and the use of resources will be greatly affected by the size of world population and how it is distributed.

Stabilising world and national population is, however, only part of the answer, because its accomplishment still leaves the question of how we use our resources and our technology. This will be affected as much by our standards and our values as by the size of the population. The problem we face in the next decade is firstly to stabilise population then to build our standards and values around the concept of ecology. There is no greater problem to be faced and surmounted. Britain has a great opportunity to set the example, but time is short.

References

1. L. DUDLEY STAMP, Our Developing World, Faber, 1968, p. 21.

2. R. ARVILL, Man and Environment, Penguin Books, 1969, pp. 189–90.

3. STAMP, pp. 19–21.

4. EDWARD J. KORMONDY, Concepts of Ecology, Prentice-Hall, 1969, p. 167.

5. Ibid., p. 171.

6. 'Pollyanna to Cassandra', The Guardian, 25 June 1969, reporting the views of Lewis C. Frank, Executive Director of the Information Centre on Population Problems in New York.

7. A. C. FRASER and P. S. WATSON, 'Family planning – a myth?', The Practitioner, 201, Aug. 1968.

8. (a) Sunday Times, 20 July 1969, article on sterilisation, and 3 Aug. 1969, letter headed 'Vasectomy'. (b) Nova, Aug. 1969, pp. 32–7.

9. Registrar-General's estimate, The Times, 24 Sept. 1969.

10. PAUL R. EHRLICH, The Population Bomb, Ballantine Books, 1968.

11. The Guardian, 23 Sept. 1969, reporting on FAO statistics.

12. R. CARSON, Silent Spring (Hamish Hamilton, 1963), Penguin Books, 1965, pp. 162–7.

13. L. REID, The Sociology of Nature, rev. edn., Penguin Books, 1962, p. 130.

14. CARSON, pp. 56–9.

15. 'Not so Easyrider', The Guardian, 18 Oct. 1969, Peter Fonda talking to John Walker.

16. CARSON, p. 162.

17. Report on fly-killers, Which?, July, 1969.

18. CARSON, pp. 242–55.

19. KENNETH MELLANBY, *The Soil Association and the Scientist*, pamphlet.

20. *The Soil Association's Research Facilities*, pamphlet issued by the Soil Association, New Bells Farm, Haughley, Stowmarket, Suffolk.

21. ARVILL, p. 467.

22. 'Flying high – 53 million', *Evening Standard*, 16 Sept. 1969.

23. L. DUDLEY STAMP, *Land of Britain – its use and misuse*, Longmans, 19, p. 438.

24. Ibid., p. 467.

25. ARVILL, chap. 6.

26. 'Poisoned air is Britain's free gift to Sweden', *The Guardian*, May 1969.

27. 'The prosperous polluted society', *Industry Week*, 1 Aug. 1969.

28. J. DAVY, 'Management today', *The Environmental Crisis*, Sept. 1969.

29. LORD RITCHIE CALDER, 'Hell upon earth', Presidential address to the Annual General Meeting of the Conservation Society..

30. KORMONDY, p. 186.

31. 'Tighter control the answer to pollution accidents', *The Times*, 25 June 1969.

32. 'One man's sewer is another's water', *Sunday Times*, 7 Sept. 1969.

33. CALDER, p. 13.

34. THE NATURE CONSERVANCY, *Progress 1964–1968*, pp. 41–4.

35. The David Davies Memorial Institute of International Studies, *Principles Governing Certain Changes in the Environment of Man*, HMSO, 1968.

36. Department of Health and Social Security, *On the State of Public Health: report of the Chief Medical Officer for the year 1968*, HMSO.

37. REX WINSBURY, 'The cost to industry, the risk to life', *Financial Times*, 22 Oct. 1969.

Corporate Strategy and the use of resources
A. Man management

17

Human relations and human resources*

R.E. MILES

'Participative' management in some form or another is likely to become increasingly popular as a remedy for the rising level of industrial conflict. Miles, however, argues that management theorists have been advocating two significantly different models of participative management. The first of these is commonly known as the 'human relations' model which managers tend to adopt in dealing with their own subordinates; the second is described by the author as the 'human resources' model which managers would like their own superiors to adopt. The models emphasise different aspects of the leader-subordinate relationship. By and large the 'human resources' model is much more concerned with the development of the talents and abilities of each individual within the organisation. Thus subordinates may have more freedom to take initiatives and develop their own lines of thought under the 'human resources' model. The successful application of the 'resources' approach depends ultimately on how optimistic a view each manager takes of his subordinates' capabilities.

The proselytising efforts of the advocates of participative management appear to have paid off. The typical modern manager, on paper at least, broadly endorses participation and rejects traditional, autocratic concepts of leadership and control as no longer acceptable or, perhaps, no longer legitimate. However, while participation has apparently been well merchandised and widely purchased, there seems to be a great deal of confusion about what has been sold and bought. Managers do not appear to have accepted a single, logically consistent concept of participation. In fact, there is reason to believe that managers have adopted two different theories or models of participation, one for themselves and one for their subordinates. These statements reflect both my analysis of the development of the theory of participative management and my interpretation of managers' attitudes towards these concepts.

My views are based in part on a number of recent surveys of managers' beliefs and opinions. The most recent of these studies, which I conducted, was begun with a group of 215 middle and upper level managers in West Coast companies,

* Reprinted from HBR July–August ©1965; 1965, by the President and Fellows of Harvard College; all rights reserved.

and has been continued with a sample of over 300 administrators from public agencies.[1] This study was designed to clarify further certain aspects of managers' attitudes uncovered by earlier research under the direction of Dale Yoder of Stanford[2] and Professors Mason Haire, Edwin Ghiselli, and Lyman Porter of the University of California, Berkeley.[3] This series of studies involved the collection of questionnaire data on managers' opinions about people and on their attitudes towards various leadership policies and practices. Several thousand managers in all, both here and abroad, have participated. This article is not intended to summarise all of the findings on managers' leadership attitudes available from these studies. Rather, my primary purpose is to construct a theoretical framework that may explain some of the principal dimensions of managers' views and some of the implications of their beliefs and opinions, drawing on the research simply to illustrate my views.

Participative theories

While the suggestion that managers have accepted a two-sided approach to participation may be disturbing, it should not be too surprising. Management theorists have frequently failed to deal with participation in a thorough and consistent manner. Indeed, from an examination of their somewhat ambivalent treatment of this concept, it is possible to conclude that they have been selling two significantly different models of participative management.

One of the scholars' models, which we will designate the human relations model, closely resembles the concept of participation which managers appear to accept for use with their own subordinates. The second, and not yet fully developed, theory, which I have labelled the human resources model, prescribes the sort of participative policies that managers would apparently like their superiors to follow. I shall develop and examine these two models, compare them with managers' expressed beliefs, and consider some of the implications of managers' dual allegiance to them.

Both the human relations and the human resources models have three basic components:

1 A set of assumptions about people's values and capabilities.
2 Certain prescriptions as to the amount and kind of participative policies and practices that managers should follow, in keeping with their assumptions about people.
3 A set of expectations with respect to the effects of participation on subordinate morale and performance.

This third component contains the model's explanation of how and why participation works – that is, the purpose of participation and how it accomplishes this purpose. In outline form, the models may be summarised as shown in Fig. 17.1.

Fig. 17.1 Two models of participative leadership

HUMAN RELATIONS   HUMAN RESOURCES

ATTITUDE TOWARDS PEOPLE

1. People in our culture share a common set of needs – to belong, to be liked, to be respected.

1. In addition to sharing common needs for belonging and respect, most people in our culture desire to contribute effectively and creatively to the accomplishment of worthwhile objectives.

2. They desire individual recognition but, more than this, they want to feel a useful part of the company and their own work group or department.

2. The majority of our work force is capable of exercising far more initiative, responsibility, and creativity than their present jobs require or allow.

3. They will tend to cooperate willingly and comply with organisational goals if these important needs are fulfilled.

3. These capabilities represent untapped resources which are presently being wasted.

KIND AND AMOUNT OF PARTICIPATION

1. The manager's basic task is to make each worker believe that he is a useful and important part of the department 'team'.

1. The manager's basic task is to create an environment in which his subordinates can contribute their full range of talents to the accomplishment of organisational goals. He must attempt to uncover and tap the creative resources of his subordinates.

2. The manager should be willing to explain his decisions and to discuss his subordinates' objections to his plans. On routine matters, he should encourage his subordinates to participate in planning and choosing among alternative solutions to problems.

2. The manager should allow, and encourage, his subordinates to participate not only in routine decisions but in important matters as well. In fact, the more important a decision is to the manager's department, the greater should be his effort to tap the department's resources.

3. Within narrow limits, the work group or individual subordinates should be allowed to exercise self-direction and self-control in carrying out plans.

3. The manager should attempt to continually expand the areas over which his subordinates exercise self-direction and self-control as they develop and demonstrate greater insight and ability.

1. Sharing information with subordinates and involving them in departmental decision-making will help satisfy their basic needs for belonging and for individual recognition.

2. Satisfying these needs will improve subordinate morale and reduce resistance to formal authority.

3. High employee morale and reduced resistance to formal authority may lead to improved departmental performance. It should at least reduce intradepartment friction and thus make the manager's job easier.

1. The overall quality of decision-making and performance will improve as the manager makes use of the full range of experience, insight, and creative ability in his department.

2. Subordinates will exercise responsible self-direction and self-control in the accomplishment of worthwhile objectives that they understand and have helped establish.

3. Subordinate satisfaction will increase as a by-product of improved performance and the opportunity to contribute creatively to this improvement.

Note: It may fairly be argued that what I call the human relations model is actually the product of popularisation and misunderstanding of the work of pioneers in this field. Moreover, it is true that some of the early research and writings of the human relationists contain concepts which seem to fall within the framework of what I call the human resources model. Nevertheless, it is my opinion that while the early writers did not advocate the human relations model as presented here, their failure to emphasise certain of the human resources concepts left their work open to the misinterpretations which have occurred.

Human relations model

This approach is not new. As early as the 1920s, business spokesmen began to challenge the classical autocratic philosophy of management. The employee was no longer pictured as merely an appendage to a machine, seeking only economic rewards from his work. Managers were instructed to consider him as a 'whole man' rather than as merely a bundle of skills and aptitudes.[4] They were urged to create a 'sense of satisfaction' among their subordinates by showing interest in the employees' personal success and welfare. As Bendix notes, the 'failure to treat workers as human beings came to be regarded as the cause of low morale, poor craftsmanship, unresponsiveness, and confusion'.[5]

The key element in the human relations approach is its basic objective of making organisational members feel a useful and important part of the overall effort. This process is viewed as the means of accomplishing the ultimate goal of building a cooperative and compliant work force. Participation, in this model, is a lubricant which oils away resistance to formal authority. By discussing problems with his subordinates and acknowledging their individual needs and desires, the manager hopes to build a cohesive work team that is willing and anxious to tangle with organisational problems.

One further clue to the way in which participation is viewed in this approach is provided in Dubin's concept of 'privilege pay'.[6] The manager 'buys' cooperation by letting his subordinates in on departmental information and allowing them to discuss and state their opinions on various departmental problems. He 'pays a price' for allowing his subordinates the privilege of participating in certain decisions and exercising some self-direction. In return he hopes to obtain their cooperation in carrying out these and other decisions for the accomplishment of departmental objectives.

Implicit in this model is the idea that it might actually be easier and more efficient if the manager could merely make departmental decisions without bothering to involve his subordinates. However, as the advocates of this model point out, there are two parts to any decision – (a) the making of the decision and (b) the activities required to carry it out. In many instances, this model suggests, the manager might do better to 'waste time' in discussing the problem with his subordinates, and perhaps even to accept suggestions that he believes may be less efficient in order to get the decision carried out.

In sum, the human relations approach does not bring out the fact that participation may be useful for its own sake. The possibility that subordinates will, in fact, bring to light points which the manager may have overlooked, if considered at all, tends to be mentioned only in passing. This is treated as a potential side benefit which, while not normally expected, may occasionally occur. Instead, the manager is urged to adopt participative leadership policies as the least-cost method of obtaining cooperation and getting his decisions accepted.

In many ways the human relations model represents only a slight departure from traditional autocratic models of management. The method of achieving results is different, and employees are viewed in more humanistic terms, but the basic roles of the manager and his subordinates remain essentially the same. The ultimate goal sought in both the traditional and the human relations model is compliance with managerial authority.

Human resources model

This approach represents a dramatic departure from traditional concepts of management. Though not yet fully developed, it is emerging from the writings of McGregor, Likert, Haire and others as a new and significant contribution to management thought.[7] The magnitude of its departure from previous models is illustrated first of all in its basic assumptions concerning people's values and abilities, which focus attention on all organisation members as reservoirs of untapped resources. These resources include not only physical skills and energy, but also creative ability and the capacity for responsible, self-directed, self-controlled behaviour. Given these assumptions about people, the manager's job cannot be viewed merely as one of giving direction and obtaining cooperation. Instead, his primary task becomes that of creating an environment in which the total resources of his department can be utilised.

The second point at which the human resources model differs dramatically from previous models is in its views on the purpose and goal of participation. In this model the manager does not share information, discuss departmental decisions, or encourage self-direction and self-control merely to improve subordinate satisfaction and morale. Rather, the purpose of these practices is to improve the decision-making and total performance efficiency of the organisation. The human resources model suggests that many decisions may actually be made more efficiently by those directly involved in and affected by the decisions. Similarly, this model implies that control is often most efficiently exercised by those directly involved in the work in process, rather than by someone or some group removed from the actual point of operation. Moreover, the human resources model does not suggest that the manager allow participation only in routine decisions. Instead, it implies that the more important the decision, the greater is his obligation to encourage ideas and suggestions from his subordinates. In the same vein, this model does not suggest that the manager allow his subordinates to exercise self-direction and self-control only when they are carrying out relatively unimportant assignments. In fact, it suggests that the area over which subordinates exercise self-direction and control should be continually broadened in keeping with their growing experience and ability.

The crucial point at which this model differs dramatically from other models is in its explanation of the causal relationship between satisfaction and performance. In the human relations approach improvement in subordinate satisfaction is viewed as an intervening variable which is the ultimate cause of improved performance. Diagrammatically, the causal relationship can be illustrated as in Fig. 17.2.

Fig. 17.2 Human relations model

Participation   →   Improved satisfaction and   →   Lower resistance
                          morale   Improved compliance
                                                                   with formal authority

In the human resources model the causal relationship between satisfaction and performance is viewed quite differently. Increased subordinate satisfaction is not pictured as the primary cause of improved performance; improvement results directly from creative contributions which subordinates make to departmental decision-making, direction, and control. Subordinates' satisfaction is viewed instead as a by-product of the process – the result of their having made significant contributions to organisational success. In diagram form the human resources model can be illustrated as in Fig. 17.3.

Fig. 17.3 Human resources model

Participation   →   Improved decision-making   →   Improved subordinate
                          and control   satisfaction and morale

The human resources model does not deny a relationship between participation and morale. It suggests that subordinates' satisfaction may well increase as they play more and more meaningful roles in decision-making and control. Moreover, the model recognises that improvements in morale may not only set the stage for expanded participation, but create an atmosphere which supports creative problem solving. Nevertheless, this model rejects as unsupported the concept that the improvement of morale is a necessary or sufficient cause of improved decision-making and control. Those improvements come directly from the full utilisation of the organisation's resources.

Managers' own views

Which approach to participative management do managers actually follow? It was suggested earlier that managers' views appear to reflect both models. When they talk about the kind and amount of participation appropriate for their subordinates, they express concepts that appear to be similar to those in the human relations model. On the other hand, when they consider their own relationships with their superiors, their views seem to flow from the human resources model. A brief review of the relevant findings suggests some of the bases for this interpretation.

Participation for subordinates

When we look at managers' views on the use of participative policies and practices with the subordinates who report to them, two points seem clear:

1 Managers generally accept and endorse the use of participative concepts.
2 However, they frequently doubt their subordinates' capacity for self-direction and self-control, and their ability to contribute creatively to departmental decision-making.

In the Stanford studies, an overwhelming majority of managers indicated their agreement with statements emphasising the desirability of subordinate participation in decision-making.[8] In the Berkeley studies, a majority of the managers in each of eleven countries, including the United States, indicated their agreement with such concepts as sharing information with subordinates and increasing subordinate influence and self-control.[9] Similarly, in my recent studies, managers overwhelmingly endorsed participative leadership policies.

On the other hand, while managers appear to have great faith in participative policies, they do not indicate such strong belief in their subordinates' capabilities. For example, the Berkeley group in their international study found that managers tended to have a 'basic lack of confidence in others' and typically did not believe that capacity for leadership and initiative was widely distributed among subordinates.[10] In my own study, managers in every group to date have rated their subordinates and rank-and-file employees well below themselves, particularly on such important managerial traits as responsibility, judgement, and initiative.

But if managers do not expect creative, meaningful contributions from their subordinates, why do they advocate participative management? A reasonable answer seems to be that they advocate participative concepts as a means of improving subordinate morale and satisfaction. This interpretation gains support from my recent studies. Here, managers were asked to indicate their agreement or disagreement with statements predicting improved morale and satisfaction and statements predicting improved performance as the result of following various participative leadership policies. In connection with each of these policies, managers indicated consistently greater agreement with the predictions of improved morale than with the predictions of improved performance.

The fact that managers appear to have serious doubts about the values and capabilities of those reporting to them seems to rule out their acceptance of the human resources model for use with their subordinates. On the other hand, the fact that they do endorse participation and seem quite certain about its positive impact on morale suggests a close relationship between their views and those expressed in the human relations model. Moreover, the types of participative policies which managers most strongly advocate seem to support this interpretation.

In my research, managers indicate strongest agreement with policies that advocate sharing information and discussing objectives with subordinates. However, they tend to be somewhat less enamoured with the policies which suggest increasing subordinate self-direction and self-control. This pattern of participation seems much closer to that of the human relations approach than to the pattern advocated in the human resources model.

Participation for themselves

When I examined managers' views towards their relationships with their own superiors, a much different pattern of responses became evident:

1 Managers in my studies tend to see little, if any, difference between their own capabilities and those of their superiors. In fact, they tend to rate themselves equal to, if not higher than, their superiors on such traits as creativity, ingenuity, flexibility, and willingness to change.
2 When asked to indicate at which levels in their organisations they feel each of the participative policies would be most appropriate, managers invariably feel most strongly that the full range of participative policies should be used by their own superiors.

More importantly, they also tend to be most certain that these participative policies will result in improved organisational performance at their own level.

Thus, when managers discuss the type of participative policies which their superiors should follow with managers at their own level, they appear to espouse the human resources model. They see themselves as reservoirs of creative resources. Moreover, the fact that they frequently view themselves as more flexible and willing to change than their superiors suggests that they feel their resources are frequently wasted. Correspondingly, they expect improvement in organisational performance to result from greater freedom for self-direction and self-control on their part.

Reasons behind views

If the evidence of the current survey does represent managers' attitudes towards participative leadership, one serious question immediately comes to mind. How can managers desire one type of authority and control relationship with their superiors and at the same time advocate another type with their subordinates? A general answer, of course, is that this pattern of attitudes is just human nature. We tend not only to think more highly of ourselves than we do of others, but also to want more than we are willing to give. There are, however, other logical, more specific explanations for managers' reluctance to accept the human resources model for use with their subordinates.

In the first place, the human relations model has been around much longer, and an exceptionally good selling job has been done in its behalf. The causal relationship among participation, satisfaction, and performance, despite a lack of empirical validation, has become common wisdom. The human resources model, on the other hand, has not been as fully or systematically developed, and has not been the subject of as hard a sell. Managers may 'feel' some of the concepts expressed in the human resources model and intuitively grasp some of their implications for their relationships with their superiors, but little pressure has been put on them to translate their attitudes into a systematic model for use with their subordinates.

A second explanation for managers' failure to accept the human resources model for use with their subordinates is that they are simply reluctant to 'buy' a theory that challenges concepts to which they are deeply and emotionally attached. There is no question that the human resources model does attack a number of traditional management concepts. Two of the bedrock concepts that are directly challenged deal with: (a) the origins and applicability of management prerogatives; and (b) the source and limits of control.

The human resources model recognises no definable, immutable set of management prerogatives. It does not accept the classical division between those who think and command and those who obey and perform. Instead, it argues that the solution to any given problem may arise from a variety of sources, and that to think of management (or any other group) as sufficient in and of itself to make all decisions is misleading and wasteful.

This approach does not directly challenge the 'legal' right of management to command. It suggests, however, that there is a higher 'law of the situation' that thoughtful managers will usually observe, deferring to expertise wherever it may be found. In this model the manager's basic obligation is not to the 'management team' but to the accomplishment of departmental and organisational objectives. The criterion of success, therefore, is not the extent to which orders are carried out but the results obtained.

Admitting that he may not have all the answers is as difficult for the manager as for any of the rest of us. He has been taught to hide his deficiencies, not to advertise them. Holding on to information, maintaining close control, and reserving the right to make all decisions are ways by which the manager can ensure his importance. Further, many organisations have reinforced this type of behaviour either (a) by failing to emphasise the manager's obligation to develop and utilise his human resources, or (b) by failing to reward him when he does make this effort.

In the area of control the human resources model challenges the traditional concept that control is a scarce resource. In traditional theory there is presumed to be a virtually fixed amount of control. This fixed amount can be distributed in a variety of ways, but control given to one group must eventually be taken away from another. Given this concept, the manager is reluctant to allow his subordinates any real degree of self-control – what he gives up to them, he loses himself. In fact, it is frequently this basic fear of losing control which limits the amount of participation that managers are willing to allow.

The human resources model does not accept this lump-of-control theory. Instead, it argues that the manager increases his total control over the accomplishment of departmental objectives by encouraging self-control on the part of his subordinates. Control is thus an additive and an expanding phenomenon. Where subordinates are concerned with accomplishing goals and exercising self-direction and self-control, their combined efforts will far outweigh the results of the exercise of any amount of control by the manager.

Moreover, the fact that subordinates desire to exercise greater self-control does not mean that they reject the manager's legitimate concern for goal accomplishment. Rather, there is evidence that they in fact seek a partnership that will allow them to play a larger role, yet also will allow for a corresponding increase in management's control activity.[11]

In all, the fact that managers are reluctant to adopt a model which forces them to rethink, and perhaps restructure, their perceptions of their own roles and functions is not surprising. It is also not surprising that some writers in this field have hesitated to advocate a model which challenges such deeply held concepts. The human relations approach is easy to 'buy', since it does not challenge the manager's basic role or status. It is correspondingly easy to sell, since it promises much and actually demands little. The human resources model, on the other hand, promises much but also demands a great deal from the manager. It requires that he undertake the responsibility of utilising all the resources available to him – his own and those of his subordinates. It does not suggest that it will make his job easier; it only acknowledges his obligation to do a much better job.

Logical implications

The nature of the evidence to date does not warrant any firm or sweeping conclusions. Nevertheless it does suggest enough support for the interpretations made here to make it worthwhile, and perhaps imperative, to draw some logical implications from the fact that managers seem to have adopted two apparently conflicting attitudes regarding participative management.

The first implication, and the easiest one to draw, is that, given managers' present attitudes, the human resources model has little chance of ever gaining real acceptance as a guide to managers' relationships with their subordinates. Managers at every level view themselves as capable of greater self-direction and self-control, but apparently do not attribute such abilities to their subordinates. As long as managers throughout the organisational hierarchy remain unaware that the kind of participation they want and believe they are capable of handling is also the kind their subordinates want and feel they deserve, there would seem to be little hope for the human resources approach being actually put into practice.

A second, and somewhat more complex, implication of managers' current views is that real participation will seldom be found in modern organisations. Participation, in the human relations model, is viewed as an 'ought' rather than a 'must'. The manager is under no basic obligation to seek out and develop talent, or to encourage and allow participation; it is something which he 'probably should do' but not something for which he is made to feel truly responsible. Viewing participation in this fashion, the manager often junks it when problems arise or pressure builds up from above – the very times when it might be expected to produce the greatest gains.

A third implication, closely related to the second, is that the benefits which the human resources approach predicts from participative management will not accrue as long as managers cling to the human relations view. From the human relations model, a manager may draw a rule for decision-making which says that he should allow only as much participation, self-direction, and self-control as is required to obtain cooperation and reduce resistance to formal authority. In the area of job enlargement, for example, the manager following the human relations model would be tempted to enlarge his subordinates' jobs just enough to improve morale and satisfaction, with little real concern for making full use of their abilities. This limited approach borders on pseudo-participation and may be interpreted by subordinates as just another manipulative technique.

The human resources model, on the other hand, does not hold the manager to so limited a decision rule. In fact, it affirms that he is obligated to develop and encourage a continually expanding degree of responsible participation, self-direction, and self-control. The only limiting factors legitimate in this approach are the basic requirements of capacity to perform and the need for coordination. The manager following the human resources model would therefore continually expand subordinates' responsibility and self-direction up to the limits of their abilities, and/or to the point at which further expansion would produce a wasteful overlap among the responsibilities of members of his department. Even these limits, however, are far from absolute. The human resources model suggests that with subordinates' broadened abilities and expanded information, voluntary cooperation can erase much of the need for specific job boundaries.

A fourth and final implication can be drawn from managers' confused and conflicting attitudes towards participative management. Managers' attitudes, as suggested earlier, in part reflect the ambivalent and inconsistent treatment which scholars have given to participative leadership concepts, and are not likely to change until theorists firm up their own thinking.

Some final comments

It must be clear at this point that I feel that management scholars should focus their attention on developing and promoting the application of the human resources approach. While I cannot, at this stage, base my preference for the human resources model on solid empirical evidence, there is one strong argument for its potential usefulness. It is the fact that managers up and down the organisational hierarchy believe their superiors should follow this model.

Critics of the human resources approach have argued (a) that its costs outweigh its benefits because in its final form the human resources model prescribes management by committee at every level, which results in wasted effort and the inability to act in crisis situations; and (b) that this approach is unsuitable for organisations or organisational groups whose members have neither the desire nor the ability to meet its challenge.

In answer to the first charge, this approach does imply a need for additional information flow to subordinates at all levels, and I admit that collecting and disseminating information increases costs. However, information collected and used at lower levels may be less costly than information collected for use at upper levels that is subsequently ignored or misused. Further, and more important, the application of the human resources model does not require – in fact, would make unnecessary – committee-type sharing of routine departmental tasks. This model would suggest that subordinates are generally willing to go along with their superiors' decisions on more or less routine matters, particularly when they are well informed and feel free to call important points to their bosses' attention. Moreover, this approach implies that many matters are to be delegated directly to one or more subordinates who, in most instances, will coordinate their own activities. At the same time, this model emphasises that full and extended discussion by the whole department will be utilised where it can do the most good – on complex and important problems that demand the full talent and complete concern of the group. One could argue that under these circumstances crises should arise less often and consensus should be more quickly reached when they do arise.

There is no quick and easy answer to the second charge that the human resources model is more adaptable to and more easily applied with some groups than with others. Note, however, that it is the human relations approach, and not the human resources model, which promises quick and easy application. The latter cannot be put into full-blown practice overnight in any situation, particularly where subordinates have been conditioned by years of traditional or pseudoparticipative techniques of leadership. It involves a step-by-step procedure wherein the manager expands subordinates' responsibilities and participation in keeping with their developing abilities and concerns. High expectations and full support, coupled with an open recognition of the inevitability of occasional shortcomings, are required to achieve successful application.

Finally, there is a familiar ring to the critics' charge that many organisation members are either unwilling or unable to contribute creatively, or to accept any real measure of responsibility. In fact, this charge brings us back once again to the heart of the conflict in managers' attitudes towards participation – their own view that subordinates are suited only for the human relations type of participation, while they themselves are well suited for the full range of participation suggested in the human resources model.

References

1. RAYMOND E. MILES, 'Conflicting elements in managerial idealogies', *Industrial Relations,* October 1964, pp. 77–91. The subsequent research with public administrators is still being conducted, and reports have not yet been published.

2. DALE YODER, 'Management theories as managers see them', *Personnel,* July–Aug. 1962, pp. 25–30; 'Management policies for the future', *Personnel Administration,* Sept.–Oct. 1962, pp. 11–14 ff.; DALE YODER *et al.,* 'Managers' theories of management', *Journal of the Academy of Management,* Sept. 1963, pp. 204–11.

3. MASON HAIRE, EDWIN GHISELLI and LYMAN W. PORTER, 'Cultural patterns in the role of manager', *Industrial Relations,* Feb. 1963, pp. 95–117, a report on the Berkeley studies.

4. REINHARD BENDIX, *Work and Authority in Industry,* Wiley, 1956, pp. 287–340.

5. Ibid., p. 294.

6. ROBERT DUBIN, The World of Work, Prentice-Hall, 1958, pp. 243–4. It should be noted that Dubin treats the concept of privilege pay within a framework which goes beyond the human relations approach and, in some respects, is close to the human resources model.

7. See particularly DOUGLAS MCGREGOR, The Human Side of Enterprise, McGraw-Hill, 1960; RENSIS LIKERT, New Patterns of Management, McGraw-Hill, 1961; and MASON HAIRE, 'The concept of power and the concept of man', in *Social Science Approaches to Business Behavior,* ed. George Strother, Homewood, Illinois, The Dorsey Press, 1962, pp. 163–83.

8. YODER, *et al.,* 'Managers' theories of management'.

9. HAIRE, GHISELLI and PORTER, *op cit.*

10. Ibid.

11. See CLAGGET C. SMITH and ARNOLD TANNENBAUM, 'Organisational control structure: a comparative analysis', *Human Relations,* Nov. 1963, pp. 299–316.

18

Corporate strategy and management by objectives

J. D. WICKENS

Management by objectives (MBO) as a technique for improving individual motivation and organisational efficiency may be a very useful aid to strategic planning. In this article Mr Wickens reviews the development of MBO as a concept and assesses its operational costs and benefits. Referring to the experience of his own company, the author explains how the application of MBO revealed serious defects in the organisational structure — notably a lack of managerial control over certain functions and operations. It would appear that the very application of MBOs even after the programme itself has been formally discontinued, can have qualitative repercussions on the whole style of management so that top executives rapidly grow accustomed to managing by objectives. The author points out, however, that technological factors may limit the success of MBO or at least make it harder to introduce. Nonetheless he concludes that MBO is likely to make corporate strategy more effective and accustom all members of the organisation to the reality of planning.

Development of the concept

In his influential book, The Practice of Management,[1] first published in the United States in 1954, Peter Drucker argued that instead of directing operations towards a single end-result, such as profitability, business managers should set objectives in 'every area where performance and results directly and vitally affect the survival and prosperity of the business'. In any business these areas would include market standing, innovation, productivity, physical and financial resources, profitability, manager performance and development, worker performance and attitude, and public responsibility.

From his contacts with such firms as General Electric, General Motors and Sears, Roebuck, Drucker reported: 'Company after company is working on the definition of the key areas, on thinking through what should be measured and on fashioning the tools of measurement.' With his great gift for interpreting trends in advanced management thinking and behaviour, he pointed out that clear objectives, derived from company goals and provided for each manager at every level, could counteract three powerful sources of confusion and misdirected management effort: the specialised work of most managers; the hierarchical structure of management, which invested the boss's least remark with great significance; and the differences in viewpoint between the different functions and levels in a business.

In order to give full scope to individual managers while achieving common direction of effort throughout the company, it would be necessary for each manager to develop objectives for his own unit, and submit them for approval by higher management, and to participate in developing those of the larger unit of which his was a part. Measurement of results could then show each manager the extent to which he was achieving his objectives.

By the late 1950s, a number of North American companies were searching for *standards* of performance for managers, and at a research seminar arranged by the American Management Association and published in 1960,[2] examples were quoted from such diverse operations as the regional sales managers of Smith, Kline & French, the pharmaceuticals firm, and area superintendents of products pipelines for Standard Oil of Ohio. The seminar distinguished between objectives, which are usually unique to an individual and a particular set of circumstances, specifying an improvement in results within a period of time, and performance standards, which define the conditions which exist when a job is being well done, either for an individual, or everyone in a particular kind of job. For example, a production manager may undertake to save £10000 by value analysis by the end of 1968, as an objective; all production managers in a company may have as a standard a certain frequency of lost-time injuries per 100000 manhours.

The concept of performance standards for management suggests an industrial engineering approach, rather than concern with strategic planning and the coordination of functional and departmental goals with the company's objectives. The interest in performance standards was not confined to process and mass production industry, however, as one might have expected, and there was a widespread tendency in the early 1960s to discount any objectives which did not share with most performance standards the characteristic of being quantitative. Objectives and/or standards tended to be set for every significant facet of a manager's job – e.g. a Standard Oil Company (Ohio) example gave thirty-seven standards, covering aspects of operations, maintenance, safety, personnel administration, communications and public relations.[3]

At about the same time, Douglas McGregor formulated two contrasting theories of industrial behaviour,[4] based on different assumptions about motivation. Theory X, assuming that the average human being disliked work and avoided responsibility, proposed that most people must be coerced into putting forward enough effort towards achieving the organisation's objectives. Theory Y, assuming that the average human being derived satisfaction from work and responsibility under certain conditions, proposed that most people would exercise self-direction and self-control in the service of objectives to which they were committed.

Theory X, which McGregor associated with the traditional, and still predominant, view of managers in American industry, made authority the central principle of organisation. Theory Y, which he derived from contemporary social science and in particular Maslow's theory of motivation, made integration the central principle, so that one of management's primary responsibilities was the creation of conditions in which members of the organisation could achieve their own goals best by directing their efforts toward the success of the enterprise.

Management by objectives, for McGregor, could be interpreted in the light of theory X as 'no more than a new set of tactics within a strategy of management by direction and control', or in the light of theory Y, as 'a deliberate attempt to link improvement in managerial competence with the satisfaction of higher-level ego and self-actualisation needs', in fact as 'management by integration and self-control'. Performance appraisal, which tended in theory X practice to be linked with task descriptions and to be used to control behaviour, would in applications of theory Y be replaced by self-control, towards the achievement of agreed target results, and self-appraisal.

The concept today

Since McGregor's influential work, a small literature on management by objectives has appeared on both sides of the Atlantic. A recent American Management Association series of reports[5] describes the American scene. In Britain, most of the papers and magazine articles appear to recount the experiences of firms who have been introduced to management by objectives by a well-known firm of management consultants, whose approach was devised by John Humble after a study of American practice. Some of these, like Humble's own booklet,[6] emphasise the development of individual managers, others[7] emphasise corporate long-range planning and its extension to departmental levels, on Drucker lines. Most treatments, however, set one overall aim against the background of the other.

The current features of the concept of management by objectives may be summarised as follows:

1 Objectives or standards are set (defined in terms of results or outcomes, not tasks or activities). The terms may be quantitative (e.g. volume, cost, profit) or qualitative (e.g. to complete a project, to establish an organisation). General terms (e.g. 'at minimum cost') are avoided so far as possible.

2 Time is specified, except where continuous duration is implied (e.g. in performance standards).

3 Objectives or standards are set only for key aspects of the organisation's operations, and for key aspects of managers' jobs, not for every task.

4 Objectives or standards may be set at all managerial levels of the organisation, which is desirable, or in particular circumstances they may be restricted to higher or lower levels. In either case, subsidiary objectives/standards must be mutually consistent (e.g. sales with output) and must contribute to the

higher-level ones (whether these are expressed or implied). Management by objectives programmes must therefore be integrated with management planning, budgeting, scheduling, etc.

5 The time-scale used must be appropriate to the organisation level – normally longer periods at higher levels – and short-term objectives must contribute to the longer-term ones. Management by objectives programmes must, therefore, be integrated with long-range corporate planning, as well as with short-term planning (e.g. up to one year).

6 Objectives/standards must be compatible with any job descriptions, organisation charts or manuals, etc., which already exist or are introduced.

7 Objectives/standards must be integrated with the control system(s), so that performance can be compared with targets by means of the regular or special management accounts, reports, etc.

8 Objectives/standards must be integrated with any systems of performance appraisal, salary review, training analysis, management development, and succession planning.

9 Objectives/standards programmes must be coordinated with the development of any services available for improving efficiency and effectiveness (e.g. industrial engineering, management services, O and M).

10 Objectives/standards must be set by procedures which do not conflict significantly with the current managerial style (autocratic, participative, etc.) in the organisation; whatever the style, however, each manager involved must know the objectives/standards for his own job, and must accept them, if the programme is to be successful.

Costs and benefits

The direct costs of introducing management by objectives usually include consultants' fees, together with the cost of one or more senior staff as advisers to maintain it, and often a small team of management services staff. In addition, a heavy investment of managers' time is usually needed to establish what are the key results appropriate to each job, and to set objectives or standards – about ten to twelve hours per job, according to one estimate (Smith's Industries).

Indirect costs may also be incurred in modifying the organisation's planning, control, training, performance appraisal and other procedures, organisation structures, policies, and so on. Recurring costs may not be so high, but will still be significant.

The benefits frequently attributed to successful application of the concept may be summarised as:

● concentration on key tasks, rather than energy-dissipating activities which tend to take up too much of managers' time
● better delegation
● clearer accountability

- better controls
- better communication between superiors and subordinates
- better coordination between departments
- better management training
- better assessment of managers' performance
- better identification of management potential
- a better basis for salary administration
- identification of problems which inhibit better performance
- higher rate of suggestions for improvement
- higher motivation and morale among managers
- improved performance by the organisation as a whole, as well as by individual managers.

On the other hand, a number of the earlier British applications have failed, in the sense that 'management by objectives' did not become institutionalised: within a year or two, objectives were no longer being systematically set and reviewed.

A case history

In my own company, a management by objectives programme was introduced in three different units between 1961 and 1964 – units in the heavy mechanical, heavy electrical and electronic industries respectively. In each, the programme produced some benefits as well as costs, but 'management by objectives' was discontinued after varying intervals. However, in 1965 a corporate planning procedure was introduced throughout the company, and this included many of the essential features of the 'management by objectives' concept. As part of the same top management strategy, the company was reorganised in late 1965 into groups of product divisions.

Since 1965 there has been a striking improvement in planning, in identification of key business objectives, and in coordination between functions. Personnel management, like other functions, has become much more results-oriented, so that salary administration, manpower planning, management training and performance appraisal have been affected. Control systems have improved, although the radical changes which are needed to take advantage of computer capabilities are in their early stages. These improvements have been masked by the sharp deterioration in home trading conditions which coincided with them, but there is little doubt that they have happened.

In the earliest and most sustained application of the management by objectives concept, about 3500 people were employed in designing, making and selling several closely related product ranges. Under a general manager, a chief engineer, a sales manager, and a works manager were responsible for operations, and six heads of department provided accounting, personnel and various technical services. Production was predominantly of small batches of capital goods, and standardisation of components and designs was limited. Budgeting was established but not standard costing, and five-year forecasts of financial results had been recently introduced. Competition, at home and overseas, was rapidly intensifying, and one product range was uncompetitive and losing money.

The general manager, aware of a number of signs of increasing organisational malaise, asked a management consultant to assist in defining the structure of authority and responsibility. The consultant recommended a programme of management by objectives on North American lines, and this was accepted. In a period of three months job descriptions were written and objectives set for nearly a hundred jobs, at six levels of management. In the following twelve months or so, performance was assessed, and these assessments were combined into a management inventory.

For each job, the job-holder wrote his own detailed description, helped by a standard questionnaire, and set objectives for each facet of his responsibilities. With the help of the consultant or the personnel manager, he then discussed job description and objectives with his immediate supervisor, and agreement was eventually reached. Part of the discussion dealt with the difficulties which prevented or hindered the manager from improving his performance in the way he, or his superior, would have liked. The whole process took ten to twenty hours for each job.

The programme showed that the organisation structure was seriously defective – for example, in many instances several managers said that they were responsible for some facet of the operations, but none of them exercised control over it. As no resources were made available for studying the organisation structure in depth and modifying it, however, few changes were made, and these were spread out over several years. In these circumstances it was naturally difficult to set meaningful objectives, and the fact that objectives were in practice being set simultaneously at several levels of organisation simply demonstrated that different levels were setting conflicting objectives – no resources to eliminate the conflicts were available, apart from the managers' own efforts, and such remedial actions as were taken were spread out over a long period.

A further difficulty emerged at the appraisal interview. Objectives had been set for the following twelve months. Even where a manager had been able to set himself some objectives which would have been feasible (among others that were not really within his control), within twelve months the markets had changed, the priority of various operations and problems had changed, and there was little basis in existence for performance appraisal, as the elaborate objectives had seldom been updated in the meantime.

Nevertheless, this first programme generated a good deal of enthusiasm as well as some resistance, probably because the new interest shown by senior managers in their subordinates' problems and goals was interpreted as a sign that life would become less frustrating because somebody would do something about the various organisational problems. A number of major organisational changes were in fact made, to group manufacturing with engineering (and for some products also commercial) operations under divisional managers.

Responsibilities were redefined in some cases. The objectives of the service departments in particular were redefined and coordinated to a greater extent with the operating departments' objectives. Awareness of the importance of each department's contribution to business was increased. More attention began to be paid to the development of subordinates, and management succession was systematically reviewed for the first time. Overall, cost reductions of about £100 000 per annum were achieved, and working capital was reduced by 26 per cent in twelve months.

Two years after the beginning of the first programme, a second was initiated on similar lines, but this time little cooperation was forthcoming from middle-level managers. The improvements which had been made were still not adequate, and in any case they were not seen to be part of the management by objectives programme. The technical inadequacies of the approach which had been used came to be more clearly recognised by top management, and it is probable that this second cycle would have been followed by more purposive action than the first, but two major changes intervened. Firstly, corporate long-range planning was formalised, and the amount of work initially involved in assembling and in many cases radically revising numerous separate and often incomplete analyses, assumptions, plans, forecasts and budgets, threw such a load on local top management that they had time for little else apart from day-to-day matters. Secondly, the company was reorganised into groups of product divisions, and the new appointments affected most of the local top management jobs in one way or another. 'Management by objectives' was discontinued, and has not been revived. Managing by objectives, in a much more general sense, is beginning to take root.

The corporate planning procedure which is now followed prescribed four aspects for each divisional management plan (the divisions have an average turnover of about £4 million per annum, though the range is from less than a million to ten or more million).

First, the outlook for the business is summarised in terms of analyses of the markets and product strengths and weaknesses. Second, the major opportunities and problems facing the business are analysed; they are limited to the three to six most important issues, and the next three to five years. Third, and of most direct relevance to management by objectives, for each of these key opportunities or problems, programmes of action are summarised. Fourth, the implications of the plan for finance and other resources are estimated, and profit and loss statements prepared for five years – the current and the next four years. After each plan has been discussed with group and central management in the light of corporate objectives, and where necessary revised, five-year financial and man-power forecasts are prepared in detail for the current and the following year, and in outline for the next four years.

The third part of the management plans in particular is intended to be reviewed periodically by the division manager, and reviewed quarterly by group management. Some division managers, though not all, use the documents as the framework for their regular meetings with their immediate subordinates, to ensure that progress is reviewed and the programmes updated as necessary. The assessment of executive performance should be based at least partly on the achievement of these programmes, though they do not necessarily deal with all the key areas for individual performance but only with those most vital to exploiting major opportunities or tackling major problems for the business.

The company has a standard procedure for executive succession planning, but each group devises its own approaches to management development, with advice available from the centre. In my own group, in which unit and small batch production predominate, a standard procedure has been applied since mid-1966 to all managerial and professional staff down to a certain job level, which at present has a salary minimum of about £2500, together with individuals thought likely to reach this level within five years. In some rapidly expanding divisions, the coverage is extended further downwards.

Most of the staff who have already reached the minimum job level are usually responsible for at least one programme or subprogramme, but for individuals at lower levels this is not the case. The Performance Review is intended to include any programmes (or parts of programmes) for which the individual was responsible in the previous twelve months together with other key results areas, which may be defined in terms of objectives, standards, or simply tasks. The review cycle is timed to begin in September each year – shortly after the new management plan has been finished – and to be completed by the year-end. It does not, therefore, fit the annual management accounting cycle, which is based on the calendar year, but information on many matters is available every four weeks. It does, however, fit the salary review quite well, because this takes place in January and February, for implementation in April.

No systematic treatment is provided for intermediate objectives or assignments to be recorded between one management plan or the performance review and the next one. It is assumed that a combination of existing correspondence or other records, and the memory of the people concerned, will be adequate – though this is perhaps not necessarily the case.

An appraisal of the concept

Neither behavioural scientists nor operations research scientists in Britain appear to have paid much attention to management by objectives, and the few Americans seem to be committed and therefore suspect as social scientists – for example, McGregor, who selected social science concepts which fitted his own predilections as an academic administrator, or Charles Hughes,[8] an industrial psychologist working first in IBM and later in Texas Instruments. If we look at the wider literature on organisational behaviour, however, there are a number of writers whose concepts and theories find an answering chord in a manager's experience of management by objectives.

For example, in opposition to those social scientists and managers who believe that industrial relations problems can all be solved by more understanding and better communications, the Birmingham sociologist Baldamus[9] bases his hypotheses on the assumption that the interests of employers and employees are fundamentally opposed. Conflict, instead of being the result of inadequate communications, is then seen as basic and unavoidable, because employers and employees are bound to disagree over the distribution of earned income between shareholders, managers, other salary-earners and wage-earners.

Two main factors determine this distribution: the labour market and administrative controls. The labour market crudely determines the worth of particular kinds and levels of knowledge, skill and experience. Administrative controls seek to determine how much effort is contributed by employees. Baldamus's main concern is with the complex network of managerial controls over the wage-earner's effort (including supervision, methods of payment, and methods of production), and with the complex network of wage-earners' countervailing controls over their own and each other's effort.

Baldamus frequently refers to wage-earners as though they were the only employees in a modern industrial organisation. In recent years, however, effort-controls such as work measurement and variable factor programming have been extensively applied to clerical work, though they have been strenuously resisted by the draughtsmen's union. Less noticeably, managers too have become subject to an intricate system of administrative controls by higher management – budgets, plans, schedules, and in a small but significant number of firms, objectives and standards. At the top levels, a considerable amount of freedom of choice remains. Further down the organisation, however, the organisational needs and objectives inevitably become dominant, and individual needs and freedom of choice inevitably are restricted.

It would not be surprising, therefore, if lower and middle level managers found some way of resisting what they might come to regard as undue pressures from higher management. The more detailed the controls, for example in the form of a management by objectives programme or detailed performance standards, the more they might be expected to resist them. It is probably true that managers identify their interests with the organisation's interests more readily than other employees do. However, as very large organisations come to dominate the economy, and as management comes to depend less on experience and knowhow and more on rational analysis and evaluation, it seems likely that managers will become more professionalised – more like engineers or accountants. If this is so, they are likely to attach less value to long service and loyalty, and more to their own interests and their quasi-professional status.

Baldamus points out that in industrial society, ethical conceptions of a moral obligation to work support the administrative controls over effort. He mentions that there is some evidence that people with middle-class backgrounds place more emphasis on 'hard work' as a means to occupational success than those from working-class backgrounds. However, this would not necessarily prevent managers, whether from middle-class or other social backgrounds, from formulating some standards of effort beyond which they were not normally prepared to go, in return for the rewards which higher managers were prepared to pay. When the effort involves a major change of working habits, indeed, many managers are clearly not willing to cooperate if the change is imposed from above or outside – for example, by management consultants. And by dealing exclusively with improved performance, management by objectives characteristically involves changing habits.

However, the emphasis placed on participation by most members of the 'management by objectives' school of thought may be said to counter this objection. Many managers in this country would endorse the views of the American managers who took part in an AMA survey: 'Participation (in setting objectives or standards) tends to increase commitment; commitment tends to heighten motivation; motivation which is job-oriented tends to make managers work harder and more productively; and harder and more productive work by managers tends to enhance the company's prosperity; therefore, participation is good.'[10]

This judgement, of course, uses the company's interests as the criterion. But many researchers have argued that participation in decisions affecting an organisation's wellbeing brings benefits to its members. For Friedmann,[11] Argyris,[12] Likert,[13] Bennis[14] and many others, participation is one of a few related developments in industrial organisation which may decrease employees' feelings of dependence, frustration and apathy or hostility, and increase the satisfactions derived from control over one's own actions, and an enhanced feeling of worth and importance. If this is so, then even those managers who seek to keep control of their own effort to obtain an acceptable deal with their employers – behaving like the other employees in Baldamus's model – might be willing to trade greater effort and improved performance for greater satisfaction.

The comments of managers quoted in many of the published case histories appear to support this. Similar comments were made in my own company in the early phases of introducing management by objectives. However, case histories tend to be selective. They very seldom include failures, and they quote comments by individuals, not by a sample of managers. In my experience, while most managers initially welcomed greater participation, others did not – some resisted the implication that their performance could be improved, some apparently wanted to keep higher management at arm's length, some acknowledged that improvement was possible but did not want to have to suggest targets or methods, some did not want their subordinates to make suggestions, and so on. These are surely reactions which are likely to be widespread.

Some social scientists recognise this, though others do not. Likert, for example, sketches in a scale of participation, from extremely low ('no information given to employees, either about the current situation or in advance of proposed changes') to extremely high ('leader and subordinates functioning as a group tackle the problem and solve it, using the best available methods for group functioning').[15] He points out that different organisations, and even different parts of any one organisation, are accustomed to a particular degree of participation, high or low. He warns us that a sudden change, or a great increase in participation, is likely to defeat its purpose; the people involved are unable to cope with it – they seem to feel that it is not 'legitimate'.

In the case of tightly controlled organisations, a move towards participative management is likely to be met with apathy and indifference, or even hostility – partly to release pent-up frustration and partly to test the superior's sincerity in opening the way to comments and suggestions. Likert suggests that as two or three years are usually required to introduce a major technological change smoothly, introducing a substantially different management system will require appreciably longer – at least three or four years to develop and test the new theory in the company, and an additional five years or more to shift the organisation to full-scale application – in large companies, longer still. Likert often writes as a partisan exponent of collaborative or participative management, rather than a scientist, but these seem to be wise practical comments.

Argyris,[16] whose researches in theory X types of organisation seem to be associated with a less liberal-democratic view of human nature than McGregor's or Likert's, discusses the difficulties in more detail, and in terms that suggest that they are very intractable. Firstly, many successful managers would have to change their basic predispositions from being directive, self-controlled, accepting frustrations, seeking success as quickly as possible, relying on their own expertise, and wanting to have other people dependent on them, to become leaders of group discussions, helping subordinates to clarify their thoughts and feelings, prepared to express their own feelings and tensions, aiming at the achievement of growth and insight by their subordinates, recognising the limitations of their own knowledge and experience, and preferring to be first among equals. This would be a major change even for those who could achieve it.

Secondly, many employees have learned to be apathetic and non-involved at work – they do not want to be responsible for their own or their group's behaviour, and they will not readily accept this responsibility from their manager even if he offers to share it with them. This probably applies to at least a minority of managers, as well as other employees at lower levels. Although some of these individuals could perhaps learn to adapt to a new managerial style, others would be prevented by deep-rooted personality factors from doing so.

Thirdly, 'effective leadership depends on a multitude of conditions. There is no one predetermined, correct way to behave as a leader'. Unfortunately, research has not yet provided us with the tools for deciding which kind is likely to be most effective in any particular situation, although Joan Woodward's early work on technological variables found that permissive or participative management, with a high degree of delegation, was characteristic of unit and process production, while clearcut definition of responsibilities and authority was characteristic of large batch and mass production firms in South-East Essex.[17]

A recent introductory textbook on organisational psychology[18] very usefully puts into perspective a number of theoretical models of human behaviour in organisations, the evidence from their validity, and the managerial strategies which would result from them. The author compares the models of rational Economic Man, dating back to Adam Smith, but closely similar to McGregor's theory X, not to mention Baldamus; Social Man, immortalised by Elton Mayo and the Hawthorne researches, and developed by some of the Michigan studies in employee-centred supervision; and self-actualising Man, created by Maslow and adopted by Argyris and McGregor. After noting that empirical research has found some support for each of these simplified models, Schein concludes that people are not only more complex than any of them but highly variable. Man has many needs, which are combined in complex patterns of motivation which vary between individuals, and for any one individual in different situations or at different times; he can therefore 'respond to many different kinds of managerial strategies, depending on his own motives and abilities and the nature of the task; there is no one managerial strategy that will work for all men at all times'. This would clearly apply to management by objectives and participative management.

Friedmann, a French engineer and administrator, mentions a final difficulty which American writers hardly ever recognise: if highly participative management, involving extensive use of group-decision, is to spread widely beyond the few successful examples which undoubtedly exist, industrial society itself will have to change its values radically from its present authoritarian/laisser-faire dependence on a mixture of coercion and competition as the mainsprings of its socio-economic system.[19]

So far I have discussed only the strong participative connotation of management by objectives, which is of course most relevant to the benefits which might be derived from improved motivation, morale and manager development. Considered as an approach to planning and control, management by objectives has equally serious limitations.

Corporate strategic planning is inherently more difficult for firms engaged in unit and small batch production than for firms engaged in large batch and mass production, and it is least difficult in process production. This is not to suggest that process industries can predict their future – their present difficulties would dispel such a belief. The process of planning, however, is inevitably more complex in unit and small batch production, in which production schedules are generally based on customer orders only, close and continuous contact between operating functions is needed, and the dominance of the development function makes close control very difficult in other functions. In large batch and mass production, longer-term production schedules are necessary, for stock as well as for orders; working relationships between functional departments need not be so close, so that each function is less heavily dependent on the others; and closer control is exercised, particularly in the dominant production function. In process production, in which the plant determines the product, long-term planning is essential because of the high capital cost of the plants, the operating functions are almost independent of each other in many matters, and control is exercised by the technical requirements of the plant rather than by the management's administrative measures.[20]

Hence, in unit production, managers are generally able to plan for only a fairly short way ahead, and they must do this in close cooperation between functions. Clear objectives for individual managers can be set, provided such cooperation exists, but achievement of the objectives in any one function will depend very much on the other functions – for example, frequent design modifications tend to delay production, and invalidate the sales forecasts as well as pushing both production and design costs above budgeted levels; and higher costs combine with lower turnover to reduce cash flow and profitability. A management by objectives programme is likely to succeed only if long-term overall objectives are rather loose, and departmental and sectional objectives are kept flexible and short-term, and frequently revised at irregular and unpredictable intervals. Nor does it seem realistic to judge managers' performance by the objectives set at the beginning of any long period of time – the detailed situation may well have changed several times in as many months. In fact, as performance will have been greatly affected by many factors outside the manager's control, including the operations of other functions, performance appraisal in terms of the achievement of objectives is necessarily highly subjective.

In mass production, it should be practicable to plan further ahead, to set firm sectional and departmental objectives, and to integrate these more closely with the corporate plans and objectives. Even here, however, changes in the environment (such as devaluation, or a change in purchase tax) may make a change of plan suddenly necessary and such possible changes have to be taken into account in the corporate strategy. Similarly, internal events such as a strike may also dislocate plans and objectives. For these reasons, predetermined plans and objectives do not provide valid criteria for measuring performance, except in the short term.

In process production there is still more stability of operations at plant level, and it is feasible not only to plan and set objectives for longer periods, but also to develop performance standards for managers. Neither the external environment nor the internal system is wholly controllable, however, and objectives and standards still need careful subjective interpretation if they are to be used not only for industrial engineering purposes but also for assessing individual performance by managers.

In view of these difficulties, it is perhaps surprising that so many firms have embraced management by objectives enthusiastically, and not unexpected that some have found that its secret eludes them. B. J. Loasby,[21] goes so far as to argue that if strategic planning is used for control purposes, it frustrates its own valuable functions, which are concerned with present decisions to take present action, and not with future action. Controls based on long-range plans may motivate managers to promise only what they are confident they can achieve, and may increase a tendency to go on doing what the plans have laid down, instead of reacting with sufficient speed to changes in the situation.

A final major source of difficulty is that in many firms, especially in unit and small batch production, the organisation is barely under the management's control, in two senses. Firstly, measures for many of the key operations do not exist, or are rudimentary: this applies not only to design and development and marketing, but even to production, so that planning and forecasting have no firm basis, either for a single function or for corporate operations. It follows that objectives and plans are unreliable guides to decisions about the present, let alone decisions for future action; and appraisal of performance against targets or objectives is unreliable history.

Secondly, the informal organisation in such firms, which is essential if anything at all is to be achieved, may be so powerful that decisions taken at higher levels have only a minimal effect on the way the organisation actually operates. The top managers may initiate actions to increase production, reduce investment in work in progress, and so on, which are wholly or largely subverted at lower levels, often in ignorance though sometimes deliberately. The complex network of working relationships, across departmental and functional barriers, is to a large extent outside formal procedures and formal channels of communication, and so formal directives may make little or no impact. Objectives, like plans and budgets, have little relevance in such organisations unless they are broken down and reapplied at every level – yet the short-term nature of the planning cycle, the frequent changes of situation, and the complex interdepartmental working relationships make this a very difficult and time-consuming task. Close personal control by the chief executive may overcome the difficulties if the organisation is small enough.

How, then, can we explain the apparent successful use of management by objectives? Firstly, in view of Likert's comments on time-scale, any period of less than (say) five years is insufficient for an evaluation, and most British papers and articles are based on less than this – often less than two or three years. It is noteworthy that in General Electric of America, one of the pioneers, management by objectives has not become fully institutionalised after ten to fifteen years,[22] and recent published references indicate a flexible and undogmatic approach[23] which is in strong contrast with many of the hymns of praise sung by the newly converted.

Secondly, firms whose corporate planning is inadequate are likely to benefit from improving it, whether in the course of 'managing by objectives' or otherwise. As Loasby suggests, 'the great value of formal procedures (of long-range planning) is in the raising and broadening of important issues that are liable otherwise to be inadequately considered'. At lower levels, similar benefit may be achieved by successful attempts to define 'key results areas', which may be far from obvious, and by providing a regular occasion for manager and subordinate(s) to give sustained consideration to what they are trying to achieve, and better ways of achieving it. These benefits are not automatic, of course, and depend at the top on good business decisions and at any level on good management.

Thirdly, some firms may be sufficiently amenable both to planning and to some degree of participation, so that they benefit from a sustained programme which concentrates on improving these processes. It may be that most such firms will be in the process or mass production industries, or small enough to be controlled by the chief executive personally.

Lastly, even in highly successful firms, efficiency is so far below the optimum that a very wide range of actions, even if they are only partially effective, may well lead to a significant degree of improvement. The involvement of competent management consultants, with a practised eye for opportunities for improvement, increases this probability.

References

1. P. F. DRUCKER, *The Practice of Management*, Heinemann, 1955.

2. J. W. EWELL and G. H. HAAS, *Setting Standards for Executive Performance*, AMA Research Study, no. 42, 1960.

3. Ibid.

4. D. MCGREGOR, *The Human Side of Enterprise*, McGraw-Hill, 1960.

5. E. C. MILLER, *Objectives and Standards*, AMA Research Study, no. 74, 1966.
E. C. MILLER, *Objectives and Standards of Performance in Marketing Management*, AMA, 1967.
E. C. MILLER, *Objectives and Standards of Performance in Production Management*, AMA, 1967.

6. J. W. HUMBLE, *Improving Management Performance*, BIM, 1965.

7. e.g. D. E. P. OWEN, 'Setting objectives', *Chartered Mechanical Engineer*, Sept. 1966.

8. C. L. HUGHES, *Goal Setting*, AMA, 1965.

9. W. BALDAMUS, *Efficiency and Effort*, Tavistock Publications, 1961.

10. MILLER, op. cit., 1966, (see ref. 5), p. 38.

11. G. FRIEDMANN, *Industrial Society*, New York Free Press, 1948.

12. C. ARGYRIS, *Personality and Organisation*, Harper Bros., 1957.

13. R. LIKERT, *New Patterns of Management*, McGraw-Hill, 1961.

14. W. BENNIS, *Changing Organisations*, McGraw-Hill, 1966.

15. LIKERT, op. cit., p. 243.

16. ARGYRIS, op. cit., pp. 193–208.

17. J. WOODWARD, *Industrial Organisation: Theory and Practice*, Oxford University Press, 1965.

18. E. H. SCHEIN, *Organisational Psychology*, Prentice-Hall, 1965.

19. See also B. L. DAVIES, 'Some thoughts on "organisation democracy"', *Journal of Management Studies*, Oct. 1967.

20. WOODWARD, op. cit., pp. 125–53.

21. B. J. LOASBY, 'Long-range formal planning in perspective', *Journal of Management Studies*, October, 1967.

22. MILLER, op. cit., 1966, (see ref. 5), pp. 48–50.

23. e.g. M. S. KELLOGG, *What to do about Performance Appraisal*, AMA, 1965.

19

Patterns of organisation change*

L. GREINER

Today many top managers are attempting to introduce sweeping and basic changes in the behaviour and practices of the supervisors and the subordinates throughout their organisations. Whereas only a few years ago the target of organisation change was limited to a small work group or a single department, especially at lower levels, the focus is now converging on the organisation as a whole, teaching out to include many divisions and levels at once, and even the top managers themselves. There is a critical need at this time to understand better this complex process, especially in terms of which approaches lead to successful changes and which actions fail to achieve the desired results.

The shifting emphasis from small to large-scale organisation change represents a significant departure from past managerial thinking. For many years change was regarded more as an evolutionary than a revolutionary process. The evolutionary assumption reflected the view that change is a product of one minor adjustment after another, fuelled by time and subtle environmental forces largely outside the direct control of management. This relatively passive philosophy of managing change is typically expressed in words like these: 'Our company is continuing to benefit from a dynamically expanding market. While our share of the market has remained the same, our sales have increased 15 per cent over the past year. In order to handle this increased business, we have added a new marketing vice-president and may have to double our sales force in the next two years.' Such an optimistic statement frequently belies an unbounding faith in a beneficent environment. Perhaps this philosophy was adequate in less competitive times, when small patchwork changes, such as replacing a manager here and there, were sufficient to maintain profitability. But now the environments around organisations are changing rapidly and are challenging managements to become far more alert and inventive than they ever were before.

* Reprinted from HBR May–June 1967; © 1967 by the President and Fellows of Harvard College; all rights reserved.

Management awakening

In recent years more and more top managements have begun to realise that fragmented changes are seldom effective in stemming the underlying tides of stagnation and complacency that can subtly creep into a profitable and growing organisation. While rigid and uncreative attitudes are slow to develop, they are also slow to disappear, even in the face of frequent personnel changes. Most often these signs of decay can be recognised in managerial behaviour that (a) is oriented more to the past than to the future, (b) recognises the obligations of ritual more than the challenges of current problems, and (c) owes allegiance more to department goals than to overall company objectives.

Management's recent awakening to these danger signs has been stimulated largely by the rapidly changing tempo and quality of its environment. Consider:

- computer technology has narrowed the decision time span
- mass communication has heightened public awareness of consumer products
- new management knowledge and techniques have come into being
- technological discoveries have multiplied
- new world markets have opened up
- social drives for equality have intensified
- governmental demands and regulations have increased.

As a result, many organisations are currently being challenged to shift or even reverse gears in order to survive, let alone prosper.

A number of top managements have come around to adopting a revolutionary attitude towards change, in order to bridge the gap between a dynamic environment and a stagnant organisation. They feel that they can no longer sit back and condone organisational self-indulgence, waiting for time to heal all wounds. So, through a number of means, revolutionary attempts are now being made to transform their organisations rapidly by altering the behaviour and attitudes of their line and staff personnel at all levels of management. While each organisation obviously varies in its approach, the overarching goal seems to be the same: to get everyone psychologically redirected towards solving the problems and challenges of today's business environment. Here, for example, is how one company president describes his current goal for change:

> I've got to get this organisation moving, and soon. Many of our managers act as if we were still selling the products that used to be our bread and butter. We're in a different business now, and I'm not sure that they realise it. Somehow we've got to start recognising our problems and then become more competent in solving them. This applies to everyone here, including me and the janitor. I'm starting with a massive reorganisation which I hope will get us pulling together instead of in fifty separate directions.

Striking similarities

Although there still are not many studies of organisation change, the number is growing; and a survey of them shows that it is already possible to detect some striking similarities running throughout their findings. I shall report some of these similarities, under two headings:

1 Common approaches being used to initiate organisation change.
2 Reported results – what happened in a number of cases of actual organisation change.

I shall begin with the approaches, and then attempt to place them within the perspective of what has happened when these approaches were applied. As we shall see, only a few of the approaches used tend to facilitate successful change, but even here we find that each is aided by unplanned forces preceding and following its use. Finally, I shall conclude with some tentative interpretations as to what I think is actually taking place when an organisation change occurs.

Common approaches

In looking at the various major approaches being used to introduce organisation change, one is immediately struck by their position along a 'power distribution' continuum. At one extreme are those which rely on unilateral authority. More towards the middle of the continuum are the shared approaches. Finally, at the opposite extreme are the delegated approaches. As we shall see later, the shared approaches tend to be emphasised in the more successful organisation changes. Just why this is so is an important question we will consider in the concluding section. For now, though, let us gain a clearer picture of the various approaches as they appear most frequently in the literature of organisation change.

Unilateral action

At this extreme on the power distribution continuum, the organisation change is implemented through an emphasis on the authority of a man's hierarchical position in the company. Here, the definition and solution to the problem at hand tend to be specified by the upper echelons and directed downward through formal and impersonal control mechanisms. The use of unilateral authority to introduce organisation change appears in three forms.

BY DECREE

This is probably the most commonly used approach, having its roots in centuries of practice within military and government bureaucracies and taking its authority from the formal position of the person introducing the change. It is essentially a 'one-way' announcement that is directed downward to the lower levels in the organisation. The spirit of the communication reads something like 'today we are this way – tomorrow we must be that way'. In its concrete form it may appear as a memorandum, lecture, policy statement, or verbal command. The general nature of the decree approach is impersonal, formal, and task-oriented. It assumes that people are highly rational and best motivated by authoritative directions. Its expectation is that people will comply in their outward behaviour and that this compliance will lead to more effective results.

BY REPLACEMENT

Often resorted to when the decree approach fails, this involves the replacement of key persons. It is based on the assumption that organisation problems tend to reside in a few strategically located individuals, and that replacing these people will bring about sweeping and basic changes. As in the decree form, this change is usually initiated at the top and directed downward by a high authority figure. At the same time, however, it tends to be somewhat more personal, since particular individuals are singled out for replacement. Nevertheless, it retains much of the formality and explicit concern for task accomplishment that is common to the decree approach. Similarly, it holds no false optimism about the ability of individuals to change their own behaviour without clear outside direction.

BY STRUCTURE

This old and familiar change approach is currently receiving much re-evaluation by behavioural scientists. In its earlier form, it involved a highly rational approach to the design of formal organisation and to the lay-out of technology. The basic assumption here was that people behaved in close agreement with the structure and technology governing them. However, it tended to have serious drawbacks, since what seemed logical on paper was not necessarily logical for human goals.

Recently attempts have been made to alter the organisational structure in line with what is becoming known about both the logics and nonlogics of human behaviour, such as engineering the job to fit the man, on the one hand, or adjusting formal authority to match informal authority, on the other hand. These attempts still rely heavily on mechanisms for change that tend to be relatively formal, impersonal, and located outside the individual. At the same time because of greater concern for the effects of structure on people, they can probably be characterised as more personal, subtle, and less directive than either the decree or replacement approaches.

Sharing of power

More towards the middle of the power distribution continuum, as noted earlier, are the shared approaches, where authority is still present and used, yet there is also interaction and sharing of power. This approach to change is utilised in two forms.

BY GROUP DECISION-MAKING

Here the problems still tend to be defined unilaterally from above, but lower-level groups are usually left free to develop alternative solutions and to choose among them. The main assumption tends to be that individuals develop more commitment to action when they have a voice in the decisions that affect them. The net result is that power is shared between bosses and subordinates, though there is a division of labour between those who define the problems and those who develop the solutions.

BY GROUP PROBLEM-SOLVING

This form emphasizes both the definition and the solution of problems within the context of group discussion. Here power is shared throughout the decision process, but, unlike group decision-making, there is an added opportunity for lower-level subordinates to define the problem. The assumption underlying this approach is not only that people gain greater commitment from being exposed to a wider decision-making role, but also that they have significant knowledge to contribute to the definition of the problem.

Delegated authority

At the other extreme from unilateral authority are found the delegated approaches, where almost complete responsibility for defining and acting on problems is turned over to the subordinates. These also appear in two forms.

BY CASE DISCUSSION

This method focuses more on the acquisition of knowledge and skills than on the solution of specific problems at hand. An authority figure, usually a teacher or boss, uses his power only to guide a general discussion, such as a case or a report of research results. The 'teacher' refrains from imposing his own analysis or solutions on the group. Instead, he encourages individual members to arrive at their own insights, and they are left to use them as they see fit. The implicit assumption here is that individuals, through the medium of discussion about concrete situations, will develop general problem-solving skills to aid them in carrying out subsequent individual and organisation changes.

BY T-GROUP SESSIONS

These sessions, once conducted mainly in outside courses for representatives of many different organisations, are increasingly being used inside individual companies for effecting change. Usually, they are confined to top management, with the hope that beneficial 'spill-over' will result for the rest of the organisation. The primary emphasis of the T-group tends to be on increasing an individual's self-awareness and sensitivity to group social process. Compared to the previously discussed approaches, the T-group places much less emphasis on the discussion and solution of task-related problems. Instead, the data for discussion are typically the interpersonal actions of individuals in the group; no specific task is assigned to the group.

The basic assumption underlying this approach is that exposure to a structureless situation will release unconscious emotional energies within individuals, which, in turn, will lead to self-analysis, insight, and behavioural change. The authority figure in the group, usually a professional trainer, avoids asserting his own authority in structuring the group. Instead, he often attempts to become an accepted and influential member of the group. Thus, in comparison to the other approaches, much more authority is turned over to the group, from which position it is expected to chart its own course of change in an atmosphere of great informality and highly personal exchanges.

Reported results

As we have seen, each of the major approaches, as well as the various forms within them, rests on certain assumptions about what should happen when it is applied to initiate change. Now let us step back and consider what actually does happen – before, during, and after a particular approach is introduced.

To discover whether there are certain dimensions of organisation change that might stand out against the background of characteristics unique to one company, we conducted a survey of eighteen studies of organisation change. Specifically we were looking for the existence of dominant patterns of similarity and/or difference running across all of these studies. As we went along, relevant information was written down and compared with the other studies in regard to (a) the conditions leading up to an attempted change, (b) the manner in which the change was introduced, (c) the critical blocks and/or facilitators encountered during implementation, and (d) the more lasting results which appeared over a period of time.

The survey findings show some intriguing similarities and differences between those studies reporting 'successful' change patterns and those disclosing 'less successful' changes – i.e. failure to achieve the desired results. The successful changes generally appear as those which:

- spread throughout the organisation to include and affect many people
- produce positive changes in line and staff attitudes
- prompt people to behave more effectively in solving problems and in relating to others
- result in improved organisation performance.

Significantly, the less successful changes fall short on all of these dimensions.

'Success' patterns

Using the category breakdown just cited as the base-line for 'success', the survey reveals some very distinct patterns in the evolution of change. In all, eight major patterns are identifiable in five studies reporting successful change, and six other success studies show quite similar characteristics, although the information contained in each is somewhat less complete.

Consider:

1 The organisation, and especially top management, is under considerable external and internal pressure for improvement long before an explicit organisation change is contemplated. Performance and/or morale are low. Top management seems to be groping for a solution to its problems.

2 A new man, known for his ability to introduce improvements, enters the organisation, either as the official head of the organisation, or as a consultant who deals directly with the head of the organisation.

3 An initial act of the new man is to encourage a re-examination of past practices and current problems within the organisation.

4 The head of the organisation and his immediate subordinates assume a direct and highly involved role in conducting this re-examination.

5 The new man, with top management support, engages several levels of the organisation in collaborative, fact-finding, problem-solving discussions to identify and diagnose current organisation problems.

6 The new man provides others with new ideas and methods for developing solutions to problems, again at many levels of the organisation.

7 The solutions and decisions are developed, tested, and found creditable for solving problems on a small scale before an attempt is made to widen the scope of change to larger problems and the entire organisation.

8 The change effort spreads with each success experience, and as management support grows, it is gradually absorbed permanently into the organisation's way of life.

The likely significance of these similarities becomes more apparent when we consider the patterns found in the less successful organisation changes. Let us briefly make this contrast before speculating further about why the successful changes seem to unfold as they do.

'Failure' forms

Apart from their common 'failure' to achieve the desired results, the most striking overall characteristic of seven less successful change studies is a singular lack of consistency — not just between studies but within studies. Where each of the successful changes follows a similar and highly consistent route of one step building on another, the less successful changes are much less orderly.

There are three interesting patterns of inconsistency:

1 The less successful changes begin from a variety of starting points. This is in contrast to the successful changes, which begin from a common point – i.e. strong pressure both externally and internally. Only one less successful change, for example, began with outside pressure on the organisation; another originated with the hiring of a consultant; and a third started with the presence of internal pressure, but without outside pressure.

2 Another pattern of inconsistency is found in the sequence of change steps. In the successful change patterns, we observe some degree of logical consistency between steps, as each seems to make possible the next. But in the less successful changes, there are wide and seemingly illogical gaps in sequence. One study, for instance, described a big jump from the reaction to outside pressure to the installation of an unskilled newcomer who immediately attempted large-scale changes. In another case, the company lacked the presence of a newcomer to provide new methods and ideas to the organisation. A third failed to achieve the cooperation and involvement of top management. And a fourth missed the step of obtaining early success while experimenting with new change methods.

3 A final pattern of inconsistency is evident in the major approaches used to introduce change. In the successful cases, it seems fairly clear that shared approaches are used – i.e. authority figures seek the participation of subordinates in joint decision-making. In the less successful attempts, however, the approaches used lie closer to the extreme ends of the power distribution continuum. Thus, in five less successful change studies, a unilateral approach (decree, replacement, structural) was used while in two other studies a delegated approach (data discussion, T-group) was applied. None of the less successful change studies reported the use of a shared approach.

How can we use this lack of consistency in the sequence of change steps and this absence of shared power to explain the less successful change attempts? In the next section, I shall examine in greater depth the successful changes, which, unlike the less successful ones, are marked by a high degree of consistency and the use of shared power. My intent here will be not only to develop a tentative explanation of the more successful changes, but in so doing to explain the less successful attempts within the same framework.

Power redistribution

Keeping in mind that the survey evidence on which both the successful and the less successful patterns are based is quite limited, I would like to propose a tentative explanatory scheme for viewing the change process as a whole, and also for considering specific managerial action steps within this overall process. The framework for this scheme hinges on two key notions. First, successful change depends basically on a redistribution of power within the structure of an organisation. (By power, I mean the locus of formal authority and influence which typically is top management. By redistribution, I mean a significant alteration in the traditional practices that the power structure uses in making decisions. I propose that this redistribution move towards the greater use of shared power.) Secondly, power redistribution occurs through a development process of change. (This implies that organisation change is not a black to white affair occurring overnight through a single causal mechanism. Rather, as we shall see, it involves a number of phases, each containing specific elements and multiple causes that provoke a needed reaction from the power structure, which, in turn, sets the stage for the next phase in the process.)

Using the survey evidence from the successful patterns, I have divided the change process into six phases, each of them broken down into the particular stimulus and reaction which appear critical for moving the power structure from one phase to another. Fig. 19.1 represents an abstract view of these two key notions in operation.

Let us now consider how each of these phases and their specific elements make themselves evident in the patterns of successful change, as well as how their absence contributes to the less successful changes.

1   Pressure and arousal

This initial stage indicates a need to shake the power structure at its very foundation. Until the ground under the top managers begins to shift, it seems unlikely that they will be sufficiently aroused to see the need for change, both in themselves and in the rest of the organisation.

The success patterns suggest that strong pressures in areas of top management responsibility are likely to provoke the greatest concern for organisation change. These pressures seem to come from two broad sources: (a) serious environmental factors, such as lower sales, stockholders' discontent, or competitor breakthroughs; and (b) internal events, such as a union strike, low productivity, high costs, or interdepartmental conflict. These pressures fall into responsibility areas that top managers can readily see as reflecting on their own capability. An excerpt from one successful change study (Guest 1962) shows how this pressure and arousal process began: '"Pressure" was the common expression used at all levels. Urgent telephone calls, telegrams, letters and memoranda were being received by the plant from central headquarters. . . . Faced with an increase in directives from above and cognisant of Plant Y's low performance position, the manager knew that he was, as he put it, "on the spot"' (p. 18). As this example points out, it is probably significant when both environmental and internal pressures exist simultaneously. When only one is present, or when the two are offsetting (i.e. high profits despite low morale), it is easier for top management to excuse the pressure as only temporary or inconsequential. When both are present at once it is easier to see that the organisation is not performing effectively.

The presence of severe pressure is not so clearly evident in the less successful

Fig. 19.1 Dynamics of successful organisation change

	Stimulus of the power structure		Reaction of the power structure
PHASE 1.	→ Pressure of top management		
		→	Arousal to take action
PHASE 2.	Intervention at the top	←	
		→	Reorientation to internal problems
PHASE 3.	Diagnosis of problem areas	←	
		→	Recognition of specific problems
PHASE 4.	Invention of new solutions	←	
		→	Commitment to new courses of action
PHASE 5.	Experimentation of new solutions	←	
		→	Search for results
PHASE 6.	Reinforcement from positive results	←	
		→	**Acceptance of new practices**

changes. In one case, there was internal pressure for more effective working relations between top management and lower levels; yet the company was doing reasonably well from a profit standpoint. In another case, there was environmental pressure for a centralised purchasing system, but little pressure from within for such a change.

2 Intervention and reorientation

While strong pressure may arouse the power structure, this does not provide automatic assurance that top management will see its problems or take the correct action to solve them. Quite likely, top management, when under severe pressure, may be inclined to rationalise its problems by blaming them on a group other than itself, such as 'that lousy union' or 'that meddling government'.

As a result, we find a second stage in the successful change patterns – namely, intervention by an outsider. Important here seems to be the combination of the fact that the newcomer enters at the top of the organisation and the fact that he is respected for his skills at improving organisation practices. Being a newcomer probably allows him to make a relatively objective appraisal of the organisation;

entering at the top gives him ready access to those people who make decisions affecting the entire organisation; and his being respected is likely to give added weight to his initial comments about the organisation.

Thus we find the newcomer in an ideal position to reorient the power structure to its own internal problems. This occurs in the successful changes as the newcomer encourages the top managers to re-examine their past practices and current problems. The effect appears to be one of causing the power structure to suspend, at least temporarily, its traditional habit of presuming beforehand where the 'real' problems reside. Otherwise we would not find top management undertaking the third stage – identifying and diagnosing organisation problems. We can see how an outsider was accomplishing this reorientation in the following comment by the plant manager in one successful change study: 'I didn't like what the consultant told me about our problems being inside the organisation instead of outside. But he was an outsider, supposedly an expert at this sort of thing. So maybe he could see our problems better than we could. I asked him what we ought to do, and he said that we should begin to identify our specific problems' (L. Greiner, 'Organisation and development' unpublished doctoral dissertation, Harvard Business School, June 1965).

Three of the less successful changes missed this step. Two of the three attempted large-scale changes without the assistance of an outsider, while the third relied on an outsider who lacked the necessary expertise for reorienting top management.

3   Diagnosis and recognition

Here we find the power structure, from top to bottom, as well as the newcomer, joining in to assemble information and collaborate in seeking the location and causes of problems. This process begins at the top, then moves gradually down through the organisational hierarchy. Most often, this occurs in meetings attended by people from various organisation levels.

A shared approach to power and change makes itself evident during this stage. Through consulting with subordinates on the nature of problems, the top managers are seen as indicating a willingness to involve others in the decision-making process. Discussion topics, which formerly may have been regarded as taboo, are now treated as legitimate areas for further inquiry. We see the diagnosis and recognition process taking place in this example from one successful change study:

> The manager's role in the first few months, as he saw it, was to ask questions and to find out what ideas for improvement would emerge from the group as a whole. The process of information gathering took several forms, the principal one being face-to-face conversations between the manager and his subordinates, supervisors on the lower levels, hourly workers, and union representatives. Ideas were then listed for the agenda of weekly planning sessions (Guest 1962, p. 50).

The significance of this step seems to go beyond the possible intellectual benefits derived from a thorough diagnosis of organisation problems. This is due to the fact that in front of every subordinate there is evidence that (*a*) top management is willing to change, (*b*) important problems are being acknowledged and faced, and (*c*) ideas from lower levels are being valued by upper levels.

The less successful changes all seem to avoid this step. For example, on the one hand, those top managements that took a unilateral approach seemed to presume ahead of time that they knew what the real problems were and how to fix them. On the other hand, those that took a delegated approach tended to abdicate responsibility by turning over authority to lower levels in such a non-directive way that subordinates seemed to question the sincerity and real interest of top management.

4 Invention and commitment

Once problems are recognised, it is another matter to develop effective solutions and to obtain full commitment for implementing them. Traditional practices and solutions within an organisation often maintain a hold that is difficult to shed. The temptation is always there, especially for the power structure, to apply old solutions to new problems. Thus, a fourth phase – the invention of new and unique solutions which have high commitment from the power structure – seems to be necessary.

The successful changes disclose widespread and intensive searches for creative solutions, with the newcomer again playing an active role. In each instance the newcomer involves the entire management in learning and practising new forms of behaviour which seek to tap and release the creative resources of many people. Again, as in the previous phase, the method for obtaining solutions is based on a shared power concept. Here the emphasis is placed on the use of collaboration and participation in developing group solutions to the problems identified in Phase 3.

The potency of this model for obtaining both quality decisions and high commitment to action has been demonstrated repeatedly in research. In three successful changes, the model was introduced as a part of the Phase 3 diagnosis sessions, with the newcomer either presenting it through his informal comments or subtly conveying it through his own guiding actions as the attention of the group turned to the search for a solution. In two other studies, formal training programmes were used to introduce and to help implement the model. For all successful changes, the outcome is essentially the same – a large number of people collaborate to invent solutions that are of their own making and which have their own endorsement.

It is significant that none of the less successful changes reach this fourth stage. Instead, the seeds of failure, sown in the previous phase, grow into instances of serious resistance to change. As a result, top management in such cases falls back, gives up, or regroups for another effort. Because these studies conclude their reports at this stage, we are not able to determine the final outcome of the less successful change attempts.

5 Experimentation and search

Each of the successful change studies reports a fifth stage – that of 'reality testing' before large-scale changes are introduced. In this phase not only the validity of specific decisions made in Phase 4, but also the underlying model for making these decisions (shared power), falls under careful organisation scrutiny. Instead of making only big decisions at the top, a number of small decisions are implemented at all levels of the organisation. Further, these decisions tend to be regarded more as experiments than as final, irreversible decisions. People at all organisation levels seem to be searching for supporting evidence in their environment – e.g. dollar savings or higher motivation – before judging the relative merits of their actions. This concern is reflected in the comment of a consultant involved in one successful change:

> As might be expected, there was something less than a smooth, unresisted, uncomplicated transition to a new pattern of leadership and organisational activity. Events as they unfolded presented a mixture of successes and failures, frustrations and satisfactions. . . . With considerable apprehension, the supervisors agreed to go along with any feasible solution the employees might propose (Seashore and Bowers 1963, p. 29).

This atmosphere of tentativeness is understandable when we think of a power structure undergoing change. On the one hand, lower level managers are undoubtedly concerned with whether top management will support their decisions. If lower level managers make decisions that fail or are subsequently reversed by top levels, then their own future careers may be in jeopardy. Or, on the other hand, if higher level managers, who are held responsible for the survival of the firm, do not see tangible improvements, then they may revert to the *status quo* or seek other approaches to change.

Thus, with these experimental attempts at change and the accompanying search for signs of payoff, there begins a final stage where people receive the results and react to them.

6 Reinforcement and acceptance

Each of the studies of successful change reports improvements in organisation performance. Furthermore, there are relatively clear indications of strong support for change from all organisation levels. Obviously, positive results have a strong reinforcing effect – that is, people are rewarded and encouraged to continue and even to expand the changes they are making. We see this expansion effect occurring as more and more problems are identified and a greater number of people participate in the solution of them. Consider this comment by a foreman in one study:

I've noticed a real difference in the hourly workers. They seem a lot more willing to work, and I can't explain just why it is, but something has happened all right. I suppose it's being treated better. My boss treats me better because he gets treated better. People above me listen to me and I hope at least, that I listen to my people below me (Guest 1962, p. 64).

The most significant effect of this phase is probably a greater and more permanent acceptance at all levels of the underlying methods used to bring about the change. In each of the successful changes, the use of shared power is more of an institutionalised and continuing practice than just a 'one-shot' method used to introduce change. With such a reorientation in the decision-making practices of the power structure, it hardly appears likely that these organisations will 'slip back' to their previous behaviour.

Looking ahead

What is needed in future changes in organisation is less intuition and more consideration of the evidence that is now emerging from studies in this area. While it would be unwise to take too literally each of the major patterns identified in this article (future research will undoubtedly dispel, modify, or elaborate on them), their overall import suggests that it is time to put to bed some of the common myths about organisation change. As I see it, there are four positive actions called for.

1 We must revise our egocentric notions that organisation change is heavily dependent on a master blueprint designed and executed in one fell swoop by an omniscient consultant or top manager.

  The patterns identified here clearly indicate that change is the outgrowth of several actions, some planned and some unplanned, each related to the others and occurring over time. The successful changes begin with pressure, which is unplanned from the organisation's point of view. Then the more planned stages come into focus as top management initiates a series of events designed to involve lower-level people in the problem-solving process. But, even here, there are usually unplanned events as subordinates begin to 'talk-back' and raise issues that top management probably does not anticipate. Moreover, there are the concluding stages of experiencing success, partly affected by conscious design but just as often due to forces outside the control of the planners.

2 We too often assume that organisation change is for 'those people downstairs', who are somehow perceived as less intelligent and less productive than 'those upstairs'. Contrary to this assumption, the success patterns point to the importance of top management seeing itself as part of the organisation's problems and becoming actively involved in finding solutions to them. Without the involvement and commitment of top management, it is doubtful

that lower levels can see the need for change or, if they do, be willing to take the risks that such change entails.

3 We need to reduce our fond attachment for both unilateral and delegated approaches to change.

The unilateral approach, although tempting because its procedures are readily accessible to top management, generally serves only to perpetuate the myths and disadvantages of omniscience and downward thinking. On the other hand, the delegated approach, while appealing because of its 'demo-cratic' connotations, may remove the power structure from direct involvement in a process that calls for its strong guidance and active support.

The findings discussed in this article highlight the use of the more difficult, but perhaps more fruitful, shared power approach. As top managers join in to open up their power structures and their organisations to an exchange of influence between upper and lower levels, they may be unleashing new surges of energy and creativity not previously imagined.

4 There is a need for managers, consultants, sceptics and researchers to become less parochial in their viewpoints.

For too long each of us has acted as if cross-fertilization is unproductive. Much more constructive dialogue and joint effort are needed if we are to understand better and act wisely in terms of the complexities and stakes inherent in the difficult problems of introducing organisation change.

References and further studies

Reporting 'successful' organisation changes:

ROBERT R. BLAKE, JANE S. MOUTON, LOUIS B. BARNES and LARRY E. GREINER, 'Breakthrough in organisation development', HBR, Nov.–Dec. 1964, p. 133.

ROBERT H. GUEST, Organisation Change: The Effect of Successful Leadership, Homewood, Illinois, The Dorsey Press, 1962.

ELLIOTT JAQUES, The Changing Culture of a Factory, New York, The Dryden Press, 1952.

A. K. RICE, Productivity and Social Organization: The Ahmedabad Experiment, London, Tavistock Publications, 1958.

S. E. SEASHORE and D. G. BOWERS, Changing the Structure and Functioning of an Organisation, Ann Arbor, Survey Research Centre, The University of Michigan, Monograph no. 33, 1963.

Showing similar success patterns, but containing somewhat less complete information:

GENE W. DALTON, LOUIS B. BARNES and ABRAHAM ZALEZNIK, 'The authority structure as a change variable', paper presented at the 57th meeting of the American Sociological Association, Washington, DC, Aug. 1962.

PAUL R. LAWRENCE, The Changing of Organisation Behavior Patterns: a case study of decentralisation, Boston, Division of Research, Harvard Business School, 1958.

PAUL R. LAWRENCE, et al., 'Battleship Y', Organisational Behavior and Administration, Homewood, Illinois, The Dorsey Press, p. 328, 1965 edn.

FLOYD C. MANN, 'Studying and creating change: a means to understanding social organisation', *Research in Industrial Human Relations*, ed. C. M. Arensberg *et al.*, New York, Harper, 1957.

G. SOFER, *The Organisation from Within*, London, Tavistock Publications, 1961.

WILLIAM F. WHYTE, *Pattern for Industrial Peace*, New York, Harper, 1951.

Studies which reveal 'less successful' change patterns:

CHRIS ARGYRIS, *Interpersonal Competence and Organisational Effectiveness*, Homewood, Illinois, The Dorsey Press, 1962, especially pp. 254–7.

A. GOULDNER, *Patterns of Industrial Bureaucracy*, Glencoe, Illinois, The Free Press, 1964.

PAUL R. LAWRENCE *et al.*, 'The Dashman Company and Flint Electric', in *Organisational Behaviour and Administration*, Homewood, Illinois, The Dorsey Press, p. 16 (1965 edn), and p. 600 (1961 edn).

GEORGE STRAUSS, 'The set-up man: a case study of organisational change', *Human Organisation*, 13, 1954, p. 17.

A. J. M. STRAUSS, 'The effects of a supervisory training course in changing supervisors' perceptions and expectations of the role of management', *Human Relations*, 15, 1962, p. 227.

WILLIAM F. WHYTE, *Money and Motivation*, New York, Harper, 1955.

20

Manpower planning at
national and company
level

JOAN COX

Discussion of manpower planning take place in the context either of national plans or of company plans. From time to time the view has been expressed that the coverage and the time scale of these two types of planning are so different that there is nothing in common between them. This paper considers whether, in practice, 'manpower' is really so different from 'personnel'. After all, the individuals regarding whom both plans are made are the same people; in both cases the planners are concerned with the posts they are to fill, with their salaries and with their mobility.

Quite obviously there must be differences of approach between manpower planning at national and company level. 'Redundancy', which may be the concern of personnel departments, has a different aura from 'unemployment' which is the parallel concern of the government planner. Similarly, the earnings of the company have only a remote connection with the gross domestic product of the country. But these are matters of scale and approach rather than of substance. It is generally recognised that the creation of new job opportunities is a concomitant of a buoyant and growing economy, but, to be itself growing and buoyant, the economy must consist of growing and buoyant companies. Similarly, if companies or public corporations are to expand, then they must also expand their personnel. It makes little difference that, in the national aggregate, it is usual to refer to 'manpower'.

The common area

It is axiomatic that the growth of the economy is no more than the growth in aggregate of public corporations and innumerable private enterprises. Thus (although there are certain differences) national manpower is a parallel activity to the company planning (implicit or explicit) of those enterprises that make up the industrial sector. It will be remembered too that national planning is unlikely to be undertaken unless the views of the public and private employers are first obtained.

Company and national planning draw further apart when policy matters are being considered. A company, looking forward five or ten years, must consider the personnel that it must employ to carry out its current short-term programme, as well as its more tentative longer-term programme and it will first draw from the pool of people it already has in its employment. A generously staffed organisation may be able simply to rearrange posts and responsibilities, whereas a fast-growing company may be involved in a sizeable recruiting campaign.

Manpower planning at national level, however, has to encompass the whole of the working population or, more precisely, that part of the working population relevant to the plan under consideration. In doing so it must take into account such factors as the level of unemployment, the availability of personnel outside the working population (such as married women), the extent of mobility between sectors and finally, migration. The national manpower planner must interest himself in the demography of the country's manpower and reflect on the government's responsibility for manpower as a whole. This makes him see the problem from a different angle. This is not to say that manpower planning at national level has 'full employment' as a primary aim, but it does mean that the manpower implications of any particular set of propositions at national level should be understood and communicated to senior officials and ministers. The manpower planner must be in a position to assess the effects of expansion or retrenchment on the economy as a whole. Thus he is concerned with an aggregate of enterprise and public sector plans and must assess whether it is likely to come into balance with the numbers resulting from past demographic trends and activity rates. And, if they do not balance in the first instance, what economic and social consequences can be expected.

It can be seen that there is a very large common area of interest between manpower planning at national and company level – planners are concerned with the same people, in the same age groups and in the same posts. It is only at the final stages of the analysis that the interests tend to diverge; while the national planner is assessing the balance between supply and demand for manpower as a whole or in broad categories, the company personnel planner is checking whether his recruitment plans are consistent with manpower costs and are providing an acceptable age and promotion structure. Economic and social considerations are, of course, of interest to both sides; it is just that the impact on their responsibilities is somewhat different.

Having identified what are the essential differences, we can now see the extent of these similarities and can study the desirability of an interchange of ideas between national and company planners in their common areas.

Decision-making

Management literature rightly puts the emphasis on decision-making. It is axiomatic that the sequences of forward planning must follow a decision and it is immaterial whether this decision to commit resources is taken by the directors of a company or the government of a country. Again, while there is no conceptual difference between the decision to commit resources by government or by an enterprise, the scale of the operation and the chain of command by which the results are obtained can be very different. Furthermore, the *direct* action taken by the company contrasts with the *indirect* action normally taken by government – with its much longer time-span.

The decision to commit resources is the starting point for planning. It is sometimes supposed that planning can take place in a vacuum but this is clearly unrealistic; such a view confuses planning with the monitoring or appraisal of events already occurring. It is equally true that the initial decision to commit resources for a particular objective is followed by a sequence of secondary decisions usually at lower levels of command and it is the appreciation of the sequence of decision-making that provides, so to speak, the chart that will guide the manpower planner.

Before going into the sequence of logical steps needed to implement a decision it is worthwhile looking at the differences and similarities between these procedures as they present themselves at national and company level. Fig. 20.1 makes a first comparison between the sequence of decisions as they will be taken.

Fig. 20.1 Manpower planning at national and company level

NATIONAL LEVEL	COMPANY LEVEL
National objective	Company objective.
↓	↓
Identification of activities and function(s). Construction R and D.	Identification of function(s) within which company must operate (R and D, production, etc.).
↓	↓
Translation into posts to work within function(s).	Translation into posts to work within function(s).
↓	↓
Identification of broad group of skills required in such posts.	Identification of job skills required in posts.
↓	↓
Using cross-analyses of job skill/subject of qualification, assess subjects likely to be called for by employers.	Translation into subjects of qualification (or job experience) required in posts.

As already observed, in practice national manpower planning tends to operate through indirect processes. Whereas the company can bear directly on the problem by moving people within the company or by recruiting from the market, at any point in time, the government must operate with a working population of a given size and with a given distribution of qualification and experience. If, for instance, the decision is to launch a new road-building programme, it is only a limited help if universities transfer resources to their civil engineering departments. By the time the additional graduates are leaving the universities, the civil engineering contractors who are responsible for the programme will have completed their recruitment.

Up to this point we have ignored one of the biggest differences between company and national planning: the speed at which plans are brought into effect. The company can act promptly; if it is prepared to raise its price, it can obtain the necessary personnel either in competition with home-based or even with overseas-based employers. The achievement of its immediate needs is a matter of economics but, except in very rare circumstances, the achievement of government plans is a matter of time and persuasion as well as money. This factor of the time lag may well prove to be the main difference between the environment of the company and the national planners. Nevertheless, there is still a considerable degree of similarity and Fig. 20.2 indicates the main points of comparison.

Fig. 20.2 Matters to be considered

Who are already in the country and available for employment?	*Who are already in the company?*
Data from Census of Population.	Planning requires that a full register of posts is made and of the people in them.
Periodic surveys of manpower.	You cannot plan ahead without full knowledge of the posts in the company at any date.
Compare numbers required overall with number in stock.	Compare number in each category required with people already employed.

Planning in the organisation

Planning is an activity which is initiated by a decision to commit resources to a given objective or goal.* The resources which now come under the scrutiny of the corporate planners comprise finance, capital facilities and people. Personnel planning concentrates on the last of these but the investigation of interplay with the investment programme and with cash flow is part of the planning process.

The personnel planning part of the total or corporate planning falls into four stages:

1 The examination of the objective.
2 The resources to be allocated to personnel.
3 The analysis of the jobs required:
  (a) in which functions
  (b) the authority of posts within these functions
  (c) the skills required and
  (d) the identification of the level at which the skills must be performed.
4 The matching of posts and people.

  * Such a decision, of course, will be preceded by a review of alternative goals – but this is not strictly part of the planning stage.

Before this last stage, the finding of the people, personnel planners must ask a number of questions:

Q.1 Who do we have in the company who could be shifted? What is their age? Qualification? Experience?
Q.2 Who shall we have to recruit?
Q.3 What does this imply for other posts in the company?

It will be appreciated that these questions cannot be answered without information. All these questions:

- who do we have?
- which posts should they fill?
- how many shall we have to recruit?
- what does this imply for other posts in the company? – require precise and, equally important, *immediately retrievable* information.

This indicates the first rule of planning, the requirement of adequate information. This must comprise:

- posts in the company at the date the planning starts
- information about the individuals who fill these posts

 and, if possible,

- the situation as it has changed over the last few years, so that wastage and promotion can be studied.

In view of its importance, why are organisations so slow to collect and retrieve information of this type?

It is odd that, while we can produce the necessary 'systems' to send men to the moon, the equivalent 'system' to do what has just been described is evolving very slowly. Why is this? Two things stand in the way of proper information: first, the sheer cost of holding, updating and sorting files on individuals and the posts they fill; and second, the difficulty of even attempting this until we have a consistent system of defining and describing posts – so that these can be recognised for what they are, and not be hidden behind different job titles.

A project to explore such a system for defining and describing posts, so deceptively simple in concept but so fiendishly difficult in practice, brought industry and government together.

Influence of the computer

As companies grow and become more complex, more information is needed about the men employed and the posts they fill. But by the laws of arithmetic the larger the number of records the harder it is to extract information from them. Five hundred punch cards need skilled handling – what if there are 10000? or 24000 as in a large government department? How can twenty people with the required characteristics for a new research team be found from such a number? It is almost impossible. This simple frustration – the absence of time, systems and resources explains why so little is known about posts and manpower utilisation in organisations.

Undoubtedly the reason that job classification came to the forefront of manpower thinking around 1964 was the intrusion of the computer into personnel work and manpower analysis. Personnel administrators saw clearly that, within a few years, they would be keeping the posts record for their company on magnetic tape. This would involve systematic description and coding of the posts that men were occupying or were to occupy. And systematic description of posts means that the main characteristics must be identified and set into a list of descriptors. The job can then be identified by the selection of the appropriate descriptor for each characteristic.

As has already been seen from Fig. 20.1, manpower planning at company and at national level is a parallel and not dissimilar activity. A number of companies who provided manpower data to government also recognised that national and company planning were not mutually exclusive exercises but were entities that were involved one with the other. They argued that the data collected for essential personnel planning by companies should be so designed that they would link directly with those used by government departments for national planning. Perhaps the most surprising thing about this statement of the obvious was that it had not been actively explored before. As yet, no complete solution to the problem has been found, but discussions between government and industry are going forward. These centre round the characteristics which derive from the processes of decision-making – and involve distinguishing the job skill, the *basic criteria* of each post, from the *associated factors*. The underlying principles of the proposed classification are derived from the planning stages (1) and (2) set out above.

Planning properly follows a sequence of decisions, thus the information to be stored and retrieved for planning should depend on a system of descriptors based on the logical processes of decision making and committal of resources. Again, since the approach to job classification accepts that top level decisions must impose their characteristics on the post being described, it follows that the information can most usefully be interpreted in a corresponding form. For instance, an initial decision to increase the R and D effort can be monitored by retrieving the number of posts (and costs) reflecting the current effort in the R and D function.

Manpower planning by government

A brief description of manpower planning at national level was given above. We can now look at two further aspects of the complexities of planning by a central authority.

The first aspect of importance for manpower planning is the cumulative build-up of stock. Large manpower aggregates such as the whole of the working population will change only slowly whatever the economic climate – for instance, the number employed in manufacturing in the year 2000 is expected to be little different from what is now. However, in small occupational groups the situation can be very different – this is because the inputs to the group from the educational system can be very large in comparison with the size of the stock. It follows that abrupt changes in flows can bring quite dramatic results.

It will be remembered that, at the height of the Apollo programme in the United States, the number of emigrants with engineering qualifications, over 6000, was equivalent to 50 per cent of the new supply.[1] Looking at this another way, if there had been neither natural wastage nor migration, the numbers in employment would have risen by 8 per cent each year. This is a sobering thought for planners. It can thus be seen that in certain circumstances, changes in flows can bring very marked changes in stock. It follows that the manpower planner must pay even more attention to this 'cumulation factor' where the body of people is small and specialised; and where the economic rewards are high, attracting even more entrants to training.

From time to time the economy experiences a very sharp increase in the number of job opportunities in a new specialism or technology; nuclear science and computers are two such examples. It is very much the responsibility of the national manpower planner to assess whether the upsurge in training that follows is meeting a long-term need or whether, some time later, the number of new job opportunities will be below the numbers that are trained each year.

This brings us to a second important factor, the dynamic characteristics of the organisation. Organisations are invariably subject to a feature of growth that might be described as the 'S curve'. They start slowly, experience a period of fast growth in employment and then tend to level off. In recent times we have seen this phenomenon occur in aviation, in atomic energy, even in the staffing of the universities following the Robbins expansion. As the growth occurs, universities and other educational institutions do their utmost to fill the gap between demand and supply; and employers, who in such situations face an inflation of salaries, will be critical if the trained people do not become available.

It is in this situation that the manpower planner has his heaviest responsibility. There is invariably a disinclination to look far enough into the future. Infrequently the extent of the shortage is exaggerated, even to the point where demand would be met by stock accumulation with no further action taken. The danger is that the new supply becomes available just when the creation of new posts requiring such skills is tailing off.

The phenomenon of the 'S curve' growth, and its effect on the provision of new job opportunities can best be illustrated by an example. Fig. 20.3 represents a sector which is introducing a new technology over a period of years, let us say 1958 to 1972. As a result, there is very fast growth in employment around the second quarter of the period shown and slightly less growth in the third quarter. In the fourth quarter employment levels off and finally declines as international competition restricts its market. The pattern of recruitment for that sector is shown in the bar chart below the line representing employment. It will be seen that the recruitment would be highest in the second quarter – corresponding to the period of fastest growth. By the fourth quarter, recruitment would be required only for the replacement of those who died or resigned; without any further growth this may level out at about $3\frac{1}{2}$ per cent, even less. (See Fig. 20.4 for calculation of necessary recruitment.)

The characteristics of these interrelated charts suggest that the planner must pay special attention to two things:

1 Pressure for raising the output of specialists can be expected to be most intense around the second quarter of any growth period: the period when advertisements for posts are most numerous and salaries are high relative to other specialisms.
2 The initiation of additional training places at this point on the growth curve almost ensures that the additional graduates present themselves just as the market weakens.

Fig. 20.3 Employment in sector adopting a new technology over fifteen years: a simulated example

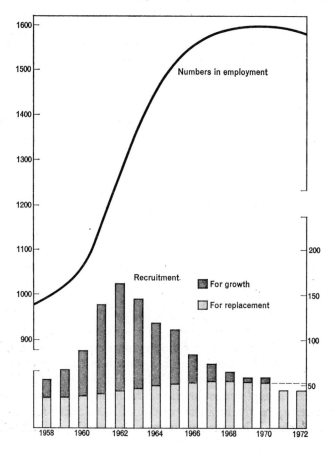

The lower bar chart also suggests that longer-term courses for specialised technologies should be planned with care; possibly restricted to no more than 5 per cent stock replacement. This would leave the peak demand to be met by overseas graduates or by crash courses. To achieve this, some estimate must be made of the level at which employment will level off – the top of the S curve – but experience has shown that economic assessments of this type can be made and are good enough to set the limits.

This task, though exacting, is not one that can be side-stepped by the national manpower planner. The risk of disappointment and frustration among young people who graduate and then find the job opportunities are not there is very considerable. At the present time the overall position for highly qualified people is such that the ability for sideways transfer between one occupational group and another is already being restricted. In the past this has largely been avoided because the number of highly educated people in the economy has been well below demand. The situation now arising suggests that some ground rules should be observed by any planner (or advisory committee) who is seeking the correct response to a rising demand for specialised graduates.

Fig. 20.4 Simulated example of a sector adopting a new technology over fifteen years

| Year | EMPLOYMENT | | RECRUITMENT | | | | |
| | At January | Change in year % | Total | For growth | To replace losses† from: | | |
					Total	Normal mobility	Wastage
1958	980	2·0	57	+20	37	20	17
1959	1000	3·0	67	+30	37	20	17
1960	1030	4·9	88	+50	38	21	17
1961	1080	9·3	140	+100	40	22	18
1962	1180	10·2	163	+120	43	24	19
1963	1300	7·7	146	+100	46	26	20
1964	1400	5·0	119	+70	49	28	21
1965	1470	4·1	111	+60	51	29	22
1966	1530	2·0	83	+30	53	31	22
1967	1560	1·3	73	+20	53	31	22
1968	1580	0·6	63	+10	53	32	21
1969	1590	0·3	58	+5	53	32	21
1970	1595	0·3	58	+5	53	32	21
1971	1600	−0·6	43	—	43	22*	21
1972	1590	−0·6	43	—	43	22*	21
1973	1580						

* In a situation of declining employment employees leaving for posts in other sectors will not be replaced.

† For discussion of natural wastage and normal mobility see Sections 11 and 22 of *Persons with Qualifications in Engineering, Technology and Science, 1959 to 1968*.

References

1. Statistics of emigration and new supply are taken from *Persons with Qualifications in Engineering, Technology and Science,* 1959 to 1968, HMSO, March 1971, Table 28.

2. For discussion of flows, see Section 22 of *Persons with Qualifications in Engineering, Technology and Science,* 1950 to 1968, HMSO, March 1971.

21

Developing a strategy in industrial relations

L. F. NEAL

One of the objections commonly encountered with regard to the feasibility of a strategy in industrial relations is that most managers simply do not have the time to sit back and develop long-range plans in a field where the pressures of day-to-day problem-solving are becoming increasingly acute. In this article the Industrial Relations Director of British Rail explains how management in this industry succeeded in breaking away from their traditionally defensive and negative postures in collective bargaining and how they have moved towards the formulation of a bargaining strategy.

Past and present practices in British industrial relations

Two to three months ago one of the railway chauffeurs came to meet me from an overnight train and in doing so gave me the daily newspapers. As I sat in the car glancing through the reports of shootings, drug raids, sex crimes, strikes, atrocities in Vietnam and the latest extravagances between Messrs Wilson and Heath – the chauffeur said to me: 'There's nothing in the papers these days, is there. We don't seem to get in the news nowadays like we used to. Not like the old days when we used to get the beds out.'

It transpired, under questioning, that collective bargaining in the railway industry until a few years ago, followed an unchanging pattern of:

1 *First stage.* Trade union claim, followed by management rejection ... increase in trade union temperature.
2 *Move to next stage,* and repeat with temperature rising sharply accompanied by violent spasms.
3 *The third stage* was associated always with a formal and icy reference to arbitration; the press dusting off its placards – 'Rail Crisis' and, even more blood-curdling 'Rail Chaos'.
4 The parties then moved to the *fourth stage* which was usually at Downing Street in the middle of the night. Just prior to this the Railway HQ had been filled with camp-beds; hotel rooms have been reserved and emergency car

249

transport rotas arranged. Offices were liberally supplied with mounds of sausage rolls, pies and other indigestible provisions.

It may be that my chauffeur friend has this in common with the great British press – he equates newsworthiness with crisis, bloodshed and disaster. And I think there can be little doubt that British industrial relations have been made to look worse than they are by the deeply ingrained belief of newspaper editors as to what is news, and what is not. Journalists seem to love to make our flesh creep with horror stories rather than to emphasise the more encouraging aspects of industrial conflict. They prefer the moaning of Jeremiah to the comforting demeanour of Isaiah. If there is such a thing as an 'English sickness' it exists more in our capacity for self-flagellation and mortification of the flesh than in anything else. Clearly, on the subject of strikes, it is possible to demonstrate that we are not much worse than some countries; and a good deal better than others and that even the good ones are now beginning to be infected by this form of conflict.

But this is beside the point and honesty compels me to admit that we would be extremely unwise to extract too much comfort from that argument. Indeed the indictment that can be made about the results that have flowed from our system (and the effectiveness of that system in regulating the relationship between management and labour) is much more formidable.

As one looks back on the last decade it seems that the two major issues of industrial relations in the 'sixties were that:

- the results of the collective bargaining system had a seriously damaging effect on our economy
- many of the mechanics of the system – which after all was broadly established in the 1930s and 1940s – failed to operate effectively in circumstances of full employment and inflation.

First, *the results of the system*. Between 1960 and 1969 earnings rose by about 70 per cent, output rose by about 26 per cent and prices rose by about 40 per cent. I do not suggest that the results of collective bargaining reflected by these figures was the only cause of our serious economic difficulties in the 'sixties. But it was certainly one of the major causes of inflation; of our failure to remain competitive; and of our failure consequently to achieve faster economic expansion.

Secondly, *the mechanics of the system*. The weaknesses of this became apparent in the 1960s. They are well analysed in the opening chapters of the *Report of the Royal Commission on Trade Unions and Employers' Associations*. The report draws attention to the institutional failings we all know.

- there is the confused system of collective bargaining below the surface of national joint councils, negotiating bodies and so on – what the Commission described as the two-tier system of collective bargaining – though this is an oversimplified description
- there are the incomplete, sometimes obscure and imprecise collective agreements including procedure agreements

- there are ambiguities and variations between unions over the functions and powers of trade union officers and shop stewards
- there is the lack of attention given to industrial relations by top management and the inadequate training and expertise of middle and lower management
- there is the confused structure of the trade union movement and the proliferation and inadequacy of employers' associations.

Behind these features of the system there were I think other developments of particular significance.

The distribution of power within trade unions changed considerably during the 1960s. Until around 1960 for historical, political and personal reasons the influence and standing of the national officers of trade unions was very considerable. This was a legacy of the decade of crisis from 1940 to 1950 when trade union leaders were in close discussion with the government about policies affecting their members and were generally agreed about the policies necessary in the national interest and in the interest of their members – concepts much easier to define and agree then than now.

Since 1960 the power within many unions at national level has decreased. This I suppose was inevitable given the continuation of full employment, inflation, the nature of our collective bargaining and the character of many wage systems. The shift of power from the national level has in the last two or three years been openly reflected by the philosophy of some of the most important national trade union figures, such as Mr Jones of the Transport and General Workers' Union and Mr Scanlon of the AEF.

This shift of power (and the increased importance of the shop steward) has had a marked effect on the position of managements. *The importance of direct negotiation between management and their employees has increased.* The importance of national negotiations between unions and employers' associations has diminished. The shelter provided for individual managements by national agreements and procedures has become less effective. (These shifts in power have led to the theoretical arguments in favour of company and plant bargaining, productivity deals, criticism of the York Engineering procedure and so forth and the sudden discovery of the advantages to the economy of these things. The academics have been justifying the facts of life.)

But the debate about the nature and effects of our industrial relations system will not be complete or fruitful unless it is also concerned with its objectives and whether those objectives can be more positive in the 1970s than they have been in the 1960s.

A further criticism can, in my view, be justly added in that most managements seem to have seen IR as a synonym for wage bargaining only. The end result of the welter of IR activities was to determine the price of labour and to do this by the most inefficient means possible. Management tended always to await the initiative of the trade unions and the actions of the labour force. The outcome was the annual ritual of wage bargaining in which no one really believed and which solved very few, if any, problems of industry, let alone of the relationship with labour. Problems seemed to explode in one's face; solutions were *ad hoc* and empiric and output was secured only during the uneasy periods of truce that painfully emerged during the actual periods of disruption.

It seemed as though management had persuaded itself that labour is a temporary problem that one patted back into place (under the carpet) when it would stay there and everything would be all right in the future. Rather like the motorist who believes that if he can only get round the queue of cars in front he'll have a clear road ahead. But it is not like that. If there is one truth that management has to accept it is that labour relations is a continuing exercise that has to constantly engage the attention of management and cannot be swept under the carpet after each new wage agreement is made and settled.

It is bound to be so for many reasons, but particularly because the therapeutic effect of a wage settlement, in any case, only lasts for a few months. In a comparatively short while people become used to the experience of more cash in their pocket and the feeling of well-being wears off. This is not merely a function of the rise in retail prices but is because people have a natural urge to reach new horizons and new satisfactions. In general, dissatisfaction is a very human attribute that we may find irritating but which we cannot eliminate.

Development of industrial relations strategy

In the railways we have found, over the years, that an *ad hoc* approach to wage bargaining so far from solving problems inevitably meant that many more were created. For example, in 1965 when we were moving out of steam traction into diesel and electric locomotion it was realised that firemen, as such, would be redundant. At that time there were 20000 firemen of whom 15000 would be surplus in about six months. The Board then entered into negotiations with the railway unions to 'single-man' the new trains. The union asked for compensation to the drivers for the loss of the firemen who were not now needed and the management agreed to this by increasing the mileage payments to drivers. Having secured this concession the unions then argued that firemen were dedicated railwaymen who should be protected against the evils of redundancy, so the firemen were given guarantees of no redundancy. It was then urged that the firemen ought to maintain their same relative position on mileage payments as they had previously enjoyed *vis-à-vis* the drivers. And so their mileage payments were increased!

By this time the 'agony' of the firemen had come to the notice of the guards at the other end of the trains and they, not unreasonably, felt that their mileage earnings should keep pace with the firemen who were also doing nothing at the front! And after some ritual posturing by both sides the guards got increases too.

None of this, however, had gone unnoticed by the signalmen ... !

Today we have drivers and guards in the £2500 to £3000 per annum class and we still have surplus firemen.

It was for this and many other similar reasons that we decided some two years ago to outlaw 'ad hockery' as such. Henceforth solutions to our problems would need to conform to a coherent pattern of bargaining which would be a continuous process. We came to the view that it was not so important to know where you stand on particular issues but in which direction you are moving.

Now, of course it is easy enough to declare one's purpose in these matters but quite a different one in achievement. We have found in fact that a declaration of this sort is a salutary exercise in identifying other needs that are not obviously associated with IR. It seems that the following stages are unavoidably involved.

1 First there are certain long-term objectives that have to be identified:
  (a) manpower – numbers and skills
  (b) wage, salary and pension policies
  (c) business plans – old activities to be closed down; new ones opened up.
2 Examine the management structure (railway and Fawley). Too many levels? Sufficient authorities? Sufficient in numbers and quality to meet objectives?
3 Negotiating machinery – is it a relic of the past, designed to deal with a different approach to bargaining? Is there sufficient flexibility? Are bargaining areas accurately defined? Are there adequate criteria for productivity bargaining?
4 Is the communication network adequate? Do managers understand their role in informing employees? Is too much reliance placed on formal machinery? Are communication activities tested for effectiveness – or are they taken for granted? Does management understand the frequency, variety and visual aspects of communication?
  Is management development a reality or a ritual? Are managers developed for their managerial qualities or because they are good technicians and salesmen?

There are many more stages like this that need to be looked at. They are not new, but if one is to bargain strategically and have a coherent plan then these elements are a part of that plan just as much as of any other.

Railway experience in bargaining by objectives

It may be of help if I now describe our practical experience in the railways of trying to apply these concepts. I am deliberately diffident about this because if there is one mistake that management seems more prone to than any other it is in slavishly copying the experience of others. In the business of labour relations we have to work out our own salvation by studying our own problems and developing our own peculiar solutions. There are no blueprints drawn up in one place that have any uniform relevance elsewhere. So with all these reservations and qualifications here is what we did.

Timetable

Being involved in the intensive transport of freight and passengers we have naturally developed a preoccupation with timetables, so our first act was to take a sort of Napoleonic decision to change the calendar. The railway bargaining calendar now divides the years into two parts – September to July and then August. That is we spend ten to eleven months in continuing informal discussions with the trade unions – their top officials and executive members. The purpose of all this activity is to identify and work on the problems that we want to clear up in the formal negotiations in August. We do this by an adherence to two principles – firstly that any person from any group can say what he likes and make any suggestion he likes. There is no waiting for the 'leader' – that habit in negotiations that makes them so defensive and negative. Here ideas are earnestly sought and participants are encouraged not to feel inhibited. This is possible because of the second principle – that of informality. No records are taken in these informal sessions so that there is maximum opportunity to retract since the discussions are completely (at this stage) without commitment.

A year-long calendar of activity of this sort fits into what we call our 'Rolling Programme' – a programme of:

- identifying problems – from either side
- examining structures – whether of wages or of bargaining or of organisation
- improving efficiency
- exploring new ideas, e.g. behavioural sciences – Herzberg, Thorsrud, attitude surveys, etc.

In addition to all this there is alongside a continuous volume of joint consultation at all levels concerned with local problems – manning, etc.; regional problems – of meeting business objectives; national problems – where the Board meets top trades union officials to discuss the total business strategy and results.

Bargaining tactics

Now, as I have mentioned before, this has led to quite dramatic changes in our bargaining tactics and it would be as well to elaborate a little further on these changes. It is probably necessary to describe why these changes have become so vital. Firstly, it is because the railway negotiating machinery had become so formal, stilted and legalistic. It had become so, as a product of the size, age and complexity of the railway industry. It is perhaps the oldest (and therefore most traditional) negotiating machinery in the country! The industry is so large – still nearly 300 000 employees; where 1 per cent increase in wages adds £3·3m to the wage bill; where the network covers the whole country; and where assset exceed £1 500m. It is also complex – railways, ships, hotels, hovercraft, property, engineering, police, ports. There are no less than thirteen national agreements that have to be separately negotiated.

It must be clear that with an industry as large and as complex as this a too rigidly formal system of negotiations can have defects as well as advantages. It can inhibit the process of agreeing about the nature of the problems and the criteria for settlement and it can become excessively tardy and non-productive. Our August negotiations therefore are:

- intensive. Residential
- informal and uninhibited, with specialist subcommittees
- brainstorming
- functional experts

Summary

If I could summarise this approach and give it the usual misleading label that we have such a gift for in this country it would be 'Bargaining by objectives' and our current objectives in this rolling programme of ours, are:

1 Settlements must be coherent and consistent.
2 Remove imbalance in earnings.
3 Devolution in bargaining.
4 Develop ideas in motivation and participation.
5 Reduction of overtime and rest day working.
6 Simplification of pay structures.
7 Extension of work measurement and job evaluation.
8 Development of agreed productivity indices.
9 Redeployment and training.

All settlements must contribute to the strategy and the strategy itself is not inflexible and immutable but is updated and refined as changing circumstances require.

So to put this strategy or policy into a few precepts. I do not think that bargaining is an activity that is susceptible to generalised policies and blueprints. Rather is it a business – from the management side – of identifying the strengths and the weaknesses in any situation or industry, and of exploiting the former and strengthening or eradicating the latter. People are different and because they are different management's approach must take into account these differences. It means identifying one's own problems and not assuming that the solution developed by one industry has a universal relevance. It also means, of course, developing jointly with employees one's own solutions to these problems. It means avoiding other people's prescriptions and resisting the appeal of current fashions – that one feels tempted to accept for their own sake.

.

PART III

B. Financial management

22

Growth and financial strategies

ALAN ZAKON

The potential contribution of the creative use of financial resources to corporate strategy is enormous, and for all but a few companies, indispensable.

Strategy concerns strengths – for growth and *against* competition. In so far as the financial officer has the most intimate knowledge of the potential magnitude and possible deployment of corporate resources, his impact on the formulation of corporate strategy should be far greater than causing or avoiding the idleness of short-term cash or enforcing quantitative limitations on the appropriation of investable resources.

The default of the financial function in the face of such potential can be disastrous:

- In evaluating the deployment of assets, the rigidity of quantification (DCF, for example) can distort the true picture of the various alternatives open to a firm seeking growth: those factors which do not lend themselves under conventional methods to numerical analysis tend to be left to intuition (e.g. risk tradeoffs)
- The reinforcement of 'minimum rates' or uniform return criteria can often result in foreclosing growth through implicitly limiting a company's strategic choices
- Failure to come to grips explicitly with risk/return tradeoffs often displaces logical strategic analysis with traditional policies or 'conventional wisdom'
- The lack of creative financial planning can, and most often does, result in conflicting goals and policies in regard to financial parameters such as growth targets, shareholders' return and liquidity.

The financial function alone can ensure that a corporation's strategic objectives conform to its long-term resources. The finance function is often the best equipped to avoid the otherwise inevitable conflicts between the necessary policies for a growth strategy and traditional – often financial – practice enshrined in the corporate culture.

Most importantly, in an environment where the perception of a corporation's worth – and hence the long-run interests of its shareholders – is largely in terms of growth, the chief financial officer possesses what for many firms are its most potent strategic weapons. The firm that grows the fastest is the one which generates enough money to add to its assets at the fastest rate. The firm that grows the fastest is the one which sustains the highest rate of return *on its equity capital* (and reinvests these funds). The firm that grows the fastest is the one that brings to bear the greatest force of resources in the face of its competitors.

In all these situations, the critical issue is sustaining the optimum mix of strategic resources in the proper place at the proper time in the proper amounts. For growth companies, especially those in capital intensive industries, these resources are usually financial, and the determination of the 'mix' most appropriately falls to the chief financial officer. It is he who must most perfectly understand what determines growth for his company and what the optimum balance is between the strategic weapons at its disposal.

The determinants of growth

A company's sustainable rate of growth depends in part on and is limited by the rate at which it can generate funds available for commitment to the growth target, and the return it can expect to earn on these funds. The sources of these funds are generally known: retained earnings, debt, and new equity. Dividend payout and capital turnover will determine the availability of these funds. Rate of return and the risk characteristics of investment projects will determine the effectiveness of their use.

Debt, risk, dividend and return policies and preferences must be determined before any statement of corporate goals can be made. The company earning 10 per cent on its assets, with a no-debt policy and a 50 per cent of earnings dividend payout obviously cannot set a goal of 10 per cent growth per year – unless it changes its financial policies: it simply cannot generate funds to support this growth.

It is the responsibility of the financial officer to develop a set of goals and policies in *financial* terms that will support the corporate goals. In fact, it is his responsibility to develop financial opportunities to attain these objectives. To do this he, and top management, must clearly understand the interrelation of the *financial* parameters that contribute to growth and the effect of their manipulation.

Rate of return

A company generally has a characteristic rate of return on assets, defined by the growth rate and objective character of the business, or businesses, it is in. Because of the essentially fixed nature of a company's traditional performance, a firm can normally raise its overall rate of return only by moving into a different business with a higher return.

However, for most companies, diversification is not necessarily the most attractive alternative for improving the return on invested resources; it involves generically higher risk exposure as well as strategically different requirements on management than encountered in traditional businesses. Another alternative exists for the firm that will turn its attention to strategic deployment of its financial resources.

While return of assets employed is important in assessing fundamental characteristics of investment opportunities, it is not the critical factor in long-run performance. Whatever the business mix of a company, and whatever the rates of return open to it, the true measure of management's success is growth in terms of the shareholder's equity committed to the company. Hence, the really important variable in deploying resources, and constructing a financial strategy, is *return on equity*

By using return on equity as a standard, a firm can often improve performance, and growth, by a careful revaluation of its own businesses. In this context, most importantly, leverage, dividend policy, and equity funds assume a strategically different interrelationship.

Fig. 22.1 Growth and rate of return

	Year 1	Year 2	Year 3
Total assets	$100·00	$110·00	$121·00
Equity	100·00	110·00	121·00
Rate of return	10%	10%	10%
Profit	10·00	11·00	12·10
Dividends	0	0	0
Debt	0	0	0
Reinvest	10·00	11·0	12·10
Return on assets	10%	10%	10%
Return on equity	10%	10%	10%

At a given level of business and, hence, return, corporate profits are equal to total assets employed times the return earned on these assets.

$$\text{profits} = \text{return on assets} \times \text{assets}$$

Corporate growth will equal the rate of return on assets if all earnings are reinvested; that is, if no dividends are paid, and no debt is used.

In the example, the rate of growth is clearly 10 per cent, where the return on assets that supports it is 10 per cent. Notice that since no debt is used, the return on equity is also 10 per cent.

Debt

The use of debt allows a firm to lever a constant return on assets to a higher return on equity, and hence, if a fixed ratio of debt to equity is maintained over time, a higher and sustainable level of growth (given a constant level of dividend payout).

The important fact to emphasise is that this is accomplished without changing the firm's characteristic return on investment. Balancing the higher return on equity and larger cash flows against the fixed cost of interest payments, a level of debt usage can be set at which growth potential is greatly increased with a proportionally lower increase in the over-all risk exposure, relative to the alternative of finding new businesses with unlevered returns of equal impact.

Fig. 22.2 Growth, debt, and rate of return

	Year 1	Year 2	Year 3
Total assets	$100·00	$117·00	$136·90
Equity	50·00	58·50	68·45
Debt	50·00	58·50	68·45
Debt/equity	1:1	1:1	1:1
Rate of return	10%	10%	10%
Profit before interest	10·00	11·70	13·69
Interest	1·50	1·75	2·05
Profit after interest	8·50	9·95	11·64
Dividends	0	0	0
Net return on assets	8·5%	8·5%	8·5%
Return on equity	17·0%	17·0%	17·0%
Equity reinvestment	8·50	9·95	11·64
Additional debt	8·50	9·95	11·64
Total new investment	17·00	19·90	23·38

If debt is introduced into the example in Figure 22.1, the results change dramatically. Assuming a constant debt/equity ratio of 1:1 and after tax interest costs of 3 per cent, the return on assets drops to 8·5 per cent (reflecting interest charges), but the rate of growth and return on equity increase to 17 per cent.

It is also important to note that this represents a level of debt usage that is usually higher than that practised by most companies. Perhaps it is the lingering memory of the liquidity crisis of the 'thirties, but debt still carries a degree of apprehension not similarly attached to new ventures, high investment in plant or other forms of 'business' (versus 'financial') exposure. The tradeoffs involved here are discussed in a later chapter, but it remains that the general aversion to debt exists and in fact offers a significant strategic weapon to those competitors able to use it.

The relatively liberal use of debt (vis-à-vis competition) can enable a firm to:

● accept lower profit margins, thus overcome short-term cost disadvantages, and capture a greater share of the market's growth
● pay more for assets, such as capacity, and achieve economic size relative to more efficient producers
● maintain a higher growth rate than the industry norm.

It can do these things because, by using return on equity as a standard, the firm can accept a lower overall return on its investments than its low-debt competitors.

In more general terms, the firm which, as a matter of long-term policy, maintains an optimal level of debt usage can be more flexible about its investment criteria. More important, the firm can accept lower return investments than its competitors and still grow at a more rapid rate. This is because a low return business financed with a significant amount of debt can generate very high returns on equity and, hence, rapid rates of growth. All this means is that the firm is adding financial risk (through debt) to a project with a low level of business risk.

Ideally, the firm's target return on equity follows directly from its growth goals. The acceptable investment is one whose return on equity invested, giving due allowance to debt usage, at least meets the corporate criterion. If all investments are accorded a debt level such that their summed business and financial risks are equal, then the return on equity allows investments to be compared to each other and to the corporate target in terms of return and risk. The debt usage applied to each investment varies, of course, with the business risk of the project. Thus, the very safe but low return investment may well offer a higher return on equity at a lower overall exposure to risk than the alternative high risk, high return commitment.

In fact – again leaving the discussion of the tradeoffs involved until later – a firm which pursues a strategic approach to debt usage can often increase its growth rate while lowering the overall risk of its business mix.

Dividends

Dividend policy is a critical variable and one which can condition an industry's entire competitive structure. If the firm in Fig. 22.2 were to pay out 50 per cent of earnings, its growth rate would fall by a corresponding half, to 8·5 per cent. This is true even if the debt/equity ratio were held constant and all remaining earnings were reinvested (see Fig. 22.3).

Fig. 22.3 Growth, rate of return, dept, and dividends

	Year 1	Year 2	Year 3
Total assets	$100·00	$108·50	$117·72
Equity	50·00	54·25	58·86
Debt	50·00	54·25	58·86
Debt/equity	1:1	1:1	1:1
Rate of return	10%	10%	10%
Profit before investment	10·00	10·85	11·77
Interest	1·50	1·63	1·77
Profit after interest	8·50	9·22	10·00
Net return on assets	8·5%	8·5%	8·5%
Return on equity	17·0%	17·0%	17·0%
Dividends	4·25	4·61	5·00
Dividend payout	50%	50%	50%
Equity reinvestment	4·25	4·61	5·00
Additional debt	4·25	4·61	5·00
Total new investment	8·50	9·22	10·00

Dividend policy can be introduced into the example in Figure 22.2. The result of a 50 per cent payout is a halving of the growth rate, although returns on assets and equity remain at the earlier level. The example adjoining illustrates this. Whereas with zero payout, a 10 per cent return on assets is levered to a 17 per cent return on equity and rate of growth, the 50 per cent payout introduced in this example drops the growth rate to 8·5 per cent, thus nullifying the leverage effect. Note that this in fact takes place despite the 1:1 debt/equity ratio. If no debt were used, the payout policy would result in only a 5 per cent rate of growth. (Verify this by introducing a 50 per cent dividend with the example in Figure 22.1.)

This means that those companies who compete with the firm in Figs. 22.2 and 22.3 can match the latter's growth rate with less debt or lower rates of return, and exceed it if they maintain the same debt/equity ratio. Assuming that the debt level used in Fig. 22.3 were the optimum for the business, the first company is powerless to retaliate without overextending itself. It can't increase its leverage because of the high incremental risk involved in committing itself to interest charges above the optimum level. It can't reallocate resources to higher return projects because the higher risks associated are compounded by the necessity – just to hold the line against competitors – of maintaining a debt/equity ratio which is appropriate for lower risk investments.

It should be clear that dividend policy is a major factor in growth strategies – that, indeed, lower payouts support higher growth rates.

There is a direct tradeoff between current and future dividends. Holding other factors equal, lower current payouts will produce a more rapid dividend growth and higher future dividends (see Fig. 22.4). If a firm earns 20 per cent on equity an 80 per cent payout will sustain a 4 per cent annual growth rate, while

Fig. 22.4 Dividend payments if a company earns 20% on equities and pays out either 40% of earnings or 80% of earnings in dividends.

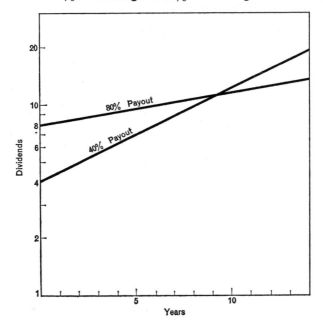

a 40 per cent payout will generate 12 per cent per year growth. In the first case if earnings were $10, the initial dividend is $8 and it will grow to $11.84 in ten years. With a 40 per cent payout, the initial dividend of only $4 will grow to $12.50 in the same period. The lower payout not only generates a threefold growth rate but produces a larger dividend in *absolute terms* by the tenth year.

Growth can be sustained at high levels of dividend payouts only if rate of return is very high or if debt levels can lever the reduced investments. If competitive pressure and risk constraints foreclose on these, the situation is more difficult. A company paying out all – or large part – of its earnings in dividends and locked into a constant debt ratio cannot grow without (a) changing its payout policies or (b) turning to the market for equity funds. The tradeoffs here are discussed in the next section. In the meantime, Fig. 22.5 consolidates the discussion so far in symbolic form.

Fig. 22.5 Derivation of the growth formula

The rate of growth is equal to the firm's return on equity if no dividends are paid. We can define the return (profit) as the rate of return on assets less interest on the debt. Symbolically, this is

$$\text{Profit} = r(TA) - iD$$

where, r = rate of return
TA = total assets
i = interest rate
D = debt
E = equity

Since total assets are equal to the sum of debt and equity, we may rewrite the expression as

$$\text{Profit} = r(D + E) - iD \qquad \text{or} \qquad \text{Profit} = rD + rE - iD$$

If the whole expression is divided through by E (equity), it becomes

$$\frac{\text{Profit}}{\text{Equity}} = \frac{D}{rE} + \frac{E}{rE} - \frac{D}{iE}$$

This can be rewritten as

$$\frac{\text{Profit}}{\text{Equity}} = \frac{D}{E}(r - i) + r, \qquad \text{or} \qquad \text{growth rate} = \frac{D}{E}(r - i) + r$$

Since dividend payments reduce this rate of growth, the effect of dividends may be introduced by multiplying the expression by p, the percentage of earnings *retained*. The growth formula thus becomes

$$g = \frac{D}{E}(r - i)\,p + rp,$$

where, g = rate of growth
D = debt
E = equity
i = interest rate
r = return on assets
p = percentage of earnings retained

External equity

The tradeoff between dividends and equity financing of growth is a telling one. This section will deal with the effect of equity dilution on growth and shareholder return. The discussion should illustrate sharply that lower dividend payouts (to allow greater use of non-equity financing and a higher level of internal equity generation) is substantially cheaper for the shareholder than dilution. The cost in dilution per share earnings is very high where equity financing is substituted for debt leverage within a high payout policy. In fact, the higher the target rate of growth, the more difficult it becomes to overcome the dilution incurred.

Anytime money can be invested at a rate of return above the earnings/price ratio of a firm's common stock, earnings per share will increase. This is what is meant by 'advantageous price'. But, as Fig. 22.6 shows, this increase in earnings per share falls short of the target rate of growth. Even though the sale of new shares contributes to an increase in per share earnings, the issuance of new shares changes the base of measurement and dilutes the growth rate (unless ever-increasing amounts of shares are issued).

Fig. 26.6 Growth, rate of return, and equity financing

	Year 1	Year 2
Total equity	$1000	$1200
Return on equity	20%	20%
Profit	$ 200	$ 240
Shares outstanding	100	$102\frac{1}{2}$
Earnings per share	$ 2·00	$ 2·34
Stock price	$ 40·00	—
Price/earnings ratio	20:1	—
Dividends	$ 100	—
New equity required	$ 100	—
New shares sold	$2\frac{1}{2}$	—
New investment	$ 200	—

Equity dilution is a critical factor if a firm attempts to maintain its growth by paying dividends and 'recapturing' the equity through the sale of new shares. In this example, dividends of $100 were paid and $2\frac{1}{2}$ new shares were sold at $40 per share to 'recapture' the $100. Total equity grew at 20 per cent and *total* earning increased by only 17 per cent, lower than the firm's characteristic rate of return and its realistic growth target.

The reason for this dilution is not difficult to see, but a detailed explanation provides a convenient way to measure the effects of equity dilution.

As a starting point, earnings per share may be defined as

$$\frac{\text{total earnings}}{\text{total shares}} \quad . \quad \text{and}$$

next year's earnings per share may be defined as

$$\text{current eps} \left(\frac{1 + \text{earnings growth rate}}{1 + \text{share growth rate}} \right)$$

As an example, if the firm in Fig. 22.6 paid no dividends and, therefore, sold no new shares, its 20 per cent return on equity would indicate a 20 per cent growth rate in earnings per share, as

$$\text{eps} = \$2.00 \left(\frac{1 + .20}{1 + .00} \right) = \$2.00 \ (1.20) = \$2.40$$

On the other hand, if all earnings were paid out in dividends and new shares were sold to increase equity by 20 per cent, shares would increase by a factor of 5 per cent (based upon the earnings price ratio of $1/20$). In this case, per share growth would be only 14 per cent.

$$\text{eps} = \$2.00 \left(\frac{1.20}{1.05} \right) = \$2.00 \ (1.14) = \$2.28$$

In Fig. 22.6, these two extreme cases were combined; that is, of $200 in total reinvestment, $100 was provided internally and $100 was provided by external equity. The resulting growth rate of 17 per cent indicated in Fig. 22.6 represents the average of 20 per cent growth from internal sources and 14 per cent growth from the sale of new equity.

Thus, the per share growth is based on the rate of growth in total earnings and the average dilution factor. The average dilution factor, as demonstrated above, is the ratio of external equity used to total new equity used multiplied by the earnings/price ratio of the common stock, or

$$\left(\frac{\text{incremental external equity in dollars}}{\text{incremental equity in dollars}} \right) (E/P) = \text{dilution factor}.$$

Earnings per share growth over any time period, then, can be calculated by

$$\text{growth in eps} = \frac{1 + \text{growth in earnings}}{1 + \text{dilution factor}}$$

Further, if the firm desires to grow at a given rate and maintain a given dividend payout, the required return on equity may be calculated. In fact, overcoming dilution can be formidable. If the firm in Fig. 22.6 wishes to grow at 20 per cent annually with a 50 per cent of earnings dividend payout, the dilution factor is $\frac{1}{2}$ (0.05) or $2\frac{1}{2}$ per cent, and the required growth in total earnings is 23 per cent, as noted below.

$$\text{growth in eps} = \frac{1 + \text{growth in earnings}}{1 + \text{dilution factor}}$$

$$1.20 = \frac{1 + \text{growth in earnings}}{1.025}$$

$$1 + \text{growth in earnings} = 1.23$$

$$\text{growth in earnings} = 23\%$$

Thus, the firm must earn 23 per cent on equity to maintain a 20 per cent rate of growth. Further, if the price-earnings ratio were lower, the required return on equity would rise dramatically.

Tradeoffs: the growth mix

Growth can be attained through many combinations of rate of return, debt, and dividends. While the individual firm's preferences have some latitude in determining the appropriate mix, it is clear that emphasis of one factor at the expense of others, or a doctrinaire aversion to a particular input, can put a major burden on corporate performance.

Fig. 22.7 demonstrates the sensitivity of the growth rate to the several variables. In this illustration, rate of return on assets (earning power), the interest rate paid, the debt/equity ratio and dividend payout are each changed in turn by 10 per cent, holding all others constant.

Fig. 22.7 Sensitivity analysis of four variables influencing corporate growth rates

VARIABLE	GROWTH RATE (%)	CHANGE IN GROWTH RATE IN RESPONSE TO A 10% CHANGE IN VARIABLE (%)
Earning Power (%)		
6·3	4·80	
7·0	5·50	12·7
7·7	6·20	
Interest Rate (%)		
3·3	5·35	
3·0	5·50	2·7
2·7	5·65	
Debt-equity ratio		
0·9:1	5·30	
1:1	5·50	3·6
1·1:1	5·70	
Earnings retention (%)		
45	4·95	
50	5·50	10·0
55	6·05	

It is not surprising that earnings power emerges as the most sensitive variable — increasing ROI is obviously the most direct route to higher growth rates, although the numerical example cannot, of course, weight the practical problem of achieving a higher level of return, nor reflect the structural problem of increased risk exposure.

More strikingly for most businessmen – although not surprising in the light of the previous discussion – dividend policy is shown to be almost as powerful a determinant of growth as rate of return. There is a clear tradeoff for the shareholder between near term profit (dividends) and equity growth.

Finally, the fact that debt/equity ratios and interest rates are significantly less sensitive variables is highly meaningful for establishing alternative growth strategies:

- small increases in debt will not have a major strategic impact on growth rates, but
- major increases in the pre-tax interest rate ($\frac{1}{2}$–1 per cent) will have even less impact; so
- a large increase in the debt/equity mix is a viable strategic alternative, even if higher interest rates are incurred along the way.

Obviously, there are limits beyond which the relative sensitivities change, although the 'normal range of operations' is much broader than commonly defined, especially in respect to debt capacity and interest charges. None the less, the limits are instructive in themselves.

If we set a debt/equity ratio of 2:1 as an upper limit for leverage of the normal ranges of business – beyond this, interest rates are apt to approach the rate of return and, in themselves, will have a major distorting effect on sensitivity – a striking tradeoff between debt and payout policy is demonstrated. The tradeoff is this – if the impact of dividend outflow on growth is to be offset by leverage, very high levels of debt are unavoidably forced on the company.

Fig. 22.8 indicates the tradeoff between earnings retention and debt/equity ratios if a firm wishes to lever a 7 per cent return on assets into a 10 per cent per annum rate of growth. The exhibit reveals that debt ratios react so explosively to changes in dividend payout that alternatives are severely limited:

Fig. 22.8 Debt/equity ratios needed to lever a 7% return on assets into a 10% growth rate at different levels of dividend payout

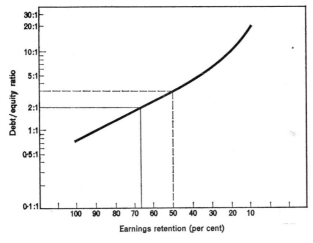

- if the company's debt ratio cannot exceed 2:1, earnings retention must not decline below 66 per cent for the company to grow 10 per cent
- conversely, if a firm feels it must pay out 50 per cent of earnings, the debt/equity ratio cannot decline below 3:1!

The implications for management are clear. Not only do debt policy, earnings retention and shareholder return have direct impact on corporate growth, but they are all inextricably interrelated. A decision to increase a company's growth rate necessitates a careful revaluation of all financial policies that have gone before. The explicit recognition of the tradeoffs involved is an absolute prerequisite to formulating the strategic alternatives open to the firm. Otherwise no alternatives will, in fact, exist.

Strategy and the growth business

There are profound interrelationships among industry growth, competitive advantage, pricing policies and financial strategies. These form a complex business system in all industries, but most dramatically in the case of a rapidly growing one:

- the characteristic return in a growth industry must be higher than that in a stable one
- the time perspectives involved necessarily tend to be long
- capital requirements are great
- the real dynamics of growth tend to be subtle and not clear from reported operating data.

Clearly, the essential difference between a growth situation and a stable one is risk. Larger amounts of money are committed to an unfamiliar and rapidly changing business with a more distant payout in the face of increasingly aggressive and shifting competition. While the increased potential for return promises spectacular growth, the stakes can prove to be too great for the firm strategically unprepared.

Growth and risk

The faster the rate of growth in industry demand, the higher the rates of return and the profit margins on sales must be to sustain that growth. If demand grows at 20 per cent per year, the industry as a whole must earn 20 per cent on investment, just to generate the funds necessary to add capacity to meet demand growth – this means that, with a once annual asset turnover and no debt, profit margins on sales *after tax* must also be 20 per cent.

The magnitude of these numbers have critical implications for management. Despite a 40 per cent pre-tax profit margin, a business that must grow at 20 per cent per year:

- cannot generate funds for dividends
- cannot spin off cash into other businesses, either for corporate earnings enhancement or for investment hedges against obsolescence
- cannot finance growth in *excess* of the 20 per cent industry average.

The risks are obvious and compound one another. While some managers and some, but fewer, shareholders have come to realise that the real value of a business derives from its *potential* ability to pay dividends, the demands of a high growth business push that potential further into the future. It is very easy to imagine growth industries in which firms show very high profit margins and report rapidly growing earnings, but which can *never realise* these earnings for the shareholder in the form of dividends.

For example, many of the firms in the germanium transistor industry reported annual earnings increases of 25 to 50 per cent per year during the early growth phases. But *all* earnings were required for investment to keep up with the growth in demand for the product.

The risks in this situation are that a firm will *not* reinvest earnings and, therefore, erode its future competitive position, or that it will reinvest earnings in assets that never pay out. The net result of a heavy investment programme must be an asset base that allows the firm to be competitive in future markets and, hence, repay the owners for the use of their money or one which cannot generate funds to repay itself. Many semiconductor firms built up substantial levels of retained earnings that represented noncompetitive assets or assets employed in a business that was becoming obsolete. As a result, none of the reinvested earnings were available for dividends.

Retained equity, built up during the rapid growth phase of a business, can be distributed to shareholders in dividends only when annual earnings plus depreciation exceed reinvestment needs. This is likely to occur only when any of the following conditions are met:

- the firm's capital structure and cost structure will sustain required growth and allow payment of dividends
  - industry-high debt levels
  - industry-low cost levels
  - at least maintenance of market share
- the firm *liquidates* its market position by growing more slowly than the industry and thereby generate more funds than it reinvests
  - a growth company can be liquidating itself by shrinking its market share even though it grows at a rapid rate
  - high profit margins may generate reported earnings but erode market share
  - slower than average industry growth can generate cash at the expense of future production costs, relative to the competition.

What this means is that reported earnings are not a reliable measure of success in a growth industry. These earnings only have value if they are converted into equity that some day will allow the payment of cash dividends to the shareholders.

When a growth company reinvests earnings it is betting that it can establish a position in a market such that the earnings from that business will ultimately be dividendable. This means that the firm must concentrate first on establishing its competitive position in terms of production costs and capital structure.

Capital structure, production costs and competitive position

Over time, all growth industries mature and settle down to a rate of growth approaching that of the national product. This is inevitable, and means that industry rates of return and profit margins must decline to levels that will just support this growth. This declining trend in ratios is accelerated by an increasing use of debt as maturity brings stability and lowers the apparent risks of the business. It is in this phase that companies can generate cash for dividends and enjoy the benefits of past investments. These benefits should accrue primarily to the leading firms and depend almost entirely upon production cost levels and debt usage.

It is well documented that production costs fall as a direct function of cumulative experience. Our studies in the semiconductor industry, for example, indicate that this cost decline follows a slope of about 70 per cent; that is, each time a company's cumulative production experience doubles, costs fall to about 70 per cent of what they were before production doubled.* This means that the fastest-growing firm in the industry will have the most rapidly declining costs, and the industry leader when the business matures will be able to pay the highest dividends. There are many examples of this. Fig. 22.9 presents some data for a mature industry – automobiles – which show the very direct relationship between production experience (market share) and profit margins.

It is clear that the firms with the most experience must have the lowest costs. Thus, the low-cost producer is not only in the strongest competitive position, but can maintain that position with the highest current shareholder returns. This is illustrated in Fig. 22.10. The automobile industry as a whole earns 17·0 per cent on equity, retains 36 per cent of earnings, and can therefore sustain growth of about 6 per cent per year. At *existing prices*, this means that each competitor can just about maintain its market share, but at different levels of dividend payout. General Motors, for example, pays 73 per cent of earnings in dividends while Chrysler can maintain its share only with a dividend payout of 48 per cent. This difference in dividend return to shareholders represents the *payoff* from General Motors' early growth; that is, its cost advantage earned from experience.

This industry is a prime example of higher-cost firms offsetting the cost advantage of lower-cost competitors through financial policies – in this case, dividend policy. It is also interesting that existing prices are apparently too low to allow American Motors to add capacity.

* Cost *versus* market share relationships are derived from Experience Curve Theory, more fully developed in the book *Perspectives on Experience* published in 1968 by the Boston Consulting Group.

Fig. 22.9 Experience and profit margins in the automobile industry (per cent)*

		AMERICAN MOTORS	CHRYSLER	FORD	GENERAL MOTORS
1961	market share	6·8	11·8	30·6	49·4
	profit margin	6·5	4·4	15·3	18·1
1962	market share	6·6	10·3	27·9	53·9
	profit margin	7·0	7·7	15·3	21·7
1963	market share	6·3	13·7	25·7	53·4
	profit margin	6·5	10·9	14·4	22·4
1964	market share	5·1	16·1	27·7	51·1
	profit margin	4·2	11·1	12·7	21·3
1965	market share	3·7	15·7	27·5	53·1
	profit margin	1·6	10·4	13·4	21·6
1966	market share	3·2	16·8	28·2	51·7
	profit margin	—	8·7	12·0	18·7
1967	market share	3·0	17·0	27·5	52·5
	profit margin	nil	7·0	10·0	17·0

* Data from Value Line.

Fig. 22.10 The Automobile Industry—1966

	AMERICAN MOTORS	CHRYSLER	FORD	GENERAL MOTORS	Industry AVERAGE
Sales	£870mm	$5650mm	$12240mm	$20208mm	$38969mm
Debt and preferred	73mm	308mm	772mm	571mm	1724mm
Equity	254mm	1701mm	4782mm	8443mm	15180mm
Debt and equity	327mm	2009mm	5554mm	8014mm	16904mm
ROI*	—	9·9%	11·6%	20·1%	15·6%
Return on equity	—	11·1%	13·0%	21·2%	17·0%
Earnings retention	—	52%	57%	27%	36%
Sustainable growth†	—	5·8%	7·4%	5·7%	6·1%

* Return on debt and equity (after taxes, before interest).
† From the model, growth = (return on equity) (per cent of earnings retained).

This analysis suggests some interesting observations:

- once the growth rate slows down, the industry leader can maintain market position with a minimum debt position and maximum dividend position
- at the same time, the marginal firm in the industry will have to maintain the highest debt levels and lowest dividend payout in the industry just to survive. (This was true in 1967 for American Motors.)

It is clear that the payoff for gaining market share is likely to be far out of proportion to the costs and risk involved. In this context, financial strategies can make a major contribution to achieving market share objectives in a growing business.

Growth and financial strategies

Market share strategies must be undertaken before a product's growth begins to slow down. It is virtually impossible to increase market share significantly by taking existing business away from competitors. The essential stability of mature and slow-growing industries such as autos, food and domestic steel reflect this. Major inroads into competitors' market position are best achieved by capturing a proportionately greater share of an industry's incremental growth. This requires that the strategy be undertaken while the incremental growth is itself significant, i.e. during the rapid growth phase of the industry's life cycle.

What this means is that market dominance must be an explicit objective in the entry *phase* of a growth product strategy. This in turn means that pricing policy must be of prime importance, and of utmost flexibility (mostly downward) at a time when capital requirements demand high margins and substantial reported earnings.

Aggressive financial management can often mediate the conflicting requirements in a situation like this.

Recall the example of the firm using a 20 per cent after-tax margin to fund a 20 per cent per year growth business. The firm rightly perceived the first rule of a growth strategy – zero dividend payout – but it still was not in position to grow any faster than the industry, and thus was locked into a constant market share. Without a fresh inflow of capital, the firm could not improve its growth rate – the only internal source of increased funds was higher profits from the business itself, but increasing its profit margin above the industry norm would foreclose future sales growth and result in loss of market share.

If the firm were to introduce debt financing in its capital structure, its position would improve on a compound basis. Not only would leverage funds increase the amount of investable capital, but also would allow the firm to pursue an aggressive pricing policy. If debt is used, required profit margins and rates of return can be lower; that is, 20 per cent growth can be sustained by a 20 per cent return on equity, which can be realised by a number of debt, return and profit margin mixes (Fig. 22.11).

Fig. 22.11 Profit margins, rates of return, and debit levels necessary to sustain industry growth at 20 % per year*

RETURN ON EQUITY %	DEBT/EQUITY†	REQUIRED RATE OF RETURN %	REQUIRED PROFIT MARGIN ON SALES‡ %
20	0	20·0	20·0
20	·5:1	14·5	14·5
20	·75:1	12·4	12·4
20	1:1	11·8	11·8
20	1·5:1	10·1	10·1

* Assuming no dividend payments to investors or other divisions in the company and no new equity financing.
† Assuming 3½ per cent after-tax interest rate.
‡ Assuming a once annual turnover of assets.

The relationship between market share requirements for eventual success and the tradeoffs among return, reported earnings and margins suggest a number of important conclusions:

● high profit margins do not necessarily indicate an attractive business; reported earnings are not always meaningful. However, since most businessmen perceive margins as an indicator to the contrary, it is in the interest of the aggressive firm to keep margins down to discourage entries into the market
● the firm using debt aggressively and withholding dividend payments can both cut price, relative to competitors, *and* finance an increase in market share. For this reason, entry into high growth businesses should be contemplated only by firms willing to compound the structural risks of full financial leverage; or by mature firms with substantial cash flows available and debt capacity based on a stable, dividendable business.

The full use of financial resources in a growth business allows a firm to achieve the lowest prices in the industry and thus leads to sustainable advantages in costs and profit margins, even at the lower prices, through growth in cumulative experience and market share. It is clear, then, that dominance in these areas obviously compounds as well, since the resulting stability of margins and sales will in turn allow the greater use of debt, and a higher degree of cash spin-off to protect future market position. Conversely the firm which underutilises financial resources gradually falls behind in costs, margins and market share and finds its strategic alternatives foreclosed.

This means that once industry growth slows, marginal firms live at the mercy of the industry leader. For example, if General Motors were to expand its debt ratio to 1:1 and cut its dividend payout to 50 per cent, it could grow at 6 per cent per year and cut price by about $220 on a $2000 car. And even if General Motors is precluded from doing this, it is a strategy that can be utilised by Ford against Chrysler and American Motors, or Chrysler against American Motors.

The net result is that the interaction among financial strategies and growth to achieve cost advantages are extremely interesting. The danger to the industry leader is that a secondary competitor can grow fast enough to become the low-cost competitor through financial strategies, unless the leader responds in kind. The danger to other firms is that the leading firm will utilise its financial strength as well as its cost position.

The system

It becomes very clear that the rewards to the low-cost producer are very significant:

- dominant competitive operating position
- dominant competitive financial power
- highest level of shareholder returns.

The cost-dominance position is essentially the payoff from growth. Even in a slowly growing industry, one firm can achieve dramatic cost improvements by increasing market share. For example, if an industry grows at 6 per cent per year, so that production doubles every twelve years, and its costs follow a 70 per cent cost/volume slope, industry costs would look as follows:

Year	Costs
0	$100
12	70
24	49

On the other hand, if one firm could grow at 15 per cent per year by increasing market share and thereby doubling experience every five years, its costs would decline much more rapidly, as:

Year	Costs
0	$100
5	70
10	49

Such a strategy, of course, is workable only if it is not matched by competitors. A key element, therefore, may well be to make the business appear unattractive to competition by aggressive capacity building and low prices; i.e. brinkmanship. Once a position of cost leadership is gained through rapid growth, the leading firm now has the most powerful financial arsenal in fact. If the leading firm has the highest profit margin, it must have the greatest debt capacity and ability to either pay dividends or fund additional growth.

Finally, this analysis provides some insights into growth patterns that have emerged in recent years. Most growth companies in industries with rapidly changing technology maintain their positions through continued product leadership. On the other hand, many companies report high earnings for a time and then fall by the wayside as new products force obsolescence of their existing products.* This is because the industry leaders can sustain their growth in one product area while *paying dividends* to another developing area. Even though research and development is a tax-deductible expense, it should properly be viewed as a dividend from one product line to another. This helps explain why the industry leader can maintain new product leadership in a dynamic industry – the leader has the profit margins to do so.

The same point can be made in terms of debt capacity. A leading firm with high debt capacity in one business is in an ideal position to fund a new business. This can be done by debt or by intracorporate dividends from one business to another; it makes no difference. The significant point is that the fledgeling growth business can be given *huge* debt/equity ratios through the capacity of the parent. As a result, it can grow much more rapidly than new firms without such backing and can attain leadership in that industry. In this context, it is no accident that General Electric aims for industry dominance in each of its lines and concentrates on new businesses whose development requires very great sums of money. A direct analogy is the funding of growth businesses through the acquisition of mature firms to gain either cash flows (intra-corporate dividends) or debt capacity. The logic behind the development of conglomerate firms in growth businesses is compelling.

Conclusion

This commentary has dealt with an enunciation of a business system which included:

- debt policies
- dividend policies
- price policies
- industry growth
- competitive cost positions.

Competitive strategy cannot be premised upon those elements taken individually. Financial strategy, including the element of brinkmanship, is integrally related to the firm's cost position and real ability to compete over time.

Failure to approach competitive strategy through an integration of financial and operating insights must result in failure to understand the real competitive system.

Decisions that produce earnings or dividends at the expense of market share are tantamount to liquidation – yet these decisions are made every day. Failure to utilise financial resources must result either in an erosion of market position or a missed opportunity to reap the returns of industry leadership.

* An interesting note is that such a company can continue to grow rapidly and show constant or declining sales. This happened in germanium transistors as price reductions premised upon cost/volume relationships offset annual growth in units produced.

23

Financial forecasting in strategic planning

A. L. KINGSHOTT

Planning to meet cash requirements is an essential management function in any business. It is not enough for the undertaking to make a profit. Cash resources must be planned to finance a negative cash flow in a period when necessary additions to fixed assets or temporary increases in working capital requirements are in excess of funds being generated by profits and by depreciation charges. In a period of surplus funds the need for a forecast of future cash levels is not less important. A forecast of available funds is a prerequisite for any investment plan. A. L. Kingshott, formerly Treasurer of Ford of Europe Inc., Ford Motor Company, discusses in detail the use of forecast balance sheets and source and application of funds statements. He also develops a cash flow model and examines the use of the computer for simulating the financial consequences of alternative policies. This paper was first presented at the University of Bradford Management Centre Seminar in October 1968.

Because it is the only common denominator for a vast range of corporate activities, the major part of any corporate plan must be expressed in financial terms. The specifically financial aspect of corporate planning, however, is the management of money. The two most important elements of this are the management of money in terms of investment and borrowing, and the protection of company assets against changes in national and international currency values by financial means. The management of a company's foreign exchange exposure position is a topical matter, but because it is of crucial significance to relatively few companies, I propose in this paper to discuss only the management of cash resources. This involves the necessity for cash forecasting. I will begin by discussing cash forecasting as a fairly short-term activity, the guise in which it is probably most familiar, and will then proceed to discuss the particular problems that emerge when cash forecasting is extended over the longer periods associated with the corporate planning activity.

Cash forecasting

Planning to meet cash requirements is an essential management function in any business. It is not enough for the undertaking to make a profit. Cash resources must be planned to finance a negative cash flow in a period when necessary additions to fixed assets, or temporary increases in working capital requirements, are in excess of the funds, being generated by profits and by depreciation charges. Many otherwise efficient and profitable businesses have encountered financial difficulties during the recent period of bank credit restrictions in which priorities for the available cash resources have been established in relation to national economic considerations rather than commercial supply and demand. The timing of a period of economic crisis may coincide with heavy cash requirements and if a business is to be assured of adequate funds to permit operations to be maintained at a profitable level a continuing examination of the forecast cash requirement for at least two years ahead is essential. Ford of Britain enjoyed a cash surplus position for many years (it was in fact the company referred to in the Radcliffe Report as holding £28m of Treasury Bills at the end of 1958) and in 1959 had surplus funds of approximately £70m. Considerable expenditures on capital facilities, which have been running at about £40m a year, resulted in a foreseeable need for borrowed funds. Cash forecasts were prepared extending three to four years ahead to identify the period when funds would be needed, to select the sources of funds most suitable for the particular requirements, and to estimate the financing costs of the various funding alternatives. In a period of surplus funds the need for a forecast of future cash levels is no less important. As a general rule the longer funds can be invested the higher the rate of return which can be earned. A forecast of available funds is a prerequisite for any investment plan.

The two best-known methods of cash forecasting are those based on an analysis of expected receipts and payments and the preparation of forecast balance sheets. The factors underlying the items forecast in both methods are of course the same (sales volumes, prices, costs of labour and materials purchased, etc.) but whereas the receipts and payments forecast lists the cash effect of these basic functions a balance sheet forecast quantifies the profit and depreciation cash flows, and reflects expected changes in the balances of such working capital items as inventories, receivables and payables as well as showing disbursements for capital expenditures, taxes, dividends, etc. The cash position emerges as the balancing item in the balance sheet. The receipts and payments forecast is most suitable for short periods and should be checked by the preparation of a balance sheet at the final date to ensure that inaccuracies in certain items have not produced balance sheet amounts which are clearly contrary to previous experience or established ratios. At Ford forecasts from one month to three to four years ahead are based on the balance sheet method.

Forecast balance sheets

Control on the accuracy of the forecast is exercised by extracting variance analyses between successive forecasts and by comparing the one month forecast with actual. When compiling the forecast balance sheets it is therefore desirable to comply with the accounting conventions in use in the company's accounts in order that comparisons are not distorted. For example, several methods of accounting for government grants are currently in vogue; Ford offsets them against the cost of the asset and sets up a receivable for the amount due. If the forecast balance sheets took grants into profit then subsequent comparisons with the company's actual balance sheet would cease to be meaningful.

The *sales and production volume forecasts* used in the cash forecast are those which are developed for the company's profit budget. These will have regard to production capacity and sales demand which will reflect forecast national economic conditions and their expected effect on industry and company volumes. Current year figures are reviewed monthly in the form of a production programme. Those for the future years are revised less frequently when significant changes have occurred, perhaps quarterly.

Profit forecasts are obtained by measuring variances from the original profit plan caused by changes in volumes, prices, manufacturing costs, administrative and commercial expenses, etc. Depreciation and amortisation charges and government grants will have been calculated on the basis of the current capital expenditure programme. As cash flow is generated by profits before depreciation and amortisation it is essential that the actual figures which have been charged for these items in the particular profit forecast are used. Because of the delay in making tax payments profits are shown before tax and tax payments forecast as a separate item. One of the items included in profit will be either investment income or borrowing expense which is itself calculated from the cash forecast. This is a chicken and egg situation which is usually resolved by using the cash forecast for the interest effect of any significant change in cash from the previous forecast. Using forecasts of profit before tax, tax, and dividends, appropriate adjustments can be made to net worth, payables and the tax liability as appearing in the balance sheet for the end of the previous period. Depreciation and amortisation of fixed assets can also be adjusted by the amounts to be charged to profit and the gross cost of fixed assets increased by forecast facility expenditures as reduced by government grants. Theoretically, retirements of fixed assets should also be forecast. As the assets concerned are probably fully written off and their scrap value may not be significantly more than the cost of removal, there would be little cash effect and we have not attempted to establish a basis for forecasting asset retirements.

The other major asset categories are *inventories and receivables*. In the motor industry inventories comprise stocks of vehicles held by domestic dealers in addition to normal work in progress items, as vehicles are distributed on a sale or return basis to protect the dealers from the effect of changes in the purchase tax rate. In compiling the sales and production volumes which I have referred to previously as the production programme, account is taken of seasonal fluctuations in consumer demand which make it desirable to hold a higher level of dealer stocks in winter months to maintain production levels in the factories. Export requirements are also seasonal, unfortunately coinciding to some extent with domestic demand, but do not usually result in increased vehicles stocks. Before the introduction of a new model, stocks are built up to ensure that dealers will have vehicles to sell when the announcement is made and this will be reflected at the appropriate times in the forecast. Forecasts of work in progress are also based on production volumes but may also reflect build up of stocks if certain production facilities are planned to be out of use, perhaps for rearrangement or modernisation.

The effect of volume changes on working capital items can most clearly be seen at the time of the annual vacation shutdown. By the end of this three-week period payables and vehicle inventories will have fallen by more than £10m.

As payment is received for domestic vehicles at the time when they become accounted sales, no receivable is generated. Dealers, however, receive normal trade credit terms for spare part sales and all exports (mainly to Ford associated companies) are payable one month after shipment. The receivable forecast, therefore, is built up by reference to the volume forecast and payment terms for the relevant items of sales and also includes unpaid government grants.

Although cash has been described as the balancing item of the exercise it is important to identify separately the amount of non-liquid cash which the business requires if the amount is significant. This may comprise petty and undeposited cash and, if the bank does not give immediate value for cheques paid in for collection, the sums in course of collection. If a borrowing requirement is indicated by the forecast this will, of course, be increased by forecasting an item of non-liquid cash. Conversely if most suppliers are paid immediately prior to the date of the forecast and the company's book position of cash reflects these cheques then actual cash or borrowing may be different by the value of the unpresented cheques. It may not, however, be desirable to reverse the cheque entries by a transfer to payables as they will undoubtedly be presented within a day or two justifying the conservative approach of treating them as presented at the bank. This factor must, however, be considered when reconciling actual borrowings with forecasts made on this basis.

The principal current liability items to be forecast are *payables and taxes.* Payables may be related to production volumes although it is necessary to take into account any proposed increases in stocks of raw materials. If capital expenditures fluctuate significantly and a detailed forecast is available then it is desirable to forecast these payables as a separate item. In relating payables to production volumes it should be recognised that the change in the provision for payables in the balance sheet from one period to the next is caused by two factors having opposite effects; cash paid to suppliers and new deliveries of merchandise. Whilst the volume of new deliveries should in the main have correlation to the preceding month's production (assuming thirty-day credit terms) cash payments should be related to the previous month, or earlier if the company is known to be dilatory in paying its suppliers. The corporation tax provisions can be built up by reference to taxes on forecast profits and known due dates for payments. Where, however, the company is a collector of purchase tax which is paid to the excise authorities periodically, then the provision for unpaid excise tax will be based on sales volumes in the appropriate period.

Additions to provisions for *salaries, wages, holiday pay, PAYE, pension costs* do not usually fluctuate significantly and can be predicted by reference to past experience without substantial inaccuracy. Having forecast all other items in the balance sheet, the identity and classification of which will have been discovered by careful analysis of a current actual balance sheet, the difference between assets and liabilities can be inserted either as cash or borrowings. When referring to the methods used for forecasting certain balance sheet items I have suggested that these should be related to production or sales volumes. These relationships are sometimes expressed as a ratio, say, inventories being a certain number of days' sales. As shown in Fig. 23.1 this ratio may not remain constant at different sales levels and a more realistic forecast may be obtained by plotting a graph line representing past experience of inventory levels at the actual sales levels and then projecting the line to the current sales forecast. In this way the changing ratio of sales to inventories at different sales levels will be taken into account. In the example on Fig. 23·1 using a fixed ratio of (say) fifteen days' sales 1968 inventories of £405 000 would have been forecast instead of £378 000.

Fig. 23.1 Scatter diagram forecast

End year	Sales per working day £	Inventory £	Inventory as number of days' sales
1964	19 000	336 000	17·7
1965	21 000	355 000	16·9
1966	23 000	364 000	15·8
1967	25 000	375 000	15
1968 (forecast)	27 000	378 000 (projection)	

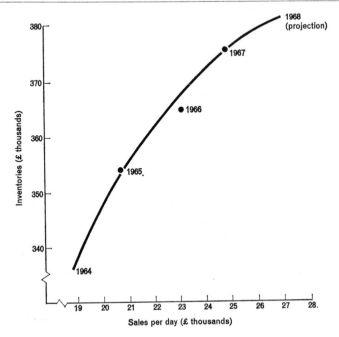

Forecast source and application of funds

Although the preparation of a forecast balance sheet (Fig. 23.2) will indicate forecast surplus cash or borrowings at particular dates, the reasons for the changes during each period can best be explained by the use of a Source and

Fig. 23.2. Balance sheet

	Actual 31 August 1968	Forecast 30 September 1968	Forecast 31 October 1968	Subsequently established Actual 30 September 1968
Cash	19 000	25 000	23 000	22 000
Receivables	619 000	622 000	625 000	614 000
Inventories	969 000	965 000	970 000	969 000
Property, plant and equipment	2 993 000	3 018 000	3 043 000	3 015 000
less: accumulated depreciation	1 123 000	1 143 000	1 163 000	1 142 000
	1 870 000	1 875 000	1 880 000	1 873 000
Total Assets	£3 477 000	£3 487 000	£3 498 000	£3 478 000
Bank liabilities	867 000	863 000	754 000	865 000
Payables	813 000	817 000	814 000	816 000
Excise and withheld taxes*	60 000	136 000	35 000	132 000
Corporation taxes	77 000	87 000	97 000	86 000
Salaries and wages	10 000	10 000	10 000	11 000
Vacation and holiday pay	5 000	10 000	15 000	10 000
Long-term debt	73 000	73 000	73 000	73 000
Net worth	1 572 000	1 486 000	1 700 000	1 485 000
Total liabilities and net worth	£3 477 000	£3 487 000	£3 498 000	£3 478 000

*Includes dividend withholding tax.

Application of Funds Statement (Fig. 23.3). This can commence with opening cash and include sections for cash additions, effect on cash of changes in working capital accounts and cash disbursements. If any new borrowings or repayments of borrowings are also shown then the final figures will be the closing cash position.

L

Fig. 23.3 Source and application of funds statement
Date of forecast – 31 August 1968. (Amount in £'s. Cash outflow in brackets)

	Forecast		Subsequently established actual at 30 September 1968	Variance analysis from forecast dated 31 August	
	September	October	September		
Gross cash and cash investment at beginning of period	19 000	25 000	19 000	–	
Cash additions: Profit before tax	24 000	24 000	22 000	(2000)	Sales £8000 lower than volume forecast – profit effect £3000.
Depreciation	20 000	20 000	19 000	(1000)	depreciation £1000 lower than forecast lower level of capital expenditures in September
Other additions – proceeds of issue of ordinary shares	–	200 000	–	–	
Total additions	44 000	244 000	41 000	(3000)	
Effect on cash of changes in non-cash working capital accounts: Receivables	(3000)	(3000)	5000	8000	lower sales level in September increased by cost of lower sales £5,000 and reduced by lower deliveries from suppliers £1,000
Inventories	4000	(5000)	–	(4000)	

Fig. 23.3 (continued)
Cash forecasting

Payables	4000	(3000)	3000	(1000)	lower deliveries from suppliers
Other (net)*	39 000	(54 000)	36 000	(3000)	lower purchase tax collections £4,000 – error in forecasting Salaries and wages liability £1,000 lower than actual
Total	44 000	(65 000)	4 4000	—	
Cash Disbursements					
Capitalized facility expenditure	(25 000)	(25 000)	(22 000)	3000	delay in delivery of new machinery
Dividends and dividend withholding taxes	(58 000)	(42 000)	(58 000)	—	
Corporation tax payments	—	—	—	—	
Total disbursements	(83 000)	(67 000)	(80 000)	3000	
Borrowing (Repayments)	1000	(114 000)	(2000)	3000	
Increase (Decrease) in cash	6000	(2000)	3000	(3000)	
Gross cash and cash investments at end of period	25 000	23 000	22 000	—	
*Comprises – purchase tax – collection	34 000	35 000	30 000	(4000)	
– payment	—	(94 000)	—	—	
Change in salaries and wages liability	5000	—	1000	1000	
Vacation and holiday pay liability		5000	5000	—	
	39 000	(54 0100)	36 000	3000	

The cash additions section will include:

- profit before tax
- dividends from subsidiary companies
- depreciation
- amortisation
- other additions.

Although balance sheet net worth will have been adjusted by profit after tax this statement will show only profit before tax as the tax charge will show in a subsequent period according to payment date. Depreciation and amortisation will show the amounts charged to profit in the period.

The change in working capital section will comprise:

- receivables
- inventories
- payables.

and will show the changes in these items during the period. Included in 'other' will be sundry provisions for wages, salaries, holiday pay, PAYE, pension costs, etc., in fact everything which could fluctuate in either direction but is not listed separately in this section.

The cash disbursements section will include:

- capital expenditures
- trade investments
- dividend payments
- income tax payments
- other disbursements.

Capital expenditures will represent gross expenditures less grants if this is the accounting practice of the company. Dividend payments should be shown net and the subsequent tax payment should appear in the appropriate period of the forecast. If the company is in a borrowing position then the final cash figure should now be inserted representing the non-liquid cash requirement and the balancing change in borrowing requirements then entered in the preceding section as additional borrowing or as a repayment.

The variance analysis

If a reasonable degree of accuracy in forecasting methods is to be achieved it is necessary to learn by past mistakes. These can best be identified by a variance analysis showing reasons for the changes in each figure between one forecast and the next and particularly between the one month forecast and the subsequent actual (Fig. 23.3). These may be due to revised forecasts of sales or production volumes, changes in credit terms, increases in manufacturing costs or even improvements in the method being used to forecast the particular item.

For the purpose of illustration, I have included a source and application of funds statement, a variance analysis and a hypothetical balance sheet (Figs. 23.2, 3 and 4) which show the transition of balance sheet figures into the source and application of funds statement and explain the changes of certain items from forecast to actual as a variance analysis.

Fig. 23.4 Assumptions for balance sheet and source and application of funds statement

	Forecast September	October	Actual September
Trading profit	44 000	44 000	41 000
Depreciation	20 000	20 000	19 000
Profit before tax	24 000	24 000	22 000
Tax	10 000	10 000	9000
Profit after tax	£14 000	£14 000	£13 000
Capital expenditures	25 000	25 000	22 000

Other working capital account changes (adverse cash effects in brackets)

	Forecast September	October	Actual September
Purchase tax – collection	34 000	35 000	30 000
– payment	—	(94 000)	—
Vacation and holiday pay liability	5000	5000	5000
Receivables	(3000)	(3000)	5000
Payables	4000	(3000)	3000
Inventories	4000	(5000)	—
Salaries and wages	—	—	(1000)

New share capital proceeds received in October – £200,000.
Dividend £100,000, paid net in September £58,000, cash withholding tax of £42,000 paid in October (included in excise and withheld taxes at 30 September 1968).

The pattern of surplus cash and/or borrowing requirements which is not available will form the basis of the company's investment policy and/or borrowing programme. The shape of future borrowing requirements will determine the sources of funds to be used and an accurate forecast will avoid over-borrowing at rates in excess of those which can be earned on surplus funds, prevent commitment fees being incurred on unnecessary borrowing facilities and may indicate a cheaper form of finance than (say) an expensive lease-back transaction.

Borrowing programme

The most usual source of short-term funds which can be used to finance a temporary requirement of working capital is bank overdraft. At the present time the banks are under severe restrictions regarding the amounts of funds they may lend and have been directed to give preference to manufacturing industry, particularly to exporters. Interest rates are usually related to bank rate and vary from the 'blue-chip' level of bank rate plus $\frac{1}{2}$ per cent pa reserved for the most credit-worthy customers, upwards. Acceptance facilities are also available from banks who will accept and discount bills of exchange to finance outstanding receivables. The minimum acceptance commission charged by the members of the Issuing Houses Association is usually 1 per cent pa and the bills are then eligible for discount at the fine bill rate, usually a fraction below bank rate. Foreign currencies, including Euro currencies, can also be borrowed subject to exchange control approval. Although interest rates on some currencies may be lower than for sterling funds the possibility of exchange loss must be considered and if a forward cover contract is arranged the total cost will usually be found to be more in line with the market rate for sterling funds. Some banks can arrange to discount notes or bills drawn against shipment of goods between two countries outside Germany. As German banks can discount this paper with the Bundesbank at German bank rate (currently [1968] 3 per cent) a favourable discount rate can be quoted and if forward cover costs are not too high the total cost may be less than for sterling funds.

Medium-term sterling loans have, in recent years, been difficult to obtain because the institutional lenders have preferred to secure what have been considered historically high interest rates for as long a period as possible. Some specialist banks have, however, been formed to make medium-term loans and Euro currencies can be borrowed for up to five years or more.

Long-term funds can be raised by issuing ordinary or preference shares, debenture stock or unsecured loan stock. Alternatively properties can be sold and leased back.

Investment policy

Investment of surplus funds can also be planned to maximise investment income if the pattern of the sums expected to be available has been forecast. It may be advantageous to invest funds presently available in investment if a subsequent period in which surplus cash levels are falling is seen to be only temporary and suitable borrowing sources are known to be available to finance the deficit. Suitable forms of short-term investments include:

(a) *Clearing bank deposits* which usually earn 2 per cent below bank rate.

(b) *Deposits with non-clearing banks.* These reflect current money market rates and can be made for periods as short as overnight. A recent spread of fixed interest rates varied from $7\frac{1}{2}$ per cent pa for overnight balances to 8 per cent pa for one year money (bank rate $7\frac{1}{2}$ per cent pa).

(c) *Loans to local authorities.* Interest rates are similar to those for deposit with non-clearing banks and loans may be negotiated through certain stockbrokers specialising in this market.

(d) *Tax reserve certificates.* These are issued in multiples of £25 and earn tax-free interest at a fixed rate applying at the time of issue (currently $4\frac{3}{8}$ per cent pa before tax). They can be used to pay corporation and other taxes due at least two months after purchase. Although TRCs can be held indefinitely they earn interest only for twenty-four months. Surrender for cash at ten days' notice is possible two months after issue but no interest is earned. TRCs are not transferable. When comparing the return with other rates it should be noted that interest is earned only to the due date of the tax which might represent a disadvantage if the company did not always make tax payments promptly on the due date.

(e) *Treasury bills.* These are issued by tender each Friday to be taken up on the date stipulated during the following week and mature ninety-one days later. The discount houses are obliged to tender to the whole amount on offer (£170m on 23 October 1968) and compete with other buyers, including Commonwealth central banks and domestic clearing banks bidding on behalf of customers. The clearing banks purchase their own requirements from the discount houses by arrangement and do not compete in the tender or purchase bills with less than eighty-four days' life to maturity. The average discount rate is normally about $\frac{1}{2}$ per cent below bank rate but can vary according to expected short-term interest rate trends and for other reasons.

(f) *Government securities.* Dealings in these securities are usually on a 'cash' (next day) settlement basis although the market is usually prepared to deal for settlement a day or so later by arrangement. Stocks with less than five years' life to maturity are dealt in on a 'clean of accrued interest' basis for which payment is made in addition to the quoted price but the price of an 'over five year' stock includes the right to interest accrued since the last half-yearly interest date. As the shorter-dated stocks currently offer a gross yield of about $7\frac{1}{4}$ to $7\frac{1}{2}$ per cent pa the return is likely to be less attractive than other forms of investment unless a period of falling interest rates is successfully foreseen and appreciation during the period the stock is held exceeds the 'straight line' expectation to maturity.

(g) *Loans to finance houses.* The larger finance houses usually take deposits for fixed periods of three months or longer at rates broadly comparable to those obtainable on loans to local authorities. Certain houses are wholly or partly owned by clearing banks which provides assurance of their credit status.

(h) *Sterling certificates of deposit.* The London market is making plans to deal in sterling certificates of deposit. The advantage of these certificates would be one of marketability compared with normal bank deposit and they will presumably earn fractionally less than straight deposits. The discount houses operating the secondary market would also have to take a 'turn' between buyer's and seller's price thus further reducing the yield if they could not be held to redemption. If the return, however, is better than 'overnight' money or treasury bills then these certificates might be a suitable form of investment in a period when temporary funds were available.

Cash forecasting in the longer term

When cash forecasting is extended over a longer period than three to four years although the basic principles are, of necessity, the same, the forecasting process rapidly tends to become very difficult. The reason for this is that in the shorter term the values of most of the variables with which one is concerned have been determined by formal management decision or else are likely to fluctuate only within a fairly narrow range: in the longer-term these same items may not have been determined at all, or else could still be subject to radical alteration.

In the shorter run for instance it is probable that all the major capital expenditure decisions have been taken; in the longer run it is extremely probable that the person making the cash forecast will have to work with a different set of person and concepts. This will require a forecast of the future product range, sales volumes, spare capacity requirements and the changes in stock levels. Not only will the cash forecaster have to take account of the capacity requirement implied by these forecasts, he will also have to consider where this capacity will come from. By the extension of existing facilities? Or by an acquisitions policy. The effect of these policies on cash forecasts will be very difficult. These forecasts will, in turn, influence another cash forecasting item, the future level of depreciation. From becoming a fairly self-contained exercise, then, the forecasting process in the longer term gradually extends its sphere of interest to cover almost the total of corporate activity.

The cash flow model

Let me illustrate how extensive the information required to prepare the long term cash forecast can become, by reference to Fig. 23.5.

As can be seen, the format of our cash Flow model is almost identical to the one we use in our short-term forecast but many, though by no means all, of the items are calculated on different bases to the short-term forecasts.

The first item, gross cash, presents some problems since historical cash levels as shown on the balance sheet, very rarely represent the actual amounts needed to run the business; for example, cash levels may be inflated during a period of rising profits, low capital investment, and restricted dividends, thus giving a misleading impression. It is necessary, therefore, to establish a level of cash required for operating purposes. Once this has been done, projections can be made on the historical relationship with a key variable such as cost of sales.

This will indicate the level of working cash required. If the independently forecast levels of receipts and disbursements generate a shortfall, it will mean that the 'previous' year's borrowings will have to be increased. If they generate a continuous surplus over the years, even when most or all long-term debt has been extinguished, it may mean that a reappraisal of debtor, creditor, and inven-

Fig. 23.5 Items included in the long-term cash flow forecast

ITEM	FACTORS DETERMINING THE FORECAST
Gross Cash and Cash Investments at beginning of Period	Forecast on basis of estimated minimum average working cash requirements.
Cash additions: – Profit before taxes	Forecast takes account of: prices, product range, sales volumes, gross margins and fixed costs.
– Depreciation	Asset level after adjustments for additions and retirements, changes in depreciation techniques, and investment grants.
Other additions: e.g. Increase in equity finance Investment grant receipts	Forecast on basis of optimum gearing structure and expected rates practice of investment incentives.

Effect on cash of changes in non-cash working capital accounts:
– Receivables
– Inventories
	Projected on basis of historical relationship with revenue.
	Forecast as function of: Raw materials
	                         Work in process
	                         Finished stocks
	Projections based upon historical relationships modified for anticipated changes in corporate level of integration.

– Payables	Forecast on basis of historical relationship with cost of sales.
– Accruals and prepayments (net)	Forecast on basis of historical experience, e.g. per cent of current assets.
Other (net) e.g. Collection payment of purchase tax Investment grants receivables	Forecast depends on expected direct indirect taxation, and investment incentive structure and rates.
Cash disbursements: – Capitalized facility expenditure	Forecast on basis of asset replacement estimates, capacity expansion programmes, and new model programmes, modified for changes in price levels, investment incentives, etc.
– Dividends and dividend withholding taxes	Forecast on basis of historical payout rates adjusted for anticipated changes in gearing and tax policies.
– Corporation tax payments	Forecast on basis of estimated rates and payment practices.
– Net interest (on loans, overdrafts, and investments)	Forecast on estimated bank market rates in major European capital markets for short/medium/long term debt/investments.
– Borrowings/investments	Determined according to the cash shortfalls surpluses indicated by the cash flow model.
– Repayments	Forecast on basis of current and estimated future medium/long term debt redemption dates.

Gross cash and Cash Investments at end of period

tory assumptions is needed, or even a fresh look at dividend policies and capital investment plans. Obviously in the long run, a company should be able to earn a better rate of return by using its cash internally than by investing it outside, so that stock market investment, which may well provide a haven for short-term surpluses, is not, in the long term, an acceptable solution.

The determination of profit before taxes is crucial, but this is not the moment to consider the techniques in detail except to say that a larger number of assumptions will have to be made relating to corporate profitability in future years. For example, what products will we be making? How will the prices of raw materials, labour, and our own products change? Will technological changes significantly affect the manufacturing cost structure? Let us take the profit as read and move on to the next item.

Although we do not forecast asset retirements in the short term, in the long term this factor has an extremely important effect on the depreciation changes and a forecast of asset retirements and replacements must be made. At Ford a large proportion of capital expenditure will be composed of new model and capacity expansion programmes, but the assets which provide existing capacity will have to be replaced sooner or later. The estimated asset lives as used for depreciation purposes may give a clue to the time at which assets will have to be retired and replaced, or it may be necessary to make an analysis of historical retirements by year of purchase. Changes in depreciation practices will also affect the timing of the cash flow in any one year, though not over a long period. A change in the investment grant structure would also have a significant effect on depreciation charges since depreciation is calculated on the net cost of the asset.

The other major sources of cash are investment grant receipts and the proceeds of equity issues, a need for the latter item being determined by ratio analysis of balance sheet relationships and, of course, the comparative cost of capital. Once more, broader issues impose themselves. For example, what effect would compulsory employee shareholding have on company financing? It is worthwhile to point out at this stage that we prepare a forecast balance sheet in conjunction with the cash flow model and use ratio analysis to indicate whether key relationships are in disequilibrium. If this is the case, some of the assumptions may have to be modified.

The next four items, receivables, inventories, payables, and accruals and prepayments do not present any particular problems, and can all be forecast on the basis of historical relationships to key variables, e.g. average debtor collection periods, although some modification to inventory levels may be necessary to reflect changes in the corporate level of integration.

Other items which have to be considered are those taxes where the company acts as an agent for the tax authorities, such as purchase tax. A change from purchase tax to a lower level of value added tax on all consumer products at a common rate would be significant, not only because of the effect on the demand for motor cars, but also because the motor industry acts as an agent for the government in the collection of purchase tax from the dealer.

With regard to capital expenditure, there is no need to enlarge upon what has already been said in connection with depreciation.

Dividend payments, withholding taxes, and corporation taxes require a number of difficult assumptions to be made, particularly when one considers the problems facing international companies. Will exchange control policies be liberalised or tightened? What will be the attitude of governments on the repatriation of profits? Could the abandonment of the corporation tax system in the UK lead to a complete change in gearing and dividend policies? What effect on national taxation policies would the British entry to the Common Market have, or even the realisation of the 'European company' concept?

The last two lines on our cash flow model – borrowings/investments and repayments – represent the balancing adjustments necessary, with forecast receipts and disbursements, to maintain cash at the level required for the smooth operation of the enterprise. It is the responsibility of the planning staff to examine whether the level of borrowings is acceptable or otherwise. If the level is too high, then another form of financing may be necessary, e.g. equity finance.

I could extend this section considerably, but I think I have written enough to indicate that in long-term cash forecasting a great deal less can be taken for granted and that there has to be speculation on a wide variety of corporate, industrial, and environmental trends. This is not just a matter of emphasis, it is a question of scale. I would go so far as to say that the skills required for success-ful long-term cash forecasting are utterly different from those required for successful short-term forecasting.

Sensitivity analysis

Let me hasten to add that the need for omniscience in long-term forecasting can be avoided by the use of some form of sensitivity analysis. This is extremely simple in concept; it is a technique designed to show the effect on the forecast of various hypothesised changes in variables which are used in the forecasting process. The result is that one can focus attention and forecasting effort on the things that matter rather than on things that merely change.

I find in practice, however, that the use of sensitivity analysis requires con-siderable precision of thought if all the implications of the hypothesised changes are to be properly thought through, and this leads me to the view that to make a real success of long-term cash forecasting it is necessary to develop a fairly rigorous mathematical model of corporate activity which can be computerised. Computerisation not only avoids the tedium of manual sensitivity analysis, but also allows one to take some account of the complexities of actual corporate decision-making.

Uncertainty

The final aspect of long-term financial forecasting on which I would like to concentrate is that of uncertainty. This is an area in which, again, the use of a computer is advantageous, and it is also an area which by its very nature is of much greater importance to long- than short-term cash forecasting. There is, I think, no area of a company's operations which is so susceptible to the consequences of forecasting error and uncertainty as cash flow. This is not only because cash flows are relatively small differences between very large magnitudes, but because errors in one variable tend to cause disproportionate errors in others. If there is an unanticipated and major change in sales volume, it is probable that one will find that variable costs will not vary as smoothly as one had been led to expect. The discussion on the variability of labour costs might be resolved quite suddenly, if not expectedly, if there are major changes in the size of the labour force, while anticipated changes in inventory costs are probably too deeply rooted in the unrealistic concept of orderly changes to be of great use. The 'surprise' or 'disruption' costs that result from errors in forecasting tend to be very high and it is not too much to say that failure to foresee this can endanger the chances of a company's survival. It is, therefore, of the greatest importance that the longer term cash flow forecast and policy recommendations be made only after the problem of the uncertainty surrounding the forecast has been formally and rigorously analysed.

It is most unlikely that a systematic examination of the probable results of the combinations of the many alternative outcomes that can be associated with the long-term cash forecasting process will leave the initial policy proposals unchanged. Because of the financial consequences of being wrong if the company is too highly geared in a period of low profitability, the development of a fairly normal system of policy making which can cope with error and uncertainty is basic to the success of long-term cash forecasting.

I would like to conclude this paper by saying that the end product of financial forecasting for corporate planning purposes is very similar to that required for shorter term planning periods. The difference between cash forecasting for the longer and shorter periods is therefore a matter of technique. This is because the longer term forecast can take much fewer facts for granted and must therefore be based on a comprehensive review of both corporate and environmental activity. As this view is potentially panoramic, it is therefore necessary to develop techniques which reduce redundant effort by indicating which surprise developments will significantly affect the forecast if they actually occur. Finally, because the view is also long term, it is necessary in addition to use techniques which can assess the robustness of favoured financial policies in the face of much larger degrees of error and uncertainty than is present in shorter term cash forecasts.

Part III

C. The management of technology

24

The changing technological climate

A. A. L. CHALLIS

In this article Dr Challis propounds the view that the inventive process has dominated the technological climate for almost two centuries but is now having less and less influence. He further argues that the importance of technological forecasting can be overestimated. First, he points out that it is still up to the planner and the organisation he represents to choose objectives and strategies to suit their own needs — technology does not advance according to the dictates of some iron law. Secondly, he argues that whatever innovation there is within the foreseeable future, it will bring surprises for which it is impossible to plan. Thirdly, he maintains that the major problems of the future will be more sociological than technological and that trying to forecast the one without the other is therefore a useless exercise.

Up to about 1920 the pattern of invention was curiously haphazard in the sense of what was invented and what was not, and what was developed and what was not. An invention usually requires the combination of identification of need, human need, with a scientific/technological innovation, usually plus the availability of the correct constructional materials and fabrication techniques. Sometimes the inventor creates his inventions by bringing together the three parts which pre-exist separately; but more often the inventor brings together only two parts and wills the third into life, as for example the primitive jet engine created the high temperature alloys for its blades and for its commercial success, or alternatively the innovation of low persistence high activity herbicides created the concept — the need — of ploughless agriculture in regions of low soil stability where ploughing was too hazardous. Often the need is long identified. For example, we need right now a chemotherapeutic agent effective against virus infection, or an agent effective against cancer. The length and the lack of success in the search for these two almost certainly indicates that what is needed is general scientific progress in the biological field before the conditions are created in which the innovation can be made.

This rather cavalier treatment of invention neglects the time factor between the inventive step itself and fruition, fruition being the use of the invention by many men. This time interval always seems inexplicably long and has many causes. Sometimes it is due to slowness in making the minor enabling inventions needed, but more often it is due to limitations in foresight, drive or capital. Even for this time interval, however, the 1920s prove to be a watershed in human progress as Figs 24.1 and 2 show. Einstein once said:

> The history of scientific and technical discovery teaches us that the human race is poor in independent thinking and creative imagination. Even when the external and scientific requirements for the birth of an idea have long been there, it generally needs an external stimulus to make it actually happen; man has, so to speak, to stumble right up against the thing before the idea comes.

If you have any doubts on this consider the time which elapsed before the man-carrying glider came into being. The desire to fly has long been there and although the flapping wings of the bird provide a false model, a bird gliding in the updraught at the cliff edge must have been seen by many inventive intelligences over a period of thousands of years. The material for the construction of models, paper and glue, have long been present, the schoolboy's paper dart shows the way. The result of model experiments in this field scale up fairly readily. The skills and necessary materials of construction for a full-scale machine have been available since at least AD 900 or even earlier. Leonardo de Vinci invented the right design in 1550, with about half the enabling ideas, yet we waited until Lillienthal in 1898 for fruition, and even he did not solve the control problems, which awaited the Wrights' fully controllable glider of 1902. This machine willed the necessary lightweight power unit into being during the following year. It is quite extraordinary to think that the Wrights then put their flying machine into a shed and left it there for three years.

The study of the creative thought process, of which material invention is only a part, is a fascinating one. The inventive process has dominated the technological climate for a long time and is now in my view doing so to a smaller extent. This, I believe, is the basic change in the technological climate and is a process which started in the 1920s but is not yet widely recognised or exerting its maximum effect. The nature of the change is complex and difficult to define accurately; let me turn to other men's words. Jantsch has said recently : 'For centuries the future has been largely determined by haphazard technical developments. Today technological forecasting is being used to outline the scope of technological innovation and to influence its direction and pace. In this way man is becoming the master of his technology where previously he was its slave.' It goes without saying that Jantsch is a technological forecaster. What he is saying in effect is that we can will the future, that there is no reasonable target which, given the time and resources, technology in its present or its immediately foreseeable state cannot attain. We can put a man on the moon or on Mars, or an automatic laboratory on the surface of Venus; even a flight to the nearest star system is not impossible, just a little too difficult to think about at this stage. This situation is quite fantastic − to have the power to create the future. The realisation that it is true − or even partially true for our world, our country, for my organisation – hit me like a hammer blow. The very fact of making long-range plans is a more powerful influence in making them come to reality, rather than any alternative. Your plans generally will come true. We are gods, but have feet of very soft clay. As soon as we start to think we come up with a number of limitations. I would like to examine some of these in more detail.

The first limitation is that we cannot do everything, at least not all together at the one time; we must choose what our targets are to be. This is another way of expressing the change in the technological climate. Not every invention need be or should be developed; there should be more primary inventions than development effort available to develop them. In this situation we must see where we are going, assess the possible alternatives, and consciously decide to go this way and not that way and therefore to develop this group of inventions rather than that group. Yet another aspect of this is the statement that 90 per cent of the scientists who ever lived are alive now: and they are all drawing their salaries. Research and development costs in the developed countries have risen from under 1 per cent of the gross national product in 1950 to somewhere between 2 and 3 per cent. At this level we already do not lack those who extrapolate the trend curve to produce the crazy answer that research and development costs will equal the gross national product in the year 1984 or 2000, according to taste. What this means of course is that between now and 2000 the present acceleration of these costs must cease, and finally some ceiling of expenditure will be reached beyond which we will not go except in so far as GNP itself increases. As a man concerned with the application of science I am bitterly disappointed at the failure of our very considerable research effort in this country over the last ten years to have any real effect on our GNP. I believe the answer to the question of 'What are we getting for the money we are pouring out?' is 'Not nearly enough'. This seems to be true over the whole world but it is especially true in this country.

Of course, there is no difficulty in finding mitigating factors such as working population seeking the delights of the age of leisure before we have actually got there – I think we must recognise that our national answer to the choice 'less work' or 'more goods' will be 'less work', but basically I believe in the very toughminded view that the main weight of responsibility rests with poorly managed research and development. The answer is not more organisation of science. I agree very strongly with the view of my distinguished predecessor, Dr Duncan Davies, who a little while ago wrote an excellent paper on 'The undesirability of a research organisation'.[1] The answer is not the application of some set formula of evaluation to each and every research project followed by a vast rushing round turning projects on and off like taps. This converts poor management into bad management. Of course, selection and its corollary rejection followed by concentration on the selected projects, is the essence of the development end of research and development. But R and D is a very human occupation involving men at full mental and physical stretch. The myth of the cold-blooded, white-coated scientist or technologist is an extraordinary one. All the good scientists I know are highly passionate and emotional men, certainly about their science, and often on many other things. It takes time for a man to become effective on a new project. It takes time, so to speak, for him to invest his own personal capital in it. He cannot be turned off and on like a tap. Yet selection and rejection are vitally necessary. The only way out of this dilemma is the complete involvement of the working scientist with the whole project. He must be fully part of the selection and rejection process. He must know the full background of the project and be an essential part of the continuous evaluation of progress which is essential. However, I am digressing here a little from my essential theme of the limitations.

Sometimes major alternatives are not attainable simultaneously. Let me return to my favourite example – I do not think we can both put a man on the moon and feed the human population of the world, but for many things there is, so to speak, a list from which one can choose perhaps half the total without overstraining resources and leading to an ineffective pace of work. Sometimes two objectives could be obtained simultaneously but it might not be worth while doing so, for example, to build a supersonic transport aircraft or to build a highly safe economical subsonic air transport machine. We need here a systems analysis of air transport. One can go on and each of us make his own list. Such lists are often not very interesting but are highly instructive in telling you a good deal about their author. My own would certainly include, for example, a road guidance system for cars. Comparatively simple electronics of the high reliability possible with solid state systems combined with very little further progress in automatic transmission and power steering brings the possibility of vehicles travelling at high speed on a very narrow roadway spaced very close together. One can envisage a number of such track systems built only for vehicles of private car weight and outside which the vehicles could be driven in a normal fashion. Such an arrangement seems to me to combine the best features of the public transport system that we are all so busy rejecting by not using, and our own personal desire to possess and use that movable extension of our own homes – the car. It does seem to me incredibly stupid that anyone can seriously envisage any transport system which in fact takes the personally owned car away. Collectively we all make enormous sacrifices in money and in safety in order to use this device. Equally on my list would be the desire to solve the water supply problem, certainly for this country, possibly on a much wider scale, on say a fifty-years-ahead time scale.

This pair of scattered choices demonstrates, I hope, that the present mechanisms for outlining alternatives and making choices of this type are extremely rudimentary. The places where most progress is being made are in the large public companies of the capitalist nations, generally under the title of 'company planning', 'company forecasting', 'technological forecasting', and so on. There does not seem to be much parallel activity in our nationalised industries or, so far as I have been able to observe, in the technical planning organisations for the communist countries. Such forecasting activity is notably lacking in direct government where the rule of immediate expediency appears to hold undisputed sway. We are now at a time when we can and should be targeting our national scientific effort, which by any standards is excellent in quality, towards a number of scientific objectives, often quite small in size, which ought to be attainable in reasonable time and be valuable when attained. I am sure the conscious decision we made some years ago to pull out of the space race was right. What a pity we, the scientists and technicians did not then suggest alternative goals for our national scientific effort. Perhaps then the concept was too advanced but I do not believe it is at the present moment. Should we not try? Better to have tried and failed than just drifted.

The second limitation to the power of technological forecasting is that new inventions will bring surprises. The surprises that are going to affect us in the next twenty years have probably all been invented. This is not true for thirty years and is very untrue for forty. Primary innovation is a highly individual process. A minimum amount will always tend to occur. The rate can be increased or repressed by the society and the environment. One only needs to look at the long history of China or Europe in the Dark Ages to see that repression is possible, although even there the invention of the stirrup around the year 800 revolutionised warfare and by doing so greatly altered the whole basis of land tenure. Passing perhaps, from the sublime to the ridiculous, we are attempting to study the factors affecting creativity in my own laboratory, but so far have got little further than proving the already well-known but fascinating fact that the creativity of firstborn and only children is markedly greater than that of all other birth orders, certainly anyway for male children. There is some evidence, dealt with at length by Jewkes in his book *The Sources of Invention*,[2] that large research organisations are poor at this type of primary invention. This seems to be true, for example, in the large research institutes behind the Iron Curtain, and the West is not without its own examples. This ability to make primary inventions must not be confused with the ability to take up and develop a primary invention. I am left with the clear impression that the harder look that we must undoubtedly take at research project management will lead to more targeting of work. This is not a bad thing in itself but may well lead to some depression in the rate of primary invention. Given the number of active scientists, this may indeed be right. There should always be more than enough good ideas entering the expensive and time-consuming development process, but if one takes the present overall balance of scientists in this country, both academic and industrial, it may well be that there are too many endeavouring to make primary innovations so that there is insufficient effort available for development.

At this point a little conjecture may be in order and I will make two predictions, both of them pretty safe, as befits the organised cowardice of the professional scientist. I am sure that when the history of the twentieth century is written in say 2100, the significant event will not be the release of nuclear energy but the unravelling and understanding of the genetic code. The potential of this is terrific. By 1985 the new knowledge in this field will be being used to make further and faster progress along the already impressive path we have covered in the use of selective breeding to improve animal and plant strains for human use. In human beings the first use of our knowledge will be in the correction of genetic defects by perhaps 2000. Once we have started to make human application the process will continue. We have always hung back from selective breeding experiments of ourselves for the disposal of those carrying the unwanted traits could not be solved as simply as with animals and plants. Equally difficult is the definition of what exactly should be the wanted traits. Direct genetic control bypasses some of these difficulties and we shall certainly move by this way perhaps to control some antisocial character traits unaccept-able in a very crowded planet. This prospect frightens me but I believe it will be a fact of life in the twenty-first century with perhaps a measure of control on the level of intelligence and beauty by 2100. The other prediction is matched to it and will come as a result of the rapid improvement of communication between man and computer. I believe this will already be highly significant in another decade and will set a new and different meaning to what we understand by intelligence. In so many ways the attributes of the computer and of the human being, while very different, may be seen to supplement each other. The high speed and accurate repetitiveness of the computer is opposed to the slow speed of the brain, with its enormous capacity, its extremely random search process and its ability in a most remarkable way to see analogies often when they do not exist. Almost certainly the prime organ of computer/man communication will be, on man's side, the eye. The possibility of more direct communication still exists but is a long way off.

The third limitation to Jantsch's view is the obvious one that the prime prob-lems will be sociological and not technological, and indeed technological forecasting without sociological forecasting is irrelevant. This is the area of major uncertainty and there is growing evidence that we shall tackle the tech-nological problem of low sociological content rather than the other way round. The choice between putting a man on the moon or feeding the human race has been influenced by the realisation that the first is almost entirely technological and the second is almost entirely sociological. Not many people outside the immediate field seem to have really absorbed what so many agriculturalists have repeatedly said, that basically there is no technological problem to be solved in feeding the world. There exist already, in fact, half a dozen different solutions to the problem, any one of which fully rigorously applied would be sufficient. Any real solution would involve a mix and the optimisation procedure would identify further problems, solutions to which would enable the target to be obtained more quickly and more economically, but which in themselves would not, given the will, affect success or failure. I put it to you that our failure to act in this area is far more reprehensible than the failure of our Victorian fore-bears to deal with the appalling social and industrial conditions of their own age.

Yet how do we secure action, in this case or any other? Most of us have been brought up on the proposition that in national affairs we, the scientists and technologists, have one vote just like anyone else and this goes for scientific and technological questions as well where we are expected to say our piece and what it all means, then step smartly back into the ranks. This, of course, is nonsense; it reached its peak in the development of the atomic bomb where the scientists on the project notably failed to give good advice on the most effective and humane way of demonstrating the bomb so that it secured the political action of ending the war. The scientists concerned largely did step back into the ranks on the grounds that this was a military and political matter, but neverthe-less every member of that project team was loaded by himself and by public opinion with a heavy moral responsibility.

Increasingly, our attempts to say our piece on what we have just invented and what the consequences of its use are likely to be are being brushed aside with the remarks that 'it is all too difficult, can't you just decide yourself and carry the consequences if it doesn't work out right?' In the associations we all have with the establishments we work in most of us, I would guess, try to exert the maximum influence we can. I certainly try to move the policy of my company in the commercial as well as in the scientific field in directions which I believe to be right and I may well verge on to actions which are very close to being illegal, immoral or fattening in doing so. What is the right balance here between the opposite poles that all are equal and shall be seen to be so and the merito-cracy/technocracy, which is the inevitable result of the other view? I do not think the present uneasy balance is right and in my opinion by and large we are still too much on tap and not on top. Perhaps the present balance has evolved some features which may be right whereby we retain the principle of one man one vote in national affairs, with the scientists and technologists exerting their special influence through the activities of the industrial corporations which from some points of view at least are growing in size and influence. It has been said that by the year 2000 the three major growth areas – electronics, polymers and food/health – will be covered throughout the world by 100 large corporations, including, of course, state-owned corporations, each larger than any in existence now. I doubt the validity of this solution: for example, it seems to me from the United Kingdom experience that the large corporations cannot plan very well even over the economic swings produced by a series of governments actually trying to hold the economy stable. This particular experience may be due to the small size and will disappear as the large market groups come into being. Nevertheless, the central fact remains that the greater part of our activity is being controlled by government which will become increasingly centralised and which is able to become more centralised with the data-handling possibilities of computers.

Given this, I cannot see that the right balance for the degree of influence of scientists and technologists can be obtained when they interest themselves primarily in what is the peripheral part. It would, I believe, be a very excellent thing if the Science Research Council took a more positive lead in determining the direction of our national scientific effort. At present the SRC, through its subcommittee, tends to adjudicate between rival claims for funds. I would like to see the SRC propose national scientific targets mostly of the 'little science' type described earlier. There should be two varieties, the first group specific and aimed at profitable ends within a time period of, say, ten years, along with some more general propositions aimed at establishing centres of excellence in certain selected fields of science. Molecular biology is an obvious one, where we have the centre of excellence but are not nourishing it adequately. Polymer science could well be another. An essential part of such exercises would be the determination of the effort required and hence the funds required. The SRC should negotiate the principle of availability of these funds with government and then call for propositions within the limits defined. It could well be that such propositions could be prepared not only by academic institutions but also by government laboratories and even industrial laboratories.

Implicit in this discussion of the direct influence which scientists and technologists should have on the affairs of the world (or really on their fellow men) is a belief that we must take a much greater interest in sociology. You may ask, 'Why not encourage sociology as a discipline and encourage more and better sociologists?' It is obvious that this should be done, but technologists are used to calling on many disciplines, dabbling in them if you want to be unkind, and there undoubtedly is merit in the cross-fertilisation that such dabbling produces, whether it is realised from the juxtaposition of ideas in one mind or in a group of minds. Sociology has a long way to go before it can become even reasonably effective science able to make a useful contribution to human affairs. In the course of some rather uncomfortable contact with it I have been impressed with the lack of concern shown by many sociologists for the fate of their experimental material. Chiefly, however, I am concerned with their unwillingness to study society as a dynamic system. Considering the enormous difficulties of sociological study it is not surprising that there is a feeling it would be nice if only the system stood still for a while. This 'stop the world I want to study it' view seems to be hardening in many sociologists' minds into the view that stopping itself is and would be a good thing. This is surely wrong. The natural state of human societies is dynamic. We need to consider, as we can now, where we are going; to edge this way rather than that, to modify the pace, possibly to slower as well as to faster, but not to stop. I fear that our first measures of control to determine the future will be to try to stop, and I think stopping at this particular point in time has no merit, for our present position is still very largely the product of the accidental in invention. As a nation, we are very good at erecting and worshipping various sacred cows: that, for example, we should always mine 200 million tons of coal a year and that the London docks should always employ X men, or that the particular ratio of science to humanist places in the universities in 1939 was fixed on tablets of stone and should be adopted for evermore. I fear as a nation we will vote for non-progress and a comfortable dull life. If this will be the first major fruit of long-range planning, then down with it.

Let me finish with a quotation from Max Planck which should comfort both those who may have agreed with some small part of what I have said and also those who think this has been a load of nonsense: 'Truth never prevails but its enemies die out.'

Fig. 24.1 Narrowing interval between discovery and application for physical sciences

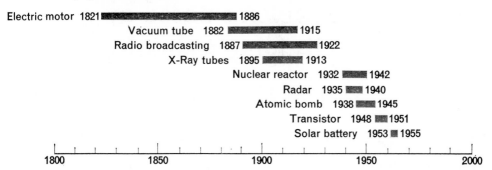

Fig. 24.2 Narrowing interval between discovery and first application for chemistry

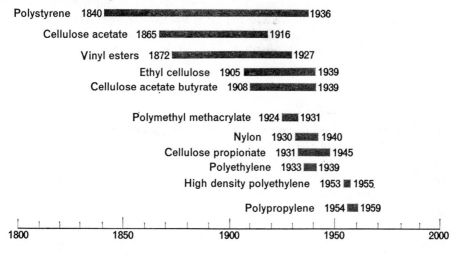

References

1. D. S. DAVIES, *Metals and Materials*, August 1967, 'The undesirability of a research organisation', p. 259.
2. J. JEWKES, D. SAWERS and R. STILLERMAN, *The Sources of Invention*, Macmillan, 1958.

25

Problems posed by changing technology

H. M. FINNISTON

How can the corporate strategist take account of technological change? How may a general manager interpret trends in a highly complex field which is growing at an exponential rate? Dr Finniston discusses the relationship of the technologist to the rest of industrial society and outlines the factors which are tending to insulate the subject from its economic and social environment. He criticises the present system of technological education and advocates a closer relationship between industry and the universities. He concludes that the increasingly important role of technology in society will place the technologist under an obligation to broaden his knowledge and deepen his understanding of those activities of industrialised societies which are not science-based.

What is technology?

In a stable society which for purposes of definition is one in which changes of any kind, whether political, social or technico-economic are minimal or slow moving, a new equilibrium in the life of a community can be established and accepted comparatively easily. In a modern industrial society wishing to sustain expanding standards of living, changes may have to be accommodated with a continuing, deeper, more challenging and disturbing influence on the industrial and social structure than the minor discontinuities experienced in earlier agrarian eras. This situation derives essentially from the establishment of the scientific method as a technique for at least being informed of and at best understanding the mechanics of nature as a preliminary to technological modification and control leading to the (non-uniform) improvement of the material standards of societies.

In this context, technology is conceived as the application of science-based methods, information, data and knowhow to the production of materials and goods and to the provision of services with the primary intentions that the technical objectives should (in the accounting sense) be achieved economically and in a free market profitably (not necessarily maximised). Technology is thus concerned with objectives which extend beyond those commonly associated with research or academic development; whereas these latter activities are more directly involved with the technical content of problems, technology has also to operate within constraints imposed by the technostructure of industry – the combination of management and technologists, finance, labour, sales, etc. – and is also concerned with the interaction of technical solutions with the economic considerations of an industry or organisation.

The qualification on profitability in the definition of technology is a refinement influencing the operations of industry. Independent of the political colour of society, maximum economy in industrial practices is a criterion rarely challenged though capable of various interpretations; but although industrial goods and services are normally geared to sell at maximum profit, the profit element may be intentionally reduced for good commercial reasons, or through provision of services or benefits with an amenity or social content either on a national, industry or company basis.

The problem of growth

The first major problem with which technology is faced is the exponential growth in knowledge. This growth is not confined to the sheer increase in volume of scientific communication; modern techniques of classification, storage and retrieval of information might in time cater for this, though there are problems of the timelags between determination of the knowledge and its communication, interpretation, rationalisation, adoption and use. What are perhaps more difficult to assimilate are the increasing complexities and subtleties of science and technology at refined levels of experiment and theory. It is chastening how little understanding, much less appreciation, there is by the trained individual of a very large proportion of the scientific knowledge emerging from more and more fields of human activity. As an example, the titles of some twenty papers chosen at random from the contents list of four internationally reputable journals are appended. It would be an interesting exercise for the reader to determine how many of the articles he could understand or how much of the jargon he could recognise; and even if understood could he guess at the potential application of the information which is one of the responsibilities of the technologist? The *World List of Scientific Periodicals*, 1966, cites over 70 000 titles of periodicals (not articles) which are only one medium through which scientific information is communicated. Yet developments in the electronics, electrical, chemical, metallurgical, engineering and every other industry known and to be generated could be significantly affected by the content of any article to a greater or less extent, either immediately or in the longer term. Such complexity detail is leading scientific practitioners to greater specialisation with greater fragmentation of interests, thus making communication across the boundaries of specialisation more difficult at a time when future technological developments are requiring improved access to specialist fields.

Two palliatives

There are two features which may tend to stem this trend or provide palliatives. The first is the attempt now being made by non-specialist journals to acquaint scientists, technologists and laymen in simple terms with what is happening across the technical board. Such journals as the New Scientist, International Science and Technology, Nature, Science Journal, Fortune and specialist articles in newspapers or magazines are examples of this trend to inform specialists outside their field. So far as technology is concerned, this 'information service', which can give a general view of the findings and thinking in specialisations which are outside technical interests but may have a bearing on them, reflects the realisation that for most industries, processes, products and services may be advanced further and faster from a knowledge of the disciplines and the workings of industries outside the immediate ambit. In this context, steelmaking can be seen as a special application to which thermodynamics and thermochemistry are relevant; some aspects of physical metallurgy can be related to theories of the solid state; logistics can be viewed as a specific example of linear programme theory; and some medical engineering as exercises in the inanimate fields of fluid dynamics and diffusion phenomena. Furthermore, the multifarious techniques and know-how which are accepted as routine by some specialists but are completely unknown to other disciplines may be adaptable and of considerable value to these latter; for example, apparatus and techniques developed by and familiar to chemical engineers are now beginning to be adapted by metallurgists for high rate processing; simulation through the analogue computer, though long used by engineers, is now being increasingly adopted by physicists; and instrumentation in general is finding invention by one discipline and innovation by others.

It may be argued that specialisation tends to stultify or prevent the broad view; this can happen if it is allowed to happen. The second palliative, however, is the capability of people to move from one technology to another without previous experience. This feature is one of which less than full advantage is taken in staffing. By such movements, pollination of new ideas and dissemination of established technology are achieved in one package deal. Libraries can be of men as well as of books. This explains the sometimes startling successes which attend placing a trained physicist or chemist in an essentially chemical- or physics-based industry, and why teams of mixed disciplines may be much more effective than single discipline units. In the UK some of the best examples in support of such measures have been in the movement during the war of scientists practising various conventional disciplines (mathematics, physics, chemistry and biology) to radar, and from radar to nuclear energy, and since the war from nuclear energy to computing or other technical industrial activities.

The compromise of coexisting specialists

The economic criterion

A second major problem which the technologist has to face is the economic attitude now pervading the operations of industry, including its research and development activities. Today, detailed evaluation of the probable economic outcome of technical projects is as much expected as part of the case for entering into these projects as is definition or explanation of the technical objective. Cost benefit analysis is being increasingly adopted by governments supporting industrial and military developments, and by the larger science-based industrial companies in determining forward policy on technical developments. Nor does economic control and audit stop there. Even after decision to engage in any specific research or development has been taken there is as an economic constraint, almost automatic application of critical path analysis to the detail of the programme; and if direction is strong, continuing reassessment of the economic value of major developments will bring a quick end to those which are not going to pass the final test.

There is an important implication deriving principally from this economic criterion. This is that the final say on the viability of a project in industry is not the sole responsibility of the technologist. It is true that his view on the technical (and perhaps other) aspects of any development will carry considerable weight, but a strong technical case does not necessarily mean a strong commercial case. Many elegant processes which are scientifically satisfying never see the light of day because they cannot compete with 'cruder' but existing processes based on plants which can still serve their purposes technically and economically. They may be galling to the technologist, particularly in an industry or company alive to new ideas, but the introduction of modernity for its own sake is not sufficient justification in a competitive industrial world. Other criteria, e.g. market research, labour difficulties, lack of management or finance, etc., may also argue against adoption of a technological advance.

This raises the question of where the technologist stands in a company. The old idea that scientists in industry should be seen but rarely heard appealed to traditional industrialists (generally in traditional industries) who felt that the backroom was the proper quarter for scientists in industry. Fortunately, there is now an increasing demand for the voice to be heard and the scientist to be seen in the prestigious laboratories and the works. In some respects the pendulum may have swung too far, since many scientists and technologists believe that only by listening to them will the ills of industry be solved. It would be foolish to deny that technologists should have a voice in affairs which involve their expertise; but it is only one of a number and the weight to be placed on it depends on the circumstances of a situation which is never simple and may in the end depend on the judgement of an entrepreneur rather than on scientific analysis which is either not possible or too uncertain. The technologists of modern industry must learn to discriminate between confidence in their ability to solve their problems and arrogance in deciding what use should be made of their solutions. The operations of a company has its complexities outside the technical area.

Understanding other experts

The requirement for interdisciplinary exchanges on the technical side, to which reference was made in the previous section, extends to the non-scientific skills which make up industry – its management, accountancy, finance, labour and marketing. Each of these disciplines (however undisciplined its practices) has its role to play and its opinion to give, but it is the sum or rather balance of these views in conjunction with that of the technologist which determines the final outcome of whether or not to proceed with the latter's aspirations. It is a salutary experience to find that accountants can so modify their presentation of an economic argument that technologists can find their cause supported or rejected (in some cases at one and the same time!) in the 'independent' views of their colleagues. If technologists are not infallible, neither are their non-scientific colleagues. In the case of economists or accountants, assumptions relating to depreciation, tax reliefs, investment grants, write-offs, etc., should not be assumed to be inviolate but require of the technologist that he appreciates the assumptions on which the economic assessment is made, even if he does not do the calculations himself. To lose a technical argument through non-technical misrepresentations seems to be a poor way in which to advance one's case. It may be for this reason that the mysterious economic jargon which filtered into industry some years ago is no longer confined to economists but is understood (if vaguely) by non-experts affected by such considerations.

The complexity of industry and of its decision-making involves technostructures with different viewpoints and opinions expressed in special 'languages', terms, expressions, jargons and techniques. If decisions are to be arrived at as a result of mutual understanding by experts and not through blind acceptance of a forcibly-expressed view or the status of authority, then there is a need on all sides to present one's contribution to decision-making in a form which makes the situation clear to all parties, and on the reader a requirement to educate himself in the expertise of his colleagues. This latter objective should not be misunderstood. It is not to be interpreted as requiring one to become expert in the affairs of all one's colleagues; rather is it that one should understand the essential point of someone else's argument in a language which is different from that normally used in one's own expertise. This whole problem of the techniques of argument and debating orally or in writing in industry for industry, and the apparatus required to arrive at a decision based on a variety of relevant viewpoints, including the technical one, is perhaps one of the most pressing problems with which the technologist in particular is faced in industry, since his jargon is the most diverse and least understood by people.

Reacting to changes

To meet a single change is one thing; more difficult to accommodate is the rate of change. If one compares the rate at which changes in society and industry have been introduced in the individual quarters of this century the pace of the third quarter can be seen to be significantly greater than the previous two. This increase in rate of change has the effect of reducing the life cycle of a product or radically modifying it so that it looks and behaves with markedly different performance from its predecessors; or it may involve changes in production with consequences on management and labour. Accommodation to this rate of change in the succeeding quarter-centuries may well become the greatest problem of all, since it is a problem unlikely to decrease with the passage of time. On the contrary once a state of mind in a society is reached at which people are prepared uninhibitedly to look at all ideas and to experiment without deferring to past procedures as a precedent, the acceleration of change will itself increase.

So far attention has been paid to the technical problems associated with the introduction of changes, but these changes themselves modify accepted tenets of thought, methods and procedures which have not always found ready acceptance. Negative reaction to innovation is partly compounded of various human failings and partly of conventions obtaining in the system under which society operates. One would expect the technical man, perhaps more than any other, to be the most open-minded, but even technologists suffer from such human obstacles to change as fear of the unknown (which includes a fear of the long-term consequences of their innovations), inertia, the NIH (Not Invented Here) factor, and sheer complexity. Besides the political, legal and fiscal determinants which industry must recognise, there are other system conditions which inhibit economic technological advances. These include such features as the isolation of research (and development) in universities or government establishments; concentration on research which is subsequently rendered nugatory by the very large requirements of capital required to meet development and later production costs; and lack of decision or delay in decision to proceed with or withdraw from projects, a particular source of irritation in government–industrial relations.

Improving the odds

In recent years the complexities of change have led to the creation of planning departments, one function of which is to consider various alternative actions which may be taken by a company in the light of its own situation and of developments of theoretical or experimental work in progress in laboratories throughout organisations operating in the same or ancillary technical fields. (Here again, the importance of access to communicable information emphasises the comments made above.)

The decision what to make and when, the specification to which the article has to be made or service provided, and the most economic means of achieving the technical ends are problems to which the technologist can make a contribution of varying worth. In the first of these (i.e. what and when), his role may be one of shared responsibility with a large number of other experts. However, as new ideas, new concepts and new inventions are generated more rapidly and with increasing competitiveness, technical assessments of the merits of new products, processes or procedures throws increasing responsibility on the technologist, as does specification of product and production machinery. (To offset the burden, the technologist has always a second-best chance to repair the failure of early entry into the market by taking out licences.)

Many major projects are started without full technical information to enable detailed assessment of the magnitude of the problems still unresolved to be determined. If complete probability of technical success is desired before projects are approved, it can almost be taken as read that the project is obsolescent and likely to have reduced economic advantages in relation to existing processes; if, however, any project is entered into too early, the chances are that the costs of manufacture, installation and commissioning of the plant will far outrun the budget set aside for the venture. The best examples of this nicely balanced situation where things most frequently hit the headlines when they go wrong are in advanced military projects undertaken by governments. Timing advances into new fields is therefore a critical decision point, not necessarily to be determined by the date of the invention of the initiative of the innovator. Any technically advanced undertaking should by definition carry with it an appropriate contingency factor in the initial estimates which allows for more uncertainties than can be dreamed up. If greater realism in costing were associated with advanced schemes in industry the pace of technology would certainly ease, and it has been argued that industry might not long survive such caution. If this is so, perhaps the financial criteria for return on investment or the incentives to enter into advanced schemes should be related to the degree of technical innovation and its possible impact upon the future rather than upon the immediate economy of the industry – and the country.

Since the monies involved in introducing major changes can be considerable and an unfortunate technical choice can adversely affect the financial status of a company for many years before the position can be recovered, can the technical men devise some means by which he can more certainly decide the chances of success? Modern techniques of decision making based on the provision of improved statistical data, games, model-making, mathematical manipulations, following-my-leader (not too far behind) and the continuing interplay of communications with people who have something to contribute towards understanding and appreciating the various factors which make up the future, are developing to give greater confidence in the value of these technological tools.

Sharing the risk

Whether one believes with Professor Galbraith that the technostructure determines what the consuming public should have, or whether the consuming public determines what industry shall make, the consuming public is always a factor.

There are two different types of public who must be satisfied with the products of industry. There is the technically sophisticated public (generally concerned with capital goods in the civil field and durables and consumables in the military), whose technical knowledge and understanding of the equipment being sold to them is at least the equal of those selling it; and there is the consuming public who can be satisfied without understanding the technical subtleties of their purchases. To a large extent the technical problems of improved or novel capital equipment are capable of definition or specification and of solution. In such cases the technological form of the future is compounded by agreement between the supplier and the purchaser, more particularly if the purchaser is a government-controlled body or its agency. The general similarity of developments in advanced nations in nuclear reactors, heavy electrical machinery, aircraft or much military equipment, is evidence of the existence of informal but reasonably universally 'agreed' general opinions defining the technical directions likely to be taken by processes and products for the future. Differences in the outcome are in details, important though these might be.

In a consumer market where aesthetics tend to obscure or highlight the technical requirements of the product, the decision of the technologist is much less valuable in deciding upon the specification although his contribution may be considerable in relation to production at acceptable cost. Motor-cars and television sets are good examples of the important roles the non-technologist can play in determining the supporting effort required of the technologist.

Breeding the technologist

Besides the problems which technologists have to face, there is the problem of creating the technologist himself. This involves consideration of the whole system of education, a matter on which there is considerable divergence of views and practices throughout the industrial nations of the world. The first degree in science should be broadly based and should not attempt any specialisation until the very last moment, probably the last year of the course. This general grounding should be in English, history, economics, mathematics, physics, chemistry and biology, and should attempt to deal with the principles, concepts, philosophy and logic of science rather than with the factual detail of specialist subjects which can always be referred to in books or gained through experience. Since it is in industry that technologists practise their art and science, the last year of the first degree course in science should preferably be operated through a sandwich system by which experience in industry is gained.

For all but the brightest academics (and these constitute less than 10 per cent of the total number taking first degree), any postgraduate continuation of studies should be deferred until the scientist has had a full-time period in industry proper. The creation of modern industrial laboratories with high-grade staffs and modern equipment certainly provides the framework within which the university-trained scientist can expect to learn the techniques and problems of industrial research. If it is argued that the kinds of research done in industrial laboratories are more of a development nature than they are of the pure variety, it is worth determining how much basic or fundamental work is really done in the applied science departments of any university and how much R and D has a great similarity to the kinds of work which obtain in industrial laboratories. The differences are more apparent than real and suggest that the balance of power in R and D does not lie with the universities. It could also be argued that there can be too much research at the expense of too little teaching or application development.

Because of the growth of knowledge, and because of the rapid changes in technology, there is a considerable requirement for refresher courses for technologists through periods of return to university and deferred postgraduate work. These refresher courses should bring individuals up to date on the latest thinking of academics who by definition should be in the van of their professional expertise. Refresher courses for experienced technologists (and particularly technologists practised in industrial problems) may have to be organised in a very different way to that accorded the first degree student. It could involve varying degrees of collaboration between the company's problems and the university departments; it could involve the use by the university of the company's facilities; it could involve lectures, courses or tutorials given on the premises of a company to a number of its employees; in fact, it can be any technique which brings the knowledge of the university to the industrial recipient knowledgeable in the ways of industry and the technical details of his profession, but who has not perhaps managed to acquire or sustain awareness of the background or of advanced concepts permeating the discipline in which he is specialising. These arrangements bring other benefits to industry in their train. There is perhaps a greater awareness of this in Europe and the US than in the UK. If we are witnessing a revolution in the advance of science and technology we will also have to witness a revolution in the education of scientists and technologists catering to their changing needs throughout a professional life which is far longer than the first four years they spend in a university.

The technologist and society

Finally, there is the major problem of the role of the technologist in society as a whole. There is an unwritten rule based on rational considerations that the scientists' views on scientific matters should carry greater weight than lay observations, but that outside the field of science, e.g. on matters political, the scientist is no more expert than any other inexpert or non-professional individual. In a world, however, which is increasingly basing its decisions on scientifically based principles and which is adopting standards and ways of living which are determined in large measure by the thinking and products of the scientist and technologist, it is becoming increasingly difficult to determine when and where the line on technological views and action should be drawn. Such technological products as the H-bomb and the oral contraceptive are accepted by society notwithstanding the complex social implications; and on a lesser level, to realise that the third generation of supersonic transport planes is now under development while society is arguing whether it should allow the first generation to fly is a more recent test of the conflict in which the technologist again looks like getting his own way.

It is clear that the views of scientists and technologists are being accorded greater acceptance (if not consideration) over a wider field of human activity. The increasing importance attaching therefore to technological thinking in determining the structure and conditions under which human beings are to live in cities and work in industry is placing considerable responsibility upon the technologist in an area in which he cannot always apply with confidence the techniques of science. In the next few decades it may be on this problem that the technologist through such institutions as the Pugwash conference, for example, might find himself expending most thought, since it is in this period that a new balance will be struck between the science-based and non-science-based activities of industrialised societies.

M

PART IV

Corporate strategy and the small firm

26

The future of the small firm

L. V. D. TINDALE

At a time when the business environment appears to be increasingly identified with a small number of large corporations, what appears to be the future prospect for small business? Mr Tindale enumerates the environmental factors which may be expected to determine the fortunes of the small firm — notably rising real incomes, the progressive internationalisation of business, the changing organisational scale of industrial activity and finally the character of government fiscal policy. He then analyses some of the operational strengths and weaknesses of the small firm and discusses the problem of developing a strategy for setting up a new business. He concludes that the continued existence of a large and dynamic small business sector is of crucial importance if the country's industrial structure is to be saved from ossification.

I have now spent over ten years of my life as a general manager of Industrial and Commercial Finance Corporation working with and for and learning about the small firm, and as a member of the Committee of Inquiry into the Small Firm under the Chairmanship of John Bolton, I spent a considerable part of 1969 in hearing from and about small firms and in considering statistical and research studies commissioned by the committee. The only firm conclusions that I have come to is that to pontificate about 'the small firm' is as unrewarding as to do so about 'the Frenchman'. It may be possible to draw some conclusions about the future of the small business sector, just as it may be possible to do so for France, but this has little relevance to the individual component. It is not very comforting to the traveller who drowns fording a stream to know the average depth is only three feet.

Small firms certainly number something over 750 000 units and employ some $4\frac{1}{2}$ million people. They account for 18 per cent of the gross national product. There are, of course, widely differing proportions in the different industrial classifications and some idea of this is given in Figs. 26.1 to 3 below. Remember though that industrial classifications and some idea of this is given by the tables. Remember though that industrial classifications themselves cover a wide range. Thus, if baby-sitting featured as a separate service industry it would presumably be 100 per cent the province of small business. Many of us would agree that its

319

value far exceeds the minute share of the gross national product which would be attributed to it. This can be applied to a lot more activities than baby-sitting.

The dynamics of change

So much for my apologia and for the static snapshot. Let us now turn to the dynamics of change, the changing environmental factors which are affecting the small firm. Once one turns to the macro level one experiences a sense of relief and throws off generalisations with an easy conscience.

The first, and probably the most important, of the factors to which I shall refer is that we as a nation, and the mass of individuals in it, are getting richer in real terms. Productivity is rising at some 3 per cent per annum and although this figure does not sound large it means, other things being equal, that we shall be about a third better off at the end of the decade than at the beginning. We are also getting poorer in comparison with our continental neighbours as well as with our transatlantic and antipodean cousins. It is possible that increasing exposure to this fact will itself lead to a sufficient change in work attitudes to increase still further the rise in living standards.

This rise in wealth will affect our expenditure patterns in many different ways, all of concern to the small firm. A cycle may well take the following form. A new idea starts by being individually produced – the plaything of the rich and the province of the small firm (whether or not part of a large group). It then spreads downwards into the mass market, probably being considerably improved in the process, but becoming very much a creation of the large organisation – maybe carrying some of the small firm originators up in the process and causing casualties to the remainder. Then the mass market itself revolts against uniformity and leaves room once more for the smaller firm to supply in one way or another some part of the demand. Alongside this, increase of wealth permits demands for goods to be satisfied while leaving a surplus in the hands of the consumer. This surplus occasions an increase in demand for service and, of course, growth in leisure and service trades is a characteristic of all developed economies today.

Although the growth in productivity which was the starting point of this section will almost certainly take place, I have made one almost unconscious assumption in the rest of these paragraphs. This is that there will be no change in trends and that the underlying motivations which are turning us increasingly into a hedonistic society will continue. Every forecaster secretly dreads a change of trend – except presumably those who point out that if present trends continue by 1980 we shall all be civil servants. Nevertheless, there are signs that our young – and here I speak of the young of the entire developed world – are rejecting some, if not all, of our satisfactions and hence of our consumer demands. Who can say if this is enduring or, indeed, correct and if so what effect this will have in the next few years. Undoubtedly, a major change in attitudes could upset any forecasts now being made.

The second factor is the continued improvement in communications and the internationalisation of business which accompanies it. Attitudes of mind are slower to change than the physical means of transport and probably slower than government policies. Today Copenhagen is a nearer market in terms of time and no more disadvantageous in other ways to a firm in Harrogate than London was in the 1940s. It is still remote in our thinking, to most of us at least. These attitudes of mind are now breaking down with effects both good and bad for the small business.

The third is the change in scale of activity which is almost always thought to favour size. Perhaps it does, but it is by no means certain. For example, the development of tape-controlled machine tools has restored a great deal of flexibility in operations which were otherwise remorselessly moving towards major inflexible layouts and bringing the possibility of reestablishing sub-contract machining as a fully economic activity.

Another interesting possibility arises from the development of management science, of which a byproduct is a change in the attitude of the manager to entrepreneurship. There is increasing evidence that managers successfully employed in large firms do from time to time long for the greener grass of self-employment. They believe that the talents which they are being encouraged to use in their large organisation, or in the use of which they are being frustrated, could be better employed under their own direction. Moreover, they are increasingly working at all levels in teams covering every aspect of management and find that their colleagues have similar aspirations. They also find that with a change in attitude to job mobility a false start would not forever damn a career, leaving the unfortunate's family to perish in the gutter. They discover that today's financial institutions are aware of this type of thinking and are prepared to back well-thought-out plans. All this means that there is an increasing number of groups of great ability prepared to look at opportunities for establishing or acquiring and expanding small businesses. These are quite apart from the traditional sources of family dynasties and men starting as individual tradesmen. Defection from large industry has now reached substantial proportions in the United States and many enlightened companies there are helping executives to set themselves up by taking an interest in the breakaway firm – presumably on the famous dictum 'if you can't lick 'em, join 'em'.

Fiscal policy and the small business

There are, of course, many environmental factors which will influence small business. I have picked out a few interesting and I believe important ones. I will only mention one more, namely the major one of fiscal policy. Since this is in the province of government it is even more unpredictable than the others. Broadly speaking, it means and is likely to continue to mean that success in small business will be encouraged by a combination of our capital market and fiscal system. This is an unpopular statement with my friends in small business who regard themselves as hard done by, and so many of them are. Nevertheless, the prizes for the few who really succeed are glittering indeed, and our own portfolio at ICFC includes many companies whose owner/managers have made themselves millionaires in well under twenty years. I know of no other method of attaining to this aim in the United Kingdom today without substantial capital to start with. However, even the most convinced equalitarian would find it difficult to change this position and the possibility of the glittering prize without ruining the entire small business sector. It is therefore probably reasonable to assume that this chance will continue as a motivator encouraging the potential entrepreneur to take the risk. On the other hand, it becomes increasingly difficult to hand on ownership of a business of any size to one's family, and the ambition to found a dynasty must be a dwindling force over the decade. Again I cannot foresee any major change in trends already established.

Personnel control and flexibility

So much for the environment, but what does the smaller organisation bring to bear on its problems? By far the most important is that it is the creation of the owner or the small team who are the owners. Although theoretically perhaps this could be either a strength or a weakness it must in fact be a strength, for even survival as a small firm demands above average ability. For example, the small firm will be acting at all times with a sense of purpose which is often lacking in a large unit even after elaborate efforts are made to disseminate information about policies and objectives. Even assuming devotion to customer service as an objective it could only have been a small firm which gave in response to an inquiry as to whether they could supply ten tons of a particular chemical – 'Yes – what is it?' Not perhaps the most scientific method of building a business, but effective and certainly the mark of singleness of purpose. Incidentally, the perpetrator, who was and is a good friend of mine, built a highly successful business which he eventually sold. He says the story is apocryphal. Whether it is or not, that it can be told and believed is significant. No one doubted the dedication to customer service of the firm in question while it remained small. Today as a large concern they would know what they were asked to supply, but their devotion to service would not come through the telephone with anything like the clarity of the early days – even after they had found the right person to reply to the inquiry.

In addition to singleness of purpose the small firm can obtain its advantage from flexibility (even opportunism), responsiveness to market shifts, low cost overhead structure. When the small firm loses this flexibility – for example, the retail establishment with a large percentage of its capital tied up in ownership of its shop – it can be very vulnerable. Its weaknesses are also its sheer lack of resources and of buying power. A single wrong decision even in a matter of relatively small moment may be a serious setback if it occurs at a bad time in other respects. Not only its own decisions, but those of major competitors can have substantial, possibly fatal, effects. For example, a price war between two majors which both survive with comparatively small discomfort and little disturbance of eventual market shares may mean 'curtains' for the small unit in the same market. Apart from these general characteristics there will be other strengths and weaknesses just as in any organisation. It may be technically strong, but poor on production, strong in marketing, but poor in financial skills, excellent at merchandising, but poor at advertising. This is what makes it an individual unit and the field one of such fascinating diversity.

Objectives and opportunities

Of course, these individual strengths and weaknesses are important elements in attempting to put together a strategy for the individual concern. Equally important are the desires and objectives of the owner – will he be content to settle for continuation as a small firm or does his ambition lie in becoming a big firm? Does it indeed lie in developing something which can be sold to a large concern? Incidentally, do not let us despair of the small company ever becoming a giant – the founder of Thorn Electric is still its presiding genius, Marks and Spencer is only just moving out of that condition, Tesco and other supermarkets are creations of a relatively few years as are Slater Walker and a number of property companies. Looking outside this country IBM, Xerox and Polaroid are all creations of, or were brought to fruition during, our own and their presiding geniuses' lifetimes. Whatever other prognostications we care to make we can be safe in assuming that the top hundred companies in 1980 will differ widely from those of 1970 – despite the advancement of management techniques and the development of takeover bids.

Any business strategy, of course, depends on identifying a market for a product or service – a market which is not being satisfactorily filled by other and more powerful contestants. The competition looked formidable when the John Stevens and Mary Quants first established themselves, but in fact it was not – there was a substantial market which was not being served at all in the terms in which it looked at itself. The tale can be told over and over again – the past twenty years have seen a revolution in eating out, in holidays and travel, in dry cleaning and laundry services, in road transport, in chicken and egg production and marketing, in office cleaning. Small companies were pioneers in all these fields – I know because in ICFC while I have been there we have backed at least one successful contender in all of them. In these areas many small firms have grown to substantial size and others have carved out a successful niche while remaining reasonably small.

Again experience in manufacturing suggests that growth goes more easily to the firm with its own products and that growth from very small beginnings is most easily obtained if based on a technological development. We have a fascinating time in this connection with our subsidiary Technical Development Capital which in the jargon of the day is now referred to as a 'venture capital' organisation, but which more irreverently used to be known internally as the mad inventors' club. The biggest lesson I have learned from what I see in TDC is that regrettably so many inventors do not have market considerations in mind. However original or advanced an invention, it is difficult for it to be the foundation of a business of any description, if the total latent world demand is calculated at £1000 per annum. So much effort falls into this category, only equalled by that spent inventing what has been invented before, or slightly worse and more costly methods of doing things which are being done already.

Although technological advance is the best and most certain basis for progress in manufacturing it is by no means the only one. Increasingly, specialisation by leading manufacturers in large volume products, even in capital goods, is leaving a field in some market sectors which is being happily and profitably filled by the smaller concern. By looking at the total world market it is sometimes possible to find sufficient demand for these special products for their exploiters to emerge eventually as a major producer of a not so small speciality.

The one strategy which I find it difficult to believe in as a sound basis for the 1970s if growth is the object, is one which is based solely on the ability to quote lower prices than competition because overheads are lower. As growth comes so overheads grow and there is indeed a difficult situation to deal with.

I am conscious that in all this I have not been able to answer the 64 000-dollar question which any small businessman – present or in embryo – might reasonably ask, namely 'What business should I be in?' I suppose the answer is that if I knew that I would be in there making a fortune instead of vetting other people's ideas – a development perhaps of the old tag that 'those who can, do and those who can't, teach'. Nevertheless, people are having novel concepts every day, backing them with their own resources of money and effort, obtaining additional resources for development and, in a substantial proportion of cases, succeeding.

I seem also to have dealt with the subject of strategy in terms of setting up a new business whereas the great majority of small businesses start from an existing position. In some cases this may be more difficult than starting *ab initio*. I certainly believe that it is easier to drive a small business based on a sound idea through its early years than to develop a medium-sized business producing too wide a range of products into the efficient producer and marketer on a worldwide scale which playing in the big league in today's conditions demands. I see too much of this kind of pattern, or opportunity, in my work on the Economic Development Committee for the Mechanical Engineering Industry for my, or the nation's comfort. However large, medium or small, we can be sure that marketing will remain the key to the 1970s.

National policies

Finally, let us consider what effect changes in national policies may have on the small company and indeed what changes in national policy small business might reasonably request. Some of the matters I shall be referring to here, indeed most of them, were within the purview of the Bolton Committee 1969 and I must, therefore, explain that the remarks I am making are my own and not the result of committee deliberation. Indeed, my own views may well be amended as a result of the research now in hand, the oral evidence which we still have to hear and the Committee discussions which will follow.

At present the majority of owners of smaller businesses appear to be disenchanted with their lot in today's conditions. It was put very succinctly in one instance in the phrase 'we are overtaxed, overgoverned, under-rewarded and under-appreciated'. Probably many engaged in management of large companies and indeed in other activities feel the same way. To what extent the malaise described is affecting performance in the sector is probably impossible to determine. Nevertheless, if one regards the need for an active small business sector as of major importance then this attitude demands consideration.

I do regard the maintenance of such a sector as of extreme importance primarily because it seems the only way in which the industrial structure of the country can be prevented from ossification. The man who is unable to persuade his large company to move, or move sufficiently fast, always has the opportunity of going it alone. Even if the small sector does no more than pinprick the giant into retaliatory action it serves a great purpose.

Our friends in smaller businesses are reasonable in their requests and, as befits a section of the business community devoted to private enterprise, they are almost unanimous in declaring that what is required is removal of disadvantages – not subsidies or special treatment. They would like government to be neutral between big and small, but this concept is difficult to spell out. It is perfectly possible for an action which appears to be equal in its burden (a fixed percentage tax, for example) to be completely biased in its application.

It will, perhaps, be possible to look forward to a better understanding of the problems of small business in Whitehall and, over the years, to this having some effect on removing annoyances in legislation and administrative action. It is also possible that some way will be found to open more government contracts and particularly research and development contracts to this sector. It may also be possible to find a way to prevent a semi-monopoly power based on purse strings damaging the smaller man.

Turning to the financial field which is again one of substantial concern to many small businesses, it is reasonable to assume that in any future credit squeezes methods will be found to prevent an undue and disproportionate burden being placed on small business – indeed, on the contrary one might hope for more favourable treatment. Institutional arrangements for the supply of finance are constantly developing, and there is undoubtedly increased interest and awareness of the opportunity which exists. I am sure that the requirements for development and establishment of new enterprises will be taken care of, either through existing methods or by new ones to be developed. I do have some doubts about the availability of private finance to enable the buying and selling of moderately substantial units by individuals – which is still a major factor in the requirements of the sector – to be arranged. No doubt, if the problem is proved to exist some method will be found to meet it.

In the field of taxation there may, of course, be a major switch from income taxation to some other form of taxation – e.g. value added tax. Otherwise, although there may be some modification of detail which will help with particular problems I believe there will be a little change. A reduced rate of corporation tax on say the first £10 000 of profit for all businesses, large or small, and also perhaps a method under which taxation does not differ substantially according to incorporation or non-incorporation may be within the bounds of possibility despite considerable technical difficulties in implementation. Changes of this nature would be a substantial relief to the smallest units as well as an encouragement to all.

Relief from estate duty is probably too much to hope for, but again a payment by instalments over a substantial period as is already granted for forestry and in certain circumstances for capital gains tax would be of substantial help without going against the principal of inheritance taxes. Just conceivably, the nation could be so convinced of the value of small business that the 40 per cent relief extended to agriculture and to a limited range of business assets would become more generally available to unquoted companies.

So we come to the end of my look into the future. What is certain is that in 1980 the small business sector will still be large and, as ever throughout our nation's history, will still be contributing substantially to the wellbeing of the nation. In part at least it will be doing this in ways which most of us – including me – do not visualise today.

This is what small business is all about.

Fig. 26.1 Small firms in the UK economy

	Year	Number of enterprises/ organizations			Employment in 000's			Net output £ million		
		All %	Small %	Small as % of all	All %	Sml %	Small as % of all	All %	Sml %	Small as % of all
TOTAL	(1963)	100	100	87	100	100	31	100*	100*	29
(a) Manufacturing	1963	6	6	94	54	34	20	26	14	16
(b) †Retail	(1963)	50	55	95	18	37	66	24	49	60
(c) Wholesale	(1963)	3	3	77	5	4	24	31	12	11
(d) Construction	1963	8	9	89	12	10	27	4	4	23
(e) Mining/Quarrying	1963	‡	‡	81	‡	‡	21	‡	‡	20
(f) Motor Trades	1962	7	7	90	3	— NA —		9	11	35
(g) †Misc. Services	1966	5	6	99	3	5	72	1	1	65
(h) Road Transport	1965	4	4	85	2	— NA —		—	— NA	
(i) †Catering	1964	16	11	59	4	— NA —		5	9	— 49

(Year) – Figures are estimates for year shown.   * – Excluding road transport
      †   – Figures for establishments.   NA – Not available
      ‡   – less than 0·5%.

Small firms are defined for each sector (a)–(i) above as follows:
(a) under 200 employees
(b) turnover not exceeding £50 000
(c) annual receipts not exceeding £250 000
(d), (e) under 25 employees
(f) turnover not exceeding £100 000
(g) virtually all
(h) 5 or fewer vehicles owned
(i) estimate, excluding multiple hotels, brewery owned public houses, etc.

Fig. 26.2 Analysis of the manufacturing industry (1963)

	Number of establishments			Employment in 000's			Net Output £ million		
	All %	Small %	Small as % of all	All %	Small %	Small as % of all	All %	Small %	Small as % of all
TOTAL MANUFACTURING	100	100	85	100	100	30	100	100	26
III Food/Drink/Tobacco	8	8	81	9	8	27	12	11	24
IV Chemicals/Allied manf.	4	4	84	6	4	23	10	7	20
V Metal manufacture	3	3	80	7	4	17	8	4	16
VI Eng./Electrical goods	19	19	84	24	18	23	23	20	23
VII Shipbuilding/Marine eng.	1	1	84	3	1	15	2	1	15
VIII Vehicles	2	2	72	10	2	7	11	2	6
IX Other metal goods	13	12	89	6	9	44	6	9	41
X Textiles	8	8	82	10	12	39	7	10	35
XI Leather/Fur, etc.	2	2	87	1	2	74	‡	2	75
XII Clothing/Footwear	9	9	82	6	11	53	4	7	51
XIII Bricks/Pottery/Glass/	6	6	89	4	5	41	4	6	40
Cement	10	9	90	3	8	69	3	7	67
XIV Timber/Furniture									
XV Paper/Printing/Publishing	12	14	88	7	10	41	8	10	35
XVI Other manufacture	4	4	84	4	4	33	4	4	29

(1958 SIC)

Fig. 26.3 Analysis of the retail trade (1966)

	Number of establishments			Employment in 000's			Net output £ million		
	All %	Small %	Small as % of all	All %	Small %	Small as % of all	All %	Small %	Small as % of all
TOTAL RETAIL	100	100	94	100	100	65	100	100	57
Grocer/provision dealers	24	24	92	20	21	68	26	26	58
Other food retailers	21	21	95	18	21	77	19	22	67
Confectionery/tobacco/news	13	13	98	12	17	96	9	15	93
Clothing/footwear	16	16	94	16	16	63	16	14	52
Household goods	14	14	92	12	13	69	12	12	59
Other non-food	11	12	95	10	11	72	9	10	65
General stores	1	‡	14	12	‡	1	9	‡	1

27

Developing corporate strategy for smaller businesses

A. E. B. PERRIGO

Is the concept of strategic planning as applicable to the small firm as to the large corporation? In this article the author suggests that this is indeed the case, but he also points out the special difficulties which the chief executive must overcome before a strategy can be successfully adopted. The most pressing need is for the chief executive to be able to stand back from his firm and make a full appraisal of all its operations before objectives and strategy can be determined. The author suggests how this preplanning stage might be tackled and how strategies for small firms might best be developed.

The smaller business and its economic significance

Unfortunately, there is no general agreement as to what constitutes a small, or smaller, business. Among the criteria which come to mind are the number of employees, the annual sales turnover, total emoluments, and the characteristics of the organisation structure of the firm. For the purpose of this article we will consider a smaller business as one with less than 200 employees. In the manufacturing area alone, ignoring firms with no more than 10 employees, 47 000 out of a total of 54 600 establishments in the United Kingdom have less than 200 employees, and they account for approximately 31 per cent of the total employees and 27 per cent of total sales. It therefore follows that the smaller-business sector in which we are interested makes an important contribution to the national economy. In consequence, any improvement in performance which can be effected through long-range planning – a practice which up to the present has largely been restricted to large companies – would significantly reflect itself in our overall national performance.

Change and the smaller business

A characteristic of many smaller businesses is that their day-to-day activities virtually absorb the whole energies and attention of management, in consequence of which practically no time is given to their longer-term interests and needs. This is particularly serious in these days of accelerating change – technical, social, and economic – since such businesses are likely to fail to recognise the opportunities or the risks to their individual prospects which such changes create. In consequence, they neither plan to take advantage of the unfolding opportunities available to them, nor prepare to take action to minimise or avoid the risks which threaten them.

It therefore follows that, before corporate strategy can be developed in the typical smaller business, attention has to be given to the day-to-day operating situation, and the essential steps taken to free the chief executive from its pressures, to permit him to devote the necessary time to the longer-term requirements of the business. Experience has shown that the implementation of these steps is usually a far more difficult task in the smaller business than it subsequently is to introduce an effective corporate strategy. Often it means the developing of a completely new style of management in the business, and the breaking down of habits of a lifetime – particularly for the chief executive, but also to a lesser extent for his subordinates. Furthermore, these steps alone, if they are implemented properly, can have a profoundly beneficial effect on the business, apart from being an essential prerequisite to the development of a sound corporate strategy. It will, therefore, be worth our while, before considering corporate strategy itself, to give some thought to the sort of situation which exists in many smaller businesses, and how this has to be changed before there is any possibility of successfully developing a sound corporate strategy.

The major problem of many smaller businesses

Probably the greatest problem of the chief executive of the typical smaller business, and from this stem many other problems, is that he is so preoccupied with its day-to-day activities, of which he only too often carries out many of the direct operating chores himself – sometimes for apparently overpowering reasons of overall economy – that he gives little or no time to appraisal and improvement of current performance, or to the longer-term needs and prospects of the business. This frequently results in crisis management and *ad hoc* decisions – the antithesis of strategic planning. Furthermore, it creates a vicious circle. Current pressures and crises are largely due to the lack of foresight shown in the past, and they in turn absorb energies which should be directed to preparation for the future.

The need for greater delegation

How can this vicious circle be broken? Unless it is broken, the introduction of corporate strategy measures will only add to the problems of the chief executive and his staff, without providing corresponding benefits. It can only be broken by first rectifying those operating weaknesses which have given rise to such a situation. When corrected, a climate results in which the development of corporate strategy, and its successful application, is a practicable possibility.

Before such a programme can be initiated, the chief executive must be prepared to reorganise and to delegate the day-to-day activities of the business to that degree necessary to permit him to spend adequate time on appraisal and improvement of current performance, and on preparation for the future. Most chief executives find the first step of reorganising the activities of their subordinates, to be logical and valuable. What they usually find much more difficult is to learn the skills of delegation and to impart these to their subordinates. They appreciate the logic that the purpose of delegation is to make it possible for one man to extend his effectiveness and discharge his responsibilities through his subordinates. They may also realise that these subordinates to be as effective as possible need to be aware of the chief's objectives, and to be suitably motivated and capable of assisting him to achieve these objectives.

The need for corresponding feedbacks

Since delegation does not mean abdication, he also has to teach them that, in delegating responsibility to a subordinate, a manager does not in any way abrogate his own responsibility for the decision. He therefore has to ensure that all necessary information is fed back to him in good time, so that he will learn of important matters when there is still time for him to take effective remedial action. His subordinates have to learn that any responsibility delegated to them places them under the obligation of keeping their chief informed of what is happening, or of the decisions they have taken or propose taking – to whatever degree the chief may indicate necessary to ensure the discharging of his own responsibilities to the company.

Some chief executives do not know, and seem incapable of learning, how to delegate authority and responsibility. If a subordinate does not achieve the required results, no matter why, they see the firing and replacement of him as the only solution, rather than the necessity of determining where the fault lay, and taking remedial action. It is interesting to note that the good subordinate, whose history is that of little going wrong, is not necessarily the most knowledgeable person available for the job. He is usually the one who most willingly and habitually provides good feedback to his chief, and happily informs his chief of the decisions he proposes to take. In this process, the chief executive will find that the degree to which he can safely delegate will depend upon the extent to which he has introduced effective controls – i.e. routine systems of feeding back essential information to him concerning operating performance. He will find the more reliable the control the greater the degree of delegation which can prudently be introduced.

Differentiating between style and substance of performance

A serious restriction to delegation is where a chief executive believes that, if he does not do the job himself it will not be done properly – and by 'properly', he means exactly as he would have carried it out and to a standard which he fondly imagines he always maintains.

One of the first secrets of delegation which a manager needs to learn is that the style of every man is unique and that, to enjoy the fruits of delegation, one has to be prepared to live with and accept (a) a level of performance from one's subordinates which may be lower than (or lower than one thinks) is one's own level; and (b) 'styles' of operation which might be different from one's own or from that of a successful predecessor in the subordinate post. This necessitates one being able to differentiate clearly between the style and the substance of a person's performance, an essential step if the chief executive is going to weld a good team out of the relatively meagre resources usually available to him.

Developing the management team in readiness for corporate strategy

Even when the chief executive has delegated responsibilities to his subordinates within a suitable organisational pattern, the degree to which he will enjoy the fruits of this will depend on the quality and the results of the training he gives them in the decision-making process and the efficient discharge of executive routine tasks.

Sometimes, with the best of intentions, a chief executive will endeavour to provide the former training by letting the subordinate 'sit at his feet' for the purpose of learning from the decisions the chief makes during the course of the day. It is much more effective (though more mentally demanding) for the chief executive to think out and define the objectives of the company and the consequent criteria against which the various decisions have to be made. This is because it is a much easier task for a subordinate to interpret what decision his chief would make in a given situation when he knows the criteria upon which the chief would base his decision, than if he has to try to unravel these criteria himself from a welter of decisions which have been fortuitously made in his presence. (Besides being of great value to the subordinate, this exercise on the part of the chief executive of defining criteria is of equal value to himself – irrespective of whether he is delegating simple office duties in a very small firm, or the responsibility for a key area of activity in a larger company.)

Improving subordinates' judgement

Until the chief executive has taught his subordinates how to make the day-to-day routine decisions of the firm, and has confidence in these decisions, he is not likely to be able to begin to spend the necessary time on the development of corporate strategy. It follows, therefore, that he needs to develop the judgement of his subordinates, and time spent on this will amply repay him. Wherever there is a problem, he should train them to consider all the solutions possible and then objectively to assess the advantages and disadvantages of each. If this is established as a rigid discipline within his subordinates, it is surprising how simply good judgement will usually follow in all but the most complicated of cases.

One of the greatest hindrances to good judgement is the common habit of not exploring all possible solutions to the problem before assessing the advantages and disadvantages of each, but of stopping at an early solution and then ingeniously gathering together as many advantages as possible for this solution, rather as an advocate would prepare a case for his client.

Reviewing current performance to determine possible future trends

Having taken the above first and vital steps of freeing himself sufficiently from the day-to-day activities of the business, the chief executive should next make a diagnostic review of performance to date. To this end, information should be gathered regarding the profitability and performance of the business over the past few years. The trends which these reveal help towards an understanding of what has been happening and also, what is equally important, of why it has occurred. The data required for this purpose include capital investment, sales turnover, profit, return on capital investment, added value per employee, inventory turnover, and accounts receivable. Why these trends have occurred will best be determined by an investigation into the relevant activities of the business. For example, what are the products, what contribution to the gross margin has each product made, what are the sales of each product in relation to its market potential, what are the trends of the markets for each of the products?

The review should also extend to the costs and other pertinent factors of all aspects of the operations which constitute the business – manufacturing, service, selling, development and administration. The trends established for the past few years, and particularly their relevance to sales turnover, volume, growth and profit, should be studied for each individual product and the activity as a whole.

Some of the information will probably be found not to be available – or only so after a lot of digging and reconstitution of figures. In such circumstances, 'guestimates' may have to be made, but it is as well for the chief executive to weight up carefully the economic pros and cons of henceforth having this provided on a routine basis.

Such a review often leads to a number of surprising, and sometimes some disturbing, findings concerning the direction in which the firm is heading, and the relative importance of various products and their markets to its well-being. Some of these findings indicate necessary changes which can easily be implemented in the short term, while others suggest improvements which can only be made in the longer term. Other findings may highlight problems – or opportunities – for which there is currently no foreseeable course of action, but will henceforth need watching carefully.

Questions requiring answers

Armed with the results of this review, and having taken steps to implement the changes which can be made in the short term, the chief executive should seek answers to the following questions.

1 What are the firm's objectives?
   In the smaller firm, where ownership and management are so closely linked – and often indivisible – this is not always an easy question to answer. This is particularly so where the owner-manager wants to satisfy personal and family requirements which are different from the requirements of the firm itself, when viewed as an entity with its own opportunities and its own resultant needs to realise these opportunities. These different requirements can be in conflict, and in some cases mutually exclusive. In consequence, in the case of owner-managership, it is worth some hard soul-searching to determine which needs are to be met, or what compromise is to be made, so that the defined objectives of the firm will have real meaning.

2 What business is the firm really in? Does it basically offer a product or a service, or is it a mixture of these? If a mixture, which contributes most to the firm's reputation?

3 What are the firm's markets? Which are expanding, which are contracting? Which have the most promising (and which the least promising) long-term potential? What if any, economic, social, political and technological changes are affecting the business or its markets?

4 Who makes the purchasing decision in these markets? Could the firm create better linkages with these decision-makers?

5 What products are providing
   (a) a satisfactory contribution to fixed expenses and profit?
   (b) an unsatisfactory contribution?

6 What steps, if any, could be taken to improve the contribution of those products of 5(b) above
   (a) in reducing direct costs?
   (b) in price changes?

7 What manufacturing processes could be improved, and how?

8 What services to production could be improved, and how?

9 Could the selling arrangements be improved?
   (a) supporting services   (c) intensity
   (b) coverage   (d) pattern of distribution

10 Are management services adequate? If not, in what directions should they be improved?

11 Where are overhead expenses too heavy?

12 Where would an increase in overheads provide an economic return?

13 In what areas do the strengths of the company lie?
  (a) market   (e) technical
  (b) financial   (f) production
  (c) product   (g) personnel
  (d) service

14 What are the weaknesses in each of the areas (a) to (g) above?

15 What is the inventory turnover, and what ought it to be?

16 What is the firm's buying policy?

17 What are the strengths and weaknesses of the key personnel and their subordinates?

18 Which members of the above staff have potential for carrying greater responsibilities?
  (a) in the short term   (b) in the long term

In answering some of the above questions, the chief executive will almost certainly find that he needs information from outside sources (e.g. government statistics, trade associations, chambers of commerce, banks, etc.). One very useful first contact in the search for such information is the local industrial liaison officer, whose address can be obtained from the regional office of the Ministry of Technology.

The small company very often finds it difficult to collect or generate sufficient information about changes in markets and in technology and in applying modern research techniques at a scale to meet the economic needs of the business. Often, the local industrial liaison officer can prove of assistance in indicating where useful outside advice can be procured at a moderate price to 'set the firm up', to make proper use of the information available within the firm (e.g. old sales records, etc.) and to be able to tap outside information of relevance to the firm's future. This difficulty experienced by the small firm, however, is more or less counterbalanced by the advantage of flexibility it possesses and the fact that, in its scale of operations, planning on a two- or three-year basis may well be as appropriate as is that on a five-year basis in the larger firm.

Setting objectives and developing corporate strategy

During the above exercise, which may spread over several months, the chief executive should take his employees into his confidence and open up dialogue with them in those areas in which they are respectively involved and have detailed knowledge. Many chief executives, when going through this process, are agreeably surprised at the amount of previously untapped information to which they gain access. While all the information so obtained is not uniformly reliable, it does stimulate thought on the part of the chief executive.

Once the exercise is completed, the chief executive should be ready to define the corporate objectives for the following three, four, or five years – as the case may be, according to the type of business – and thence to define the strategy to attain these objectives. The strategy is most likely to succeed if each of those who have a part to play in ensuring its success knows clearly what is expected of him and is aware of the significance of his contributions to the whole operation. Furthermore, the more each is committed to the plan through involvement in the decision-making process, the more he is likely to exert himself to ensure its success, and the more intelligent will be his endeavours.

Expressing objectives in budgetary and key-task terms

The chief executive has two extremely useful mechanisms available to him to ensure that each member of the management and supervisory team will be aware of the part which he is expected to play within the corporate strategy. One is that of budgetary control, and the other is in the allocation of key tasks within the job descriptions which are an essential part of an organisation structure. A number of industry training boards have recognised the value of job descriptions and have encouraged firms to make use of them.

Budgetary control is much more than an accounting procedure – though many firms unfortunately regard it in this light. It is a statement of management intent for the period to which it relates. It is expressed in the least common denominator – i.e. monetary terms – and it states in these terms the resources which management proposes to make available and the return which management expects to obtain from their use – and the budget authorises executives and supervisors to expend these resources in the manner thereby approved, providing the programme is attained.

Therefore, when the chief executive has decided with the various employees involved what improvements can be effected in market penetration, product range, pricing and sales mix, manufacturing efficiency, inventory turnover, and suitability of product to meet market needs, and has agreed dates by which these improvements could reasonably be effected, he can develop a long-term programme incorporating these proposed changes, and delegate responsibility for the achievement of various aspects to individual members of his staff. He will, of course, need to monitor the implementation of these aspects with each of the subordinates delegated the specific tasks.

His next step, in consultation with his sales manager or members of the sales department, is to prepare a sales budget in accord with the programme, and thereafter production and other departmental budgets necessary to realise the programme. A composite budget can then be drawn up, detailed monthly for the following twelve months and quarterly for each of the next two, three, or four years, according to the needs of the situation. This budget should be in accord with the corporate strategy developed to attain objectives. In each case, cash-flow statements should be developed so that the chief executive will be aware in advance of future cash needs and be able to arrange for the necessary funds as required, or trim activities accordingly. In parallel, the objectives should be reflected in the key tasks of those members of the staff to whom the chief executive had delegated responsibility for the individual projects encompassed by the total strategy.

Progress towards attaining the objectives ought regularly to be reviewed by the chief executive and action taken as considered necessary. Furthermore, he should also frequently review the objectives of the firm against performance, and in the light of external and internal changes. As found necessary, objectives should be modified or changed and the strategy to attain the revised objectives adjusted accordingly. These changes should reflect themselves where practicable within the budget, which one must never forget is the servant and not the master of the business.

Performance and long-term planning

Recently, the Small Business Centre, University of Aston, when carrying out a survey of fifteen small companies to determine their management training needs, made a subjective assessment of the managerial strengths and weaknesses of each firm with respect to their use of recognised and accepted management practices and techniques. Assessment of each firm's use was the simple one of S for strong, F for fair and W for weak, for each of the constituent management techniques. The firms were then ranked in order of their added value per employee (i.e. total sales revenue less material costs, divided by the total number of employees) and the assessments of the management strengths were entered. Two firms were not ranked because they were units of larger concerns and were not selling at 'arm's length' prices. The assessments were then given a simple weighting – 1 point being allowed for strong, $\frac{1}{2}$ point for fair and 0 for weak. A table was then constructed (Table 27.1), from which it will be seen that the firms in the top quartile of performance scored significantly heavier than those in the bottom quartile. Furthermore, and most interesting, is that it was in the area of attention to future needs – i.e. forward planning – that the greatest difference was revealed.

Table 27.1 Analysis of Managerial Strengths and Weaknesses

Ranking of firm by added value	VITAL TO CURRENT OPERATIONS							OTHER ASPECTS								FUTURE NEEDS			
	Financial control	Cost control	Technical aspects	Stock control	Marketing	Total score	Maximum possible score	Production control	Budgetary control	Labour control information	Job descriptions	Method study and layout	Work measurement	Total score	Maximum possible score	Forward plans	Succession plans	Total score	Maximum possible score
1	1	1	1	1	1	5		1	1	1	0	½	1	4½		1	½	1½	
2	1	½	1	1	½	4		½	½	1	0	½	0	2½		1	1	2	
3	1	1	0	1	0	3		½	1	½	0	1	0	3		1	1	1	
Score	3	2½	2	3	1½	12	15	2	2½	2½	0	2	1	10	18	3	2½	5½	6
% score						80	100							55	100			92	100
4	1	1	1	½	1	4½		½	½	0	½	1	0	2½		0	0	0	
5	0	½	1	½	0	2		½	0	½	0	½	0	1½		0	½	½	
6	1	1	1	1	1	5		1	1	1	½	½	1	5		1	1	2	
7	0	0	½	½	1	2		0	0	0	0	½	0	½		0	0	0	
8	½	½	1	1	½	3½		0	1	0	0	0	0	1		0	0	0	
9	½	½	1	1	1	4		1	½	0	0	½	1	3		1	½	1½	
10	0	0	0	0	1	1		0	0	0	0	½	0	½		0	0	0	
Score	3	3½	5½	4½	5½	22	35	3	3	1½	1	3½	2	14	42	2	2	4	14
% score						63	100							33	100			25	100
11	1	1	1	1	1	5		½	½	½	0	1	0	2½		½	½	1	
12	0	0	1	0	0	1		0	0	0	0	0	0	0		0	0	0	
13	0	0	1	½	0	1½		½	0	½	0	½	½	2		0	0	0	
Score	1	1	3	1½	1	7½	15	1	½	1	0	1½	½	4½	21	½	½	1	6
% score						50	100							22	100			17	100

Note: Weighting given is 1 for strong; ½ for fair; 0 for weak.

28

The planning experience of Serck Radiators Ltd

D. R. PORTMAN

Serck Radiators employ about 1600 people in offices and factories occupying a floor area of just under 500 000 square feet. The company came to Birmingham over fifty years ago and the site it purchased in 1913 had been progressively extended and developed in the years which have passed since. While the company possesses a number of large modern workshops, there remain a few smaller and less suitable buildings which were constructed in its early years.

Serck Radiators started by manufacturing car radiators and at one time dominated the market, but over the years the commitment to the motor car industry has lessened and the company had progressively diversified into other industries, such as shipbuilding, aircraft, oil engine, chemical, electrical, gas, and railway locomotive amongst others. Throughout this diversification the company's policy has remained basically the same. Although the product which has been sold has varied in size, shape and materials, whatever the industry or the application, the company has always been selling its knowledge of the art and science of heat exchange. This knowledge is being continually extended as a result of the company's research and development programme. The word 'art' is used advisedly as all things to do with heat exchange cannot be quantified, so much depends on knowhow and experience.

Serving industries as diverse as aircraft and process engineering means that the products vary in size from six inches in length weighing a few pounds to equipment 35 and 40 feet in length weighing many tons. The materials worked vary widely and include aluminium, copper, brass, stainless steel and titanium, as well as mild steel. The quantities produced range from single units to the flowline production of radiators for the automobile industry. The manufacturing processes used include metal machining, steel fabrication, press work, sheet metal work, process plating and fitting. Serck Radiators, in common with much of industry, is confronted with multifarious problems of diversity and complexity which have to be taken into account in the development of a long-range plan. The company is not operating in a highly automated one-product industry which is relatively easy to assess and quantify.

As mentioned earlier the product policy of Serck Radiators is to sell to many industries its knowledge of the art and science of heat exchange in appropriate physical forms. It was to one of these industrial outlets, namely the aircraft industry, that the company first applied long-range planning techniques.

Although the term 'long-range planning' is now being used, there was no formal decision to start using the techniques as such. The first attempt at planning was by no means comprehensive and exhaustive. Planning reached its present level of comparative sophistication in a number of well defined steps. Each step forward was taken to overcome those limitations in earlier work which had become apparent in the light of experience. It is only relatively recently that the first long-range plan covering the whole of the company's activities in depth, was prepared, but the lessons learnt in planning the company's aircraft heat exchanger business were invaluable and contributed much to the success of the work which has been done since. The first steps were taken in 1962. It so happened that that part of the company organisation which manufactured heat exchangers for the aircraft industry was clearly identifiable within the organisation at large, commercially, technically, and from the manufacturing point of view. It was therefore possible to assess it as an entity and plan its future. The decision to plan forward was precipitated by the confused situation which arose in the aircraft industry following the cutbacks in the military programme when Mr Duncan Sandys was the Minister in Charge, and the problems which followed after as a result of the cancellation of a number of other aircraft projects culminating in the termination of the TSR2, although the latter was finally cancelled some time after the long-range planning exercise had commenced.

These events forced the company to appraise the future of its aircraft heat exchanger business. The company's status in the market and its standing in the industry were reviewed. Many factors were taken into account including:

- the product itself
- trends in the design and performance of aircraft, engines and systems
- new requirements for aircraft heat exchangers
- the availability of engineering staff
- management strength
- the availability of skilled labour
- the company's manufacturing capacity and methods
- the market penetration achieved by the company
- the likely growth in the aircraft industry and the requirement for aircraft heat exchangers
- profitability, return on capital employed, and financial implications
- our competitors
- governmental policy.

An attempt was made to quantify all the factors it was considered had some bearing on the future of the company's business; this was combined with a critical appraisal of the company's strengths and weaknesses.

It was decided, notwithstanding the immediate problems with which the industry was beset, to develop the company's aircraft heat exchanger business more actively than in the immediate past as it was thought that there would be sustained growth in the use of aircraft for transportation purposes and that manned aircraft would continue to be required for military purposes for the foreseeable future. In the long run the British aircraft industry would grow and prosper, particularly that part of the industry in which Britain is strong and in which Serck Radiators has a deep commitment, the manufacture of aircraft engines.

Detailed plans were prepared for developing the company's resources to meet the growth in business which the plan showed as likely. The company's manufacturing facilities were enlarged and the management, sales staff, engineering staff, and production labour force were strengthened. The first attempt at long-range planning was relatively successful and had made it possible for the company to cope satisfactorily with the rapid growth in its aircraft heat exchanger business which has taken place since 1962.

The first plan had, however, a number of limitations. Problems arose both due to the quality of the information which went into the plan and the validity of the conclusions drawn from it. Further long-range plans were, nevertheless, developed for the aircraft heat exchanger business in 1964, 1965, and 1966. There was a progressive improvement in the comprehensiveness and validity of approach, the quality of the information used, and the conclusions reached from an assessment of the strategic plan. The practicability and accuracy of the tactical plans have also increased. An attempt was made right from the beginning to quantify everything that lent itself to quantifying, however inaccurate the source figures may have been. By doing this a closed learning loop was created. This latter technique made a major contribution to the progressive improvement in the quality of successive long-range plans.

The preparation of a plan for aircraft heat exchangers prompted the development of similar plans for those other areas of business which could be clearly identified within the company structure. These included the motor vehicle and process engineering equipment industries. Having prepared plans successfully for certain areas of the company's business, it was then decided to carry the technique a stage further and develop a plan covering the whole of Serck Radiator activities.

As the development of the long-range plan for the whole enterprise proceeded, it became increasingly evident that major changes in the organisation and procedures were necessary to make them capable of accommodating change with the necessary flexibility and speed to meet the growth and profitability called for in the plan. The company organisation, with certain exceptions, was of a functional nature at the time the plan was first formulated. It was decided that as Serck Radiators deals with a number of quite separate and distinct industries the commercial and engineering organisation should be reshaped on a divisional basis, with a separate division servicing each major industry such as vehicles, marine, aircraft, oil engines, electrical, process engineering and so forth. While the commercial and engineering side of the company was to be divisionalised on an industrial basis it was decided on the manufacturing side that a self-contained production unit would be set up for each of the company's principal products whenever volume justified. In doing this it would be possible to use manufacturing methods and control techniques appropriate to the product and the volume in which it was required. Although the company had been moving towards self-contained production shops for its principal products for a number of years this now became part of an overall company strategy and was formally incorporated into the long-range plan. The first long-range plan for the company thus came to call for major changes in organisation and procedures. The organisational changes have now been made, although the improvement in the control and financial systems is an ongoing exercise which will take a number of years to get to the level of sophistication demanded by circumstances and the plan.

The strategic and tactical plans which have been prepared include the following:

- product market strategy
- finance
- personnel
- material
- organisation
- resources development
- facilities
- manufacturing
- diversification
- research and development
- divestment
- integration
- cash flow.

I would like to end with a few somewhat disconnected comments. It is essential that long-range planning is introduced from the top as it involves an overall appraisal and activation of the enterprise. In Serck Radiators long-range planning is one of the managing director's principal activities, although much of the detailed work is offloaded to a senior executive who acts as a long-range planning officer reporting to the managing director.

Another prerequisite of success is the continual review of progress against the plan and the persistent and consistent maintenance of objectives together with the insistence that these objectives are achieved despite the day-to-day problems of running a business.

Improved performance is predicated on better management information and adequate systems. Serck Radiators is giving particular attention to this at the moment and EDP is being extended and developed to give a completely integrated control system.

If a long-range plan had not been prepared it is unlikely the company would have approached its organisational and systems problems strategically, but would have moved step by step empirically with the result it would have taken very much longer. It is also unlikely that the overall concept would have been so well developed.

Long-range planning highlights the need for management training and a management succession plan. Work on this was started six years ago when there was a dearth of young men of management potential. As a result of the introduction of training programmes, combined with judicious recruitment of young men, there is now sufficient talent and to spare at middle management level and within three or four years we expect that most senior appointments within the company will be filled from within. Of recent years this latter has been done largely from outside.

The company has also become very much clearer on the difference between marketing and sales. The need to look forward, to quantify the market, to determine market penetration, to find opportunities, and to define product and sales policies, has highlighted this as an activity very different from selling. Marketing has developed within the company practically entirely as a result of long-range planning. On occasion, however, market research is bought outside as there are certain jobs which cannot be carried out by one's own market research team.

In closing there is no doubt in my mind that the long-range planning technique has added dynamic to Serck Radiators. We are very much clearer on what we are trying to do. We are very much clearer on our product policy, the opportunities which exist, and the steps which we must take to exploit them. We are in the process of creating an organisation which is very much more attuned to the problems of the day. It has been forcibly borne in on us that a company is a living dynamic and changing thing.

PART V

Corporate strategy in a multinational perspective

29

UK entry into the
Common Market:
the implications for
strategic planning

DEREK EZRA

What impact may corporate strategists expect British entry into EEC to have on the industrial environment? Mr Ezra reviews the predictions and opinions on this subject put forward by the Government White Paper and the CBI. He then refers to the European Commission's Memorandum on industrial policy and concludes that the possibility of complete integration over the whole range of economic activities within an enlarged EEC is a very real one. The implications for strategic planning in British industry are clear — managers may expect a growth in their opportunities for expansion but also a general increase in competition. Thus strategic planning will have to be formulated on a European basis.

Negotiations for United Kingdom entry into the Common Market have already begun. If acceptable entry terms can be arrived at the United Kingdom could be a member of the EEC by early 1973, to be followed by a transitional period which could last for, say, five years. It is very appropriate therefore that in a book on strategic planning for the 'seventies we should consider what would be the implications for British business of joining the EEC. The topic is of particular importance because of the emphasis which has been placed, in the great debate on whether or not we should join the Community, on the central role which would have to be played by British industry in maximising the economic advantages and offsetting the costs of entry. This aspect emerges strongly in the two basic appraisals made in the United Kingdom this year: the Government White Paper, *Britain and the European Communities: an Economic Assessment*, and the report *Britain in Europe* by the Confederation of British Industry.

I intend to deal in particular with an issue of major importance to British industry which can now be looked at more fully in the light of the most recent developments. I refer to the question of the industrial policies and environment within which industry might be operating in an enlarged Community. The desiderata in this respect from British industry's point of view, compared with present realities in the Community, were set out in the CBI Europe Report. Since then the European Commission has published its proposals for a Community industrial policy designed to promote an integrated industrial development. It is of great relevance to consider what is likely to come out of the adoption of a policy on the lines proposed by the Commission and what this could mean for British industry.

The White Paper

The White Paper attempts to estimate the costs of entry which would result from adopting the Community's common agricultural policy, contributing to Community finance (mainly agricultural financing), the effect on trade and industry, capital markets and invisible trading. For each of these headings a range is given and the result of putting all these estimates together is an overall balance of payments cost lying between £100m and £1100m a year. But the White Paper itself points out that this is not a reliable guide to the total effect because there are certain potentially favourable factors which could not be quantified, notably in the field of industry and trade. The effects of Common Market entry on British industry and trade are shown in the White Paper as falling into two groups. First there are what the White Paper calls the 'impact effects', i.e. the changes in the patterns of cost and trade which would necessarily result from joining the Community. These would stem from the reactions of producers, traders and consumers to the changes in tariffs, and from the effects of higher food prices on British wage levels. The White Paper estimates that these impact effects would bring about an adverse movement in our visible trade balance of between £125m and £275m a year.

On the other hand there would be a second group of effects on British industry, namely the 'dynamic' effects. These would be the consequences of belonging to a customs union of 300 million people, giving a 'home market' several times larger than the present UK home market (including EFTA) and much faster-growing. Membership of this new enlarged Common Market would provide for British industry the stimuli of greater business opportunities and sharper competition, with the resultant pressure for greater efficiency and the reduction of unit costs; as well as scope for benefiting from the advantages of specialisation and larger-scale production and a wider and more secure basis for sales and investment planning. These potential benefits would be reinforced as the Community developed (as appears to be its intention) from the customs union which it has now achieved, into a fully integrated economic union. The White Paper can see no way of quantifying the dynamic effects of entry on industry or trade 'because this depends essentially on the vigour of British industry in exploiting the opportunities undoubtedly offered by joining the Community and its response to greater competition'. What the White Paper does make clear is the importance of these dynamic effects for the overall economic picture, and therefore the responsibility which would rest on British industry to make United Kingdom membership economically worth while. The continuing debate must thus be whether or not the benefits of entry secured by British industry in terms of balance of payments improvements and faster industrial growth will make a sufficient contribution towards offsetting the direct balance of payments costs of entry, notably those arising from the common agricultural policy and its financing.

The CBI report

The report of the CBI's Steering Committee which was issued at the beginning of this year was intended as a basis for consultation with CBI members and this consultation has recently been completed. The director general of CBI has indicated that some 70 per cent of CBI membership have broadly endorsed the conclusions of the report. These were as follows:

(i) It remains to the advantage both of British industry and of the industries of other European countries for a single trading and industrial area to be created in place of the two areas (the EEC and EFTA) at present coexisting;

(ii) the elimination of tariffs between the two areas is no longer (after the Kennedy Round) of such importance as the elimination of other barriers to trade and the application of measures of economic integration – this is of particular importance in the rapidly developing technological field;

(iii) the enlargement of the European market, through the progressive removal of trading barriers and integration of its industries, should provide greater opportunities for industrial and commercial enterprise and in turn lead to higher and more sustained rates of economic growth – this should be of particular significance to Britain whose growth has lagged behind that of the EEC;

(iv) ..., the enlargement of the EEC to encompass all the applicant countries with suitable arrangements also for the other members of EFTA would appear to provide the most appropriate means for achieving these objectives – subject to the two important considerations below:

(v) the committee considers it essential that the policies of the enlarged community should be progressive and outward-looking, and that any restrictive arrangements (such as some features of the Common Agricultural Policy) should be progressively eliminated; the traditions and interests of Europe and especially of Britain in world trade make this a vital consideration;

(vi) the committee also considers it essential that the initial burden of membership should not be such as to place undue strain on the economies and living standards of the applicant countries. It will in any case be necessary to establish transitional periods during which the economies of both the applicant countries and the Community can be adapted to one another so as eventually to achieve arrangements which would be in the best common interest.

At the centre of the CBI's thinking is the potential offered to the United

N

Kingdom by membership of the Community for achieving a greater and more sustained rate of growth than has been realised in the past fifteen years, thus making possible an increase in living standards despite increases in the cost of living resulting from the adoption of the EEC agricultural and fiscal policies.

Two main points flow from this. First, the CBI report considers that entry into the Common Market must not involve costs to the balance of payments which could not be sustained without internal deflation or restrictive policies that would prevent the achievement of a faster growth rate in the future. This issue can only be resolved in negotiation. Secondly, the report makes plain the concern of the CBI that the Community which British industry would be joining should be clearly heading for economic and industrial integration on a European base. The implication is that, so far, progress has been slow within the EEC itself towards creating in reality a more unified market and towards establishing an industrial policy to promote the rational and integrated development of the Community's industries as a whole. The report hopes that enlargement will provide a stimulus to the implementation of European industrial policies. It emphasises the need to create more companies of European dimensions and to pursue this on a wider basis than national mergers. A sound European strategy must be developed for the technologically based sectors in order to compete effectively with the United States, and to this end advantage should be taken of the possibilities offered by the enlargement of the European Community to secure a coordination of research and development programmes in the main European countries.

The report also stresses the importance, particularly for the advanced technology industries, of coordinating public purchasing in order to encourage a European approach; and of 'cross-border collaboration' with the ultimate objective of forming multinational companies. Above all, it is necessary to press on with the creation in the Community of a harmonised environment in which industry can operate effectively on a European scale.

This [the report says] we consider is essential for several key industries based on the advanced technologies; such industries can no longer assemble on a purely national basis the resources, financial or human, that they require, but there is every prospect that even the most advanced and exigent among them can operate profitably in the setting of an enlarged Community throughout which uniform legal, fiscal and financial rules and regulations apply. The enlarged market and uniform rules are hardly less essential for many other industries for whom economies of scale in production, marketing, financing, etc., are of great importance. If Western Europe is to compete effectively in world markets industrial restructuring from a European, rather than a national, base is essential. British firms through their efforts in recent years in research, development and re-organisation, are now in a strong position to make a substantial contribution to the wider arrangements on which future industrial progress in Europe depends.

The European Commission's memorandum on industrial policy

Against this background the appearance in March this year of the Commission's memorandum on industrial policy was a timely one. The memorandum has been described by the director general of CBI as 'the first bold and really comprehensive attempt to formulate a strategy for the development of industry in the Community' and is almost entirely consistent with the views expressed in the CBI report about requirements in the industrial policy field. The initial purpose of the memorandum is to serve as a basis for extensive discussions within the Community, i.e. in the Council of Ministers and the other Community institutions and with interested parties in the economic and social spheres. Following these discussions the Commission is to make proposals to the Community's Council of Ministers for the implementation of an industrial policy.

The memorandum sees the formulation of a common policy for the industrial development of the Community, leading to the establishment of a European industrial structure, as a vital requirement if Europe is to be prosperous and to become reasonably independent technologically of the major world powers. The Commission also links the need for a common industrial policy with the problems of the enlargement of the Community: progress on industrial policy would show public opinion in the applicant countries in which directions the Community was heading in this field, and success in arriving at an industrial development strategy would make the Community more attractive than one which remains at the stage of a customs union and agricultural policy.

In an examination of the present situation of Community industry the memorandum underlines the scope which exists for improving industrial efficiency, pointing out that in 1968 value added per person employed in Community industry in terms of real purchasing power was 61 per cent of the United States figure, and that in many sectors companies are below optimum size. The memorandum also refers to the tendency in the Community for industrial mergers to take place between firms in the same country or with firms in non-member countries, rather than with firms in other member countries; and warns against the centrifugal effect, prejudicial to industrial integration, which could establish itself as a result of national mergers and takeovers by outside firms.

The Commission's guidelines for an industrial policy call first of all for the rapid removal of technical barriers to trade which still weigh heavily on industry and are an obstacle to expansion. Although the Community has already adopted a general harmonisation programme on technical requirements and standards for industrial products, progress has been slow and the disparities which still exist remain a major hindrance to achieving the basic objective of an industrial development policy: to enable all firms and all products to benefit fully from the existence of a large-scale market. Another essential requirement of industrial policy is to work towards opening public contracts to tenders from anywhere in the Community. The practice in Europe has been and still is for governments to reserve public contracts for firms of their own country, and this deprives key industries of the advantages offered by a large common market. The industries concerned are notably the capital goods and public transport industries and industries manufacturing many types of technically advanced equipment. In such sectors as nuclear power plants and aviation equipment, public contracts represent a major outlet for firms, and the Commission proposes that arrangements would be made to concert purchasing policies in these sectors. This would help to ensure the effective establishment of a single market in technically advanced products.

The memorandum points to the need to speed up the unification of the legal, taxation and financial framework within which large firms operate, in order to promote larger-scale operations and greater cooperation throughout the EEC area. The work which has been started on European company law should be vigorously pursued, with the object of providing at national and Community level a legal framework that permits EEC companies to cooperate, make contracts, establish themselves or merge on a Community-wide basis under straightforward and secure legal conditions. Tax obstacles to multinational mergers should be removed and the harmonisation of excise, direct corporation and value added taxes is necessary to make conditions of competition as uniform as possible between member countries and frontier controls to be completely eliminated. Arrangements should be made to facilitate the provision of capital for Community firms requiring it in order to expand; this underlines the need for a true common capital market and calls also for the modernisation of banking systems as well as for financing techniques adapted to the requirements of the small faster-growing company.

The memorandum has a good deal to say about the restructuring of Community industry, pointing out that although a strong tendency towards mergers is already in progress within the Community, the relative lag in European industrial development and the keen competition from outside firms make a higher degree of concentration necessary, and especially the creation of transnational European enterprises. Transnational mergers, particularly in the advanced technology industries, are essential and urgent if European companies are to compete effectively. Member states should stop opposing such mergers and policy should be directed towards removing the political, psychological, legal and other obstacles at present standing in their way. The European investment bank could help by financing transnational merger operations, and in the advanced technology sector Community development contracts could be introduced, with priority for firms embarking on transnational cooperation and restructuring.

In a special section on the promotion of advanced technology industries the Commission indicates other reasons why operations on a European scale are essential to success in this sector. In particular it points out that there are 'minimum thresholds' of industrial, financial and technical resources below which the production of certain technologically advanced goods, e.g. large nuclear, electronic, aviation and space equipment – is doomed to failure or permanent unprofitability. After making comparisons between the relative size of American, Japanese, UK and EEC firms, the Commission attributes the Community's disappointing record so far in technological cooperation to an absence of homogeneity and a failure to organise projects on the most rational and efficient basis. It reports that successful cooperation between European firms can only be achieved through the framework of an open market for technologically advanced products within the Community and with the creation of transnational European companies. In view of the vast expenditure involved in developing advanced technological equipment – expenditure fast becoming beyond the means of individual Western European countries – European cooperation in such ventures is essential. The Commission proposes that Community industrial development contracts should be awarded for the development of viable industrial products of benefit to the development of the Community's industrial sector and the cost of which, because of the complex research and development involved, is beyond any one member state. In choosing contractors, priority would be given to companies involved in European cooperation agreements. The Community would guarantee (through Community funds) the financing of contracts although part of the financial risks would be carried by industry. Projects would be initiated by member governments, the Commission or industry, but decisions on the selection, content and financing of projects would be taken by the Community's Council of Ministers.

The Commission proposes measures to improve business management, in particular through the establishment by Community firms of a 'European management and training foundation' where modern management techniques would be studied, specialists developed, and contacts maintained at Community level between industry, the universities and specialised institutions. Measures are also suggested for disseminating information on technical innovations and research results, and encouraging their application.

Much of what the Commission is pressing for in its memorandum – the removal of non-tariff impediments to trade, the harmonisation of environments, free access to public contracts – stems from the commitment of the Six under the Treaty of Rome to create a single economic area. Other proposals are intended to guide and assist industry in adapting its structure to operating in a European dimension, in order to achieve optimum efficiency and competitive strength. The memorandum both reflects and reinforces an awareness and recognition in the existing Community of how much remains to be done in the field of economic integration. Progress will call for the solution of a whole set of problems, involving in many cases – such as the abandonment of national discrimination as regards access to public contracts, and the promotion of cross-frontier mergers and other cooperative ventures – a radical change of attitude by governments, which will not be easy to bring about. Much will depend on initiatives undertaken and pressure applied by industry itself, based on its own appreciation of the advantages of operating freely on a European scale. The CBI

Report has shown that British industry is fully seized of the benefits to be gained for itself and the British economy as a whole from a large integrated market. This has already been demonstrated in a practical way by initiatives such as the Dunlop–Pirelli link-up and the ICL proposals for a European computer group, as well as by British industry's ready cooperation in studying the Aigrain proposals for policies for technology in Europe. These things are happening before we are in the Common Market, and with the development of the attitudes of mind reflected in the CBI Report, and the intensive restructuration of British industry which has been taking place in recent years, British entry should certainly give an impetus to the adoption of policies leading to a modern, highly efficient and competitive European industry.

Implications

What, more particularly, are the implications for British management planning? These will be a function of the conditions in which industry can expect to be operating when Britain is an integral part of an enlarged Community. British producers will find themselves exposed to more competition in the home market as European firms take advantage of the abolition of tariffs and increase their sales to Britain. British firms will find that their export goods which have already been able to compete successfully in EEC markets will become more competitive, while goods which had previously been uncompetitive might be able to find new outlets in Europe. The British producer will gain freer access not only to a very large market but to a market which has been growing – and is expected to go on growing – much faster than our own. While British production (GNP) has advanced by 3 per cent per annum over the past twelve years (at constant prices) EEC production has risen by 5 per cent per annum. The increased competition of the wider European market will call for increased efficiency in British industry. Increased sales will give scope for economies of scale – not only in production, but also in marketing and in research and development. The competitive opportunities of Common Market entry will provide a much needed incentive to industrial investment in Britain. A substantial increase in investment will be required to provide the additional productive capacity and increased efficiency necessary to make British goods fully competitive in European markets.

Operating as part of the EEC market will be of great significance for management training and development. More British business executives will be stationed on the Continent, in British subsidiaries, or in joint enterprises, and as the common industrial policy emerges they will need to acquire a sound knowledge of the background to the new system of industrial arrangements as well as a much closer understanding of their colleagues in business in the other countries of the Community.

30

The multinational enterprise* and UK economic interests

JOHN H. DUNNING

It is now commonplace to find large companies operating on a multinational scale with wholly or partly-owned subsidiaries spread throughout the world. While this is a trend that can hardly be reversed it does pose a number of complex problems for national economic policies and, in turn, for the corporate strategist of the multinational company. Professor Dunning argues that a mutually rewarding balance of interests between national governments and multinational corporations may be achieved, but it is up to the former to take the initiative. He concludes that foreign direct investment cannot be anything other than highly beneficial to the British economy and that a chauvinistic attitude towards the multinational company must be avoided.

An earlier version of this paper was presented at a Conference on International Business in the 1970s – organised by the Society for Long-Range Planning in November 1970.

At the end of 1969 the value of the direct capital stake of UK companies abroad amounted to between £8400–£8500 million: the corresponding investment by foreign companies in the United Kingdom was just one-half of this amount, viz between £4200 and £4300 million. Over the seven-year period 1962–9, the value of UK investments abroad has risen by three-fifths; that of foreign companies in the UK has doubled. Excluding the investments of oil, insurance and banking companies, UK enterprises had just over £6000 million invested overseas at the end of 1969; the corresponding investment by foreign companies in the UK was £2930 million.[1]

What is the contribution of these international companies to UK economy? The answer is a very important one. In 1969 more than 25 per cent of the profits earned by UK manufacturing companies were directly derived from their foreign operations (excluding exports); while foreign owned enterprises in British manufacturing industry accounted for about 18 per cent of the total profits earned. Something approaching one-half of all UK manufacturing exports are accounted for by goods sent abroad by UK firms to their foreign affiliates, or by

---

* We define the international or multinational enterprise as one which owns or controls producing facilities (i.e. factories, mines, oil refineries, etc.) in more than one country. Such an enterprise may or may not be multinationally owned or controlled.

foreign subsidiaries operating in the UK. In recent years, these latter firms have been responsible for one-third of the increase in UK manufacturing exports. In the 1960s, they also accounted for between 15 and 20 per cent of all net fixed capital formation in the UK, while British firms invested abroad the equivalent of about one-fifth of net domestic investment. Investment by foreign companies in the UK is currently rising at twice the rate of (UK) gross national product (GNP); investment by UK companies abroad – in spite of the restrictions on capital exports of recent years – about half as much again. On current trends, between 1968 and 1980, the stock of direct foreign investment in the UK, as a proportion of GNP, is likely to rise from 7·4 to 13·3 per cent; and that of UK direct investment overseas from 15·2 to 18·3 per cent. One last set of figures; in 1968–9, the income earned by UK firms overseas amounted to 18·1 per cent of visible exports, compared with 16·8 per cent in 1955–6. The corresponding figures for the income of foreign firms in the UK expressed as a proportion of visible imports were 11·4 and 10·2 per cent.

Whichever way one looks at the figures, they all point to the important role of the international companies in the British economy. If we add together the UK share of the income earned by British owned companies abroad and the (estimated) net output of foreign firms in the UK less the income (i.e. profits and interest) accruing to the foreign owners, we arrive at a figure of about 10 per cent of the gross national product UK (GNP). These calculations take no account of the indirect or spin-off effects of the operation of such companies on the rest of the UK economy, about which we shall have more to say later; neither do they pretend to estimate their *net* economic benefits to the national economy.

The economic significance of the international company

What are the economic implications for the UK of the facts just catalogued? If we make the convenient and, on the whole, plausible assumption that, independently of the level of inward or outward investment, the UK government is successful in maintaining a policy of full employment, the question of the contribution of international companies to UK economic welfare is mainly one of their impact on the level, distribution and rate of growth of GNP; and the extent to which they make possible a more or less efficient allocation of resources.

Much of the content of this article will be concerned with these questions, and their implications on Britain's role in the world economy. Since the mid-eighteenth century, the UK has been deeply involved in the international trade of goods and services and, for many years now, visible exports have accounted for 15 to 20 per cent of GNP and visible imports for 20 to 25 per cent. But more recently, and particularly since 1950, international companies have developed new marketing strategies, one result of which is that in place of exports they have increasingly tended to supply foreign markets by the production of goods produced in these countries from factories and plants under their ownership.

World growth in international direct investment is now running at twice the rate of international trade, while in 1969 the value of manufacturing sales produced by US foreign subsidiaries was more than five times the exports of foreign subsidiaries.

One consequence of this phenomenon is that the character of transactions between economic agents in different countries is changing. Instead of (or in addition to) exporting goods, companies are exporting the capital and know-how to produce those goods, for which they receive a payment of profits, interest and royalties. Instead of (or in addition to) importing goods, countries are importing the capital and knowhow to produce those goods for which they make a payment, profits, interest and royalties. More and more international trade is becoming a trade in the 'right' to produce goods rather than trade in the goods themselves. We shall see later in this article the important repercussions this development has had on both exporting and importing countries.

It is not the purpose of this article to try to explain the pattern of international direct investment, or the operations of multinational companies, throughout the world, but perhaps the most satisfactory approach is that which derives from the comparative cost theory of international trade.[2] If I might try to put this in one sentence: *Companies and countries will tend to export capital to produce goods outside their national boundaries in which they have a comparative innovatory advantage and, initially at least, a comparative production and/or marketing advantage; this investment will be directed to those countries, which for one reason or another, over time, are likely to develop a comparative advantage in the production and/or marketing of these goods.*[3] Factors such as economic nationalism, tariffs, other restrictions to the movement of goods and multiple currencies may affect the timing and extent of such movements, but in general, they will not invalidate the general principle I have mentioned – which essentially reflects the comparative cost advantage of international direct investment.

I believe if we were to examine the pattern of inward and outward UK direct investment we would find that, in general, this hypothesis is borne out. It would certainly largely explain the domination of US firms in certain sectors of UK industry as well as the general structure of outward investment.

For the purposes of the discussion which follows, I propose to consider first the economic consequences and policy implications of foreign owned international companies operating in Britain and, second, those arising from the overseas operations of UK-owned companies.

The UK as host to international companies

The UK has always adopted a welcoming attitude towards inward direct investment and, subject to certain safeguards, now rather more explicitly laid down than in the past, official policy is still liberal. Nevertheless, warning voices have been raised that the benefits of foreign participation in UK industry may be not quite so unequivocal as was once thought. This concern is aroused not so much by the size of the present stake of foreign owned companies but by certain of its characteristics, notably its very marked concentration in certain industries, its geographical origins and its very fast rate of growth.

The facts have been documented elsewhere[4] and need only be very briefly summarised here. About 70 per cent of the value of the direct foreign capital stake in the UK is US-owned. More than one half of this amount is accounted for by the largest fifty subsidiaries and about three-quarters by the largest hundred. Investment is strongly concentrated in the technologically advanced industries, in motor vehicles and in oil refining and distribution. In most of these industries, which also tend to be dominated by a few large firms, foreign subsidiaries are among the leading three producers; in several, they supply more than one half the total output. Since these are often the most rapidly expanding industries in the economy, and, within them, foreign firms are growing faster than their competitors, the stake of these companies in the national economy is increasing. It had been estimated that by 1981 between 20 and 25 per cent of UK manufacturing output and up to one-third of exports will be supplied by foreign-owned firms.[5]

The question then arises; given these facts, what is their implication for government policy? In particular, is there any need for the introduction of policy measures either to stimulate or to curb the operation of these firms or to otherwise control their behaviour? To answer this question, I think we need first to distinguish the ways in which the economic impact of foreign-owned enterprises is different from that of indigenous firms and, second, to evaluate the extent to which they react differently to government policies. In doing so, we shall mention just three possible areas of differences, under the general headings of *objectives, organisation* and *operational impact*.

Objectives

However much a subsidiary of a foreign-owned enterprise may seek to identify itself with the UK economy, its primary responsibility must be the management and shareholders of its parent company. Where it is to their advantage that the subsidiary should behave in a way consistent with achieving the host country's economic goals, then no conflict of interest will arise. On the other hand, whereas, in the final analysis, the foreign company will judge the success of its subsidiary by its contribution to its own objectives, the host economy is best served when the contribution of that subsidiary to its own economic goals is maximised; here, income remitted by the subsidiary to the parent company represents a price which has to be paid for the resources provided by it. What is regarded as a *reasonable* price will obviously vary according to the type of investment made and its contribution to GNP. It will also depend on the price offered (e.g. in the form of tax rebates, investment incentives etc.) by other countries interested in attracting the investment. But, basically, host governments can do little about influencing the objectives of foreign subsidiaries, except that, by providing a favourable economic environment, they can steer their behaviour towards growth and stability.

Organisation

Even a *national* multiplant firm has certain advantages over a single plant firm — for example, the choice of whether to produce similar products in the separate plants, or to engage in lateral and/or vertical specialisation. As the locational choice is widened across national boundaries, the differences in economic environments become more pronounced; hence, the added incentive to the firm producing internationally to increase its product or process specialisation. Such evidence as we have suggests this kind of territorial division of labour exists more in high technology than in low technology industries.

The economic implications of international integration for the organisation of subsidiaries of multinational firms are numerous and far-reaching. From a functional viewpoint, the most significant is that it usually requires highly centralised and carefully harmonised decision-making. Apart from products produced for local markets, decisions on what and how much each subsidiary should produce, where new factories should be located, the geographical allocation of R and D activities and, very often, the amount and form of intra-group trading are taken with global needs and opportunities in mind. To an extent, all international *trade* is similarly oriented; but the fact that *production* is internationalised introduces a completely new dimension.

In theory, any enterprise which wishes to maximise its return on capital should buy from the cheapest and sell in the dearest world markets. In practice, they do not always choose to do this, partly because they are not physically present in these markets, and partly because of the constraints imposed on the trade between two (or more) parties across national boundaries. But the multi-national producing enterprise is better equipped to overcome both these difficulties, as it can transfer resources across national boundaries without actually engaging in trade. Since, in this respect, it will generally act as a cost minimiser, it helps to introduce an element of 'perfection' into world markets. For example, the shifting of funds between subsidiaries in order to take advantage of differential interest rates, tends to make for a more, rather than less, efficient world capital market; the specialisation of foreign operations in labour or capital intensive activities according to the factor price structure of the recipient countries narrows rather than widens the international differential of factor prices; increasing the supply of goods to areas where they are most highly priced relative to other markets makes for a better, rather than a worse, deal for consumers.

There may, however, be costs involved in these intragroup activities which not all national economies are prepared to accept. Foremost of these is the surrender of a certain degree of economic sovereignty. However much the movement of capital between the UK and another country by the international company might help world capital markets, it may also weaken the impact of domestic monetary policy and at times, too, exert pressure for exchange rate adjustment. It has, for example, been estimated that speculative movements of capital by multinational companies into Germany in 1969 accounted for one-half of the total capital inflow in that year. In other words, the more completely multinational enterprises take advantage of differences in national economic environments, then, subject to the constraints of competition, the nearer they will come to maximising world real output.[6] But in so far as the policies of nation states are inconsistent with this end (and/or each other's objectives), conflicts of objectives and interests are bound to arise.

This then is the first reason why governments find themselves concerned about the international company. In one sense, it is no new story; it is a continuation of an old story about the relationship between national and world economic welfare. Having said this, we must now enter a caveat. Even accepting that, if left to its own devices, the multinational enterprise might help to distribute more efficiently from a world viewpoint, there are two reasons why the market, as it is at present organised, cannot fully ensure this. The first arises from the action of governments and the second from the *externalities* or *social spin-off effects* of international companies.

Actions of governments to protect or advance the economic welfare of their citizens can affect the behaviour of foreign controlled firms in a variety of ways. Perhaps the most obvious is the way in which they tax their income and generally treat foreign inward investment. One aim of all international companies is to minimise their total tax burden. As a general rule, the greater the differential in tax rates between countries in which the international company operates (including the 'home' country), the greater the incentive of tax avoidance in high tax countries by the manipulation of intracompany transfer prices. And the more efficiently this is done, the more the high tax countries lose. Enterprises may also wish to charge other than arm's length prices, to insure against possible exchange rate changes, dividend restrictions, expropriation of assets, and so on.

Second, government policies towards trade, as shown in tariff structures, exchange controls, export credits, etc., can and do affect the flow of goods and services both traded between international companies and other economic agents, and transferred *within* international companies – as well as the structure of their operations. One recent example is the effect which the formation of the EEC has had on the distribution of US investment between Britain and the EEC countries.

Third, there is the question of extraterritoriality. This arises wherever the government of the investing company imposes rules and regulations which apply not only to the operations of that company within its boundaries, but to the foreign subsidiaries of these companies. The most quoted examples of extraterritoriality, which may not always be in the interests of the recipient countries, are controls exerted by the US government on the import and export trade and dividend policies of US subsidiaries, and antitrust legislation, which may outlaw mergers between foreign subsidiaries and locally incorporated enterprises.

Operational impact

The second issue relates to externalities, viz the 'spill-over' or 'spin-off' repercussions of inward investment. In our present context this is the effect which subsidiaries of foreign-owned multinational firms operating in the UK economy have on the efficiency and growth of other firms, and is part and parcel of the third possible area of conflict and tension, which arises from the operational and economic impact of international companies. Assume, for the moment, that we are interested in measuring the direct and indirect effects of inward direct investment on the gross national product of the UK. Such direct investment brings with it a package deal of entrepreneurship, capital and knowledge. If this, when added to local resources, produces a contribution to GNP greater than that of any other use of these resources (after deduction of any income remitted) then its economic worth is justified.

Such information as we have, from a variety of sources, suggests that foreign firms in the UK have indeed made a very positive contribution in this respect. They employ about 150 000 people in the development areas of the UK who might otherwise have remained out of work. The productivity of US subsidiaries is, on average, about one-third higher than their UK competitors, their industrial relations are generally good, and they have almost certainly assisted the balance of payments. No less valuable, however, are the spill-over effects of the imported expertise on competitors, suppliers and customers of foreign firms, and on local management and labour practices. Though quantitatively difficult to assess, these effects are known to have been very farreaching. Indeed, the assimilation of improved production and management techniques by UK firms has been one of the main reasons for the narrowing of the profitability gap between US subsidiaries and indigenous UK firms by more than one-half since 1955.

Improved productivity is undoubtedly a benefit to the British economy. What about the costs? First, it is possible that foreign firms might lead to a less efficient and/or less competitive industrial structure. There is no reason to suppose that this has occurred. It is true that US firms have probably encouraged a more concentrated structure in UK industry, but this has generally aided rather than retarded rationalisation. Second, the production methods of foreign firms may not always be suitable to the resources and/or market structure of the recipient country. Foreign (and particularly) subsidiaries tend to be more capital intensive than their UK competitors, but again usually this is to their advantage. In the case of foreign participation in some of the less developed countries this is likely to be a more important issue: not always do such firms appear to make the best use of the most plentiful local resources. Third, inward investment may bring with it certain technological drawbacks. We have dealt with some of these in more detail elsewhere.[7] but much of the problem arises because US firms are able to buy UK knowledge below the appropriate 'social' price.

Policy implications of inward investment

These then are some of the important issues surrounding the participation of foreign-based international firms in British industry. What do we conclude are the policy implications for the UK authorities? Empirically, the evidence is that foreign subsidiaries have considerably benefited the UK economy *operationally* and that from an *organisational* viewpoint there is little immediate cause for concern: this is not to deny that, in certain instances, considerable friction has arisen – the Roberts Arundel affair of 1968 is a case in point – but most of the anxiety so far expressed arises from possible rather than actual situations.

At present, as we have seen, apart from certain safeguards required from foreign firms about, e.g. the amount of local capital they wish to raise, policy towards exports, etc., the UK government's attitude has been relatively free and easy. But with the growing role of foreign firms how long can this last? The following comments consider this question, first, fairly generally, and, second, in relation to several distinct types of economic policy. First, what are the basic policy alternatives open to the UK authorities? These are many and varied, and range from the outright rejections of inward foreign investment, e.g. the course followed by Japan until recently, to doing nothing about it! Most governments adopt a midway approach and try to operate a policy which minimises the costs and maximises the benefits of inward investment. But this, to be really meaningful, involves an extremely complex and difficult cost-benefit analysis. While many of the benefits are measurable, only a few of the costs are. What, for example, is trade-off between an increase in GNP and a loss of economic independence or an encroachment on political sovereignty? How does one put a value on sovereignty, and in what terms? What of the conflicting interests between nation states, which may arise as a result of the operation of inter-national companies? Certainly, few governments have yet formulated clearly defined and comprehensive policies towards inward investment in these terms; most have been content simply to introduce *ad hoc* and/or piecemeal measures to try to ensure that the behaviour of foreign firms conflicts as little as possible with their broad economic objectives. But whatever the basic philosophy or policy alternatives adopted by host governments, it is no less important to distinguish between the different types of policy measures which might be introduced to implement this philosophy.

The first of these is between policy measures taken by authorities in individual countries, or sectors of these countries, which we might call *unilateral* measures and those which involve more than one country, i.e. *bilateral* or *multilateral* policies. Secondly, we need to distinguish between *general* policies which are designed to affect the behaviour of all firms in the UK including foreign subsidiaries, and *specific* policies designed to affect the behaviour of foreign subsidiaries only. Third, there are the type of measures which it may be desirable to introduce, irrespective of the effect which foreign subsidiaries may have on the economy. We label these *unconditional* policies in contrast to *conditional* policies, the character of which will vary according to the nature of the impact made by the foreign company. Finally, it is important to distinguish between policies directed towards altering the behaviour of foreign subsidiaries to conform to some stated macro-economic objective, and policies the purpose of which is to change the economic environment in which foreign firms operate.

UNILATERAL POLICIES

Of the general and unconditional policies measures, one of the most obvious is to encourage a market environment, such that foreign firms should not be able to exploit any economic power or influence they possess to the detriment of the UK economy. In some cases, this may involve the government assisting native firms to compete more effectively, even to the extent of backing intra-European mergers (e.g. the Dunlop–Pirelli case). In others, the existing Monopolies and Restrictive Practices legislation is adequate. It also implies that the governments should try to ensure that when a foreign enterprise takes over a UK company it pays a fair 'social' price; that sufficient information is published about the operations of firms, including foreign companies, to help firms and governments make the right decisions; that it should try to minimise the barriers to the dissemination of knowledge; and that it should help provide publicity to UK firms on the alternatives to inward investment (e.g. licensing agreements, etc.).

Specific and unconditional policies only become necessary where there are differences between the behaviour and/or economic impact of foreign and domestic firms. To allow for these, and to counteract any imperfection in market conditions which might result, use may be made of discriminatory fiscal, monetary or direct controls. It has been argued, for example, that foreign companies have certain technological advantages over indigenous firms: if this is so, it may be questioned whether some of the incentives given to such companies, e.g. to go to development areas, are really justified. Similarly, the government may wish to introduce selective measures in order to ensure the income remitted by foreign subsidiaries to their parent companies is no more than that necessary to achieve the desired level of investment. *Inter alia* this implies that the authorities should keep a watchful eye on all intragroup transactions of foreign subsidiaries to see that they are not remitting income by manipulating transfer pricing. Less desirable (or effective), in my opinion, is any *general* attempt to lay down a code of 'good' corporate behaviour, partly because it is difficult to determine what this is, as it varies between firms and over time, and partly because it may encourage actions on the part of foreign firms which may not be in the country's best interest.

Of the specific and conditional policy measures, these by definition, assume either that it is felt, in general, there is too much, too little or the wrong sort of foreign direct investment in the UK economy, and/or that there are certain areas of the economy in which the activities of foreign companies should be stimulated or curbed. Various aspects of the operational impact of the international company come to mind – its effects on the balance of payments, on industrial relations, on its ability to circumvent certain fiscal or monetary controls, and so on. One of the reasons commonly given for introducing a code of good behaviour is to minimise these effects.

Of course, in response to the effects of foreign direct investment it may be preferable that general economic policy should be changed. A *general and conditional policy* is particularly appropriate where foreign investment makes an important marginal impact on certain areas of macroeconomic policy, e.g. the balance of payments. Rather than try to discourage this investment if it is shown to have an adverse balance of payments effect, it may make better sense to modify general economic policy, so as to make it unimportant whether or not it has these effects.

MULTILATERAL POLICIES

We now turn to illustrate some bilateral and multilateral policy measures – which essentially arise not from any conflict of interest between international companies and national states but from a conflicting of national interests. Sometimes these may involve two or more investing countries; but more usually, in so far as inward investment is concerned, the investing country and two or more recipient countries. Again, it is possible to classify types of policy according to the headings used earlier but here we shall content ourselves with one or two broad observations.

Most issues of extraterritoriality involve the governments of both investing and recipient countries, and can only be settled by bilateral or multilateral general or specific unconditional policies. On the other hand, attempts to prevent recipient countries from using 'unfair' practices with respect to encouraging (or discouraging) inward direct investment, require bilateral or multilateral general policies. Outside the economic sphere there is a need for harmonisation of policy with respect to the legal and accounting procedures of international firms: still most important the principles by which the costs and benefits resulting from their operations are shared among the participating parties.[8] The concept of a 'European' company is already firmly established; the possibility of a world company is no longer a pipe dream. Accompanying this, there may well be need for a parallel to the International Court of Justice to deal with international disputes arising from the operations of international firms.

Finally, brief mention should be made of a group of problems arising out of the multilateral enterprise, which only a sectoral unilateral or multilateral policy can resolve. Of these the best example is the attitude of labour to the international company. There are three main issues here. First, trade unions may well seek for a general harmonisation of wage rates in all countries in which the company operates; second, there is the question of the effects of the foreign operations of the international company on domestic employment; third, trade unions are worried lest their bargaining power and/or participating role is weakened. Each of these issues could raise serious problems in the not too distant future; a glimpse of the feeling of British trade unions is shown in the TUC *Economic Review* for 1970.

Conclusion

To summarise this section: from a purely economic standpoint, any host country has to pay a price for inward direct investment. But as with trade, both parties may benefit from the exchange. The question is what is the 'right' price? As far as possible this should be a competitive 'social' price, i.e. the market price adjusted for spill-over effects and government action. In international trade, the General Agreement on Tariffs and Trade exists to control 'unfair' trading practices between countries. There is reason to suppose that something similar may eventually be needed for international firms.[9] But, in general, I believe that it is up to governments, rather than international companies, to take the initiative in this respect – and also to encourage the international harmonisation of law, accounting and tax procedures.

The UK as an overseas investor

Since the publication of the Reddaway study[10] nearly two years ago, there has been comparatively little public discussion on the costs and benefits of UK overseas direct investment.[11] Such evidence as we have suggests that the restrictions imposed by the British government on capital exports in the 1960s, and more particularly since 1965, have not materially affected the foreign operations of UK companies. In 1969 investment by such companies was greater than in any previous year and the trend is still upwards. This is not to deny that the controls have not led to the cut back or abandonment of some investment schemes, and it cannot be entirely coincidental that a number of the leading foreign investors have noticeably diversified their domestic activities since 1965. But, in general, it seems that the main result of the measures taken has been to make it more difficult and costly to do what was being done before, and, in the process, cause businessmen to waste a good deal of time and energy. These inconvienence or 'nuisance' consequences have almost certainly led to a less efficient allocation of resources, without producing any real gain to the balance of payments.

It is not the purpose of this part of our paper to reopen this particular debate, but rather to look, more generally, at the role of British-owned international firms in the world economy, with a view to suggesting some possible guidelines for UK government policy in the 1970s.

The growth of direct foreign investment

Since the nineteenth century Britain has always been a substantial international investor, and by World War I several UK companies, e.g. Coates, Lever and Courtaulds, were already operating sizeable foreign manufacturing outlet. But until around 1950, apart from the activities of a few oil mining and manufacturing companies, by far the greater part of UK capital exports consisted of the buying of foreign securities. In the last two decades the situation has dramatically changed and direct investment has accounted for at least three-quarters and probably four-fifths of all new private investment abroad. Between the end of 1957 and 1969, the value of the assets held by UK companies overseas, excluding those in insurance, banking and oil, rose from £2360 million to just over £6000 million; in 1969, more than one-fifth of all the earnings of UK manufacturing enterprises were derived from their foreign operations, compared with about 10 per cent in 1958.[12] This remarkable growth has arisen as part of a worldwide trend towards the internationalisation of production facilities. Both to protect and exploit its foreign markets, yesterday's leading exporters are today's leading multinational producing enterprises.

Although in a few cases, foreign direct investment and trade are substitute for each other, usually, and particularly where a company is already engaged in foreign manufacturing, the relationship is much more complex. This was amply demonstrated by the Reddaway report and its American counterpart produced by Professors Hufbauer and Adler.[13] Rarely is the textbook case of a firm faced with a straightforward choice between exporting or producing abroad met with in practice, though the relative attractions of each may well affect the balance of a firm's strategy towards its foreign operations. This is because we are living at a time, not only when the majority of the leading world exporters are already well established as multinational producing enterprises, but when an increasing number are seeking to integrate and harmonise their trade and production throughout the world.

This has two implications. The first, which we have already touched on, is the growth of non-traded exports – those which flow across national boundaries but are not bought or sold; in 1968, about one-quarter of British exports were dispatched to affiliates of the exporting firms. The second is that, for many companies, investment and trade are not only ingredients of a common overseas marketing strategy; they are also an essential prerequisite for international competitiveness.

I believe that governments – particularly governments of investing countries – have yet to appreciate the implications of these developments. In the effort to secure a balance-of-payments equilibrium, the export of goods has usually been treated as an unqualified blessing. The export of capital, on the other hand, has been seen as a drain on foreign exchange in the short run and of rather dubious advantage in the long run, and always a second best for exports. My own reading of the situation is such a policy is misconceived as it assumes much greater flexibility of choice on the part of the businessman in his overseas strategy than is, in fact, possible. Moreover, there is little evidence that, except as a stopgap measure, curbing foreign investment will aid the balance of payments and even if it did that this is the best way to achieve this particular objective. The medium to long-term effects of such curbs on Britain's economic position could be quite serious.

Some of the secondary benefits of the foreign operations of international companies to the investing country have been considered by Professor Reddaway and others, and many, e.g. feedback of technical knowhow, have been shown to be quite significant. Others are difficult to quantify, yet, in the long run, these may be the most important. Essentially they arise from the growing inter-dependence of the domestic and foreign activities of firms in the economies of scale and integration this makes possible. Where these economies are important it follows that anything which inhibits the growth and efficiency of the foreign operations of a multinational enterprise may rebound to the disadvantage of its domestic operations, and probably that of the investing country as well. The reason for this is partly that the foreign operations of UK international companies are an increasingly important part of their total business (e.g. nearly one-half the sales of the leading UK chemical firms are now accounted for by their foreign subsidiaries) ; and partly that, since there is an increasing tendency for companies to plan their worldwide operations as an integrated whole, any adverse effect on foreign production may well have unwelcome repercussions on home production as well.

In recent years, British-owned international companies have grown rather less rapidly than their US or Continental European competitors. Between 1962 and 1967, the largest 500 US industrial companies (which include all the leading foreign investors) increased their sales by 55·6 per cent; the corresponding increase for the largest British companies was 46·0 per cent and for the largest Continental European companies 47·3 per cent.[14] One reason for the slower growth of UK companies appears to be the slower growth of their foreign activities. For example, the increase in sales of American companies with strong foreign interests was 68·2 per cent compared with 52·6 per cent for companies with minor foreign interests. The corresponding figures for British companies were 51·4 and 33·5 per cent. The former enterprises, i.e. those with strong foreign interests, were also within the most rapidly expanding industries. Other data reveal that, as compared with American firms, British firms have grown rather more by diversification at home.

All this seems to point to the conclusion that one of the main ways in which large companies have grown in recent years is by expanding foreign production. Moreover, this is the route particularly chosen by research-intensive industries. Obstacles to this form of expansion may weaken not only the individual company's competitive position in world markets, but also that of the industries of which they are part.

The gain from specialisation

Why should this be so? The answer lies in the advantages of size and the economies of specialisation and integration which follow from this particular avenue of growth. Notwithstanding the evidence that there is little link between the profitability of a firm and its size, the advantages which size confers seem usually sufficient to enable the largest firms, at least, to maintain their market position. Moreover, few studies distinguish between the ways in which firms grow, and how these affect its competitive position. For example, an enterprise that grows by setting up (or purchasing) foreign production facilities is able to exploit a variety of advantages which may not be open to it at home. These may not only enable it to enlarge its market for a particular product or process, and in consequence, better spread some of its (domestic) overheads; but, because it is producing in widely differing economic environments, also allow it to engage in widespread geographical, product or process specialisation. These advantages may not be available to the firm which grows by diversification in one country

It may be argued that some countries have managed to do very well in recent years without investing much overseas. This is true, but not for the reasons usually advanced. We have suggested that most manufacturing investments are made to exploit a particular comparative advantage which the inventing firm has over its competitors (or potential competitors) in the host and/or investing country. Sometimes this advantage takes the form of a new product or process of production (often protected by patent); sometimes superior management or organisational skills; sometimes the economies of integrated production and marketing; sometimes of access to multiple currencies. The key in each case is a combination between knowledge (or access to knowledge) and the economies of size and integration possessed by the investing company. If this analysis is correct, then it follows that economies which have a comparative advantage in the production of knowledge will be potentially important foreign investors; and that the inducement to invest will be particularly marked in small countries which wish to extend their markets, which, for one reason or another, cannot be exploited by other means.

This approach would help to explain why the two leading foreign direct investors (the United States and Britain) are, relative to their gross national products, the leading spenders on research and development; and why some smaller industrial nations, such as Holland and Switzerland, have been the cradle of some of today's leading international concerns. Japan and Germany on the other hand, which have been the most substantial net importers of technology in recent years, have invested little overseas. But the position is changing. As these countries develop their own research efforts, they too are seeking production outlets overseas. Moreover, both Japan and Germany, and, to a lesser extent, other European countries, took a great deal of time to recover from the last war; and quite a sizeable part of their rapid growth is a consequence or a spin-off of this, and of the fact that they were able to re-equip themselves with the latest technology and machinery.

We have not sufficient space to develop this theory in more detail, and it is tempting to read too much into it. For example, one reaction might be that Britain should follow the Japanese example, run down her indigenous research and overseas investments, and devote the resources saved to buying and adapting foreign knowhow, and providing the necessary software of skilled personnel and equipment to do this. But a moment's thought suggests that, for a variety of reasons, both strategic and economic, this is not really a feasible proposition, although a case might be made for the rationalisation of UK research and development activities. Britain is already committed to her enterprises overseas and cannot suddenly reduce them overnight, without jeopardising the prosperity of those which remain. Moreover, as the domestic economy in Japan approaches the maturity of that of the US and UK economies, Japanese companies are increasingly turning overseas for new markets, not only in South America and the Far East, but in Europe as well.

My own interpretation of these trends is that, over the next two decades or more, the challenge to the UK's competitive position in the world economy will come not primarily from traditional trade in manufactured goods. It will come, less obviously, as a direct result of the operation of non-UK international companies – particularly those of Japanese and Continental European origin – extending their production operations throughout the world. As a result, I foresee a higher proportion of world trade being 'tied' or directly associated with the operation of these companies, as well as being affected by them; and the competitive position of advanced industrial countries being linked to the extent to which they are involved.

If this diagnosis is correct, any emphasis by the British government on fostering manufacturing exports, at the expense of UK investment overseas, could prove extremely shortsighted. Whatever the balance-of-payments advantages of such a policy may be in the short run, in the long run it could be to the detriment of the British economy, because international companies of foreign parentage would exploit the opportunities abdicated by UK companies.

Concern over the balance of payments in the last decade had led the government to take measures that are extremely difficult to justify on grounds other than expediency – or on unrealistic assumptions about the value of investing (or not investing) overseas. This is not to deny that restrictions on capital exports are probably one of the most immediately effective ways of reducing a balance of payments deficit. Professor Richard Cooper, accepting the Reddaway calculation that the return on British overseas investment gave the UK a net gain in real income of 3 per cent for every £100 invested, has estimated that any similar improvement in the balance of payments from an import surcharge of 4 per cent, or by appropriate deflation, would be very much more expensive in terms of loss in real income.[15]

At first sight, Professor Cooper's figures look very persuasive; though there are other ways of curing a balance of payments deficit which are much less costly, for example, a cut in foreign defence commitments or selected import controls. More important, however, are the questionable assumptions underlying the calculations; and, in particular, the way in which the loss of real income arising from a fall in foreign investment is calculated.

Elsewhere[16] I have expressed the view that the loss of the returns arising from reducing UK foreign investment are quite considerably underestimated by Professor Reddaway. Partly, I believe, this is because he does not sufficiently allow for the repercussions which any cutback may have on the earnings of the investing enterprise as a whole – particularly if its domestic and foreign operations are closely integrated. Secondly, it ignores the effect of reduced investment on the existing profitability of the subsidiary's investment; third, the long-run effects on the UK's competitive position are completely overlooked. On Reddaway's own hypothesis, if British firms do not invest other foreign companies will do so, and this will weaken the position of existing British firms in these (and other) markets.

Any rational policy towards the British-based international company must take into consideration both the secondary income earning effects and the time profile of any earnings generated. What really matters, of course, is its effect on future income flows. The balance of payments criterion is only relevant in so far as it may act as a constraint on growth. But even if overseas investment does lead to a drain in the balance of payments, if it still leads to a gain in real income greater than could be achieved elsewhere, then clearly the balance of payments problem should be tackled by other means.

Conclusions

We may now summarise our conclusions and link these with the results of other researches.

1 In recent years, the average rate of return earned by the foreign affiliates of UK firms, net of tax, has been running about the same, or slightly higher than the equivalent return on domestic investments. However, when one takes into account, on the one hand, the way in which these investments are financed and the effects of reducing investment (or the rate of new investment) on the profits of the parent company; and on the other, the fact that part of the tax revenue previously lost to the UK exchequer would not be recouped, it seems very probable then that the loss from any indiscriminate reduction of investment overseas would be considerably greater than the gains from investing more at home. But this is not to deny that there may be many unprofitable UK ventures overseas; much depends on the industries and/or countries in which they are producing. Since the profitability of foreign firms in the UK economy generally exceeds that of their indigenous competitors, this 'trade' in international capital would seem to be of considerable net gain to the UK economy.

2 It has been calculated that the medium-term and long-term effects of UK foreign investment on the balance of payments of the investing country are generally favourable – although not markedly so. In the short run, this is obviously not the case, and much of the discussion has been about the 'trade-off' between balance of payments costs in the short run and the real income gain in the long run. Research now being conducted for the Board of Trade suggests that the operation of foreign firms in Britain has also benefited the UK balance of payments.

3 Neither of these types of calculation adequately allows for the dynamic advantages of international investment in a world in which a larger proportion of both production and trade is being concentrated in the hands of international companies. In this paper we have sought to suggest that, for a highly

advanced industrial country with a comparatively small domestic market, whose main resource is the skill of its people and which competes in a world in which trade in goods is increasingly controlled by giant enterprises and customs unions, foreign direct investment is both an essential medium of growth and an essential prerequisite for prosperity.

4 It is from this viewpoint, and recognising that exports and foreign production are complementary parts of the strategy of the international company – they are not alternatives to each other – that future policy towards the UK-based international companies should be framed. At the very least, these companies are one of Britain's most important invisible exporters. But more than this: foreign direct investment is one of the means by which this country can maintain and strengthen its world competitive position in trade and increase its real income. A full appreciation of this fact would suggest a radical change in the attitude that the authorities have shown in recent years. It may be before long we shall be forced to take a lesson from the Japanese in this respect, who are now actively encouraging the activities of some of their leading companies overseas.

My last comment is this. From what has been said, I consider that the object of UK government policy towards inward and outward direct investment should, in general, be both liberal and encouraging. Such evidence we have suggests that the UK economy is better as a result of the foreign operations of British companies and those of foreign companies in the UK, than if there were no investment (or less investment) in either direction. *Par excellence*, Britain is a two-way international investor. Its combined income received and paid as a proportion of its GNP is considerably greater than that of any other advanced country. In my submission it cannot afford the (dubious) luxury of economic nationalism towards the international company, any more than it can towards international trade in general.

Notes and References

1. The data here and in the following paragraphs are obtained from a variety of sources, the most important of which are the *National Income Blue Book 1970*, *Business Monitor* and *Bank of England Bulletin*, Sept. 1970.

2. See also C. KINDLEBERGER, *American Business Abroad*, Yale University Press, 1969.

3. This hypothesis applied primarily to foreign *manufacturing* investments; investment in resource exploitation and marketing activities are differently motivated.

4. See, for example, J. H. DUNNING, 'Foreign investment in the United Kingdom', in I. A. LITVAK and C. J. MAULE, eds, *Foreign Investment: the experience of host countries*, New York, Praeger, 1970.

5. DUNNING, *op. cit.*

6. But not necessarily world economic *welfare*, which is also influenced by the way this

output is shared among nation states. See J. BEHRMAN, 'Governmental policy alternatives and the problems of international sharing', in J. H. Dunning, ed., *The Multinational Enterprise*, Allen & Unwin, 1971.

7. J. H. DUNNING and M. STEUER, 'The effects of United States investment in Britain on British technology', *Moorgate and Wall Street*, Autumn 1969.

8. BEHRMAN, op. cit.

9. See the evidence given by Professor Kindleberger to the Hearings before the Sub-Committee on Foreign Economic Policy of the Joint Economic Committee. Congress of the United States 91st Congress, part 4, *The Multinational Corporation and International Investment*, 27/30 July 1970.

10. W. B. REDDAWAY, *Effects of UK Direct Investment Overseas*, Cambridge University Press, 1968.

11. See, however, Industrial Policy Group, *The Case for Overseas Direct Investment*, January 1970.

12. The increase in US direct foreign manufacturing investment has been even more impressive; it rose by 329 per cent between 1957 and 1968.

13. *US Manufacturing and the Balance of Payments*, US Treasury Tax Research Policy Document, no. 1, 1968.

14. J. H. DUNNING and R. D. PEARCE, 'The world's largest companies: a statistical profile', *Business Ratios*, no. 3, 1969.

15. R. COOPER, 'The balance of payments', in R. Caves, ed., *Britain's Economic Prospects*, Allen & Unwin, 1958.

16. J. H. DUNNING, 'The Reddaway and Hufbauer/Adler reports on the foreign investment controversy', *The Bankers Magazine*, 1969.

31

Strategic planning for corporate growth in developing countries

ANDRE VAN DAM

This article is concerned with one of the less publicised aspects of planning, that of change and growth in areas where the multinational corporation is about to enter. The so-called developing countries constitute a rewarding challenge to the corporate planner. It is the accurate and, above all, timely appraisal of economic growth that is called for in 'the third world'.

The multinational corporation faces a specific problem in its strategic planning. It must anticipate how, when and in which countries to enter which type of markets with which products. This problem becomes really complex in the so-called developing countries. There are more than sixty developing countries worthy of corporate planning, compared with about twenty industrialised countries. The actual number, of course, depends upon the type of product made and marketed. Corporate planners must have deep insights into the manifold aspects of national and regional development in order to exploit, timely and accurately, the growing yet often complex opportunities of the 'third world'.

Historical comparisons

Development may well be gauged in the framework of historical comparisons. In many respects, the United States, Canada, the United Kingdom, Europe and Australia were, back in 1869, poorer than the underdeveloped countries of today. A century ago, for example, human and animal muscles still accounted for most of their total energy output, whereas half their population was engaged in tilling the land. In fact, these countries had then just emerged from the iron age into the machine and steel age.

Since then, the population of the now industrialised world has trebled and its output has increased almost thirty times. This is an impressive growth record until one realises that the *per capita* product of these countries increased by only 2 per cent per year. In our age, the United Nations consider 3 per cent as a realistic growth objective for the developing countries. Illustratively, Taiwan, Ivory Coast and Ecuador are today roughly where Australia, Canada and Italy must have been a century ago – and they will be, at the above growth rate, in the year 2000 where Yugoslavia, South Africa and Mexico are today.

Statistics

Per *capita* statistics may, of course, drown the corporate planner, inasmuch as they exclude regional and other discrepancies in the levels of living within each country. Table 31.1 showing an example for the United States is self-explanatory.

Table 31.1

(per caput product in US $)	1929	1950	Annual (%) increase
Delaware	920	1910	3·4
South Dakota	415	1310	5·6
Mississippi	275	700	4·6

Professor W. W. Rostow called the planners' attention to the stages of economic growth, which in a way determine the cycle of imports, assembly, manufacture, specialisation and exports of manufactures, in the developing countries. The main yardstick for measuring such stages is the gross national product, but that may be quite misleading to planners. A few instances suffice.

The gross national product does not measure the degree of climatic satisfaction of needs. Sunshine in most of the developing countries constitutes free energy, whereas the peoples of northern Europe spend a good part of their national product on fuel, housing, calories and clothing. In the developing countries, the rental value of owned houses, the housework of the married woman, farm produce consumed on the farm, are not included in the gross national product. The gross national product does not reflect discrepancies in market prices, as witnessed by the cost of a haircut in Chicago and Chiclayo. And then, how is it possible to compare the 'purchasing value' of a coin in the hands of a peasant of Patmos and that spent by a Manhattan tycoon?

Planners must more often than not see through the monetary veil of the cold statistics to determine which developing country will move, and when, into their five-year planning cycle, and how. They must look at such yardsticks as the propensity to save and to invest savings efficiently – this was a secret of Japan's meteoric rise. The exploitation of natural resources can boost a whole economy beyond takeoff in a short time, as in Venezuela. But natural resources do not assure the corporate planner of a market (e.g. Chile) nor does their absence impede development (Switzerland). Senegal and Burma are good examples of the fact that countries do not take off until their rural sector is modernised – yet a low proposition of arable land is no obstacle to prosperity: as is demonstrated by Puerto Rico and Japan.

Table 31.2 Yardsticks of modernization

No. of telephones per thousand inhabitants (1965 data)		Protein intake 1965 (per capita per day)		Life expectancy at birth (in full years) (1965 estimate)	
Sweden	430	New Zealand	108	Norway	74
Australia	240	Uruguay	98	Australia	69
Japan	140	United Kingdom	88	Costa Rica	64
Turkey	100	Poland	78	Algeria	59
Argentina	70	Mexico	68	South Korea	54
South Africa	60	Pakistan	58	India	49
Greece	50	Ceylon	48	Ghana	44
Jamaica	30	Liberia	38	Ivory Coast	39
Yugoslavia	20				
Peru	15				
Iraq	10				
Saudi Arabia	5				
Tanganyika	2				
Ethiopia	1				

Non-economic criteria

The corporate planner who scans the globe for geographic expansion, must also look at the infrastructure, the distribution of income and other economic data. However, often the non-economic criteria are more important to the cold appraisal of the planner. Human resources are of vital importance. Except Japan, every one of the world's twenty-five most developed countries is European, or inhabited by people of predominantly European origin. None of the world's fifty poorest countries has ever had a substantial European population. Climate, geographic and physical isolation often are the underlying causes. On the other hand, the mere size of population has little bearing upon economic development as witnessed by Ireland and Indonesia. Density of population has little correlation with poverty or wealth, as pointed up by Bolivia and Taiwan. The distribution of population is important as it affects urbanisation, education and industrialisation, e.g. the cost of distribution.

Corporate planners for the world markets have many other criteria to consider. They realise that most advanced nations have access to the ocean. Yet landlocked Switzerland is rich and the island of Ceylon is poor. Life expectancy is most influential upon economic development and vice versa. The affluent nations are composed of 22 per cent children compared with 44 per cent in the underprivileged nations. This will affect the product-mix and other parts of the corporate strategic plan, e.g. in terms of size of the labour market, need and cost of education, size of families and *per capita* income levels, demand for food and so forth.

Ranking developing countries

The Paris-based Organisation of Economic Cooperation and Development, New York's Columbia University and Philadelphia's Marketing Science Institute have applied different criteria and techniques to measure the degree, direction and level of economic growth of up to one hundred nations. The writer has made a similar study, using almost exclusively yardsticks related to long-range corporate planning in the manufacturing sphere. There is near-consensus as to the relative ranking and progress of the twenty most industrialised countries. However, as the analysts penetrate the less developed nations, their appraisals widen and differ.

In eastern and southern Europe, virtually every country is now one of a good growth rate with regard to modernisation. Yet, in Europe's periphery there are still few modernising countries, e.g. Iran, Lebanon and Israel. In Latin America, the greatest degree of modernisation takes place in Argentina, Mexico and Venezuela, as also in Brazil's industrial heartland. In Asia, the star performers seem to be, besides Japan, Taiwan, South Korea and, to a lesser extent the Philippine Islands. In Africa, we cite Rhodesia and Kenya as examples of the modernisation trend.

New trends

New trends develop which will require the attention of the corporate planner. Regional economic cooperation, timidly, yet decidedly, takes place in Asia, Africa and Latin America. In the next generation, new countries will come to the fore, such as Colombia, Thailand, Pakistan and the Maghreb countries. The corporate planner must specifically watch such candidates as India, Indonesia and Nigeria, where takeoff may assume gigantic proportions. Yet, even the less dynamic countries may, on closer analysis, assume specific importance to the corporate planner, either by their newly acquired rights in regional integration, (e.g. Paraguay), by their resource potential (Ghana) or by political develop-ments (United Arab Republic).

As the 'third world' modernises, whetting the appetite of the multinational corporation, we anticipate different rules in the international investing game. The international transfer of the factors of production, so aptly described by Jean-Jacques Servan-Schreiber, will meet new hurdles on its route towards the developing countries. The third world is increasingly aware of its political power and will demand more liberal treatment by the advanced nations, as demonstrated at the Unctad conferences.

The diminishing return of import substitution will compel many multinational corporations to gauge the export potential, in terms of manufactured goods, of the developing countries. The traditional risks of investing in 'new' countries, such as nationalisation, inflation, non-convertibility of currencies, diminish gradually. In its stead the multinational corporation faces rising demands to transfer technology, to share it with local enterprise, to contribute to the foreign exchange earnings of the host country and to adjust investment plans to local natural and human resources.

Timing geographic expansion

In this era of accelerated technological innovation, a curious and contrasting pattern arises in the developing countries. Modernisation may jump from donkey to jet plane, skipping the railroad stage altogether, for example. The computer, the satellite communications system, television and radio, modern chemicals and other phenomena of advanced technology are superimposed upon a traditional infrastructure and often upon a backward mode of life. This is a challenge to the corporate planner, to predict accurately and in good time, the impact of the revolution of rising expectations. The most difficult decision a corporate planner faces in the third world is no doubt the timing of corporate geographic expansion. An early foothold may depress returns, yet promise a leading market position when takeoff occurs. It is tempting to hold a foreign market by exporting from the home country – but a slightly premature transfer of the factors of production can pay handsome dividends in government goodwill, consumer and dealer loyalty and lasting market domination.

The third part of the twentieth century will witness the rise of strategic planning and that of the third world as an economic power. Corporate planning may, in consequence, be most effective and rewarding where growth and change will be fastest – in the developing countries.

Table 31.3 Stages of economic growth: Iran

Iran is about ready to take off. Below, raw data are ranked for forty criteria, in descending order, then measured in a geometrically progressive stage. The resulting ten stages resemble those of Professor Rostow.

Nr	Description of Factor	NA	I	II	III	IV	V	VI	VII	VIII	IX	X
1	Gross national product – *per capita*					x						
2	Non-agricultural GNP – *per capita*								x			
3	GNP – purchasing power – *per capita*				x							
4	Hypothetical GNP – *per capita*					x						
5	Growth rate GNP				x							
6	Energy consumption – *per capita*							x				
7	Steel consumption – *per capita*						x					
8	Cement consumption – *per capita*							x				
9	Fixed capital formation as % of GNP					x						
10	Interest rate of Central Bank											
11	Proportion labour force in agriculture		x									
12	Proportion labour force in manufacture				x							
13	Proportion of urban population								x			
14	Density of population					x						
15	Life expectancy at birth	x										
16	Mortality rate											x
17	Fertility rate								x			
18	Growth rate of population		x									
19	Degree of literacy				x							
20	School enrolment							x				
21	Ownership of wireless sets					x						
22	Ownership of television sets						x					
23	Ownership of telephone connections				x							
24	Readership of newspapers				x							
25	Mobility index	x										
26	Passenger railroad traffic – *per capita*					x						
27	Freight railroad traffic – *per capita*					x						
28	Ownership of motor vehicles						x					
29	Ownership of commercial vehicles					x						
30	Exports – per capita								x			
31	Exports as % of GNP									x		
32	Imports – per capita					x						
33	Foreign reserves as % of imports										x	
34	Foreign reserves as % of GNP											
35	Proportion of arable land							x				
36	Arable land – *per capita*								x			
37	Food outlays as % of total budget					x						
38	Intake of calories – *per capita*	x										
39	Intake of proteins – *per capita*	x										
40	Corn production – *per capita*			x								

PART VI

Quantitative and analytical aids to strategic planning

32

Management science and strategic planning

B. WAGLE

The author aims to illustrate how management science models can be used in strategic planning. He emphasises that there is similarity between strategic planning in the private sector and in the public sector and that the same broad principles of management science can be applied in both the sectors. Various types of computer models incorporating management science techniques which can be, and have been, successfully applied in this activity are described.

Peter Drucker, who is often regarded as one of the pioneers in the development of the philosophy of long-range planning, in his thought-provoking paper published over ten years ago concluded:

> So far it must be said management science has not made much contribution to long-range planning. Sometimes one wonders whether those who call themselves management scientists are even aware of the risk-taking character of economic activity and of the resultant entrepreneurial job of long-range planning. But in the long run management science and management scientists may well and justly be judged by their ability to supply the knowledge and thinking needed to make long-range planning possible, simple and effective.[1]

I do not believe we have progressed very far since then. Management science, which is defined as the application of the scientific method incorporating operations research techniques, econometrics and mathematical statistics to aid managers in their decision making, has yet to make a significant impact in the area of strategic planning and policy formulation. On the other hand, management science techniques are being increasingly used to solve tactical and operational problems of ever-increasing complexity and scope. The models have been successfully developed for application in inventory situations for deciding how much to order and when to order. In transportation problems these models have been developed to minimise freight costs and to establish optimal routes of travel to various points in terms of cost and time, in developing optimal scheduling patterns, in location studies, sales planning and several such areas. The reader will notice that almost all these problems deal with functional areas. It is a basic premise of this paper that management science can be just as profitably used in areas such as strategic planning, policy formulation and decision making at the corporate level as they have been in the operational fields. The formulation concepts, mathematical techniques and computer technology which will be needed to develop these management science models are now available, and yet these methods have not made a significant impact. The reason for this is not far to seek. It is essentially the difficulty of communication between the management science expert and top management often leading to mutual distrust. The following remark which is attributed to a managing director of a large firm in Europe speaks for itself. He defined operations research as 'an expensive way to invite insults from inexperienced people half your age'. A second reason is that traditionally strategic planning is largely linked with financial planning, which has been the monopoly of the accountant who often is not trained in management science techniques, whereas the management science manager usually does not really understand the complexities of finance. The purpose of this paper is to bridge the gap and to illustrate how management science models can be used in strategic planning.

What is strategic planning?

Strategic planning, and in particular corporate planning, has become a fashionable term over the last few years. There is no lack of literature on the subject as a result of the vast proliferation of articles, books, seminars and conferences dealing with it. In spite of this a recent survey carried out at the Stanford Research Institute and summarised in a paper by Ringback[2] concludes that organised corporate planning is neither as well accepted nor as well practised as one would expect. That although planning is carried out in a great majority of organisations it is lacking in coordination and is not formalised, and certainly not as sophisticated as the literature would indicate. The study goes on to say that although substantial advances have been made, there are major developments necessary before the true potential of strategic planning can be judged. A recent publication by Ackoff[3] seems to have reached a similar conclusion.

But then, what is strategic planning? What is so special about it, how does it differ from the planning which companies have been doing for so many years? We define strategic planning as the determination and implementation of corporate business strategy, a business strategy being defined as the course of action designed to optimise future profit over a series of years by deploying limited resources in a changing environment and in the face of increasing competition in the pursuit of certain management goals.

Various arguments have been raised against the principle of 'maximisation of profits'. Ackoff goes as far as to say that profit is a figment of the accountant's imagination and that by changing one's accountant one can easily create or destroy profits. Although in theory Ackoff is right we believe that he is taking an extreme viewpoint. In practice an organisation which tries to manipulate its balance sheets and P/L accounts to show good profits may succeed in fooling the shareholders for a year, perhaps two years, but certainly not for long. It is also more than likely that such a firm would suffer a takeover or be forced to make radical changes at the top of the organisation. Argenti[4] argues that the overall job of the organisation is essentially to make a profit which will satisfy the shareholders. He discusses methods of arriving at the target DCF return which will satisfy the shareholders of the company, and says that the fundamental objective of the corporation is to make that level of profit which will ensure that this target rate is achieved. The book is largely concerned with corporate planning for public companies. However, there is no reason why the approach could not be employed for strategic planning in the public sector.

Why strategic planning?

Why has strategic planning suddenly come into vogue? We believe that increasing competition, the fear of being taken over, need to keep pace with rapid technological developments, scarcity of good management, limited availability of capital and environmental constraints, are some of the major factors which have contributed to the growing need of strategic planning. Top management has been forced to realise that 'driving by the seat of the pants' and 'wait and see' attitudes can lead nowhere.

Every aspect of the organisation's work, whether it be in the private sector or the public sector, is concerned with estimating what will happen in the future. The time horizon may be a week, a month, a year or ten years ahead. Decisions on where to locate the plant, what to produce, how much to produce, how much labour to employ, how to finance investments, which investments to make, and so on necessitate looking into the future anywhere between one to twenty years ahead. The future is always uncertain and it needs to be studied in order to decide upon the decisions to be taken today. After all, decisions can only be taken in the present, the rest are only pious intentions. And yet we cannot make decisions for the present alone. It must be remembered that decisions taken today will have important consequences for tomorrow. Most strategic decisions will commit the organisation on a long-term basis. This is the *raison d'être* of strategic planning.

The aim of strategic planning is to integrate and coordinate the operations of several autonomous and semi-autonomous divisions to ensure that different parts of the organisation are not working at cross purposes. It is essentially concerned with strategic problems associated with defining objectives in the overall interest of the organisation and then developing corresponding courses of action required to realise these objectives. In this respect because of its strategic nature it should be clearly differentiated from tactical planning. The latter is short-term, and is chiefly concerned with functional planning and not with the setting of corporate goals. Tactical planning is carried out largely by functional management, whereas strategic planning, because of its very nature, must be the prerogative of top management. For effective strategic planning it is essential to get top management support and the active participation of both corporate and operational line management. The strategic plan must cover all aspects of the organisation's activities in an integrated manner. The basic data and assumptions required in the planning process should be developed in a systematic manner and explicitly stated.

The plan should be comprehensive enough to cover all the major aspects concerning corporate success. It should have a regular control and monitoring system. It will be helpful at this stage if we briefly outline the major components of the strategic plan and then indicate how 'management science' can be used in evolving this plan.

Strategic plan

We believe that for effective decision making the strategic plan should usually cover the following elements:

1 Outline of the broad objectives for the corporation as a whole, and also for the individual subfunctions. These objectives should be as quantitative as possible. While functional objectives can be set with a great deal of clarity the concept of 'corporate objective' is a broad and imprecise one and by its very nature will involve some degree of compromise between conflicting functional aims. Setting of corporate objectives is thus a difficult task and management science techniques can provide an invaluable aid in this area. We shall discuss this later in the paper. Corporate objectives, since they deal with the corporation as a whole, should generally be expressed in financial or economic terms.

For example, one overall corporate objective of the organisation may be to earn after tax a DCF return of over 15 per cent on all new investments. Another objective may be to reduce overall operating costs by 10 per cent by a given year. A third may be related to the increase in overall productivity and so on. In addition to the corporate objectives the plan should have a set of functional objectives which are consistent with each other. Functional objectives should be set in various areas such as production, marketing, research, employee-relations, external affairs and so on. These objectives too should be explicitly defined and as far as possible expressed in quantitative terms. Thus to state that the objective of the company is to seek to attain 'leadership in its industry' or 'good public relations' or 'exploit opportunities', etc., are vague and do not provide any meaningful information for taking action.

Targets are required for each major activity. For example, for the marketing sector the objective should clearly indicate for each product target sales-volumes and the corresponding sales-price to be achieved over the plan period. In the manufacturing sector the objective should set targets for variables such as reduction in operating costs, increases in productivity, increases in investment, etc. For the research department the objective should indicate the target level of expenditure on research activities as a proportion of sales and so on for the other sectors. This list is by no means exhaustive. It is merely included here to illustrate the basic point we are trying to make that it is possible to express in many situations both corporate and functional objectives in quantitative terms and this should be done as far as possible. Care must be taken to ensure the consistency of the functional objectives in evolving the overall strategic plan.

2 A study of the environmental factors such as marketing trends, political developments, technology and general economic factors which are likely to affect the business. The plan should include forecasts of these variables over the planning period. All environmental assumptions should be clearly justified. These forecasts and assumptions will form the essential basic ingredient of all the planning operations of the company and should embrace all those elements concerning which top management believe detailed knowledge is essential. The more obvious elements would appear to be:

(a) rate of economic growth of UK combined with the most likely social and political developments

(b) total industry demand for the products or services of interest to the organisation. Consider, for example, the oil industry. It is essential that a strategic plan for an oil company should contain an overall assessment of the total energy market with a breakdown into individual components, viz.: coal, gas, electricity, nuclear power and oil

(c) breakdown of the total industry into sectorial demand. Take again the case of the oil industry, the total demand for oil is made up of requirements by different sectors such as domestic, transport, agricultural, commercial, etc. The breakdown of the total demand into demand by these individual sectors can provide useful background information for decision-making purposes

(d) availability and cost of alternative sources of raw materials

(e) effects on the business of competition – large competitors, small competitors and foreign competitors

(f) selling prices and quality of products manufactured

(g) effects of growing technology leading to obsolescence of the company's products, development of new products, processes, plant and equipment

(h) capital investment requirements

(i) availability of funds both internal and external.

The above list merely indicates the type of environmental factors which need to be taken into account in building a strategic plan. It must be emphasised that all the forecasts which are built into the plan are subject to error and forecasts should not usually be made without giving some indication of the possible range of errors associated with these. This information can be used to provide a systematic evaluation of the uncertainty involved in pursuing a given strategy and in drawing up contingency plans.

3 An audit of the organisation's existing resources to indicate its relative

strengths and weaknesses. These strengths and weaknesses are internal to the company; for example, the organisation may be strong in the quality of its staff, may have an outstanding research department, excellent labour relations, etc. These strong points will naturally have to be exploited in the company's overall interest. Similarly, weaknesses should also be defined; for example, low productivity in a certain sector or alternatively a significant proportion of ageing board members, bad union relations, etc. The purposes of this list are to aid the strategic planner in formulating the overall plan so that he can exploit the strong points and overcome the weaknesses in the future.

4 A systematic analysis of constraints within which the organisation has to operate. There must be a clear distinction between objectives and constraints. Whereas the former are decided upon by management, the latter are imposed upon the organisation as a result of environmental conditions such as moral pressures resulting from society, public opinion and government legislation. The greater the number of these constraints the lesser the flexibility available for making profit. Top management must therefore decide which of the constraints are valid in its opinion and which are not and the degree to which the organisation will be governed by these constraints. The constraints can largely be classified into two categories; moral constraints and government constraints. Moral constraints are usually described in terms of attitude towards employees, government officials, suppliers and customers and even shareholders. In many cases it will be possible to quantify these constraints, for example the attitude towards suppliers may be that the organisation will buy raw materials from the cheapest supplier or it may buy raw materials from a domestic supplier providing the price differential between the domestic supplier and the foreign supplier does not exceed 5 per cent. The attitude towards customers may be reflected in the quality of the products manufactured, etc. All other operational constraints should be clearly defined and incorporated within the plan.

The second type of constraints are those imposed by the government. For example, a constraint may be that the proportion of raw materials imported should not exceed a certain level. Another constraint may be concerned with distribution rights of the organisation, viz. restriction on the number of owned outlets. Government may also enforce financial constraints by imposing upper limit on debt/equity ratio and so on. The important point is that many of these constraints can be quantified and whenever possible be explicitly stated so that the relationship of the organisation with its employees, customers, suppliers, competitors, government, shareholders, etc., is clearly defined.

5 The set of strategies and action programmes to enable the organisation to meet its overall financial target. These action programmes will form the basis of the corporate and functional objectives which are usually summarised in the first section of the strategic plan. This stage is the most critical part of the exercise because it is essentially concerned with answering basic fundamental questions such as what should the organisation do? What markets should it operate in?

How much of each product should it sell? Whether and when should additional capital investments take place? What pricing policy should the company adopt? Is it necessary to diversify; if so in which areas should it expand? Should the organisation integrate backwards or forwards? How should the organisation exploit its strength and overcome weaknesses, and so on? The heart of the strategic plan is in the answers to these questions.

An important question which arises at this stage is what period should the strategic plan cover? We believe that the period chosen should be such that reasonable forecasts of technology and costs can be made over that period but at the same time it should be long enough to ensure that one's vision is not inhibited by the existing plant, investment and markets. For most organisations in the private sector a period of ten years would appear reasonable. The plan should be reviewed annually, and a system of control and monitoring should be built in. The plan is based on various assumptions both internally and externally. If any of these turn out to be significantly different from those incorporated in the plan then the action programmes may need to be revised. Similarly, changes in government policies, etc., may necessitate regular revisions to the plan. However the strategic plan should not be revised too often, otherwise it may lose its value. Revisions should only be made when some major variables are affected which in turn could involve major policy decisions. To ensure that the actual annual targets are being achieved it is necessary to have a system of control. Control can only be exercised if information towards achieving the desired results is available. To do this, one needs a system of monitoring. This can be readily achieved by comparing the expected values of the critical variables (which should be defined well in advance) with the actuals on a regular basis and if the difference is likely to significantly alter the profits situation then detailed analysis should be carried out to rationalise the difference and to recommend what action is necessary to counteract its effect on profits.

To summarise: the strategic plan should cover five major elements – long-range corporate and nonconflicting functional objectives; basic assumptions and forecasts of environmental factors likely to influence the business during the plan period; an audit of the organisation's existing resources, strengths and weaknesses; a systematic analysis of constraints within which the organisation operates; and finally, the set of strategies and action programmes which will enable the organisation to achieve its objectives. A system for revision, control and monitoring should be appended.

Management science tools

Strategic planning involves a great number of interrelated variables and the object of the exercise is to determine the values of each of these in accordance with some economic criterion such as maximisation of profits or net cash generated or minimisation of costs subject to certain constraints. This then is the basic characteristic of all planning problems where one has to decide on the optimal combination among a large number of interrelated alternatives. And intuitively, it is logical to turn to management science methods and high-speed computers to solve problems of this kind.

Leaving aside the organisational and administrative aspects, strategic planning (or for that matter departmental planning) can logically be viewed as equivalent to the solution of a set of simultaneous equations. The variables entering into these equations represent the operational levels and the amount of funds to be allocated to the different activities. For example, the volume of a given product sold would be one such variable, quantity of raw materials used would be another, a particular type of equipment installed would be a third and so on.

As for the equations, these describe the constraints and interrelations within the system. For example, a constraint may be that the expenditure incurred in a given activity cannot exceed available funds; another constraint may be that the sales of a particular product should not exceed the total industry demand. The mathematical representation of a planning problem would thus consist of a set of variables and equations. This is essentially what the 'management science' approach attempts to do. It represents the planning problem in these terms and then uses sophisticated mathematical techniques to arrive at the solution. In technical jargon the mathematical representation of the system is termed 'a model'.

Model building

There are five basic steps involved in model building:

- definition – purpose of the model
- formulation – technique to be used, detail to be included, and so on
- data collection
- testing the model
- documentation.

The strategic planning model would necessarily represent all the operations of the organisation from buying of raw materials to selling of the finished products. It would include all financial, moral and government constraints to the extent that these can be mathematically represented. The model would need to be dynamic in its character, that is cover a sequence of time periods. The level of detail will depend upon the need and the purpose for which the model is built. However, for any sizeable organisation, particularly when it is considered through successive time periods the number of variables and equations can be impressively large, quite easily of the order of 5000–10000 variables and 1000–5000 equations. Several of these equations will be inequalities of the type that something must not be greater (or not smaller) than something else. For example, sales of a particular product should be less than or equal to demand for it or alternatively quality of a particular product must lie between certain specified limits. These inequalities, in the mathematical formulation in effect reflect the 'indefiniteness' which is the basic characteristic of all planning (strategic or operational) problems and give rise to the multiplicity of possible solutions from which the planner has to choose the optimal one.

There are essentially three approaches which can be used in formulating management science models: optimisation, simulation and regression. Combinations of these may also be utilised. The choice of the approach will largely be determined by the problem under consideration and the resources available, for developing the model. As the name itself suggests, optimisation models are designed to analyse alternatives and provide the solution so as to optimise a given objective function. The model will choose one strategy which is considered to be the best from the whole host of alternatives available. A significant by-product derived from the application of linear programming which is perhaps the most widely used technique in optimisation models is the large amount of analytical information which it provides. This includes in particular the 'marginal cost' or 'shadow prices' which describes the financial effects of possible changes in resources or money availability or other constraints. This information can be of great utility to management in their decision making.

The simulation approach to model building as the name suggests, does not optimise. Essentially the model simulates the operations of the organisation on a computer under given set of conditions. It may be used to provide a reasonably good solution by evaluating alternative strategies on a case study basis. The inequalities which in mathematical programming models are automatically dealt with need to be converted into sets of rules of the type 'if x then y' for the simulation models. Although these models do not optimise they are comparatively easy to develop, take very little computing time and can be of considerable value in overall financial planning. For details of this approach reference may be made to the article by Dourn and Salkin.[5] The regression approach essentially estimates relationships between the critical variables by analysing historical information or cross-sectional data to provide a basis for strategic decision making. For example, statistical relationships estimated between market share for a particular commodity and the amount of advertising expenditure for this commodity incurred by the organisation could be used as a guide in formulating future policy for advertising expenditure.

The next question is how can these different approaches be usefully employed for strategic planning in the private and public sectors?

Strategic planning in the private sector

The use of management science tools for strategic planning in the private sector will best be illustrated by the following hypothetical example. Consider an oil company with several refineries in Europe. These can refine various crude oils of differing qualities coming from alternative sources to produce various final products. The procurement of crude oil can take place in different sizes of tankers from different sources along alternative routes. The refineries themselves have a wide range of equipment. In each refinery several cutting schemes are available for each crude and intermediates from primary distillation can be processed in various ways. The distribution of products made from refineries to the many distributors and retail outlets scattered over the countries is made using alternative modes of transportation such as tankers, pipeline, rail, road, etc. The objective of corporate management is to decide on how to balance all these operations and produce a strategic plan for investment decisions in manufacturing, transportation and marketing over the total planning period so as to maximise the net return on investment. Management may be particularly interested in knowing which of the existing refineries should be expanded and which, if any, should be closed down, from the company's overall point of interest. An optimisation model using dynamic linear programming could be formulated to deal with this complex problem. It will need considerable skill in formulation and a vast amount of basic information. Given this, a model would not be difficult to construct. For each time period the model would need a representation of the system incorporating the different sectors, viz.: marine transportation, refining, product distribution and a financial sector. The level of detail to be included would depend on the data available, computing power and the purpose of the model. For each time period the model will thus have a submodel representing the operations dealing with that period. In addition the model will have a number of interconnecting equations which link the different time periods. This linkage is critical because it reflects the fact that any investment in the first time period will exert an influence in the succeeding time periods, similarly investment in the second time period will influence operations in the third, fourth, fifth time periods and so on. The inclusion of the time dimension is a very necessary part of strategic planning as it is required to evaluate the sequence of timing of investments. This is the distinguishing element of strategic planning models as against purely operational models. The latter rarely deal with investment opportunities. Specific investments will be included in a particular time period if the net effect of its installation in that period would be to lower the cost of the operation. This cost is expressed as the discounted after tax cost during the total time covered by the model. The model will of course take into account any financial constraints on the availability of funds for expansion purposes.

Thus the model represents in a simplified form the range and type of choice available to the organisation in its planning operations. It *tells the planner which of the available crude oils to buy, how to transport them, how much of each product to sell, when should refineries or marketing units be expanded, how should the final products be distributed and so on, under a wide range of assumptions as to product prices, policy constraints, etc.* The criterion used in the choice is to maximise the amount of cash generated after paying for all fixed and variable costs and providing not just for depreciation but also generating sufficient funds to give over the plan period a given rate of DCF return on each piece of equipment used. It will be readily appreciated that a model of this type would be of considerable value in evolving the strategic plan.

It covers all essential aspects of the plan from setting of objectives to formulation of the investment strategies. The model would be useful in pointing out each of the areas that need more detailed investigation which could be carried out at the functional level.

An organisation which does not have the resources to build dynamic optimisation models, may decide to develop simpler models of the simulation type, for use on a computer. As indicated earlier, these models are essentially used to analyse the financial implications of alternative policy decisions and changes in environmental conditions on the organisation over a series of years. The models simulate the operations of the company over the years and produce the outlook in financial terms for each year under various assumptions of forecasts concerning sales, production, planned investment, and other financial data such as interest rates, credit policies, availability of external funds and so on. The cash balance in each year interlinks the basic financial factors such as revenue, costs, dividends, credits, tax and so on. Various constraints are included in the model expressed in the form 'if x then y and if not x then z'. For example, a dividend policy may be formulated in the following terms: if earnings in a given year exceed last year's earnings by over 20 per cent pay out a 10 per cent increase in dividends: if however earnings are less than last year's earnings then dividends should be maintained at the same level. A significant portion of the model must be devoted to the detailed representation of revenues and expenditures. Similarly the model will need to include separate sets of equations for the calculation of annual depreciation and tax. Various capacity restrictions characterising the size of the company facilities should also be incorporated in the model. Restrictions on financial ratios can also be built into the system.

Table 32.1 presents an illustration of the type of results which the model would present.

Similarly summaries of the balance sheets, financing tables and various important profitability ratios for each year are typed as output of the model. In addition the model can be used to provide detailed information on any of the individual categories as required. An example would be the individual depreciation calculations, or the calculation of tax allowances for any given year.

This model does not optimise and to that extent does not provide optimal solutions automatically. However, it can be used on a case study basis to analyse the effects of alternative assumptions and policy decisions. Questions of the type – What is the effect on profit if sales are below projected level by say 5 per cent? or What is the effect on earnings if production costs are higher than forecast by say 3 per cent? or What is the effect on profits of expanding a certain plant in the fifth year of operation?, can readily be handled by the model. The model also provides an extremely useful tool for carrying out sensitivity studies. It is comparatively easy to develop and takes very little computer time. Financial models of this type can also be useful in formulating acquisition policies by analysing financial implications of alternative takeover strategies.

The third type of model, which we believe to be useful in strategic planning in the private sector, consists of regression models which can be effectively used for

Fig. 32.1 Output of a simulation model

P/L account	Year 1	Year 2	Year 3	. . . .	Year 10
Sales revenue					
Exports					
Other revenue					
Duty					
Net revenue					
Cost of raw material					
Cost of imports					
Operating costs:					
1 Production					
2 Marketing					
3 Distribution					
Depreciation					
Operating profit					
Interest payments:					
1 Short-term					
2 Debenture					
3 Other					
Gross profit					
Tax					
Net profit					
Dividends					
Transfer to					
reserves					

forecasting variables such as product demand, prices, costs and general economic factors. The models can be used to investigate different price-volume and cost-volume relationships. A regression model essentially estimates the set of relationships between two sets of variables on the basis of historical data using statistical methods of regression analysis. These relationships then provide a basis for projecting one set of variables under alternative assumptions concerning the second set. Consider for example the oil industry: demand for gasoline will depend on several factors such as car ownership, price of gasoline, cost of alternative modes of transport and several other secondary factors such as the state of roads, weather and so on. The regression model can be used to estimate the relationship between sales of gasoline and these other explanatory variables by statistical methods from past time-series data and any other available information. This relationship may then be used to forecast gasoline sales under various assumptions about car ownership and the other explanatory variables which are included in the model. As an illustration from historical data, one may be able to determine that for every 1 per cent change in car ownership demand for gasoline on average increases by x per cent and for every 1 per cent increase in the price of gasoline, the demand is decreased by y per cent.

Under alternative assumptions about car ownership and price of gasoline it is now possible to make forward estimates of the demand for gasoline. This is, of course, a very simple example. In practice, one would have to consider several explanatory variables. It may also be necessary to consider more than one relation. The form of the relationships can also be complex and various technical problems in estimation can arise. The approach, however, is of considerable value and has been successfully applied, not only in demand forecasting on a company level but also in large-scale national economic models developed for planning purposes. For a further discussion of some of these models and their applications to an oil company, reference should be made to the author's paper.[6] A similar quantitative approach to long-range planning has also been described in a series of articles by Hetrick.[7]

Strategic planning in the public sector

There is a definite parallelism between the type of problems which a strategic planner in the corporate sector has to deal with and those of his counterpart in the public sector. This will readily be appreciated for corporations such as the National Coal Board and the Gas Council. We maintain that this is also true in the case of strategic planning by the local authorities and government. Both have to consider fundamental long-range objectives and decide on strategies to achieve them. Both are dealing with a vast number of interdependent activities and operating within certain broad constraints. Both attempt to maximise well-defined objective functions. In the private sector as we have already seen the objective function would be the discounted value of net cash generated over a series of years. In the case of the public sector the objective would be the maximisation of some other well-defined public welfare function or an overall measure of economic growth or some such criterion. The only real difference between the two sectors lies in the size of the problem. No doubt strategic planning in the public sector will involve far more variables, some of them very difficult to define and constraints operating on the system may be considerably different from those in the private sector. Nevertheless, the conceptual framework will still be the same. This leads us to believe that management science models incorporating optimisation, simulation and regression could be appropriately used to deal with these problems.

Consider, for example, the problem of national economic planning. If we accept the basic premise that the fundamental objective of the plan is the development of the economy along a particular path which provides maximum growth of the gross national product (or some other measures of economic growth), then it will readily be seen that the overall problem of economic planning can essentially be reduced to the following terms. Given a set of initial conditions which include existing capacities and technologies – the problem is to decide on how products and capital goods should be generated through time so as to achieve maximum economic growth rate, bearing in mind the various limitations on natural resources of the country. Of course, there are various other constraints arising from specific factors such as land availability, labour availability, social policies, cash requirements, balance of payments and so on. These would most certainly have to be represented in the model. The formulation would also raise considerable problems in data collection and interpretation but we believe that conceptually it should be possible to develop such a model. Most of the basic data should be available from the central statistical office and the main interlinks between the different economic activities would be obtained from input – output tables of economy. The objective function which the model would aim to optimise is growth rate of the economy over a series of years. Research along these lines to develop large-scale economic models for planning could prove fruitful, and a management science model of the type developed for the private sector would provide a convenient starting point.

The second important area in the public sector which we believe management science models would be useful, and where very little impact so far has been made, is in the strategic area of investment decision making for regional and subregional planning. Plans are being formulated today setting out proposals for future locations of housing, industry, offices, shopping centres, major recreational facilities, road building, and so on, incorporating decisions on fundamental policies such as major urban renewal opportunities and schemes to attract industry. These problems are extremely important and would be amenable to management science models. Unfortunately the techniques currently employed in this area leave a great deal to be desired. This type of strategic planning is carried out as a one-off exercise by consultants or by a team of specialists set up for the purpose by direct recruitment or secondment from the authorities and departments concerned. Most of the management science models used in this area are static, in that they deal with only one year in the long-term future. They do not optimise, neither do they simulate. The approach employed essentially consists in starting with basic projections for the target year, such as 1991. These population projections are then converted into employment projections by type of industry and jobs. The potential which will be available in the target year for different development purposes taking into account various environmental factors is also assessed. On the basis of employment projections and the various physical, economic and political constraints operating in the region, the planning team draws up a number of intuitive plans based on knowledge, experience and statistical tools to obtain an overall balance. These plans generally set out proposals for the future location of housing, industry, offices, shopping centres and main roads, to suit the needs of the population in that region. The plans are then examined, taking into account any additional environmental constraints, and the one most satisfactory as a whole is put forward. In practice it is generally believed that the final plan put forward tends to be substantially biased towards reduction in road costs, as these are more easily measured than other social benefits of regional planning. For a further discussion of this topic reference should be made to Thorburn,[8] who incidentally concludes that there are only about a dozen planners in Britain who are capable of building mathematical models for planning purposes and not many more who know how to use them but the field is expanding rapidly. The progress being made is nowhere near as fast as it should be considering the pace in the development of management science techniques and computer technology. From the examples already discussed above, one will readily appreciate that there is a great need of developing dynamic models for strategic planning in the public sector.

A discussion of strategic planning in the public sector without any reference to the planning – programming – budgeting – system (PPBS) would be incomplete. This method was originally devised by the US Government/Defence Department. The basic principle of PPBS is a systematic cost benefit analysis of alternative programmes so as to arrive at better decisions on the allocation of resources to attain already established government objectives. A detailed description of PPBS would be out of context here but reference may be made to a paper by Dougharty.[9]

Conclusions

In spite of the proliferation of literature on the subject of strategic planning, there is still a great deal of confusion over what a strategic plan should contain, how it should be evolved and how maximum benefits can be secured from it. We believe that management science models can play a useful role in overcoming some of this confusion and also provide top management with a valuable tool for evaluating alternative strategies and arriving at the optimal overall plan.

In particular these models incorporating methods of optimisation, simulation and regression, can be used in various areas of strategic planning:

1 Exploration of long-range corporate objectives.
2 Provision of a framework for testing alternative policies for the organisation.
3 Evaluation of the impact of alternative government policy decisions such as changes in tax regulations, changes in investment grants and other monetary and fiscal changes.
4 Consistent and coordinated analysis of all aspects of the organisation.
5 Sensitivity studies and contingency planning.
6 Evaluation of expansion opportunities and testing alternative investment plans.
7 Evolving the long-range strategic plan.

In addition to the above benefits the management science approach brings about a new way of thinking within the organisation. By making managers analyse in a systematic manner all the interacting variables it leads to better decision making. The models deal with the organisation as a whole and thus overcome problems of suboptimisation or inconsistency in functional objectives. It is obvious that the economic motivation for dealing with problems of interfunctional dependences are far greater than concentrating on the optimisation of the effectiveness of a single functional activity and 'management science' making use of computer technology can provide valuable tools for decision making in this area. By securing the participation of different functional management in the definition and formulation of these models a deeper understanding of the business and environment is generated thus leading to more effective planning. Managers of different functions begin to understand and appreciate each other's problems and accept that at times it may be better to adjust their own departmental plan in the overall interest of the organisation. If it is accepted that it is better to have integrated planning of investments through time rather than evaluate separately the returns for individual projects, then there is a strong case for use of management science models which attempt to do this. It is worth stressing that some of these models provide a measure of the improvement in overall cash earnings or some other corporate objective if a given constraint imposed on the system were to be relaxed. This thus provides management with a measure of the true corporate incentive for removing that particular restriction. For example, the corporate incentive for investment in additional plant or the corporate incentive for increasing the sales of any particular product in any of the areas and time periods under consideration can be readily obtained. The particular value of this type of information lies in the fact that it provides a tool for appraisal of various expansion opportunities from an overall viewpoint of the corporation taking into account all the interplay between the various activities and resources throughout the company.

Management science models may just as effectively be used in the public sector as in the private sector. The problems may be more difficult to formulate, constraints may be more difficult to quantify, the number of variables significantly greater, but nevertheless, the underlying philosophy of strategic planning in both the sectors is the same, viz., to determine the particular allocation of funds and resources which will ensure that the effectiveness of the overall system is maximised within the set of certain constraints.

References

1. P. DRUCKER, 'Long-range planning – challenge to management science', *Management Science*, 5, 1959, pp. 238–49.

2. A. RINGBACK, 'Organised planning in major US companies', *Long Range Planning*, 2, no. 2, 1969, pp. 46–57.

3. R. L. ACKOFF, *A Concept of Corporate Planning*, Wiley, 1970.

4. J. ARGENTI, *Corporate Planning – A Practical Guide*, Allen & Unwin, 1968.

5. P. J. DOURN and G. R. SALKIN, 'The use of financial models in long range planning', *Long Range Planning*, 2, no. 2, 1969, pp. 27–32.

6. B. WAGLE, 'The use of models for environmental forecasting and corporate planning', *Operational Research Quarterly*, 20, 1969, pp. 327–36.

7. J. C. HETRICK, 'A formal model for long range planning', in three parts, *Long Range Planning*, 1, no. 3, 1969, pp. 16–23; 1, no. 4, pp. 54–66; and 2, no. 1, 1969, pp. 12–21.

8. A. THORBURN, 'The modern approach to sub-regional planning', *Long Range Planning*, 2, no. 3, 1970, pp. 60–6.

9. L. A. DOUGHARTY, 'Developing corporate strategy through planning, programming and budgeting', *Long Range Planning*, 2, no. 3, 1970, pp. 24–30.

33

Forecasting and strategic planning

COLIN ROBINSON

While it is now generally accepted that governments should attempt to forecast trends in the economic environment, in the business world – especially among the medium-sized and smaller companies – there is still a certain amount of scepticism about the value of forecasting. The author argues that forecasting is an essential part of any planning exercise and describes how this technique might be applied to different functional areas of a business. He emphasises, however, that the specific technique used is less important than a scientific and systematic approach to forecasting.

I want to put forward some rather general views on the subject of forecasting and long-range planning, concentrating on the ways in which forecasting can be used by and can be useful to the individual company. As a background for this detailed discussion I start with a brief account of what appears to me to be the underlying philosophy of forecasting and of the way in which forecasting should be approached.

The place of forecasting in business

A mistake which is sometimes made is to believe that forecasting is some specialised and esoteric technique that is practised only in large companies, in government departments and in research institutions, by people who have somehow acquired the gift of looking into the future – through astrology, palmistry, or even economic theory. The rest of humanity, not possessing these magical powers, simply has to accept what the race of forecasters says. In fact, as those attending this kind of seminar will all recognise, forecasting is a much more down-to-earth process than this. In a sense, forecasting is something which comes naturally to all of us as individuals living in an environment dominated by the existence of time. At every moment of time, each of us is having to make forecasts of how the future will turn out, based on his experience of the past. Having made that forecast, he can then plan to meet expected conditions in the future. This is how life goes on – we are all continually making decisions about future actions which are dependent on our estimates of the future conditions which will affect those actions.

The forecasts an individual makes can be very simple, relatively unimportant ones – such as whether a train, an aeroplane or a car will get him to a given spot most quickly. Or they can be the foundation for the kind of vital decision most of us have to make in our mid or late 'teens when we need to decide between different careers. On the basis of our past experience (for example, our performance at school) and the experience of our parents we then have to decide where our best prospects lie – in other words, we need to forecast the earnings and the satisfaction we would derive from each of the different occupations it is within our abilities to take up so that we can choose between them. Of course, most of us do not explicitly make these kinds of forecasts and plans, which have similar characteristics to and are at least as difficult to make as the major investment decisions of a firm. We simply make a judgement based on our best guesses about the future and the best guesses of those who advise us. But the point I want to stress is that this career plan, because it concerns the future, is something that can only be made with the aid of some kind of view of the future, even if only a crude one. If someone decides to become a doctor rather than a lawyer, or teacher, a barber or a dustman, this decision must be based on some kind of estimate of how his life as a doctor will turn out as compared with the alternatives open to him. Of course, it is always possible that the forecast will be wrong and that the prospective doctor would have been happier and/or earned more as a barber, but I am concerned at present with pointing out that forecasts are made rather than with their accuracy.

So far I have been intent on removing some of the mysticism which sometimes surrounds forecasting by trying to show that as individuals we all spend our lives making forecasts and then making plans on the basis of them. Man has a natural need for forecasts and a natural ability to make them, and the institutions which he has set up – such as the modern company or the government – share these needs and abilities. They also have to make forecasts and to plan ahead by making and implementing decisions based on their forecasts.

There are not many people nowadays who would question the forecasting function of the government. For a long time we have been used to budget forecasts for at least a year ahead of how much money is likely to be collected in taxes, how much is likely to be spent by the government, and how much it expects to need to borrow. People have also become used to the idea that the government will attempt to influence the course of the economy – in the budget and at other times – by forecasting what will happen on the basis of existing official policy, and, if it does not like the forecast outcome, altering policy in an effort to shift the economy on to what it considers to be the right lines. Though there are doubts on how good official forecasting has been, there are very few people who would suggest that the government should move out of the economic forecasting business altogether.

In the business world, however, and especially among the medium-sized and smaller companies, there is still a certain amount of scepticism about the value of forecasting. Using the term 'forecasting' in the broad sense in which I have used it so far – as any attempt to take a view of the future – this is not a position which can be maintained. A company, like any other human institution, has to make forecasts. It is continually making estimates of what is likely to happen in the future so that it can decide how much to produce and what to produce, how much to invest in fixed assets and in inventories, how much labour to employ and so on. It makes decisions about the future and therefore it must make forecasts. Even in companies which think they do no forecasting the managers must make forecasts all the time – though rather than looking explicitly at the future they are probably unconsciously making some simple projection into the future of their experience in the recent past.

Nevertheless, though it is true that forecasting is an integral part of business decision taking, one has to admit that there is an element of truth in the arguments of the sceptics because of the fundamental point that forecasting is, strictly speaking, impossible. None of us knows exactly what will happen in the future and so we cannot, except by chance, make forecasts which are right in all respects. Reverting to our previous example of the individual choosing a career on the basis of relatively little knowledge about his own abilities and great uncertainty about the future, he or his advisers obviously need to be gifted and/or fairly lucky if he is to make a wise choice. In business, by systematic accumulation and analysis of knowledge, the amount of uncertainty is typically less than in the career choice case but some uncertainty is inevitably associated with the future. To my mind, one of the unfortunate characteristics of many forecasters is that they tend to assume away the uncertainty of the future. They and their managers expect far too much precision from forecasts. Business forecasting should not be regarded as a means of arriving at a detailed and precise view of the future: it only provides a means of assessing future probabilities in an attempt to reduce the uncertainty which must always surround the future.

From these general remarks about the place of forecasting in business, there are three conclusions which can be drawn:

1 *Forecasting is essential.* One can argue about who should do it, how much time and money should be spent on it and so on, but however it is done, forecasting is inevitably associated with business decision making: short- or long-range plans have to be based on forecasts. The question of the size of the resources it is worth devoting to forecasting is difficult, but one way to proceed is to compare the results of the forecasting system actually employed with what the results would have been had the company used some 'naïve' forecasting technique (e.g. assuming that this year's sales always increase at the same rate as last year's sales). Such a comparison will, over a period of years, enable a judgement to be made on whether or not the forecasting system in use is more than paying for itself in higher profits. It is only worth spending money on forecasting so long as the revenue return from forecasting exceeds that expenditure.

2 *Forecasting has to be carried out systematically.* It is no use relying on intuition. The assumptions made and the logical processes used in constructing the forecast have to be made quite explicit. In this way it is possible to learn from experi-

ence by analysing the reasons why forecasts made at various times in the past have been wrong. This process of holding inquests on forecasts develops one's understanding and judgement and turns people into successful forecasters. Anyone who relies on intuition or on shortcut methods of one sort or another cannot do this and therefore has no means of improving his abilities.

3 *The usefulness of 'single number' forecasts is very limited.* Forecasts which say that this or that 'will' happen, without any qualifications – e.g. that company sales of product X will be 10 per cent higher next year than this – have little value. Such forecasts – which, in effect, try to exclude all uncertainty from the future instead of just trying to reduce uncertainty – are very misleading, because they give the impression that we can be more certain of the future than we really can be. Our only source of knowledge about the future is the past, and history does not repeat itself precisely. Errors are bound to creep into forecasts – for example, because we have not identified all the variables which influence sales of X in the past or because in the future other explanatory variables become important. Strictly, forecasts should always be expressed in terms of probabilities (which must mainly be assessed subjectively) but, of course, one has to be sensible about this and avoid producing vast numbers of statistics all with probabilities attached. This confuses the management of a company. Perhaps the best way of dealing with this problem is for the forecaster to pick on the forecast to which he would assign the highest probability and put this forward as the most probable number, at the same time indicating other fairly probable numbers. Unless one does indicate these other possibilities, there is always a danger that what may be a very uncertain future may appear relatively risk-free because of the manner of presenting the forecast, and the company will not retain the flexibility to deal with the future.

Building a forecasting model

Forecasts enter into every aspect of business life. A company needs forecasts of such factors as financial conditions, prices and wages, and manpower requirements. But perhaps the basic forecast, because all the others depend on it to some extent, is of company sales. For this reason and for the sake of brevity, I shall devote most of the rest of this article to a discussion of a model for forecasting company sales – not directly, but by forecasting the environment within which the company can expect to be operating. In the model future sales are derived from assessing explicitly the future business environment, this environment being defined as those variables not within the immediate control of the company – for example, the growth rate and pattern of development of the economy, government policy, and the actions of its competitors. The idea is to bring together within one model all these external factors and to use them along with information about the actions of one's own company, to forecast sales.

But why is it necessary to go such a long way round to get at a forecast of sales? Many forecasters try to forecast sales (or some other variable) directly by using various statistical devices. It is an inviting thought that by getting hold of a past time series of sales, analysing it to extract a trend (or trends) and some seasonal variation factors and making some kind of projection, one can estimate future sales without going through the tiresome process of actually trying to understand the determinants of sales.

Up to a point purely statistical methods can be useful – for example, in estimating very short-term movements in sales, or sales in markets which are fairly static – and some interesting methods have been developed (e.g. exponentially weighted moving averages of various types). Nevertheless all such methods, however complex the statistical analysis, are naïve methods of forecasting since they tell one nothing at all about the reasons why sales have changed in the past and are expected to change in the future. If sales have varied in the past there must have been reasons for these variations. In principle, one can discover these causes and it is surely only right to make an attempt to isolate these factors and what their effects have been. Unless one can do this, there are serious risks that changes in these underlying factors will go unnoticed and that this will make the forecasts go wrong. I am not arguing against using statistical methods in forecasting: the model explained below depends on using such methods. But forecasting depends on developing an understanding and on learning from experience and unless one is prepared to try to analyse the reasons why things have happened rather than just projecting the past into the future one is unlikely to have much success in forecasting. Statistical knowledge needs to be used as a means of defining useful relationships between variables, not as an attempt to bypass the process of understanding by mechanical extrapolation. Another reason for using the type of model described below is that it is not just a way of estimating future sales. It is useful also for such purposes as exploring the effects on the company of different marketing strategies and is a useful basis for company planning in general.

Working in two environments

The kind of model described below is really just a simple framework, which derives from the economist's view of the company, built round the concept that the individual company is part of two interdependent environments – first, the economy as a whole, and second the market or series of markets into which it sells (defined as the area(s) within which its goods are in close competition with the goods of other companies). Taking the example of a single product company (say) carpets, the forecaster in that company could, in making his estimates, look first of all at the environment which is common to all companies – the economy as a whole – and secondly at the environment which is specific to his own company and its competitors – the carpet market.

A company selling oil would provide a more complicated example. Having looked at the economy as a whole, the company would then have to define the market into which it is selling. In this case, the market would not be oil but 'energy' – including coal, gas and electricity as well as oil – since on the whole people demand energy rather than one particular form of it. In other words, because there are a number of fairly close substitutes for oil, the market has to be extended to include these. Only after examining the energy market could one with any confidence start to analyse the oil market.

This idea of the two environments leads naturally to a three-stage forecasting model. The first stage involves forecasting general economic conditions; the second stage forecasting market demand based partly on the first stage; and the third stage forecasting market share from which, together with the forecast of market demand, the individual company derives its sales.

The economic forecast

Most people recognise now that what happens to the economy at large is likely to have some impact on the operations of their own company. This is particularly true for companies in the UK which, because of the precarious state of the British economy over the past ten or fifteen years, have become used to being affected by the shock effects of economic events and the reactions of successive governments to these.

The first stage in any forecast of the business environment, therefore, needs to be an economic forecast which can then be linked into the other stages of the forecast. To deal first, briefly, with national income forecasting, the economic forecast should contain both an assessment of what will happen in the absence of government action, and an explicit analysis of what the government may do. The result will then provide a forecast of what is likely to happen, after taking into account government policy. I stress this point because government economic policy is in some industries (for example, consumer durables) one of the most important variables affecting the individual company. Moreover, contrary to popular opinion, government economic policy is not quite unpredictable. If you can forecast reasonably well what is likely to happen if the government continues its current policy you can usually guess fairly well in broad outline how it will react to the economic situation which then arises (though this is, of course, one area where it is important to look at the effects of different government policies and assign probabilities to each). Towards the end of the thirteen years of Conservative rule the government's economic policy was, in fact, one of the most easily predictable variables in the business environment.

Forecasting market demand

Given an economic forecast extending a certain period into the future (how long is a question which I will deal with later), the next stage of forecasting involves analysing the future market within which one's company can expect to be operating – that is, to estimate aggregate market demand for the product(s) it is selling. The final stage of forecasting involves the question of the individual company's share of that market in a competitive situation.

The economist's theory of consumer demand provides the best starting point for this aggregate market demand forecast. Many learned books and complex papers spell out this theory, but in essence it all springs from two simple relationships: these are that, given an individual's tastes the main factors affecting his choice of products in the market will be his income and the relative prices of the goods and services available to him. More specifically, the individual's demand for commodity X will be positively related to his income and negatively related to the price of X relative to other goods and services. If my income rises, I will normally buy more of most goods (though there are some exceptions to this) and if the price of some goods rises, compared with other things, I will normally buy less of it than if its price had remained constant.

These two simple relationships represent the point of departure for forecasting aggregate market demand: take the example of a single product company selling a consumer product X. Assume that it has information on the sales of other producers of X for a number of years in the past, which can be added to its sales to give aggregate market demand. This time series of market demand contains certain fluctuations – perhaps it goes up in some years and down in others. Certainly the rate of growth, or of decline, is likely to vary from one year to another.

As an initial assumption the company decides to test the hypothesis that these fluctuations result from fluctuations in consumer incomes and in the price of X relative to other prices (perhaps X has changed in price compared with most closely competing goods Y, or compared with some other consumer goods). Therefore the company gathers information on consumer incomes (such as is published in the UK national income statistics) and on price, and sets the income and price time series alongside the time series of market demand. The company can then carry out a statistical analysis on the effects of income and price on market demand using multiple regression.

Perhaps I should digress briefly to explain the concept of regression in case this is unfamiliar. Regression is a technique for examining relationships between variables and as such is the basis of much econometrics. The idea is probably familiar from school mathematics. Let us suppose we theorise that a variable Y is dependent on another variable X

$$Y = F(X)$$

We want to know whether or not our hypothesis is consistent with what evidence we have and also, if it is, to quantify the relationship between Y and X. We collect data – say time series – on X and Y and plot them on a scatter diagram.

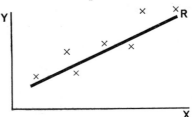

We then calculate the regression line R (line of best fit) which is usually obtained by a technique (described in the standard text books in statistics) that minimises the squares of the deviations in the Y direction, from R. In other words, the regression line is an average, or a summary of the statistical data. The closer the points lie to the line, the better the fit (the less the dispersion around the average). The equation of such a line can be written as

$$Y = a + bX$$

where a = the intercept on the Y axis and b is the slope of the line (the change in Y for a given change in X)

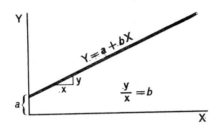

Given any value of X (the 'independent' variable) we can calculate the corresponding value of Y (the 'dependent' variable). Often it is useful to use the logarithms of the two variables so that b represents the percentage change in Y for a given percentage change in X.

The above is simple linear regression with only two variables but the technique can be extended by means of multiple regression to deal with larger numbers of variables. The regression coefficients (b_1 b_2, etc.) will then measure the relationship between the dependent variable and each of the independent variables separately.

To return to our case, our theory is that demand depends on income (Y) and price (P)

$$D = f(Y,P)$$

and if we apply the multiple regression technique we come out with an equation of the form

$$D = a + b_1Y + b_2P$$

From this we can see how close the fit of the equation is and obtain quantitative relationships between income and demand (b_1) with price held constant and between price and demand (b_2) with income held constant. For example, it may be shown that a 1 per cent increase in income in the past has resulted in a 0·7 per cent increase in demand (the b_1 relationship) and that a 1 per cent increase in price has resulted in a 1 per cent reduction in demand (the b_2 relationship). As well as these average relationships between Y and D and between P and D which cover the whole past period under review, we can also estimate the extent to which these relationships have in the past diverged from these averages.

Of course, this type of statistical analysis is much more complicated in practice than I have indicated. It is extremely unlikely that changes in market demand will be completely 'explained' by changes in incomes and prices. For simplicity, I omitted an error term from the multiple regression equation but some error is likely to be present, due, for example, to errors in measuring the variables or to the influence of other explanatory variables (which may or may not be quantifiable). It is probably vain to imagine that, in a field where one is dealing with human behaviour, one is ever going to be able to identify all the independent variables which influence demand, so it is necessary explicitly to recognise the presence of error – in other words, stochastic models have to be used. Then there are some considerable statistical problems involved in making unbiased estimates of the coefficients of the regression equation (for example, because Y and P may themselves be correlated so that it is difficult to obtain estimates of their separate effects). These kinds of statistical problems and presently-available means of dealing with them (by no means as satisfactorily as one would wish) are analysed in textbooks of econometrics such as Johnston, *Econometric Methods*; Klein, *An Introduction to Econometrics*; or Walters *An Introduction to Econometrics* and a simple account of some of the problems is contained in Chapter 1 of *How Business Economists Forecast*, a very useful American book on the practical aspects of business forecasting.[1] At one time the amount of work involved in calculating regression relationships for a lot of variables was also a problem, but fortunately there are now standard multiple regression computer programmes available.

The kind of model-building approach to market demand forecasting which has been suggested thus has its problems. Apart from the statistical problems, in practice income and price movements will generally not be sufficient to explain market demand movements. Other variables, such as the size and composition (in terms of age and class) of the population, and the distribution of income, may influence demand significantly. In some markets changes in taxes or consumer credit terms are among the most important factors affecting demand – in other words, the government's general economic policy directly influences variations in the market. In durable goods markets, the level of stocks will affect demand. Over the long period changes in people's tastes will also affect demand. The situation is further complicated by many companies selling to other companies or to the government or to overseas buyers as well as, or instead of, direct to the final customer in this country, so different economic variables will be necessary to establish demand models for these different markets. Therefore, we will have to add extra variables to the very simplified income-price model described above, if it is to deal with the forecasting problem. But a great deal of the art of setting up the model is to be able to decide which variables are likely to be of real significance in influencing demand and which are not. These problems of the model-limiting approach appear to me to be outweighed by its great advantage – that we have a properly thought-out model which sets out certain assumptions and relationships. When we come to make a forecast we can use these relationships (or modify them if there are good reasons for doing so) along with some assumptions about the income and price variables. We then have a properly constructed forecast, and, if it goes wrong, we will have a means of checking back on why this was – perhaps assumptions about future income and price movements were wrong or perhaps the relationships between D and Y or D and P changed from what they had been in the past. Once we have a model we have a means of learning from experience.

It is the person who takes the trouble to try to understand the situation of his company's product(s) within the country's economy, rather than the pure statistical manipulator, who is likely to achieve most success in forecasting.

Forecasting market share

The final stage of the forecasting process is in many ways the most difficult, but it is also potentially the most rewarding. This is the stage at which, having determined the size of aggregate market demand, we attempt to forecast the individual company's share of that market.

This is also the stage at which many companies give up the attempt to make explicit forecasts in which the assumptions and the logic are made clear. Instead they prefer to rely on the judgement of their marketing staff. This attitude is understandable since the marketing men are obviously in close touch with the market and one might suppose that they are the only people in the company who are in a position to assess future market share. Certainly one cannot forecast market share without the cooperation of the marketing men: nevertheless there is a strong case for making explicit market share forecasts in the same way as I have suggested one should make economic forecasts and market demand fore-casts. The great danger of a judgement forecast is that no one knows the basis for it, and it is therefore impossible for a company's management to know whether the forecast is soundly based or not, or to analyse why it has gone wrong, if it has. Furthermore, one danger specific to market share forecasting lies in the tendency to confuse what can realistically be expected with what one hopes will happen. One can avoid these problems, to some extent, if one makes the market share forecast within a logical framework which minimises the chance of people becoming carried away by their own hopes.

However, I am not in any way suggesting that the use of quantitative tech-niques alone will give good forecasts of market share. Obviously there is a large area in which those closely in touch with the market can exercise 'judgement'. But there is much more scope than is generally recognised for statistical analysis and for ensuring that people's judgement is quantified as far as possible.

One must always precede the use of statistical analysis in this field by develop-ing understanding – understanding of those things which make a company gain or lose sales in the market relative to its competitors – for example, differences in price, in advertising expenditure or advertising effectiveness, in quality, in the numbers of retail or wholesale outlets. One can quantify many of these variables, and it is always worth trying to make estimates of their effects on market share by building a simple model such as I have described above and estimating by multiple regression the coefficients (for example, the effects of price and advertising expenditure on market share). Some people have obtained very helpful results in this way using quite simple models;[2] if one can quantify the effects of such things as price and advertising changes there are, of course, considerable rewards for the company outside the pure forecasting field since this allows one to deal with many problems of marketing strategy. Even if the statistical analysis yields little, it is a great gain just to get everyone who makes market share forecasts to think out the factors which influence that share and then attempt to quantify the effects of those factors.

The broader environment

Though it does not fit neatly into the sales forecasting model I have been describing, there is one other important area for forecasting which I should mention for the sake of completeness, and it is one in which more and more companies who are concerned in long-range planning are becoming interested. This is a natural extension of the model I have been describing, which was based mainly on economic variables which affect sales, into a broader view of the company's future environment – the political situation and the social situation in which it is likely to be operating. Let me pick out the future political situation as an example. In these days of considerable and increasing government intervention in industry, relations with the government are of critical importance for many firms – especially the large ones. If one can make some useful guesses about such things as the likely degree of official intervention in the future, anti-monopoly policy, government policy towards foreign firms in Britain and so on, this is of obvious value in forewarning and forearming one's company.

Setting up a forecasting operation

Two other questions often come up in discussions of forecasting. The first concerns the numbers of people engaged in forecasting in a company; there is always a danger in writing about any management technique that one conjures up a vision of great armies of people busy using it. The sort of forecasting discussed in this article requires only a small amount of manpower. Of course, everybody in a management position in a company is forecasting in one way or another and it is always as well if they recognise the general aims and the pitfalls of forecasting. However, for the type of environmental forecasting discussed here, the company needs only a few professionally trained forecasters. They can provide an explicit forecast of the business environment and how this will affect the company and the mass of operating decisions can then be taken within this framework. The forecasters do not need to be inside the company: small companies will probably find it cheaper to buy forecasts from outside consultants, whereas large companies may prefer to run small forecasting departments. The forecast for the economy, in particular, is something which many companies will prefer to buy from outside rather than employing economists within the firm to make it. Fortunately, the National Institute of Economic and Social Research's *Economic Review* provides an excellent source of short-term economic forecasts.

The second question concerns the lengths of time ahead which one needs to forecast. Most companies need to forecast a year or so ahead (with the year split into months, weeks, days, or hours, as may be relevant) for the purposes of production and sales planning – that is to plan the use of existing capital assets. However, beyond this short-period forecasting, the necessary time period for the forecast is likely to vary greatly from company to company. One of the principal objects of medium- and long-term forecasting is to look beyond the period in which capital equipment can be treated as more or less fixed, to determine how much capital to invest in the longer term; since the periods necessary to plan and construct new capital facilities and for those facilities to bear fruit vary considerably between companies one would expect the forecasting time period to vary also.

Even within a company there may be large variations in the time needed for planning different sorts of facilities. In the oil industry, for example, refineries can be constructed fairly quickly, but investment in new oil fields (which is very risky) needs to be planned many years in advance of the time when the oil supplies may actually be needed in the market place. So once one moves beyond the short run the forecasting time period becomes, to a large extent, a function of the time taken to bring in new fixed assets and the time period over which those assets are likely to be operating.

Conclusions

I have attempted to show that business forecasting is a matter neither of intuition, nor of mechanical extrapolation. It is simply a matter of trying to understand how one's own immediate business world works and how it fits into the wider business world. One may acquire this understanding in a variety of ways – by economic and statistical analysis or by simply sitting down and thinking out what are the relevant variables in a given situation. Always, however, it means approaching the forecast scientifically, quantifying as far as possible, and being willing to learn from experience. The techniques one may use – which usually amount to more or less sophisticated ways of showing whether and to what extent something depends on other things – are, of course, important. But one should not think that after learning a few techniques of forecasting everything is straightforward. It is the relatively slow process of improving one's own understanding which really matters.

References and further reading

1. J. JOHNSTON, Econometric Methods, McGraw-Hill, II.

   L. R. KLEIN, An Introduction to Econometrics, Prentice-Hall, 1962.

   A. A. WALTERS, An Introduction to Econometrics, Macmillan, III.

   W. F. BUTLER and R. A. KAVESH, eds, How Business Economists Forecast, Prentice-Hall, 1966.

2. See, for example, PHILIP KOTLER, 'Marketing mix decisions for new products', Journal of Marketing Research, Feb. 1964.

   JOEL DEAN, 'Does advertising belong in the capital budget', Journal of Marketing, Oct. 1966.

   KRISTIAN PALDA, The Measurement of Cumulative Advertising Effects, Prentice-Hall, 1964; and Economic Analysis for Marketing Decisions, Prentice-Hall, 1969.

   DOYLE L. WEISS, 'An analysis of the demand structure for branded consumer products', Applied Economics, Jan. 1969.

3. B. WAGLE, 'Some recent developments in forecasting techniques', Journal of the Institute of Petroleum, May 1966.

4. C. ROBINSON, 'Some principles of forecasting in business', Journal of Industrial Economics, Nov. 1965.

34

Developing corporate strategy through planning, programming and budgeting*

L. A. DOUGHARTY

The corporation needs a planning framework that aids in clarifying objectives, identifying the alternatives open to the firm, and measuring the effectiveness of those alternatives towards the attainment of the objectives of the corporation. To cope with this problem of integrating objectives (i.e. sales) with resources (in plant, capacity, personnel) the government of the United States — the biggest conglomerate of them all — is employing what is termed 'Planning, Programming and Budgeting' (PPB). This article examines how PPB may be of use to the corporation. The author reviews the features of the system, constructs a PPB planning framework for the corporation, then shows how the system may be applied to a specific strategic problem.

A corporate strategy is a plan for producing and selling selected goods and services to a particular segment of the market. The longrun health of the firm depends upon the implementation of a strategy that selects the proper mix of products that it can both produce and market successfully. Much has been written about market research that selects the type of product and product characteristics that can be successfully marketed. However, the problem of integrating the results of this market research with the resource capabilities of the firm has been given less attention.[1]

This omission may have been partly based on the premise that if a product can be sold, then it can and should be produced. However, with the increase in conglomeration and integration within the corporate structure, product profitability cannot be examined and decided upon in isolation from the rest of the firm. The number of product-mix decisions and the interdependence among decisions has led to a resultant complexity in the development of corporate strategy.

* Any views expressed in this paper are those of the author. They should not be interpreted as reflecting the views of the Rand Corporation or the official opinion or policy of any of its governmental or private research sponsors.

In brief, the corporation needs a planning framework that aids in clarifying objectives, identifying the alternatives open to the firm, and measuring the effectiveness of those alternatives towards the attainment of the objectives of the corporation. To cope with this problem of integrating objectives (i.e. sales) with resources (i.e. plant capacity, personnel), the government of the United States – the biggest conglomerate of them all – is employing what is termed 'planning, programming and budgeting (PPB). To examine how PPB can be of use in the development of corporate strategy, it is necessary to review its most important features. This review is presented in the next section. The concepts of PPB are then applied in the construction of a planning framework for a corporation. This construction illustrates the difference between PPB and the more conventional type of corporate planning, and the implications of those differences on corporate strategy development. To further clarify the PPB process, an example is presented in the last section that employs PPB in strategy development.

Planning, programming and budgeting (PPB)

PPB has two important aspects for developing strategy for the firm.[2] The first aspect is programme structure of development. In the structural part of PPB, the activities of the organisation and the resource consumption of those activities are classified by functional area. Table 34.1 presents a programme structure

Table 34.1 Programme structure of the United States Government

Programme area	Planned budget allocation						
	1969	1970	1971	1972	1973	1974	1975
I. National defence	XX	XX	XX	XX	XX	XX	XX
II. International affairs and finance	XX	XX	XX	XX	XX	XX	XX
III. Space research and technology	XX	XX	XX	XX	XX	XX	XX
IV. Agriculture and agricultural resources	XX	XX	XX	XX	XX	XX	XX
V. Natural resources	XX	XX	XX	XX	XX	XX	XX
VI. Commerce and transportation	XX	XX	XX	XX	XX	XX	XX
VII. Housing and community development	XX	XX	XX	XX	XX	XX	XX
VIII. Health, labour and welfare	XX	XX	XX	XX	XX	XX	XX
IX. Education	XX	XX	XX	XX	XX	XX	XX
X. General support	XX	XX	XX	XX	XX	XX	XX
Total	XX	XX	XX	XX	XX	XX	XX

Source: 'The Federal Program by Function', The Budget of the United States Government, 1969, US Government Printing Office, Washington, DC, 1968, p. 79.

for the US Government. It illustrates how the resources of the government (measured in dollars) are allocated to the various broad programme areas such as national defence, education, etc.

Under each broad programme area, the programmes of the government agencies that contribute towards the attainment of the broad programme area objective would be arrayed. Education programmes, for example, would be arrayed under the education category, rather than under the sponsoring agency. Selecting from among the competing programmes in each broad programme area involves the second aspect of PPB – the analytical part. Analysis is shorthand for a variety of quantitative techniques for exploring the cost and effectiveness of programme proposals over an extended time period.[3] The most prominent example of the use of PPB is in the US Department of Defence, where the new planning structure clarified objectives in defence and pinpointed weaknesses in the then current strategy for defence.

Prior to the introduction of PPB in the Department of Defence in 1961, planning and budgeting were essentially done independently by the three services – the army, the navy, and the air force. In previous times when the objectives of the United States could be stated as supremacy of the land, sea and air, planning by organisation was essentially the same as planning by objectives. However, with the advent of the nuclear weapon, intercontinental missile, and the emergence of the guerrilla, the objectives of the US and the role of the services have changed.

Objectives are now stated in terms of strategic offence, strategic defence, tactical, etc. Each service is no longer solely responsible for the attainment of its own objectives. The navy with its Polaris submarines, and the air force with its land-based intercontinental missiles and bombers, offer alternative ways of gaining strategic superiority. Moreover, the effectiveness of one strategic missile will depend upon not only its own characteristics, but the quality and quantity of the other strategic missiles in the force. The army and navy missile systems must be treated as complements,[4] as well as alternatives in the planning process. The decision on a missile force posture should be made by comparing various mixes of these alternatives, and not by letting each service contribute to this force in isolation from the others.

The complexity of war has also required the close cooperation of the services in the support of each other. Those programmes that are designed to support another service may be unjustly cut back if the services were to plan and budget separately. The problem in the Department of Defence was that the organisational structure did not reflect the objective of the department. The planning and budgeting that was done within the organisational structure, therefore, did not reflect the objectives of the department. PPB corrects this deficiency of the organisational structure in recognising the objectives of the entity. The objectives of the entity prescribe a programme structure (planning and budget format) and the lower levels of organisation compete for resources within that structure.

In the case of the Department of Defence, the programme categories that reflect the military objectives of the US are set by the department and not by the

P

services.[5] The services then compete for funds within these categories on the basis of cost-effectiveness for the limited budget of the department. Moreover, by making alternative and complementary system trade-off decisions explicit in the analytical phase of PPB, the decision maker has a greater realisation of what he can attain and how it can be attained.

The transition of the PPB concept used in government planning to corporate planning is not difficult to make. The parallel between business and war is remarkably close, so it is not surprising that planning techniques of the two can be quite similar. To be more precise about how PPB can be applied in the development of corporate strategy, the next section discusses the PPB process in the context of the corporation and its implications for corporate planning.

Applying PPB to the development of corporate strategy

The two important parts of PPB in the development of corporate strategy were outlined in the previous section. In the first part, structuring of the activities of the corporation along the line of its objectives, several principles must be observed. First, and most obvious, is that the programme structure should reflect the objectives of the firm. Second, the programme categories should be independent so that alternatives can be analysed within one programme category without regard to major effects on the other programme categories; and, third, programme categories should be selected that can reflect complementaries within the system trade-off decisions.

To illustrate how these principles are applied in the structuring process, we have represented a typical corporation that has the facets of both conglomeration and vertical integration. Fig. 34.1 presents the organisation of the firm which we will call the General Products Corporation (GPC). GPC consists of three subsidiaries: subsidiary 1 produces two brands, X and Y, of essentially the same product for the same general market segment – toothpaste could be the example. Subsidiary 2 produces product Z which is used in the manufacture of both X and Y, but also has other industrial uses. Subsidiary 3 manufactures a product, W, that does not compete with any of the other products. Each subsidiary is organised into the four functional divisions – marketing, sales, manufacturing, and finance. Subsidiary 1 is further broken down below the functional level by type of product and then by sales district.

Budgeting under this type of organisation is likely to start with the sales estimates that are made at the district level. Estimates are then further refined in the finance department to correspond with its view of what can be sold and what can be produced. These sales and production estimates are then the basis for the more detailed budget for the marketing division (what type of promotion will be needed?), the sales division (how much selling expense will be involved at this sales level?), manufacturing division (what will the production schedule and cost be?), and the finance division (what will be the cash flow requirements?).[6]

Fig. 34.1 The organisation of General Products Corporation

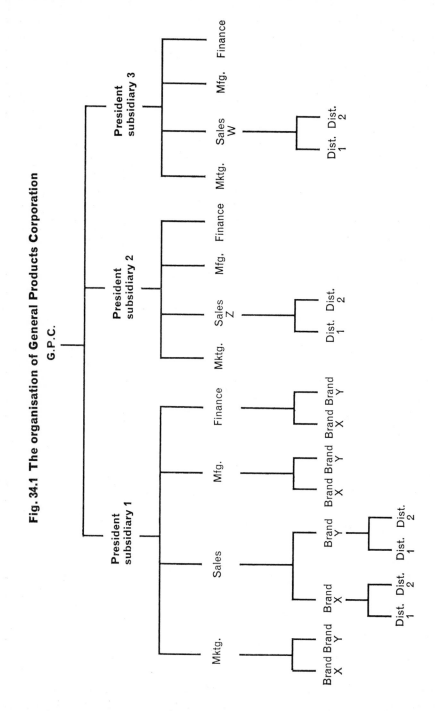

Under this type of planning sytem, three important features of a planning process are omitted. First, alternatives that contribute to the same objective are not explicitly analysed together. For example, sales estimates for product X and Y in each of the districts are made independently. Certainly the sales of X have an impact on the sales of Y, since they are direct competitors. The interdependence of the sales of these two products mean that profit rates for the products cannot be estimated independently. A resource allocation method using independent estimates of profit rates would not necessarily tend to maximise actual profits. Secondly, the sales estimates are made without regard to the complementary systems such as marketing and pricing policy that are made independently in the marketing and finance divisions. A planning system that does not provide for the thorough examination of various combinations of sales, marketing, and pricing policy narrows the perspective of top management and eliminates what could be highly profitable alternatives from consideration. Third, no attention is given to alternatives that are not already part of the firm. The systematic evaluation of the possibilities for replacing or adding new products is not an integral feature of this type of planning system.

One programme structure for the GPC could look something like that presented in Table 34.2.[7] The programme areas correspond to the product areas. Each product area is nearly independent from the other. That is, decisions in one area should not have a large impact upon programmes in the other product areas. This format arrays all of those programmes that compete with each other in the same category. Various mixes of products X and Y, for example, would be evaluated for their effectiveness in penetrating the market in each sales district. Regional differences in income, sales history, and distribution facilities would be considered in the evaluation of the alternative product mixes. The allocation of the scarce resource, in this case money, can be portrayed in this framework for as many alternatives as management wants to evaluate. Using rate of return as a criterion for programme selection, adequate analysis within the framework of the programme structure should provide for a production mix tailored to the desires of the market and the capabilities of the corporation. In the planning by organisation presented previously, each product pushes for large production, independent of the plans for the other product. A satisfactory mix of the two products is not assured because attaining such a mix is not an integral feature of that type of planning process.

The structure also reveals how complementary systems fit within the programme structure. A programme for product X, for example, is not a sales projection but consists of elements from sales, marketing, and manufacturing. In this programme formulation alternative types of sales and marketing strategies can be compared, for resource requirements and relative effectiveness. This is contrasted to the previous case where marketing services were designed after sales quotas were made.

There is increasing evidence that the necessity of central planning for organisationally independent parts but operationally dependent parts is being recognised. Several of the major US airlines have recently reorganised their marketing efforts to have the previously independent sales, passenger service, scheduling, and advertising departments in one department and under one man.[8] Whether this change will make actual passenger service more like advertised passenger service, one can only hope for. In any event, planning will not be done separately by the advertising and passenger service groups. The new head of the marketing department will now have the explicit trade-off decisions concerning the relative effectiveness of advertising and passenger service in increasing passenger revenue.

To reiterate, in strategy development and programme selection, the components of the business system must be evaluated together to achieve a proper mix of the complementary systems.

The implication of vertical integration for corporate policy is also made explicit within this framework. Under programme area II, the corporation analysed the effects of selling product Z to subsidiary 1 or selling the product to other industrial users. The alternatives are analysed in the usual type of 'make or buy' analysis. New programmes can be introduced within the existing programme categories or by creating new programme categories. Where they compete within the product areas already established as programme categories, they are included as a new alternative. If new product areas are proposed, new categories are established, and alternatives are selected from within those new categories.

The longer term implications of current budget decisions are reflected in the programme structure. Table 34.2 reflects the net demand for funds (expenditures-revenue) for the next ten years for this set of programmes. The net change in scarce resources shown in the programme structure need not be money. Forecasts of the needs for personnel, raw materials, and manufacturing capacity could just as easily be shown if there were some indication that these resources could not be purchased at the prices reflected in the net funds forecast.

Though the most effective mix may have been selected within each category, it is likely that there are not enough resources to fund all of the selected alternatives. The final decision on the corporate strategy must be made centrally. The amount of funds committed to each product area would depend upon the amount of funds available and the rate of return of the individual programmes within each category. Alternatives with low rate-of-return would be eliminated until the resources required by the remaining alternatives match the resources available to the firm. The marginal contribution of acquiring more capital can be seen by examining the different programmes that could be adopted if the capital constraint were relaxed.

In summary, PPB is a process for systematically arraying and selecting programmes. It presents choices to the decision maker by making the alternatives explicit. It puts the decision in proper context by ensuring that alternatives that contribute to the same objective are analysed together; and, finally, PPB illuminates the decision in its analytical part by examining the relative effectiveness of the alternative and its total system cost.

Table 34.2 Programme structure for GPC

	Net funds year									
	I	2	3	4	5	6	7	8	9	10

I. *Product area 1 (product X & Y)*
   District 1
      Product X
         Costs
            Sales
            Marketing
            Manufacturing
         Revenue

            Net funds
      Product Y
         (Same as product X)
   District 2
      (Same as district 1)
II. *Product area 2 (product Z)*
   District 1
      (Same as district 1, product
        area 1)
   District 2
      (Same as district 1, product
        area 1)
   Sales to subsidary 1
III. *Product area 3 (product W)*
   District 1
      (Same as district 1, product
        area 1)
   District 2
      (Same as district 1, product
        area 1)
IV. *General support*

         Net funds required

The next section presents an example that integrates the two components of PPB, programme structure and programme analysis, in strategy development. Since PPB has only been formally applied in government,[9] the selection of a comprehensive example is somewhat restricted. The example presented concerns the development of a strategy for a state government in the field of health. The processes of decision making in the public and private sector should be similar enough to make the example a relevant illustration for corporate planning.[10]

Example of strategy development

One of the more rural states in the US is concerned that its citizens are not getting adequate health care. Indicators of the health of the community such as infant mortality, reported syphilis cases, and mortality rate justify this concern. It is felt that the main reason for this lack of adequate health care is the shortage of doctors. The doctors *per capita* in the state is only 25 per cent of the national average. The government, therefore, adopts as an objective the increase in the stock of doctors in the state.

To achieve this increase, programmes are proposed by the university, the Health Department, the Welfare Department and the Administration Department. Without PPB, each department would make a decision on these programmes without regard to the relative effectiveness of each of the competing programmes. With PPB, each of the alternative programmes are arrayed and analysed together

Table 34.3 Abbreviated health programme category

I. *Increasing the medical personnel programme*
  A. Doctors
      1. Training facilities (university)
      2. Pecuniary reward for medical service in state (administration)
      3. Lower entrance requirements (health)
      4. Health insurance (welfare)
      5. Construction of health facilities (health)
II. . . .

to develop the most viable strategy for the state. Table 34.3 presents the abbreviated Health Programme Category that reflects only the programme for increasing medical personnel.

Programme 1 would have the state increase its training of doctors at the University Medical School. Programme 2 is a method of raising the compensation to the doctor, sponsored by the Administration Department. Programme 3 would lower the requirements for obtaining a licence to practise medicine in the state. Programme 4 would increase the demand for health services by providing health insurance, and subsequently increase the supply of doctors within the state. Programme 5 would build facilities for the practice of medicine. The state would then lease these facilities to doctors at a moderate price. Facilities are used as an indirect subsidy to attract and retain doctors.

The structure exemplifies what is meant by arraying all alternative programmes together. While medical education is often considered in the budget deliberations of the university (where the tradeoff is with other types of education), the real impact of this education is in the health area. Therefore, the medical school competes for resources with alternatives for increasing the health care for the community and not against programmes for raising the quality and quantity of education within the state.

Before the analysis proceeds, it is decided that programmes 3 and 5 are untenable solutions. Programme 3 is eliminated because the state has delegated its responsibility in setting standards to the medical profession itself. The state does not feel that it wants to incur the political costs of reassuming this responsibility. Programme 5 is eliminated because there is no way of insuring that it will increase the number of doctors in the state. It is more likely that current residents will apply for the better facilities, so that there may be no net change in the number of doctors in the state. Alternative 4 is set aside for the moment since the Federal Health Insurance programme has not been finalised and therefore the possible course for state action in this field is unclear.

Alternatives 1 and 2 are analysed to test their feasibility. The first step in the analysis is the construction of a model that will estimate the number of doctors in the state as a function of the number trained at the medical school and the average income of a doctor in the state expressed as a percentage of the national average income of this group. These are considered the policy variables in this analysis. (Policy variables are ones that the state can change through a change in policy.)[11]

One alternative for increasing the stock of doctors is to double the capacity of the medical school. It will be three years before facilities can be built, and doctors recruited, and larger classes can be admitted. Therefore, it will be ten years (three years for start-up, four years of medical school, and three years of residency) altogether before this increase in production has any effect on the health of the community. The estimated increase in the stock of doctors in the state using this alternative is shown in Table 34.4.[12] The incremental system cost to the state for this alternative is also shown in Table 34.4.

Table 34.4 shows that the state will be spending $80 million to procure this increase in doctors over the next sixteen years. If this money were spent to increase the average income of the doctor, what would be the increase in the doctor stock? To make this estimate, it is assumed that the annual sum of $5 million is distributed among the doctor stock, $D(t)$, over and above keeping pace with an income that is 80 per cent of the national average. This alternative produces the doctor stock shown in Table 34.4. Both alternatives cost the same but have different expenditure time patterns, as shown in the table.

The figure shows that the alternative, to increase the income ratio, is the dominant solution. That is, for every year under consideration, more doctors are practising in the state under this alternative than if the alternative to increase enrolment at the medical school were adopted. However, there are several arguments against such a proposal.

Even if the model is correct, there is no assurance that the doctors will be distributed within the state to service those in the rural areas where the medical personnel shortage is greatest. Secondly, if the state starts giving tax concessions to one profes-

Table 34.4 Stock of doctors

Year	No change in policy No. doctors	Increase no. of graduates No. doctors	Increase	Cost (m. $)	Increase income ratio No. doctors	Increase	Cost (m. $)
0	1500	1500	0	10	1500	0	5
1	1452	1452	0	10	1481	29	5
2	1411	1411	0	10	1467	56	5
3	1378	1378	0	9	1457	79	5
4	1351	1351	0	2	1450	99	5
5	1330	1330	0	3	1447	117	5
6	1314	1314	0	4	1446	132	5
7	1303	1303	0	4	1446	143	5
8	1295	1295	0	4	1449	154	5
9	1290	1290	0	4	1453	163	5
10	1288	1344	56	4	1458	170	5
11	1288	1386	98	4	1464	176	5
12	1290	1420	130	4	1471	181	5
13	1294	1448	156	4	1478	184	5
14	1298	1471	173	4	1486	188	5
15	1303	1491	187	4	1495	192	5
				80		2063	80

sion, it may be forced through political pressure to give it to other groups – teachers and engineers, for example. Thirdly, it may prompt other states (i.e. competitors) to grant equal subsidies so that the end result would be higher cost for doctors and no change in the stock of doctors. Lastly, the high cost of \$38 800 per doctor-year seems high. The state is subsidising all the doctors but only influencing migration on the margin. For these reasons, this alternative is not considered feasible.

The analysis has been enlightening to the decision maker, even though its results were not adopted. It showed that subsidising all doctors in the state was not a practical way to increase the doctor stock. Since the graduates of the medical school are the most mobile in the first three years, and this mobility is the most sensitive to income, it seems reasonable to subsidise this group alone. Using this approach, a third alternative is generated. It is suggested that tuition to the medical school be raised to more closely approximate the cost of that education, while at the same time offering student loans to those who qualify for entry into the school. The loans can then be forgiven for years of service in the state (e.g. 25 per cent is forgiven for each year of service in the state).

If the medical school graduate perceives a 10 per cent increase in his salary through this mechanism, the model predicts the doctor stock as shown in Table 34.5. Since the incremental cost to implement this alternative is low – tuition is almost free currently – the alternative is adopted. Moreover, if the programme succeeds, increasing the size of the medical school should be reviewed since indigenous production of doctors would be more efficient in increasing the stock of doctors than previously.

Table 34.5 Forecast stock of doctors

Year	Number of doctors	Net increase	Cost (m $)
0	1500	0	·1
1	1459	7	·1
2	1424	13	·1
3	1396	18	·1
4	1373	22	·1
5	1356	26	·1
6	1342	28	·1
7	1333	30	·1
8	1327	32	·1
9	1323	33	·1
10	1322	34	·1
11	1322	34	·1
12	1324	34	·1
13	1328	36	·1
14	1332	36	·1
15	1337	34	·1

It has been noticed that increasing the doctors *per capita* is not the objective of the state. The real objective of the state is to ensure that reasonable health standards are maintained for all its citizens. The analysis presented was too narrow in its focus when it accepted the stock of doctors as a proxy measure of the attainment of the real objective. Further analysis in this area must include the other alternative of broadening health insurance coverage so that the disadvantaged can have access to medical resources that the state may create.

This example is not similar to those found in many textbooks. No easy solution is presented. The goal and objective formulation are not clearcut. It represents the type of thinking that PPB should force upon the analyst and the decision maker. What are my objectives? Am I measuring the right thing? It is an iterative process by which many alternatives can be generated and evaluated in the framework of the objectives of the firm. It does not ensure success, but if performed properly, it does ensure illumination.

Notes

1. General Motors' strategy for penetrating the automobile market was based on producing automobiles in all price ranges that were economically feasible. This strategy has been generally credited for General Motors' success in the automobile

industry. The acceptance of the General Motors' cars showed that the public preferred the product and price differentiation offered by General Motors over the black, low-cost vehicle produced by Ford. Just as important, however, was that General Motors also had the resources to implement this strategy, since it was a conglomeration of automobile manufacturers that already produced cars in most of the price ranges. (See A. P. SLOAN, *My Years with General Motors*, McFadden-Bartell Corporation, 1965, chap. 4, 'Product policy and its origins'.)

2. PPB also includes a third part that is an information system that reports on the cost and effectiveness of the implemented plans. While this is an important aspect for strategy implementation, it is not necessary in the strategy development phase. For a fuller exposition of the concept of PPB, see D. NOVICK, *Program Budgeting: Program Analysis and the Federal Budget*, 2nd edn, Harvard University Press, 1967.

3. See E. S. QUADE and W. I. BOUCHER, *Systems Analysis and Policy Planning: Applications in Defense*, American Elsevier Publishing Co., Inc., 1968.

4. Complementary systems are those that contribute to the same objective and where the total output of the two programmes is not a linear combination of the separate outputs of each programme. For example, if the output of two complementary programmes were O_1 and O_2 the output of the combined programmes might be expressed as equal to
$$O_T. = O_1 + O_2 + KO_1O_2, K > 0$$
Since the resource allocation process is designed to maximise output for a given level of inputs, failure to recognise complementary systems will mean a degradation in the performance of the resource allocation process.

5. These military objectives are set within the guidelines of the national security policy established by the President and Congress.

6. See MOORE and JAEDIKE, *Managerial Accounting*, South-Western Publishing Co., Cincinnati, 1963, chap. 16, 'Budgets – sales and Production'. In their chapter the authors explicitly separate the type of budgeting process described above from the broader aspects of business planning. However, the annual budget is the financial translation of the first year of the plan. Therefore, it is difficult to separate the budgeting and the planning process.

7. There are many possible programme structures — one for each set of corporate objectives. For example, the programming structure for the corporation interested in public service projects will certainly look different from that of the corporation that believes that the conduct of such projects is not a proper function of private business.

8. CAROL J. LOOMIS, 'As the world turns on Madison Avenue', *Fortune Magazine*, Dec. 1968, p. 193.

9. The concepts of PPB have been used in industry without being documented. For a fuller discussion, see NOVICK, *op. cit.*, 'Introduction: origins and history of program budgeting'.

10. For a discussion of the differences in the corporate and government planning environment, see CHARLES HITCH and RONALD MCKEAN, *Economics of Defense in the Nuclear Age*, The Rand Corporation, 1960, chap. 7.

11. The model is of the form:

$$D(t) = D(t - 1) - D(t - 1)E(P) + d(t - 1)I(P) + G(t - 3)S(P) - R(t) \text{ where}$$

      $D(t)$ = stock of doctors in the state in year t,

         P = ratio of average doctor's income to national average,

      $E(P)$ = percentage of doctors in the state that immigrate as a function of P,

  $d(t - 1)$ = stock of doctors in the country in year t − 1,

      $I(P)$ = percentage of national doctor stock that immigrates to the state as a function of P,

$G(t - 3)$ = number of graduates from the medical school in year t − 3,

    $S(P)$ percentage of graduates that immigrate from the state before three years after graduation (i.e. before they complete residency and can be licensed),

    $R(t)$ = number of doctors that retire from active practice in year t.

12. The increase is the number of doctors in the state using the alternative minus the number of doctors in the state with no change in policy. The projection of the number of doctors if there is no change in policy is shown in Table 34.4.

PART VII

Conclusion

35

The future of corporate strategy

BERNARD TAYLOR

Mr Taylor reviews the present state of the art of corporate strategic planning and discusses future trends in the development of the subject as a field of business practice and as a topic for research, teaching and consultancy.

Definition

Whatever terms we use, it seems to me that we are concerned with the application of rational, systematic, or scientific approaches to the work of top management, i.e. individuals, boards of directors, or executive committees whose job it is to manage a total business or profit centre. This may be a small- or medium-size firm, or it may be a division, a subsidiary company, or a large diversified multinational organisation with an income as large as a sizeable nation.

The term 'corporate strategy' is often used to describe this area because modern approaches to the study of business policy or general management have tended to focus around the idea of 'developing and implementing corporate strategy'.

The state of the art

Business policy

'Business policy' has been studied at Harvard since 1911, and it is a core course in major US business schools, yet it has only recently been studied analytically. Traditionally, business policy has been studied through the discussion of descriptive cases, and the Harvard School stated that general management is in no sense a discipline.[1] As recently as 1967, the Harvard Business School faculty decided against the idea of starting a new academic Journal of Business Policy, because they felt that there was not sufficient theory and good research available in the area.

425

Corporate planning

However, the 1960s have seen a growth of interest in systematic approaches to corporate strategy among large business firms and consultants. Under the banner of corporate planning or long-range planning, 'blue chip' companies in industrialised countries have established planning committees, and planning departments in an attempt to produce coordinated plans for their businesses.

Consultancy

Simultaneously, major consultancy organisations such as McKinsey, Boston Consulting Group, and Stanford Research Institute, have built a worldwide reputation by specialising in top management, corporate strategy, and long-range planning, rather than competing in the longer-established fields of management accounting and management services. This shift of emphasis to strategy formulation has led to a reorientation of the approach to top management consulting. Studies of the prices of major US consultants in the early 1960s suggested a changeover from an *ad hoc* situation-analysis or 'size up' to a continuous process of strategic appraisal (see Figs. 35.1 and 35.2).[2]

Theory and research

This outburst of activity in corporate planning has prompted a response from universities, business schools and research institutes, and a wide range of books, articles, and new journals have been published about long-range planning and business policy.[3]

Two new trends are apparent in the literature on formulating and implementing corporate strategy. Management scientists have attempted to model the process of strategy formulation to the point where no self-respecting article is without its flow diagram. On the other hand, the behavioural scientists have tried to improve the implementation of plans by encouraging discussion about the effect on motivation of different styles of leadership, and by emphasising the need for 'change programmes' designed to survey, diagnose, and solve the human relations problems which exist in an organisation.

Planning in practice

Current research into corporate planning suggests the following conclusions:[4]

1 *Corporate planning is rapidly becoming accepted in industrialised countries throughout the world as fundamental to good management in a large progressive organisation.*
Corporate planning has grown with the speed of previous management fashions, such as work study, operational research and marketing. New management theories and practices seem to follow a similar pattern of diffusion. They usually start in large technology-based companies in the United States and spread quickly

to large manufacturing organisations in Europe. Only in the second phase are they taken up by other organisations in the economy, i.e. central government departments, the service industries, small businesses and local government.[5]

In the case of long-range planning, the major agents for the new approach have been first American and later British consultancy organisations.

2 *Corporate planning is at an early stage of development.*
Recent studies in Europe and in the United States show that a small proportion of companies are practising corporate planning, and even in those companies with a reputation for planning, i.e. the large manufacturing companies, the activity is in the start-up phase. This phase has these characteristics:

- top management is paying lip service to the idea, but it is still uncommitted
- line management is in the process of being sold the idea, and planning is not yet a part of its way of managing
- the main effort is on putting together a system of plans which can be consolidated and compared on a company-wide basis.
- the information system is tailored to the needs of the accounting group and new information has to be generated in the form of profit contribution by product, personnel statistics, and information about markets and the business environment.

3 *Outside the financial area, planning is largely informal and short term.*
In the present state of the art, corporate planning appears most frequently as extended budgeting. The emphasis is placed on operational plans and budgets, and strategy is neglected. Outside traditional economic forecasting, environmental analysis is rudimentary. Technological forecasting and sociopolitical forecasting are in the pilot stage. Market analysis and product planning are generally unsophisticated although there are important exceptions, especially among large consumer goods manufacturers. Plans for personnel tend to be in broad quantitative terms and it is still difficult to find evidence of formal planning for personnel strategy, industrial relations policies, and management development. Planning is probably weakest of all in the area of new ventures, i.e. planning for research and development, new product development, acquisitions, mergers, and international operations.

4 *There is ample evidence of planning failures and false starts.*
The main reasons for failures seem to be:

- an attempt to start up planning in a functional area such as finance and accounting, marketing, or management services and computers, without first winning the support of top management
- sometimes the corporate planner sees his role as doing the planning rather than coordinating the planning efforts of operating management. This is seen by line management as ivory tower planning and empire building
- frequently, planning is introduced by an outside consultant as a package rather than as a process, and not enough effort is made to produce a planning

system which is tailor made to meet the management style of top management and the needs of the organisation. Often the consultant puts in a system of planning which is too sophisticated and too detailed for the management who must maintain it

● the most common reason for planning failure is simply that top management and line management do not understand the concept, do not see the need for the enormous effort which is involved in planning, and either will not, or cannot, develop the skills – which are required before useful long-range planning can take place. As one planner is quoted as saying, 'The Board thought they could buy six yards of corporate planning'.[6]

5 *Corporate planning often requires a fundamental change of attitude on the part of management.* The attempt to produce formal written-down plans and to use them as a basis for managing a business involves certain assumptions about top management which hold true for only a few companies.

(a) *Top management must be able and willing to produce an explicit strategy.* This implies a capacity for analytical thinking, candour and self-confidence, which is rare.

(b) *Top management and operating management must be prepared to work as a team,* to enter into a dialogue about the objectives of the organisation and the likely directions for development. This kind of dialogue, e.g. between group headquarters and division management, is only possible when there is fairly close understanding and trust. Otherwise, planning becomes a gaming or bargaining process with everyone keeping cards up his sleeves.

(c) *Corporate planning is in effect a philosophy of change.* Its aim is to set up a process which will enable the organisation to adapt continually to changes in the environment. It will work properly therefore only if the management generally feel that there is a need for change. The need for a change of attitude was emphasised in a recent investigation which showed that in a sample of companies practising long-range planning, one-third had had recent changes in top management.[7] There is a suggestion here that a major crisis sometimes is required before management will make the effort to adopt long-range planning.

Teachers and courses

There are some similarities between the position of marketing in 1960, and the position of corporate strategy in 1970. In 1960 marketing was already well established in leading US companies such as Proctor and Gamble, and General Electric, and it was becoming accepted in large consumer goods companies in Europe. The development of marketing as a business practice and as an academic discipline in Britain proceeded slowly from 1960 when there were 2000 part-time students, no full-time students, no full-time lecturers, and no marketing professors to 1970, when there were 14 000 part-time marketing students, around 500 full-time students, about 100 full-time marketing lecturers, and eight marketing professors. The Marketing Society was established at about the same time. The *British Journal of Marketing*, an academic journal, appeared in 1968.

In 1970 corporate planning was well established in leading US companies and was becoming accepted in large progressive companies in Europe. In Britain, the development of courses in corporate strategy and corporate planning may be expected to grow slowly from the present situation, i.e. around 2000 part-time students, about 100 to 200 full-time students, 20 to 30 full-time lecturers, and 1 professor of business policy. The long-range planning society was established in 1967, and now has over 1000 members. The *Long-range Planning Journal* appeared in 1968, and the *Journal of Business Policy*, an academic journal, in 1970. There are at present three separate study groups examining the future development of teaching and research in corporate strategy.[8]

Future development

The prospects for corporate strategy and corporate planning look good, both as an area of business practice, and as a field for consultancy, teaching and research. The question is how and at what rate will corporate strategy develop? We may consider this question from several points of view:

- the functions of top management
- developments in basic disciplines, and business functions
- management in different industrial sectors
- management in different geographical areas.

The functions of top management

There are many variations on the Harvard approach to general management. The following list seeks to combine the Harvard models with the basic elements of corporate planning.

1 Environmental appraisal.
2 Company appraisal.
3 Objectives and policies.
4 Strategies and plans.
5 Organisational structure.
6 Executive development and motivation.
7 Management information and control.
8 New ventures.

1 ENVIRONMENTAL APPRAISAL

Interesting developments may be expected over the next decade in long-range forecasting. The broad lines of advance are already established, i.e. the forecasting of alternative futures or sociotechnological systems.

Long-range forecasting studies. Recent studies by the OECD and the Council of Europe,[9] indicate the growing expenditure and the wide range of institutions active in long-range forecasting. Two broad types of consultancy are available – the 'package' of reports and advisory services such as the Stanford Research Institute Long-Range Planning Service which is bought for an annual fee, and the special investigation which may be circulated among a syndicate of non-competitive clients. Long-range forecasting studies have already been completed for the watch industry, medicine in the 1990s, the computer industry, space satellites, the ocean environment, and the household in the year 2000.[10] Another aspect of work in this area is the construction of econometric models for national economies and for free trade areas such as the EEC.

Impressive progress has been made in the past decade in the development of forecasts for technology. The stage is set for further development and research in sociopolitical forecasting and the development of marketing models which will enable companies and government departments to simulate the behaviour of consumers, competitors, and national governments.

2 COMPANY APPRAISAL

A major advance in recent years has been the changeover from an *ad hoc* situation analysis, or 'size up' to continuous strategic appraisal (see Figs. 35.1 and 2).[11]

Analysis of strengths and weaknesses. Even so, the assessment of company strengths and weaknesses is still virtually at the check list stage. The McKinsey Economic Analysis[12] and the Stanford Research Institute SOFT (Strengths – Opportunities – Faults – Threats) analysis are representative of the present state of the art.

Inter-firm comparisons. One important assessment technique which offers much room for development is inter-firm comparisons. There is ample scope for professional institutes, industrial associations, and consultants to provide comparative business ratios for particular sectors of industry. Within larger firms, the inter-branch comparison will probably be used more widely.

3 OBJECTIVES AND POLICIES

The theory and practice of setting company objectives seems likely to change radically over the next decade. The traditional profit criteria are increasingly being questioned because they are clearly at odds with the personal values of managers and with considerations of social responsibilities.

Assessing personal values. The Harvard Business policy approach includes considerations of 'personal values' but it is only in recent years that specialists have attempted to assess the personal values of managers and relate them to business objectives and strategies. We may be approaching the time when consultants will be able to assess the personal values of a top management team and so help in the formulation of corporate objectives which represent a fair consensus of management viewpoints.[13]

Fig. 35.1 Sizing up the situation of the company as a whole

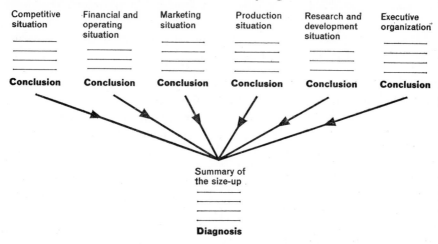

Fig. 35.2 New approach to strategy formulation

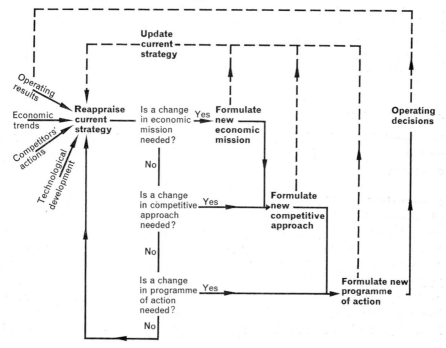

Social responsibilities. The 1960s have seen a social reaction against business and an increased concern that business enterprises should help to preserve the 'quality of life'. Possibly social priorities are changing, and as people become more affluent, so they place a relatively higher priority on non-economic considerations such as preserving the environment.[14]

Government planning. As business organisations get bigger and more powerful, inevitably government becomes more involved with business. It seems inevitable therefore that businessmen will have to become more familiar with governmental techniques of planning, programming, and budgeting, with considerations of social cost and social profit, cost-benefit analysis, and cost-effectiveness analysis. Businessmen may cherish the myth that businesses exist for the good of the shareholders. In practice, it is clear that in the 1970s, businesses will be run for the benefit of other stakeholders too. The various interest groups are organising to make their influence felt; the shop floor worker, the white collar workers, the customers, institutional shareholders, large distributors, suppliers, national and local government, and the public.[15]

Survey research. Survey research techniques are now being used more widely to keep top management in touch with influential groups inside and outside the company. In the next decade, shareholder surveys, employee surveys, and public opinion polls must surely become a regular feature of corporate life.[16]

Worker participation. Worker participation is another important trend which shows every sign of growing. Already major companies are abolishing the distinction between hourly paid and monthly paid workers. We may presumably expect to see more experiments with co-partnership employee shareholding, and worker directors on the way towards a form of business organisation which is more compatible with modern democracy.[17]

4 STRATEGIES AND PLANS

Igor Ansoff has analysed the process of strategy formulation rigorously.[18] The next stage appears to be to simulate the process of strategy formulation by computer.

Corporate planning models. Some progress is being made in the use of corporate planning models which attempts to include explicit judgements about the firm's external environment, the possible reactions of the work force, and other interested parties. One of the most sophisticated of such models is in use at Anheuser Busch,[19] and there is evidence that a substantial group of companies in the United States and in Europe are experimenting with the use of simulation models which allow the executive to examine the financial implications of a much larger number of alternatives than would be possible without the computer.[20] However, so far there seems to be no system of logic capable of conducting a search process for business ideas, nor is it realistic at this time to involve the computer in the formulation of objectives and strategies on the basis of which business ventures will be assessed. There is a considerable difference between actual organisational objectives, and the kinds of goals which tend to be used in operational research techniques. However, considerable progress is being made in the use of operational research models – for financial planning, and for planning and scheduling production and transportation systems.[21] In the next ten years, it will probably become standard practice in large companies for executives to model parts of the planning process and examine the implications of alternative strategies on remote access terminals.

5 ORGANISATION STRUCTURE

At present companies seem to arrive at organisational structures by a process of trial and error. Fashions change from centralisation to decentralisation and back again. The current vogue is for divisions based on business areas except where problems of transfer pricing and group control become too severe. Indeed, the corporate planning movement may be seen partly as an attempt to ensure some semblance of coordination between divisions and product groups in highly diversified organisations.[22]

The 'theory of corporate development'. During the 1960s, some progress has been made in the development of theories about organisation. A theory of corporate development seems to be emerging which relates different organisational structures to companies at different stages of development. It is possible that in the 1970s, this theory will be more widely accepted, and substantiated by research which relates appropriate systems of executive development, executive compensation, and management information and control to organisations at certain stages of growth. We have at least the origin here of a system for classifying organisation.[23]

Project groups. An interesting new trend in organisation structures is the appearance of more flexible organisation structures which ignore theories about responsibility and authority and enable project groups to form as required. Matrix organisations and venture groups are one symptom of this approach, which aims to make large organisations more entrepreneurial and innovative whilst at the same time maintaining the usual advantages of large-scale operations.

This arises partly from attempts by top management to create more innovative organisations. One result of this concern may be the more extensive use of group task force for new product development, merger and acquisition, organisational development and other changes which may be crucial to the future survival of the business, but cannot easily be handled by one department within the organisation. In other words, it may be necessary to create a separate organisation which will be concerned with moving the organisation to a desired future state, because most established organisations are designed to manage an existing system, and they seem to be particularly inefficient at innovation.[24]

6 EXECUTIVE DEVELOPMENT AND MOTIVATION

The field of executive development and organisational development seems to be earmarked for rapid growth.

Executive development. Good management is one competitive advantage which every company must try to achieve, and such evidence as there is suggests that even large sophisticated companies are only now beginning to use modern techniques to forecast manpower requirements, to plan for succession, and to identify and develop management potential.[25]

Recent surveys of British companies suggest that under 10 per cent of British managers receive even a one-week management course each year; the vast majority of managers are regarded as untrained and untrainable.[26] The picture is rapidly changing. The market for external management courses is doubling every five years, and internal training is growing much faster.[27] By 1980, surely every large company will have an executive development service, as an established arm of the corporate planning and development activity.

Organisational development. Another hopeful sign is the use of behavioural scientists in a small number of US and European companies and a much wider use of behavioural science techniques, mainly in the form of 'packages' such as the managerial grid and Kepner Tregoe. Possibly management by objectives also in some form may be classified under this general category which is sometimes called organisational development.[28]

One aim of organisation development specialists is to produce and implement programmes for organisational change and it is generally held that managers who are called upon to implement such programmes should be asked to participate in the planning process. Organisational development seems likely to change the style of management, and therefore the style of planning in many organisations before the end of the decade. This will make the task of corporate planning far more complex. One senior executive said recently of a company undertaking an organisation development exercise which had taken over three years: 'We have the largest planning group in the country. We have 400 executives involved in planning.' In fact, these managers in their work teams had been asked to develop five-year plans for their part of the organisation. On the other hand, providing the process can be adequately coordinated and controlled, one might expect that the plans which are produced are more likely to be carried out than plans developed under a more autocratic régime.

Executive incentive schemes. Another approach to executive motivation is being made through the use of executive incentive schemes. Companies in North America regularly involve their senior management in stock option arrangements which ensure that they will benefit from any 'super growth' which they engender. In Britain and some other European countries, stock options are not available to executives, but elaborate schemes have been devised to give top management a greater incentive to work a regular fourteen-hour day for improved profitability. With the present punitive tax system and the increasing complexity of top management problems, it seems likely that there will be a growing need for research and consultancy relating to executive motivation payment and incentive schemes.[29]

7 MANAGEMENT INFORMATION AND CONTROL

The introduction of corporate planning almost always reveals to top management the inadequacy of the existing information system as an instrument for controlling the organisation. If we assume that the aim of a top management information system should be: (a) to anticipate problems, detect causes, and implement solutions in good time; and (b) to provide autonomy for subordinates and some insurance and control for supervisors, then the traditional accounting system is completely inadequate and the annual budgeting system leaves much to be desired.[30]

Top management information systems. Corporate planning seeks to develop an information and control system which is designed for top management. It should help them:

- to coordinate, delegate, and control large complex organisations
- to anticipate problems and business opportunities in a rapidly changing environment
- to make a rational allocation of resources between competing projects in diverse operations
- to set realistic objectives and targets which may be translated into operational standards for monitoring performance
- to produce a strategy which will guide the choice of products and markets both in planning for existing operations, and in assessing project for expansion and diversification.

The development of the business planning system tends to be the main focus of planning effort in the first few years after the introduction of corporate planning simply because planning cannot go ahead until the basic data are available. It is usual to find that data on environment are inadequate, that personnel records have to be created and market research is necessary to obtain up-to-date information about the market and the strength of competition. In the finance and accounting area, prolonged investigation is sometimes necessary before it is possible to make meaningful comparisons of profitability between different divisions and product/ market groups.

New research. Top management information and control systems seem to offer a rich field for researchers and consultants. Aguilar has made a start, analysing how top management obtain information on the environment. Another project in Pilkington Glass aims to analyse the problem of developing an 'integrated' information system which is consistent horizontal, i.e. across divisions;

vertically, i.e. up and down the organisation, and in time, i.e. short term and long term.[31]

Use of computers. The use of the computer will improve the information system beyond recognition, reducing the response time and enabling top management to operate with the key facts about the business at their fingertips. This is happening slowly. A further development is for managers to be able to use operational research packages, e.g. linear programming, critical path methods, sensitivity analysis, and risk analysis, via remote access terminals. There is evidence that a start is being made in this direction, at least at the operational level though there seems to be little progress in using operational research packages on overall strategy problems. The time when top management work at the hub of an integrated planning and information system which is continually updated and available at the press of a button is still far away, though it seems quite possible that during the 1970s top management will have access to dynamic models of distribution systems, sales forecasting and stock control systems, and other information and control modules.[32]

8 NEW VENTURES

Diversification, research and development, new product development, international markets, mergers and acquisitions, these are the glamorous areas of corporate strategy. New ventures are obviously key areas for top management effort; research continually underlines the importance of organised corporate development in achieving increased growth and profitability.[33]

The field of new ventures is one that has attracted a great deal of interest in the 1960s. Ansoff and others have introduced more structure and system into diversification. Schuchman and a whole generation of marketing academics and practitioners have pioneered more systematic approaches to new product development and marketing experimentation. Bright is representative of those academics and executives who have sought to make the management of research and development more professional. Du Pont have introduced venture management – the entrepreneurial group inside the large firm. The top management of Litton and other conglomerates have demonstrated the extraordinary potential of acquisition as a route to corporate growth and Ansoff and others have confirmed that mergers and acquisitions frequently do not fulfil their early promises, particularly if they are unplanned and intuitive. The field of new ventures presents impressive openings for research teaching and consultancy. It is a primary concern of top management which straddles across all functional areas and frequently cannot be conveniently handled inside the organisation because of the special skills required and the question of security. One must predict continued growth of activity in this field in an attempt to improve the unimpressive record of major companies in new product development in mergers and in acquisitions. McKinsey in the US and the Acton Society in the UK have already sponsored sizeable research projects concerned with mergers and acquisitions.[34]

Developments in basic disciplines and business functions

In the 1970s, we may expect to see more interaction between top management, trying to develop strategies and plans for the total organisation, and the managers of functional areas, behavioural science consultants, and management science consultants who will be obliged to spend rather more time working on problems of strategy than they do at present.

BUSINESS FUNCTIONS

There are already indications that accountants are becoming more concerned with finance policy and management information systems which are related to formal long-range plans. Marketing management are developing a total systems approach to physical distribution; leading marketing companies are producing models of markets and advances are being made in distribution channel theory which could facilitate a more structured approach to channel strategy decisions. Personnel management are starting to generate more useful records which could lead to progress in manpower planning, and there is evidence of interest in formulating personnel strategies and industrial relations policies. As research and development management and purchasing management become more professionalised, these activities too will no doubt produce formal plans and strategies. In the planning and control of production operations, impressive work has already been done in the application of capital budgeting techniques, critical path methods, and other quantitative approaches. In the future one may expect to see more attention paid to production policy.

BEHAVIOURAL AND MANAGEMENT SCIENCES

In the past few years, businessmen have become much more closely involved with academics from operational research and from the social sciences. There may be a tendency during the 1970s for more academics to move up the organisation and to examine not simply work on the shop floor, but also the tasks and problems of top management, e.g. the impact on an organisation of different management styles, and the possibilities of incorporating management science techniques into top management decision making.[35]

Management in different industrial sectors

Surveys in the United States, Britain and Eire suggest that professional management is practised mainly in large manufacturing companies. The demand for management training, research and consultancy services, etc., is mainly concentrated in large industrial companies and even within this group there are whole sectors of traditional industry, e.g. shipbuilding, and textiles, where modern approaches to management have made little penetration.

Size is a major factor influencing the use of management services. At about

500 employees, there appears to be a threshold. Companies with less than 500 employees show significantly less interest in modern management methods.

During the 1970s, we should see an increasing demand for advanced management services from financial institutions and to a certain extent, government departments. Demands from other industrial sectors will probably grow dramatically too, but the need here will be for basic management techniques. Small businesses, local government, construction, distribution, hotel and catering, the hospital service, and other professional and miscellaneous organisations will fall into this category.[36]

Strategic planning in service organisations

Corporate strategy should presumably be regarded as an advanced management service, compared with, e.g. budgetary control, work study, and stock control. Demand for teaching, consultancy, and research in this area may be expected to come mainly from large manufacturing organisations. Interest is also being shown already by large financial institutions and by central government. For small manufacturing industry, distribution, construction, local government, and other service industries, the requirement will probably be rather for basic planning systems. From the point of view of corporate strategy theory and practice therefore, a most interesting new field of activity may be the application of approaches and techniques developed in manufacturing industry to service activities and to government activities.

Much investment has already been made in the United States in programme budgeting and in the application of management techniques in financial institutions. This should have the effect of accelerating the penetration of these techniques in Europe, and we will probably see more training, research and consultancy programmes concerned with top management problems in government and in financial institutions.

Specific industries

Another emerging trend is a demand for consultancy teaching and research programmes relating to the strategic problems of a specific industry.[37] In Britain, NEDO and the Industrial Training Boards have pioneered industry studies and courses for top management in a number of industries including: wool textiles, construction, lace and knitting and machine tools. In other European countries, e.g. Norway, Holland and Switzerland, trade associations have initiated research into the future prospects of industries such as carpets, boatbuilding, and watchmaking. In industries which are dominated by small firms, all working with inadequate data on economic, social and technological trends, such syndicated studies and specialist courses for top management would seem to be an essential prerequisite for good corporate planning and could mean the difference between improved profitability and bankruptcy for the entrepreneur in the smaller company.

Small business

Corporate strategy in the small business is a field of special interest to many governments. In the US the small business administration is maintained by federal funds to sponsor research, training and consultancy, and there are postgraduate courses in the management of new ventures and in entrepreneurship, at major business schools such as Harvard and Stanford. In the UK money has been found for a Centre for Management in Small Businesses, and a government committee is at present studying the need of small businesses.

In certain countries, e.g. Eire and Denmark, business is almost entirely in the hands of small businessmen and work in the field of strategy is inevitably focused on the needs of the entrepreneur. In the future, we may expect continued government support for research, training and consultancy in the emerging field of entrepreneurship, particularly where specific industries and whole nations are dependent on small business for their prosperity.[38]

Management in different geographical areas

If we see management technology as a combination of knowledge, skills and attributes, it is clear that new managerial technology tends to originate mainly in the US. Certainly we find the major centres for management research and development in the large US companies and in American business schools.

In terms of personnel, facilities and investment, the US alone must account for at least two-thirds of the world's research and development in management technology. There are currently 650 US universities offering degrees in business studies and of these 250 are separate business schools; 90 000 first degrees, 20 000 master degrees, and about 500 doctorates are awarded each year.[39]

Because of American dominance in management thinking and practice, and the relative affluence of the US compared with other countries there has been a tendency to assume that management practice in Western Europe and elsewhere will follow the American pattern. Businessmen talk of management practice in Europe being 'five years behind the Americans'. In fact, as other countries have developed their management expertise, it is apparent that the American style of management is only one of many. We can distinguish distinctive approaches to management in Japan, Eastern Europe, Western Europe, and in various less developed areas in Africa, Asia and South America.[40]

In the application of management techniques, e.g. management accounting, production control and market research, the differences between practice in various regions may simply reflect an earlier stage in the evolution of business management and in the growth of industry. In other fields, e.g. organisational behaviour, and corporate strategy, it seems that in Japan or Western Europe, the eventual pattern of management theory and practice may vary considerably from the North American tradition. Japan presents a striking example of a way of doing business which is in marked contrast to the American approach, e.g. in terms of finance and personnel, but is equally, if not more successful.[41]

In Western Europe, too, personal values and ideas of social responsibility and political and social traditions are different from the US. In Scandinavia there is close cooperation between industry, government and unions in planning a socialist society. In Britain, a substantial part of industry is nationalised. In Ireland and in southern Europe, the Roman Catholic Church is still strong. Throughout Western Europe, the idea of the welfare state is widely accepted.

The developing countries and the communist world are so far in their traditions and levels of economic development from the Western industrialised nations that the Japanese or the Israeli approach to business may serve as a better initial model than industry in the US or in Western Europe.

In the 1970s, as management technology spreads throughout the world we shall expect to see a diverse pattern of business philosophies and strategies as top management in different countries search for styles and strategies which are appropriate in their particular environment. An opportunity of new work in teaching, consultancy and research will consist in adapting the basic approaches to corporate strategy and corporate planning to conditions primarily in Western Europe, the British Commonwealth and Japan, but also in Eastern Europe and in the third world. As more large companies become truly international, so we may see a growing demand for teaching, consultancy, and research concerning the problems of top management in multinational organisations.

Trends in teaching, research and consultancy

The field of corporate strategy presents intractable problems for the teacher, the researcher, and the consultant, because of the nature of the subject.

(a) LACK OF STRUCTURE

Corporate strategy is concerned with the total business system; therefore it deals with problems which are complex and ill-defined. The research for general theories and models of corporate strategy is likely to take a long time. At Harvard, the field has been studied and researched for over fifty years, and progress in developing concepts and theories has been painfully slow. At this stage the teacher or consultant has little more to offer than a general approach and experience in the analysis of a wide range of strategy problems.

(b) SECURITY

Strategic issues are near to the heart of the business, and therefore confidential. Cases and research studies are frequently written but not released, and consultancy can rarely be publicised.

(c) PRESSURE OF WORK

Top managers are frequently the busiest men in the organisation, with many people and projects competing for their time. Interviews, when obtained, are given under pressure. Questionnaires remain unanswered. Top managers, as a group, rarely attend management training courses.

(d) PROCESS NOT PRODUCT

The teacher or consultant in corporate strategy is concerned not with selling a package but with assisting in a process. He is concerned with ends as well as means, with the long term rather than the short term. He cannot therefore assume his client's problem. He must start with the client's values and objectives and help him to resolve his own problem. In many cases the consultant in corporate strategy fills the role of confidant to top management. He is a neutral outsider who is there to help the management to move to where they want to go.

It may with some reason be claimed that in the field of corporate strategy teaching, and consultancy, must of necessity be less directive than in other fields, where problems are more easily defined, objectives may be assumed and set solutions are readily available.

New developments

However, the techniques of process consultancy are developing quickly owing to the work of behavioural scientists involved in organisation development. One authority lists the stages in process consultation as follows:[42]

   (i) initial contact with the client organisation
  (ii) defining the relationship, formal contract, and psychological contract
 (iii) selecting and setting a method of work
 (iv) data gathering and diagnosis
  (v) intervention
 (vi) reducing involvement
(vii) termination.

Corporate strategy is a similar field to organisation development in that the consultant is facilitating a process rather than selling a package, and he is concerned with helping the top management to change their organisation. In the future, it would seem likely that consultants in strategy and organisation development will work together. Otherwise, it is difficult to see how the corporate strategy consultant will acquire the behavioural skills which he requires to work with top management.

Corporate strategy consultants should make an increasing contribution in the future in step (iv), data gathering and diagnosis. One could envisage the greater use of consultants for environmental forecasting and analysis and in corporate appraisal. Presumably there will be more opinion and attitude surveys inside the organisation and among interest groups such as shareholders and the public.

Teaching will no doubt be supported by more research into the actual behaviour, the problems, and the decisions of top management, also there are indications that top management problems may be more carefully classified according to industry, size of organisation, stage of development, the cultural environment, and the top management style.

It seems likely that cases will continue as the main teaching method, but with increasing reference to the sizeable literature which is emerging on corporate planning, and using the computer as a tool to simulate the effects of different strategies.

In terms of subject matter, there is surely no doubt that corporate strategy will grow as a field for consultancy, research and teaching. More attention must be paid by business executives and by students to the role which business plays in society – civil rights, air and water pollution, the impact on the physical environment, redundancy, the effect on employees and on consumers, and shareholders.

Summary

We set out to examine the present state of the art, and likely future trends in the emerging fields of corporate strategy and corporate planning, in business practice, as a topic for research, teaching and consultancy.

There are many indications that interest in corporate strategy and corporate planning will continue to grow. Business planning systems are at an early stage of development, even the pioneers in planning are only just beginning to produce comprehensive plans and strategies.

There are mounting pressures from shareholders, employees, customers, government, and the community in general for a say in the running of business. There is also concern in many quarters that large businesses should become more innovative, and entrepreneurial.

Strategic planning could become a predominant concern of top management in the 1970s, just as marketing was in the 1960s.

The following predictions may be made with a fairly high degree of confidence:

- business, government bodies, and trade associations will invest in huge syndicated studies aimed at forecasting the shape of future sociotechnological systems and assessing the possible impact on business and on society of 'alternative futures'
- it will become standard practice for external and internal consultants working with management on operational problems to start not with ad hoc situation analysis as at present, but by making an appraisal of current strategy. This will reduce the chaos which results from the efforts of management consultants and management services groups to install packages of techniques without considering the likely impact on the total business
- top management in large and progressive businesses will accept the need to monitor the opinions of shareholders, employees, and the public through continuous attitude surveys

- senior business executives will build computer models of the company – its finance, production, markets and manpower – which will enable them to check the likely effect of many alternative strategies instantaneously on a teleprinter terminal in the office
- organisation structures will be classified according to technology, size, stage of development, and cultural environment, so that an appropriate form of top management may be designed on a systematic basis
- the social scientist will become an accepted member of top management staff and will work alongside the corporate planner in diagnosing organisational problems and planning programmes for change among executives and increasingly with the work force
- ~~executive development will become professionalised with the emergence of~~ more scientific methods of identifying executive potential and designing incentive and development programmes to meet the specific needs of individual groups
- corporate planners will become deeply involved with accountants and operational researchers in constructing information and control systems, designed for top management. This will require the creation of comprehensive long-term plans and information systems for personnel, marketing, technology, as well as for management accounting
- large- and medium-size business organisations will be radically reorganised to accelerate corporate growth by spawning entrepreneurial project teams and venture groups
- the new interest in corporate strategy will prompt managers in the functional areas and consultants in operational research and the behavioural sciences to become more concerned with the development of policies and strategies
- as professional management spreads outside large manufacturing industry, so interest will be focused on the use of programme budgeting, and cost-benefit analysis in government and in large service organisations
- we are likely to see the development of specialist training, research and consultancy services for strategic planning in specific industries, and in small businesses
- as more businesses become truly international, there will be a growing concern with the problems of top management in different countries and cultures
- the problems of top management are ill-defined, difficult to research and are not susceptible to ready-made solutions. The teacher, consultant, or researcher in corporate strategy will continue to be concerned in facilitating a process rather than selling a package.

References

1. See, for example, E. P. LEARNED et al., *European Problems in General Management*, Homewood, Illinois, Irwin, 1963, p. 24.
   E. P. LEARNED et al., *Business Policy Text and Cases*, Irwin, 1969, pp. 6 and vii.

2. F. F. GILMORE, *Formulation and Advocacy of Business Policy*, Cornell University Press, 1968, pp. 8 and 20.

3. MELVILLE C. BRANCH, *Selected References for Corporate Planning*, New York, AMA, 1966.

4. P. IRVING, 'Corporate planning in practice', M.Sc. dissertation, University of Bradford, 1970.
   J. M. HEWKINS and T. KEMPNER, *Is Corporate Planning Necessary?*, British Institute of Management, 1968.
   K. A. RINGBAKK, 'Organised planning in major US companies', *Long Range Planning*, 2, no. 2, Dec. 1969.
   J. K. BROWN et al., 'Long range planning in the USA. An NICB Survey', *Long Range Planning*, 1, no. 3, March 1970.
   R. PERRIN, 'Long range planning. The concept and the need', *Long Range Planning*, 1, no. 1, Sept. 1968.
   E. K. WARREN, *Long Range Planning: the executive viewpoint*, Prentice-Hall, 1966.
   G. A. STEINER, ed., *Managerial Long Range Planning*, McGraw-Hill, 1963.
   R. MAINER, *The Impact of Strategic Planning on Executive Behaviour*, Boston Consulting Group, 1965.
   C. O. ROSSOTTI, *Two Concepts of Long Range Planning*, Boston Consulting Group, 1965.
   W. H. STRIGEL, 'Planning in West German Industry', *Long Range Planning*, 3, no. 1, Sept. 1970.
   B. W. DENNING, 'Organising the Corporate Planning Function', *Long Range Planning*, 1, no. 4, June 1969.
   G. A. STEINER, *Top Management Planning*, Macmillan, New York, 1969.
   R. M. WORCESTER, 'Planning for growth in leading US companies', *Long Range Planning*, 2, no. 3, March 1970.

5. See D. G. CORK, *The Industrial Manager: his background and career pattern*, London, Business Publications, 1966
   B. TAYLOR, 'A seller's market for management education in Britain', *Management Decision*, Summer 1967.

6. IRVING, ref. 4, p. 81.

7. IRVING, ibid., p. 37.

8. The European Association of Management Training Centres (Brussels), The Association of Teachers of Management (London), and the American Academy of Management.

9. E. JANTSCH, *Technological Forecasting in Perspective*, Paris, OECD, 1967.
   Long Term Forecasting in Europe, Strasbourg, The Council of Europe, 1970.

10. These studies were made by the Swiss Watch Industry, the British Medical Council, Richard Hoskyns (London), the Programme Analysis Unit of the Ministry of Technology (Harwell), and Unilever (London).

11. GILMORE, ref. 2, pp. 8 and 20.

12. See H. PARKER, *Economic Analysis of Company Strengths and Weaknesses*, Long Range Planning in British Industry. Seminar Manual, University of Bradford, 1967.

13. W. D. GUTH and R. TAGIURI, 'Personal values and corporate strategy,' *Harvard Business Review*, Sept./Oct. 1965.

14. T. KEMPNER, K. H. HAWKINS and K. MACMILLAN, 'The role of business in society', *Long Range Planning*, 2, no. 4, June 1970.

15. C. C. BROWN, 'The fading of an ideology', *Long Range Planning*, 1, no. 1, Sept. 1968.
    G. A. STEINER, *Business and Society*, Macmillan, New York, 1971.

16. See, for example, R. J. BRISTON, 'The Fisons stockholder survey: an experiment in company-shareholder relations', *Journal of Business Policy*, 1, no. 1, Autumn 1970. Business Publications, London.
    R. M. WORCESTER, 'Managing change', *Long Range Planning*, 3, no. 1, Sept. 1970.

17. Further information is available from Industrial Co-Partnership Association, 60 Buckingham Gate, London, SW1.

18. H. I. ANSOFF, *Corporate Strategy: an analytical approach to business policy for growth and expansion*, McGraw-Hill, 1965. Penguin, 1968.

19. R. WEINBERG, *Corporate Planning and Operational Research*, Seminar Manual, University of Bradford, 1969.

20. See: ALBERT N. SCHRIEBER, ed., *Corporate Simulation Models*, GSOBA, University of Washington, 1970.
    J. L. MCKENNEY, 'An approach to simulation model development for improved planning', *Long Range Planning*, 2, no. 3, March 1970.
    Corporate Planning and Management Science, Conference Manual, University of Bradford, 1971.

21. See in particular the following articles published in *Long Range Planning*:
    J. C. HETRICK, 'A formal model for long range planning', 1, nos 3 and 4; 2, no. 1, March/Sept. 1969.
    G. R. SALKIN and P. J. DOHRN, 'The use of financial models in long range planning', 2, no. 2, Dec. 1969.
    J. A. BELL, 'Production strategy decisions: a simulation model approach', 2, no. 4, June 1970.
    B. J. LA LONDE, 'Integrated distribution management. The American perspective', 2, no. 2, Dec. 1969.
    M. H. HOYLE and R. J. STUBBS, 'Management stocktaking: an approach to manpower in banking', 2, no. 3, March 1970.
    R. TOLL, 'Analytical techniques for new product planning', 1, no. 3, March 1969.

22. DENNING, ref. 4.

23. M. S. SALTER, 'Stages of corporate development', *Journal of Business Policy*, 1, no. 1, Autumn 1970.
    B. R. SCOTT, 'A stages model of corporate development', unpublished paper, Harvard, 1968.

T. D. WEINSHALL, 'Conceptual schemes of organisational behaviour and their possible applications', unpublished paper, University of Tel Aviv, 1970.

24. See H. I. ANSOFF, 'The innovative firm', *Long Range Planning*, 1, no. 2, Dec. 1968.
P. DRUCKER, 'The innovative organisation', *Journal of Business Policy*, 1, no. 3, Spring 1971.
C. J. MIDDLETON, 'How to set up a project organisation', *Harvard Business Review*, May/June 1967.
A. B. COHEN, 'New venture development at Du Pont', *Long Range Planning*, 2, no. 4, June 1970.

25. On the inadequacy of Personnel Planning, see:
J. K. BROWN, 'Long range planning in the USA', p. 44; and RINGBAKK, 'Organised planning in major US companies', see ref. 4.
For examples of formal planning for personnel see:
H. P. FORD, 'Long range planning of managers', *Long Range Planning*, 1, no. 1, Sept. 1968.
Long Range Planning for Human Resources, Conference Manual, University of Bradford, 1969.
Industrial Relations Policies, Conference Manual, University of Bradford, 1970.
L. T. BLAKEMAN, 'Incomes, productivity and planning', *Long Range Planning*, 1, no. 4, June 1969.
W. VON NIEDERHAUSERN, 'Planning for executive development at J. R. Geigy SA', *Long Range Planning*, 3, no. 1, Sept. 1970.

26. H. ROSE, *Management Education in the 1970s: growth and issues*, NEDO, HMSO, 1970, p. 21.
A. MANT, *The Experienced Manager: a major resource*, British Institute of Management, 1969, p. 3.
See also: B. TAYLOR, 'A seller's market for management education in Britain', *Management Decision*, Summer 1967.
K. R. ANDREWS, *The Effectiveness of University Management Development Programmes*, Division of Research, Harvard GSOB Boston, 1966.

27. ROSE, ref. 26, p. 22.

28. For a range of books describing different approaches to Organisational Development, see The Addison Wesley Series: on Organisational Development, Reading, Massachusetts 1969 and 1970.

29. See *Identifying Executive Potential*, Seminar Manual, University of Bradford, 1969.

30. See particularly: RINGBAKK and WARREN both cited in ref. 4.

31. F. J. AGUILAR, *Scanning the Business Environments*, Macmillan, New York, 1968.
P. FRASER, 'Integrated planning at Pilkington Co.', Ph.D. research project, Bradford University.

32. See ref. 20.

33. See especially: P. M. GUTMAN, 'Strategies for growth', *California Management Review*, Summer 1964.
B. COCHRAN and G. CLARK THOMPSON, *Why New Products Fail*, Conference Board Record, Oct. 1964.
R. M. WORCESTER, *Managing Change*, ref. 16.

34. On new ventures, see ref. 24, also: H. I. ANSOFF, 'Does planning pay? The effect of planning on success of acquisitions in American firms', *Long Range Planning,* 3, no. 2, Dec. 1970.
    J. NEWBOULD, 'Strategic merger policy', *Journal of Business Policy,* Winter 1971.

35. See R. W. REVANS, *Final Report of the Senior Research Fellowship.* European Association of Management Training Centres, 1970.
    R. STEWART, *Managers and Their Jobs,* London, Macmillan, 1967.
    MCKENNEY, see ref. 20.

36. See especially: BREFFIN TOMLIN, *The Management of Irish Industry,* Dublin, Irish Management Institute, 1966.
    Also ROSE, ref. 26, chaps. 8 and 10.

37. Two published studies on strategic planning in specific industries are:
    J. D. GLOVER and R. F. VANCIL, *Management of Transformation: a report to top management of the telephone industry,* New York, IBM, 1968.
    W. R. PARK *Strategy of Contracting for Profit,* Prentice-Hall, 1966.

38. See P. F. DRUCKER, 'Entrepreneurship in business enterprise', *Journal of Business Policy,* 1, no. 1, Autumn 1970.
    J. BOSWELL, *Some Problems of Increasing Efficiency in Smaller Firms,* Journal of Business Policy, 1, no. 3, Spring 1971.
    TOMLIN, ref. 36.

39. ROSE, ref. 26, p. 137.

40. See H. V. PERLMUTTER, 'The international enterprise. Three conceptions', unpublished paper, IMEDE, Lausanne.
    O. H. NOWOTRY, 'American *vs.* European management philosophy', *Harvard Business Review,* no. 2, 1964.
    B. HAWRYLYSHYN, 'Preparing managers for international operations', *The Business Quarterly,* Autumn 1967.
    American Business in Italy, Boston Consulting Group, Massachusetts, 1967.

41. JAMES C. ABEGGLEN, *Business Strategies for Japan,* Boston Consulting Group, Sophia University, Tokyo, 1970.

42. See E. H. SCHEIN, *Process Consultation. Its role in organisation development,* Addison Wesley, 1969.

Index

Index